Constitutional Law in Hungary

Constitutional Law in Hungary

Fourth Edition

Zoltán Szente

This book was originally published as a monograph in the International Encyclopaedia of Laws/Constitutional Law.

Founding Editor: Roger Blanpain
General Editor: Frank Hendrickx
Volume Editors: André Alen & David Haljan

Wolters Kluwer

Published by:
Kluwer Law International B.V.
PO Box 316
2400 AH Alphen aan den Rijn
The Netherlands
E-mail: lrs-sales@wolterskluwer.com
Website: www.wolterskluwer.com/en/solutions/kluwerlawinternational

Sold and distributed by:
Wolters Kluwer Legal & Regulatory U.S.
920 Links Avenue
Landisville, PA 17538
United States of America
Email: customer.service@wolterskluwer.com

ISBN 978-94-035-1128-3

e-Book: ISBN 978-94-035-1138-2
web-PDF: ISBN 978-94-035-1148-1

The Author

Zoltán Szente is Research Professor at the Institute for Legal Studies of the Centre for Social Sciences, Budapest and Fernand Braudel Senior Fellow at the European University Institute, Florence. Since the mid-1990s, he has been a member (since 2013 the Vice-Chairman) of the Group of Independent Experts (for monitoring local and regional democracy), Council of Europe. Professor Szente is a co-founder of the Research Group on Constitutional Interpretation of the International Association of Constitutional Law. He has published widely on Hungarian and comparative constitutional law, constitutional theory, parliamentary law, local government and European constitutional history in Hungarian, English, German, Russian and Croatian. Among his recent publications are *New Challenges to Constitutional Adjudication in Europe: A Comparative Perspective* (London and New York: Routledge, 2018, co-edited with Fruzsina Gárdos-Orosz); 'Stepping Into the Same River Twice? Judicial Independence in Old and New Authoritarianism', *German Law Journal* 22, no. 7 (2021); *Populist Challenges to Constitutional Interpretation in Europe and Beyond* (London and New York: Routledge, 2021, co-edited with Fruzsina Gárdos-Orosz); 'How Not to Use History in Constitutional Interpretation: The Aborted Resurrection of the Historical Constitution in Hungary', in *Comparative Constitutional History: Volume Two: Uses of History in Constitutional Adjudication*, edited by Biagi Francesco, O. Frosini Justin & Mazzone Jason (Leiden: Brill 2022); 'The Impact of Populism on Constitutional Interpretation in the EU Member States', *International Journal of Human Rights* 26, no. 7 (2022); 'Constitutional Changes in Populist Times' *Review of Central and Eastern European Law*, 47, no. 1 (2022); 'Using Emergency Powers in Hungary: Against the Pandemic and/or Democracy?',in *Pandemocracy in Europe : Power, Parliaments and People in Times of COVID-19*, edited by Matthias C. Kettemann & Konrad Lachmayer (Oxford: Hart Publishing 2022);'From Guarding the Constitution to Serving Politics: The Decline of the Hungarian Constitutional Court', in *Constitutionality of Law Without a Constitutional Court: A View from Europe*, edited by Miroslaw Granat (New York: Routledge, 2023); 'The Myth of Populist Constitutionalism in Hungary and Poland: Populist or Authoritarian Constitutionalism?' *International Journal of Constitutional Law*, 21, no. 1 (2023).

The Author

Table of Contents

Table of Contents

List of Abbreviations

CCL	Constitutional Court Law
CEU	Central European University
EC	European Community
ECHR	European Convention for the Protection of Human Rights and Fundamental Freedoms
ECJ	European Court of Justice
ECtHR	European Court of Human Rights
EEA	European Economic Area
EU	European Union
FKGP	*Független Kisgazdapárt* (Independent Shareholders' Party)
GDP	Gross Domestic Product
HAS	Hungarian Academy of Sciences
HUF	Hungarian Forint
KDNP	*Kereszténydemokrata Néppárt* (Christian Democratic People's Party)
MDF	*Magyar Demokrata Fórum* (Hungarian Democratic Forum)
MEP	Member of European Parliament
MNB	*Magyar Nemzeti Bank* (Hungarian National Bank)
MP	Member of Parliament
MSZP	*Magyar Szocialista Párt* (Hungarian Socialist Party)
NATO	North Atlantic Treaty Organization
N.B.	Nota Bene
NEC	National Election Commission
NGO	Non-governmental Organization
NJC	National Judicial Council
NOJ	National Office for the Judiciary
OLAF	*Office européen de lutte antifraude* (European Anti-Fraud Office)
OSCE/ODIHR	Organization for Security and Co-operation in Europe/Office for Democratic Institutions and Human Rights
PBO	Public Benefit Organization

List of Abbreviations

SAO	State Audit Office
SZDSZ	*Szabad Demokraták Szövetsége* (Alliance of Free Democrats)
UN	United Nations
PM	Prime Minister

List of Figures

List of Figures

List of Tables

List of Tables

Preface

The aim of this monograph is to give an overview of Hungary's constitutional system, primarily to foreign students and scholars who are interested in the constitutional law of this country.

Hungary is a small Central European country with a long tradition with more than a thousand years of statehood. The country has been a Member State of the European Union since 2004, which was made possible by the collapse of the communist political system after four decades in 1989–1990. As a result of the democratic transition of that time, Hungary, like many other countries in the region, became a constitutional democracy. Hungary was at the forefront of both democratic change and the EU accession process of the post-communist states owing to the fact that the country, despite its turbulent and in many ways unsuccessful history, belonged culturally to the West. It might be surprising that now, partly because of its recent constitutional developments, Hungary is at the centre of international public interest, far beyond its political and economic weight. This is mainly due to the changes that have taken place in the country since 2010 and the contradiction that while the country was the champion of the Central and East European democratization process more than thirty years ago, today, as many think, it is the frontrunner of the new authoritarianism systematically dismantling the system of the rule of law.

In order to get a better picture of this process, we need an overview that analyses in detail the key institutions, principles and rules of the Hungarian Constitution, the Fundamental Law of 2011, and presents, as far as possible, the antecedents and causes of recent changes. In this context, not only the main institutions and procedures of constitutional law will be discussed, but constitutional practice will also be briefly introduced.

The constitutional law of Hungary is discussed most often in three parts – even in Hungarian law faculties, constitutional law is taught in three semesters according to the more or less traditional division of sovereignty issues, state organization and fundamental rights. This structure will be followed also in this monograph.

Kluwer International published a book on Hungarian constitutional system a decade ago;[1] since then, substantial changes have taken place in this country. This explains that this volume is not an updated version of that book but a completely new work. It is worth noting that the present-day constitutional law is an ever-changing legal area in Hungary, which requires the text to be updated again and

1. Márta Dezső et al., *Hungary* (Wolters Kluwer 2010).

again. In addition, since 2020, Hungary has (apart from a brief interruption) continuously had a special legal order in force, giving the government the exceptional power to override any law by means of emergency decrees, and the hundreds of such decrees issued over the past almost four years have significantly changed the legal system and greatly reduced the importance of the rule of law institutions and guarantees.

Since Hungarian-language sources are hardly accessible to the international public, I do not refer them, except the most important works, indicating also the English-language academic literature on Hungarian constitutional law. In spite of this, I gave the most important legal sources of the various fields of constitutional law.

Part I: Sovereignty

Chapter 1: A Short Constitutional History of Hungary

§1.01 THE ORIGINS AND THE FIRST CENTURIES OF THE HUNGARIAN STATE

1. The ancestors of Hungarians came from the Ural region to the Carpathian Basin in the ninth century, and, in the last years of that century, they conquered its whole area. According to the early medieval chronicles, the conquering Hungarians consisted of seven tribes which were united under the lordship of Árpád, who founded a ruling dynasty.

2. Géza was the first ruler who was baptized (in 972), and, since then, the Christian faith started to spread among the Hungarians. He was followed by his son Vajk, who defeated some powerful local rulers and unified the whole conquered territory under his centralized rule. After he had been crowned as King Stephen in 1000 A.D., the new kingdom of Hungary became a sovereign part of the Christian Europe. The international legitimacy of the new monarch was based on his success in founding ten bishoprics and two archbishoprics, and forcing his subjects to abandon their pagan beliefs by their systematic conversion to Christianity. Owing to the success of conversion and the military strength of the country, the monarchy was established as an independent and sovereign kingdom. Stephen divided the country into royal counties (*királyi vármegyék*) and appointed his governors (*comes*) to lead the counties. It should be noted that the Hungarian historical tradition counts the beginnings of the so-called thousand-year constitution from the age of St. Stephen's rule.

3. The first royal dynasty, the Árpád-House, ruled until 1301, consolidating the royal power and its institutions like the royal council (*curia regis*), the early feudal assembly (*Országgyűlés*), the palatine (the king's deputy in the absence of the monarch), the seneschal (the supreme judge after the king) and other court officials. Hungarian legal historians generally hold that the institution of national assemblies evolved from the days of the royal courts. The Golden Bull of 1222 stipulated that nationwide assemblies be held 'on the day of our sacred king' in the municipality of Székesfehérvár, the coronation city of Hungarian kings,[2] in the presence of the supreme ruler. Here, the king exercised his prerogative of jurisdiction, which stated that the supreme judicial power rested at all times with the king. On such occasions, royal jurisdiction was not limited strictly to passing judgments in individual cases,

2. Later on, the place of coronation changed several times.

for it soon became customary for the king to interpret, and sometimes to confirm various laws of his kingdom at these court days. Prelates were obliged to present themselves at national assemblies from as early as 1231, and a law enacted in 1267 stipulated that each *comitat* should delegate two or three noblemen to the national assembly. Eventually, a Royal Decree of 1290 obliged all noblemen to attend the assemblies in person.[3] On this basis, the roots of Hungarian National Assembly (*Országgyűlés*) are most frequently traced back to the late thirteenth century. Open-air, crowded assemblies were held until the seventeenth century. A law recognized in 1608 the practice that had already been established, according to which the National Assembly was sitting in two chambers. The 'higher table', the upper chamber, was composed of magnates (barons and counts) and prelates (of the Catholic Church), who were summoned personally by the king, while in the 'lower table', the nobility and, from the fifteenth century, the royal municipalities were represented by their delegates.

4. After the extinction of the Árpád dynasty, the kingdom became a formally elected monarchy, as all new kings were elected by the Estates Assembly, even if the monarch was often elected from the same dynasty (e.g., for almost all of the fourteenth century, the kings were chosen from the Anjou House). At this time, the so-called Holy Crown, namely the diadem with which Saint Stephen, the first king (who was canonized in 1183), had allegedly been crowned, received particular significance because, after the interruption of royal descendants, it affirmed the legitimacy of the new ruler. From then on, a king was only regarded as a legitimate king if crowned by the Archbishop of Esztergom in Székesfehérvár with the original crown[4] of St. Stephen.

5. Although the roots of feudalism can be traced back to the twelfth and thirteenth centuries, when the king started to gift royal demesne to his noble servants primarily for their military service, a well-developed feudal state emerged in the fifteenth century. The Golden Bull of 1222 – which is frequently compared to the English Magna Carta – was the first collection of noble privileges recognized by the king (Andrew II). The last clause of this Charter acknowledged the magnates' and prelates' right to resist the monarch if he did not respect the nobles' privileges. The Bull was subsequently reaffirmed by later kings on several occasions. The development of the legal institutions of feudalism, like *aviticum,* [5] the court-baron, the tithe and other feudal burdens, were completed by the laws of Louis the Great (Nagy Lajos) in 1351.

---

3. Zoltán Szente, *Functions of the National Assembly Within the Constitutional Tradition of Hungary*, 8 Hist. Const. 227, 232 (1997).
4. Although it is not possible to know the fate of St. Stephen's original crown, it is certain that the crown currently displayed in Parliament's building is not the one with which Stephen was crowned in 1000 (or 1001). The present crown was composed of two distinct parts (*corona latina* and *corona graeca*), the lower part of which came from Byzantium in the second half of the eleventh century.
5. The rule that alienation of possessions (feudal estates) was barred and instead estates were to descend directly and as of right to male siblings and their issue, whose claim was to be absolute.

6. In the late Middle Ages, Hungary was on occasion in personal union with other countries like under Louis the Great with Poland (1370–1382) or Sigismund who was also Holy Roman Emperor (1433–1437) and the king of Germany and Bohemia (in different periods).

§1.02 THE FEUDAL CONSTITUTION

7. By the regular summons of the delegates of the royal municipalities in the first half of the fifteenth century, the development of representative institutions was completed. The period between the early fifteenth century and 1526 was the heyday of the Hungarian feudal state in which power was divided between the king and the estates, and the Hungarian Kingdom became a regional power in Central Europe.

8. Hungarian customary law was collected and compiled by István Werbőczy in his *Tripartitum* which had been prepared at the king's request in the early 1500s. Though this collection was never sanctioned by the king as law, it was used by courts over centuries.[6]

9. Since the mid-fifteenth century, the European expansion of the Ottoman Empire threatened the independence of the country more and more. In 1526, Hungarian troops lost the fateful battle of Mohács.[7] After that, two kings were elected and crowned. After some turbulent years, the country was divided into three parts. In the west, Ferdinand of Habsburg reigned, while the central part of the country was under Turkish rule. The eastern part of the country, Transylvania, became an autonomous principality under the protectorate of the Ottoman Empire. The country was liberated from the Turkish occupation and was reunified only in the 1680s.

10. Although since the coronation of Ferdinand I in 1526 the Hungarian estates and orders had chosen the king always from the Habsburg dynasty (as they hoped for help from the Habsburg Empire to fight the Turks),[8] the primogenitary hereditary rights of the House of Habsburg-Lorraine was recognized by the feudal diet only in 1687. In the same year, the National Assembly cancelled the 'resistance-clause' from the Golden Bull. It is to be added that the inheritance rights of female Habsburgs were also acknowledged in 1723. The latter law was called *Pragmatica Sanctio*, and it provided that Hungary and the other countries and territories of the Habsburg monarchs must be ruled 'inseparately and indivisibly', establishing the common defence between Hungary and the other Habsburg territories.

---

6. *See*, in detail, Martyn Rady (ed.), *Customary Law in Hungary: Courts, Texts, and the Tripartitum* (Oxford University Press 2015).
7. Since then, 'Mohács' has been deeply ingrained in collective memory in Hungary as a symbol of failure and national tragedy.
8. However, due to the division of the country, in 1526 János Szapolyai, and after his death in 1540, his son John Sigismund (János Zsigmond) was elected king; so between 1526 and 1571 the country had two kings.

11. The eighteenth century and the early nineteenth century were the eras of various kinds of absolutism. From 1740 to 1790, under Mary Theresa and Joseph II, enlightened absolutism introduced social and administrative reforms, but they brought about the ignorance of the traditional feudal institutions, overshadowing the feudal diet and the noble counties. After the death of Joseph II, the Hungarian nobility tried to restore the old noble privileges, in particular, the traditional tax exemption of noblemen and their participatory rights in the exercise of public power. Although Act X of 1790 recognized the Habsburg House as the royal dynasty, it declared also that Hungary had its own state existence and constitution.

§1.03 From Feudalism to Civic Constitutionalism

12. The roots of modern nationalism can be traced back to the early nineteenth century, the so-called Reform Age, and culminated in the revolution and independence war of 1848–1849 against the Habsburg Empire. The revolutionary legislation, the 'April laws' of 1848, transformed most institutions of the feudal constitution, abolishing the feudal burdens and the tax exemptions of the nobility on the basis of the principle of civil equality. The abolition of most social privileges entailed the extension of civil liberties: censorship was abolished, the equality of religious communities was recognized, and suffrage was also broadened. In addition, the whole system of public power was also changed: the composition of the lower house of Parliament was based on the principle of popular representation, although the upper house retained its feudal character. The Act III of 1848 introduced the institution of an independent responsible Hungarian government, which took over the exercise of executive power from the imperial court authorities in Vienna. In short, the absolute monarchy of the pre-1848 period was transformed into a constitutional kingdom.

13. The revolution soon became a war of independence against the Habsburgs, in which the revolutionary legislature in 1849 proclaimed a Declaration of Independence, and declared the deposition of the Habsburg dynasty. However, the Habsburg Empire, with the military support of Russia, suppressed the uprising, and the following Habsburg rule abolished Hungarian representative institutions and tried to merge the country into the Austrian half of the Empire, on the pattern of the Austrian eternal provinces. This was unsuccessful, however, and the degrading international situation of the Habsburg Empire led to the so-called Great Compromise of 1867 between the ruler, Francis Joseph I, and Hungarians. As a result, the Austro-Hungarian Monarchy was created, with Hungary as an equal party alongside Austria (Act XII of 1867).

14. That Monarchy realized a special relationship between Austria and Hungary, one which was stronger than a confederation, but weaker than a federation (or a 'real union').[9] It did not have common legislative, executive and judicial bodies, but certain matters – foreign affairs, war and peace and the finance of these matters –

9. Zoltán Szente, *Kormányzás a dualizmus korában* (Atlantisz 2011) 175–198.

fell within common jurisdiction which was arranged by a three-membered Council of Ministers appointed by the common monarch.

15. In Hungary, most of the institutions created by the 1848 laws were restored. The principle of judicial independence was recognized by law in 1869 (Act IV of 1869), and an administrative court was set up in 1896 (Act XXVI of 1896). In the era called 'dualism', there was a kind of quasi-parliamentarism in Hungary. Although there were several parties and a vibrant parliamentary life, universal male suffrage was not introduced during that epoch (which lasted until the First World War). There was also a dominant party system without any real chance of government change: the opposition in the whole era was able to win parliamentary elections only once, in 1905, but it could form a government only by renouncing key points of its political programme.

16. The period of the Austrian-Hungarian dualism has always been seen as a golden age in Hungarian history, with a long and significant economic and cultural development and the establishing of institutions of civil constitutionalism. Nevertheless, unlike the mainstream of contemporary European constitutional movements, no written constitution was codified, but the historical constitution, even if in a deeply reformed form, was preserved.

§1.04 The Hungarian Constitution in the Twentieth Century

17. Hungary participated in the First World War as part of the Austro-Hungarian Monarchy alongside the Central Powers. In the late period of war, in October 1918, a revolution (the 'Aster Revolution') broke out, during which the provisional government proclaimed the 'Hungarian People's Republic' on 16 November. In March 1919, a Bolshevik-type coup d'etat took place. The new regime, which lasted 133 days, attempted to transform the whole legal system, including the adoption of a written constitutional statute that never entered into force.

18. After the collapse of this early communist rule, Hungary, as a belligerent country on the losing side, was forced to sign the Peace Treaty of Trianon in June 1920. As a consequence of the Treaty, the country lost more than two-thirds part of its pre-war territory, and more than half of her population. In contrast to the multinational composition of the population before the war, Hungary became a homogeneous nation-state and about 3.3 million ethnic Hungarians now fell under foreign authority.

19. Act I of 1920 restored the historical constitution and provided for the 'temporary exercise of public power' authorizing the regent to exert the power of the Head of State 'until the final arrangement' of the issue of the form of state. Nevertheless, throughout the interwar period, Hungary was 'a monarchy without a monarch' because, while the country preserved the monarchical form of the state, the throne remained vacant throughout the era. The last legally crowned ruler, Charles of Habsburg IV, was not allowed back on the throne by the Entente Powers, and after his death in 1922, no new dynasty (and king) was elected. Instead, the powers of the Head of State were exercised by Miklós Horthy as a regent elected by the National Assembly in 1920. Horthy remained in office until 1944 (later, the whole era was characterized by his name).

20. The ruling political ideas of this period were the claim for territorial revision and the restoration and legal continuity of the 'one-thousand-year' historical constitution. The core theory of contemporary constitutional law then was the doctrine of the Holy Crown because, embodying the integrity of the territory of the monarchy, it provided a historical argument for reclamation of the lost territories. In addition, according to ancient Hungarian public law theory, all sovereign power was vested in the Holy Crown. The form of government was seen as a parliamentary system, but in reality, this era was also marked by the dominance of ruling parties. Although general elections had been held by universal and secret right to vote (including women's suffrage) in 1920, a mere two years later, the secret voting system was abolished (except in the largest cities).

21. Hungary went to war against the Soviet Union as an ally of Nazi Germany – once again, it took part in the losing side of the war. The Peace Treaty of Paris in 1947 confirmed the state borders of Hungary of 1938, Hungary thereby losing its former state territories regained in 1938 and 1940.

22. At the end of the war, the country came under Soviet military occupation. However, in the period between 1945 and 1948, in the so-called coalition era, there was an aborted attempt to introduce a pluralistic parliamentary democracy. Act I of 1946 (the 'small constitution') declared Hungary a republic and openly rejected the restoration of legal continuity with the historical constitution. Multiparty parliamentary elections were held in 1945 and 1947. However, the Communist Party, effectively backed by Soviet occupation forces, became increasingly strong and practically gained political plenipotence in 1948. The new Soviet-type political and constitutional system was institutionalized by the 1949 Constitution, modelled on the Soviet, Stalin-type Constitution of 1936.

23. The first written Hungarian Constitution declared the form of state as a 'people's republic', which was intended to express the political nature of the state as a 'popular democracy' and to distinguish it from the Western-like European republics. The Constitution was deeply permeated by the postulates of Marxist ideology, emphasizing, for example, that '[t]he Hungarian People's Republic is a State of workers and working peasants', declaring the 'State … fights against every form of exploitation of man', and stating that '[t]he working class is gradually eliminating the capitalist elements and is consistently building the socialist order of economy.' In this spirit, the Constitution preferred the 'property of society' and the 'ownership of the State' vis-à-vis the private property. A centralized economy was introduced by providing that 'economic life … is regulated by a State plan of the people's economy'. The core principle of state organization was the unity of public power which was in theory exercised by the one-chamber National Assembly as 'the highest representative and public body' of the 'People's Republic of Hungary'. In fact, throughout the communist era, all members of the National Assembly represented the Communist Party having imperative mandates which meant that the MPs could be recalled by voters. In theory, the Council of Ministers, the highest organ of the executive power, had a political responsibility to Parliament, but this principle was never concretely applied. The public administration was a uniform and centralized organizational system involving the Soviet-type local and county councils. In fact, however, the real power was exercised by the Communist Party which kept the state organs under strong political control at all levels of government.

24. The Constitution of 1949 preferred second-generation (economic, social and cultural) rights at the expense of political liberties. Although the right to vote was universal, equal, secret and direct, it did not matter much because only state-party candidates could run in elections.

25. The constitutional amendment of 1972 brought about a limited democratization, but only within the institutional framework of dictatorship.

26. After the economic situation of the State gradually worsened from the mid-1980s on, the ruling party became divided between the hard-liners and the reformist wing, while in parallel, opposition movements became stronger. When the last communist government embarked on a wide-ranging reform programme that would democratize the entire public law system by preparing a new constitution, there was nothing left under the frameworks of the old socialist regime, and political developments quickly passed beyond these attempts.

§1.05 From Transition to Democracy to 2010

27. In the transition period of the Central and Eastern European countries, Hungary was the only post-communist State which did not adopt a new constitution replacing the old communist-type basic law. The constitutional foundations of the 'system change' in 1989–1990 were laid down by a peaceful negotiating process producing an agreement between the ruling Communist Party and the opposition parties and movements. The so-called National Roundtable Talks shaped a comprehensive political compromise not only on the schedule of the democratic transition from a Soviet-type, one-party authoritarian regime to a Western-like parliamentary democracy but also on the rules of the game, namely the basic institutions and features of the new constitutional system.[10] The results of this compromise were codified by the last one-party communist National Assembly as a basic revision to the existing Constitution of 1949, which brought about fundamental changes in Hungarian constitutional law. In reality, the general revision of the Constitution in

10. J.W. Schiemann, *The Politics of Pact-Making. Hungary's Negotiated Transition to Democracy in Comparative Perspective* 37–84 (Palgrave Macmillan 2005).

1989[11] changed almost all the important parts of the basic law to such a degree that many refer to it as 'an actually new constitution'.[12]

28. All references to the communist ideology were replaced by new values. For example, the communist principle of democratic centralism was succeeded by the principles of democracy and the rule of law; the centrally planned economy by a 'social market' one, and a parliamentary government was established based on a multiparty political system and free elections.[13]

29. Remarkably, the last communist government, led by Mr Miklós Németh, launched a project for preparing a new constitution. The work was managed by the Ministry of Justice, with contributions from some excellent legal experts and technocrats. But this attempt failed. The political changes were too fast for a sophisticated lawmaking process. By the time the conception was ready, the so-called reform communists had already lost their influence to get a new constitution accepted. Thus, the old Constitution remained in effect, retaining its unfortunate title of Act No XX of 1949, even if in a deeply restructured version.[14] Yet, it proved to be fairly flexible: from the general revision of 1989 to 2010, the Constitution was modified more than twenty times.

30. Despite the failure to pass a completely new constitution at the dawn of the system change, all political actors believed that even the considerably revised Constitution would only be a transitional one, as its preamble said, 'in order to facilitate a peaceful political transition to a constitutional state', Parliament established the new text of the basic law, 'until the country's new constitution is adopted'.

31. Only a couple of years later, in 1994, the leftist coalition of the Hungarian Socialist Party (MSZP) and the Alliance of Free Democrats (SZDSZ) gained a parliamentary majority of 72%. Thus, the chance arose to adopt a new constitution because in Hungary, Parliament itself was the '*pouvoir constituant*', as the constitutional amendment process required a two-thirds majority of the Members of Parliament whose decisions did not need the consent of any other body. Nevertheless, the government and opposition parties reached an agreement that they abandon the two-thirds majority requirement for constitutional amendment, and passed one

11. Act XXXI of 1989 on the amendment of the Constitution.
12. András Jakab, *The Republic of Hungary: Commentary*, in Constitutions of the Countries of the World 8 (Rüdiger Wolfrum & Rainer Grote eds., Oceana 2008).
13. István Szikinger, *Hungary's Pliable Constitution*, in *Democratic Consolidation in Eastern Europe. Volume I. Institutional Engineering* 409–415 (Jan Zielonka ed., Oxford University Press 2001); Gábor Halmai, *Ungarn*, in *Handbuch Ius Publicum Europaeum. Band I. Grundlagen und Grundzüge staatlichen Verfassungsrechts* 695–700 (Armin von Bogdandy, Pedro C. Villalón & Peter M. Huber (eds.) C.F. Müller Verlag 2007).
14. *See* Péter Paczolay, *The New Hungarian Constitutional State: Challenges and Perspectives,* in Constitution Making, in *Eastern Europe* 21–55 (Dick Howard ed., The Woodrow Wilson Center Press 1993) and István Pogány, *Constitutional Reform in Central and Eastern Europe: Hungary's Transition to Democracy*, 42(2) Intl. Comp. L.Q 332 (1993).

which required a four-fifths supermajority for adopting the special rules for preparing a constitutional draft.[15] It meant that the leftist coalition engaged itself not to use its own constitution-making capacity, but rather to pursue political consensus around the new basic law. It was not only a political gesture of the majority to the parliamentary minority: just after a parliamentary cycle with the defeat of communist rule, the post-communist MSZP was quite careful using its own power, whereas its coalition party, the liberal SZDSZ was an effective counterbalance against the socialists (who alone had an absolute majority in Parliament, so they would have been able to establish a one-party government themselves).

32. The whole process lasted more than two years, realizing an exceptionally wide-ranging professional and political coordination. As a result of the long preparatory work, a draft constitution was submitted to Parliament in 1997, but, in the final vote, it did not get the necessary support. As a matter of fact, a number of socialist MPs voted against it, so this attempt failed too.

33. In the years following, due to the growing hostility between the rightist and leftist parties, there was no real chance of putting the issue of a new constitution on the political agenda, nor was it seen as an exigent political question. The most important modifications (which were necessary for Hungary's accession to the NATO in 1997 or the European Union in 2004) were successfully adopted, and the activist jurisprudence of the Constitutional Court filled the gaps in the old Constitution.

34. Even when the possibility of a two-thirds majority of Fidesz was in the centre of the political discussions before the parliamentary elections of 2010, the question of a new constitution was not a featured issue in the election campaign. Nevertheless, shortly after his election victory, Viktor Orbán, the charismatic Prime Minister and undisputed leader of the political right, made it clear that the new coalition would use its mandate to create a new constitution.

15. Act No. XLIV of 1995. The constitutional amendment was adopted only for the period of parliamentary mandate (until 1998), but some legal collections indicated it as valid even after that time. Therefore the government majority of the new Parliament of 2010, to be sure, abolished it with a constitutional amendment.

Chapter 2: The Constitution

§2.01 Introduction: The Concept of the Constitution in Hungarian Constitutional Law

35. In ancient Hungarian constitutional history, the word 'constitution' (*alkotmány*) always meant the unwritten 'historical constitution' (*történeti alkotmány*), which evolved, according to the traditional view, since the founding of the State, and which consisted of the most important cardinal (or fundamental) laws and constitutional customs and conventions on Hungarian state sovereignty, the exercise of public power and individual freedom. In this approach, those laws were considered 'fundamental', which had been adopted by Parliament and sanctioned by the King in accordance with the rules of procedure applicable to ordinary laws (i.e., there was no separation between the constituent and the legislative power), and whose constitutional nature was recognized by custom or by public consensus.

36. In spite of this traditional conception, since the adoption of the first written constitution in 1949, in Hungarian constitutional law, the Constitution has been conceptualized as the highest normative act issued by Parliament.[16] The concept of the Constitution is usually defined on the basis of its main regulatory subjects and its formal characteristics. According to this, the Constitution is the highest legal norm containing the most important principles and rules of the exercise of public power and fundamental rights.[17] In more general terms, the Constitution expresses the relationship between society and the State.[18]

37. In academic literature, the concepts of 'material' and 'formal' constitution are often distinguished, classifying all legal principles and rules into the material constitution which govern the system of separation of powers and the fundamental rights, whereas the constitution in the formal sense involves all legal norms adopted in a constitution-making procedure, regardless of their content.

38. The Fundamental Law, which entered into force on 1 January 2012, is, by its own definition, the basis of the whole legal system (Article R) section (1)). The Fundamental Law does not classify itself as a legal norm, but this is of little importance, since the Fundamental Law is at the top of the hierarchy of sources of law in the sense that no legal norm can be in conflict with it.

---

16. András Jakab and Zoltán Szente, *Az Országgyűlés hatáskörei, 19.§* in Az Alkotmány kommentárja I. kötet (Jakab András ed., Századvég 2009) 556.
17. Barna Mezey & Zoltán Szente, *Európai alkotmány- és parlamentarizmustörténet* (Osiris Kiadó 2019) 488.
18. *Alkotmánytan* (István Kukorelli ed., 5th ed. Osiris 1998) 11.

§2.02 The Fundamental Law of 2011

[A] The Constitution-Making Process in 2010–2011

39. In the two decades after the system change, despite some political initiatives, all attempts to adopt a new constitution failed, including the constitution-making project of the mid-1990s when the Left-Liberal government coalition had a two-thirds majority in Parliament (1994–1998), one sufficient to amend the Constitution or to make a new one. However, after a conservative government coalition had gained a qualified majority again with 53% of the votes cast, everything changed rapidly. Just a year after the overwhelming election victory of the new coalition government in 2010, a new constitution was voted in by them. Even during this year, the old Constitution was amended no less than twelve times by the new governing parties.

40. The whole process of constitution-making was exceptionally rapid and lacked transparency. Although its preparation lasted for almost ten months, the ad hoc committee established in June 2010 for the preparation of the conception of the new constitution was convened only twenty times. The members took about seventeen hours altogether to prepare the final concept. In November, two opposition parties, the MSZP (the Hungarian Socialist Party) and the LMP (*Lehet Más A Politika,* the 'Politics Can Be Something Else' party) marched out the parliamentary committee as a protest against the mutilation of the competence of the Constitutional Court, and, in general, the governmental politics of 'destroying the rule of law' (and they never came back). After an uneventful period of three months, owing to the protest and boycott of the opposition parties, the conception of the ad hoc committee was declared non-binding for further work and, by a parliamentary resolution adopted on 7 March, all parliamentary factions were invited to introduce their own constitutional bills until 15 March 2011.[19] Finally, the constitutional bill, submitted by the governing party MPs, in the absence of two opposition parties, was approved by 262 votes in favour to 44 against (with 1 abstention)[20] – the MPs of the third opposition party, the radical rightist Jobbik voting 'nay'.

41. This zealous constitution-making activity did not ease even after the enactment of the new Fundamental Law (i.e., the Constitution). Together with that Fundamental Law, a long piece of constitutional legislation ('Transitional Provisions') came into force on 1 January 2012, containing a number of rules completing and detailing the new constitutional text.[21] Since then, the parliamentary majority has amended the Fundamental Law eight times, rewriting about 25% of the constitutional text.

---

19. Only two bills were submitted, one by the coalition parties and another by a deserted socialist politician, the former speaker of Parliament.
20. The Parliament had 386 members.
21. The Constitutional Court invalidated Transitional Provisions objecting, among others, the uncertain constitutional rank of this piece of legislation. Decision 45/2012. (XII. 29.) of the Constitutional Court.

[B] The Structure of the Fundamental Law

[1] General Characteristics

42. The new Constitution is a written basic law contained in a single document. From a formal point of view, it has several specific features. In addition to the traditional major structural elements, the Constitution has a motto and a *postambulum* (epilogue). Furthermore, it does not have a uniform numbering method for the paragraphs. The provisions of the first part are numbered by capital letters from A to U, the catalogue of basic rights and citizens' obligations by Arabic numerals, while the rules on public authorities are marked by Roman numbers. Interestingly, as opposed to the rules of Hungarian spelling, certain words are written with capital letters emphasizing such concepts as 'The Members of Hungarian Nation', 'Our Homeland' or 'The Man'.

43. It is even more striking that, according to its official name, it is not a 'Constitution', but a 'Fundamental Law'. This denomination is the product of a historicizing endeavour of the constitution-makers to link somehow the new Constitution to the so-called historical constitution, denying also the legitimacy of the first written Hungarian Constitution of 1949.[22] In fact, the category of 'fundamental laws' was indeed well known and admitted in past Hungarian public law, but it was understood in quite different ways: those laws were called 'fundamental' which were considered as parts of the unwritten, historical constitution, rather than a consolidated constitutional charter. According to an author of the new constitutional text, the intention was 'to rebuild the interrupted continuity' with the old, 'one-thousand-year-constitution'.[23] In this understanding, the (real) 'constitution' as such is composed of the Fundamental Law and the historical constitution. This view is also supported by the Preamble of the Fundamental Law, proclaiming that it does not recognize the suspension of the historical constitution. Whatever the original intention was concerning the name of the new Constitution, it is certain that constitutional practice does not regard the historical constitution as a source of law, but only as an auxiliary principle of constitutional interpretation, as will be discussed later.

[2] The Preamble of the Constitution: 'The National Avowal'

44. As has been said, the Fundamental Law has a motto: 'God bless the Hungarians', which is the first line of the national anthem. The reason for this solution was that the mention of God in the constitutional text triggered controversy and the constitution-makers thought that the reference to God in this way could avoid further criticisms.

---

22. Zoltán Szente, *A historizáló alkotmányozás problémái: A történeti alkotmány és a Szent Korona az új Alaptörvényben* 4 Közjogi Szemle 1, 10 (2011).

23. József Szájer, *Szabad Magyarország, szabad Európa: Újabb tizenöt év. Beszédek, írások, dokumentumok 1998–2013* (2014) 825.

45. The Preamble of the Fundamental Law is named 'National Avowal'. It is by far the longest and one of the most pathos-ridden preambles in Europe. It lists the subjects of national pride, like the achievement of King Saint Stephen to make Hungary 'a part of Christian Europe one thousand years ago', the 'forebears who fought for the survival, freedom and independence', 'the outstanding intellectual achievements of the Hungarian people', the country's role in defending Europe 'over the centuries', and so on. The Constitution secures nationalities as parts of the political community, and Hungary bears responsibility for the next generations. The conservative ideological values of the Preamble are definitely the repercussions of the one-sided preparation of the Constitution. Thus, the Preamble emphasizes 'the role of Christianity in preserving nationhood' and declares that the family and the nation are the most important bases of the 'coexistence'. In the Hungarian political context, the recognition and respect of the achievements of the historical constitution and the Holy Crown, 'which embodies the constitutional continuity of Hungary's statehood and the unity of the nation', also reflect right-wing conservative value judgments.

46. This pathetic and value-driven Preamble has raised some logical problems and legal concerns. Above all, while it does not recognize 'the Communist Constitution of 1949', and proclaims it 'to be invalid', the Closing Provisions make clear that Parliament adopted the Fundamental Law in accordance with the rules of the former Constitution for the adoption of a new Constitution. Hence, the Fundamental Law based its own legitimacy on the Constitution, whose legality was nevertheless denied. Furthermore, after the Closing Provisions, there is a declaration expressing that the constitution-maker adopted this Constitution as 'the first unified Fundamental Law of Hungary', which also seems to deny the Constitution of 1949 as a real one.

47. Due to its ideological biases and some legally questionable stipulations, the National Avowal triggered deep criticisms. Thus, the attempt to revive the historical constitution and the respect of the Holy Crown have caused a number of difficulties since the constitutional text gives a quasi-normative power for these manifestations, qualifying them as principles of constitutional interpretation. The problem is that it is not clear what can be considered to be the 'achievements' of the historical constitution which existed for centuries and changed frequently during its existence.[24] Another legal concern arose from the declaration of the Preamble asserting that the constitution-makers 'deny any statute of limitations for the inhuman crimes committed against the Hungarian nation and its citizens under the national socialist and communist dictatorships'. Having regard to the indirect normative power of the Preamble, this claim grants constitutional empowerment for retroactive criminal legislation in case of certain offences of a political nature, raising thus some rule of law

24. Imre Vörös, *A történeti alkotmány az Alkotmánybíróság gyakorlatában* 7 Közjogi Szemle (2016); Zoltán Szente, *The Doctrine of the Holy Crown in the Hungarian Historical Constitution*, 4(1) J. Eur. Hist. L. (2013).

problems.[25] Political controversy and protests were caused by the reference of the National Avowal to the German occupation on 19 March 1944 as a date when Hungary lost its sovereignty. The background reason of this outcry was that the Preamble tried to close authoritatively a long political and historical controversy about the responsibility of Hungarian authorities for the persecution of Hungarian Jews during the Second World War.

[3] Sovereignty and the Fundamental Principles of the Hungarian State: 'Foundation'

48. The first part of the Fundamental Law is called 'Foundation', which contains the basic principles of the Hungarian State and the most important provisions concerning sovereignty.

49. Although the new Constitution has changed the official name of the country from 'Hungarian Republic' to 'Hungary', the form of State has remained a republic (Article A) and B) section (2)). There has also been no change in the constitutional text defining Hungary as 'an independent, democratic state governed by the rule of law' and the principle of popular sovereignty has been preserved as the source of all public power. The principle of the separation of powers is also entrenched in the text together with the prohibition of 'the forcible acquisition, exercise or exclusive possession of power'. Any attempt at the latter actions entitle and oblige 'every person' 'to act against such an attempt in a lawful way' which is probably a recommitment to the famous resistance clause (Article 31) of the medieval charter, the Golden Bull of 1222.

50. Regarding sovereignty issues, this chapter contains the European Union clause: the constitutional grounding and empowerment of the country's EU membership. Also included in this chapter are the territorial structure of the State, the basic principles of citizenship, the state symbols and national holidays. The Constitution states that Hungarian is the official language, and the *forint* (HUF) is the official currency in Hungary.

51. This part defines the Fundamental Law as the foundation of the legal system, and together with legal rules, it is binding on everyone. Article S) specifies the constitution-making process and enumerates the legal rules, laying down the principle of the hierarchy of legal norms.

---

25. Here, first of all, the violation of the principles of *nullum crimen sine lege* and *nulla poena sine lege* can be cited, which were previously well-established constitutional guarantees of the Hungarian legal system. However, due to the passing of time, these have retained only symbolic significance. After 2010, only the *Biszku* case fell within the scope of this provision. In order to create a legal basis for the trial against Béla Biszku, the former Minister of Interior, for his involvement in the reprisals after the Revolution of 1956, a special law (which has been called 'lex Biszku' by the press) was adopted and which extended the exclusion of the Statute of Limitations, as a principle of international law, to the 'Communist' crimes under the Communist regime from 1949 to 1990: *see* Law No. CCX of 2011.

52. This part also comprises ideological commitments fixing certain values in the Constitution that are usually attributed to the conservative political creed. These include, for instance, Hungary's responsibility for the fate of Hungarians living beyond its borders, defining the traditional concept of marriage as a union of a man and a woman, emphasis on the values of work and self-responsibility, and everyone's obligation to contribute to the performance of State and community tasks.

53. The most politicized provisions are contained in Article U) which were incorporated in the text by the Fourth Amendment to the Fundamental Law in 2013, although these rules as parts of the Transitional Provisions had been annulled earlier by the Constitutional Court. In fact, this article involves a political manifesto which, among others, stigmatized the Hungarian Socialist Party, the largest opposition party at the time when the amendment was adopted, and its legal predecessors as 'criminal organizations' serving the communist dictatorship before the system change. Article U) obliterates the Statute of Limitations in case of serious criminal offences committed under the communist dictatorship 'which were left unprosecuted for political reasons'. Some other provisions, on behalf of restorative justice for human rights violations under the communist regime, impose certain restrictions (such as limitations on the right to a pension or reopening criminal procedures in case of statute-barred 'political' crimes) on the leaders of the communist dictatorship.

[4] The Constitutional Rights and Obligations: 'Freedom and Responsibility'

54. The next part of the Fundamental Law has the title of 'Freedom and Responsibility' and contains basic rights and citizens' duties. Although the title of this chapter and some general phrases of the text sound as if fundamental rights would be conditional upon the fulfilment of civil obligations, the relevant provisions – with one exception[26] – do not ground such a relationship between them. This part predicates that the protection of inviolable and inalienable fundamental rights is the primary obligation of the State, and the Constitution recognizes not only individual but also collective rights as well. Article I) section (3) specifies the proportionality-necessity test as the general method of legitimate limitations on basic rights. It is also an essential constitutional guarantee that the detailed rules on basic rights may be laid down only in acts of Parliament.

55. The Fundamental Law then lists the most classical political rights and civil liberties, circumscribing their primary content and often specifying their special safeguards. Besides those, the Constitution also stipulates a number of economic and cultural rights too. The relevant provisions were modelled on the Constitution

26. In the scope of social and welfare rights, Art. XIX s. (3) stipulates that 'the nature and extent of social measures may be determined in an Act in accordance with the usefulness to the community of the beneficiary's activity'.

of 1949/1989. However, in contrast with the former Constitution, the current provisions acknowledge social and welfare rights only as state goals rather than enforceable basic rights.

56. The part 'Freedom and responsibility' contains some rights that were not included in the previous Constitution, like the prohibition on using the human body or its parts for financial gain, human cloning, and human trafficking. Allegedly, the Charter of Fundamental Rights of the European Union was taken into account in the wording of this part of the Fundamental Law, but the text followed mainly the former Constitution's provisions.

57. In accordance with its title, this part specifies the most important citizens' duties as well. Article XVI prescribes that parents are obliged to take care of their children when minors, including providing schooling for them. Allegedly, this was taken over from the Russian Constitution that adult children must take care of their parents if they are in need (Article XVI section (4)). At the constitutional level is the novel obligation that anyone who causes damage to the environment is obliged to restore the latter or bear the costs of restoration (Article XXI section (2)). The Constitution contains two traditional citizens' duties, even if in new wording. According to Article XXX section (1), all citizens have to contribute to covering common needs in proportion to their capabilities or participation in the economy. The curious feature of this provision is that, in a unique way in Europe, the obligation contained therein has no institutional limitation, for the Constitution has deprived the Constitutional Court of its judicial review power over any public finance legislation (as described *infra* in Part II, Chapter 6, §6.03, [B]). The other classical obligation is participation in defence of the country. As to the forms and extent of this obligation, the Fundamental Law creates some differences between citizens. First, only adult male citizens are obliged to perform military service, with the exception of those whose religious beliefs cannot be reconciled with the use of weapons and who can then perform unarmed military service. Second, those bound to defend the country are only those who have a residence in Hungary, meaning, in other words, that Hungarian citizens living beyond the borders are not obliged to do so. In the framework of the obligation of national defence, citizens are also obliged to perform public work for national defence purposes, and, in the interest of performing national defence and disaster management tasks, they have civil protection obligations as provided for by cardinal acts.

58. This part of the Fundamental Law surprisingly contains certain policy decisions which usually belong to the agenda of everyday governmental politics in other countries. The purpose of these provisions was to incorporate certain basic political choices of the ruling coalition of 2010 into the Constitution and to make it difficult to change the policy measures of this government for all subsequent governments. Thus, among other things, the Constitution requires the maintenance of a uniform state pension system based on social solidarity and prohibits the agricultural production of genetically modified organisms.

[5] The System of the Separation of Powers: 'State'

59. The next part of the Constitution, which is entitled 'State', contains the basic rules for the legal status of the most important public authorities. Its provisions, which are numbered with Roman numerals, relate to the National Assembly, the President of the Republic, the government, the autonomous regulatory organs, the Constitutional Court, the (ordinary) courts, the Prosecution Service, the Commissioner for Fundamental Rights, the local governments, the Hungarian Defence Forces, and the police and national security services. Although the chapters for these bodies are not uniform in their structure, the relevant provisions generally regulate the way in which the particular public authorities are formed and terminated, their most important functions, powers and duties and major procedures. In each case, the Constitution empowers the legislature to determine the detailed rules by way of cardinal act. The lawmaking powers of public authorities are also defined by the Constitution in these sub-chapters.

60. The constitution-makers used a strange regulatory technique when they placed some chapters governing certain important constitutional procedures and activities in this part. For example, the chapter on the National Assembly is followed by the rules on national referendums; the chapter on 'Public Finances' has been incorporated between the chapters on local governments and the Hungarian Defence Forces, and after the rules on the police and national security services a separate chapter on the decisions on participation in military operations is placed. The structure of the chapter on 'Public Finances' is especially peculiar because, apart from the basic rules on the annual state budget and the so-called debt-brake rules, it also contains provisions on the legal status of the Hungarian National Bank, the Budget Council and the State Audit Office, which should be placed, according to the general logic of this part, in separate chapters.

[6] 'Special Legal Orders'

61. The Fundamental Law contains the main rules on the special legal orders. While originally six different emergency situations were regulated by the Constitution, the Ninth and Tenth Amendments simplified the emergency regime, the importance of which was increased by the fact that the country has had a special legal order in force continuously since March 2020, with a short interruption for various reasons. This part of the Fundamental Law includes both common rules for all special legal orders and provisions governing certain exceptional situations specifying which bodies or officials in each case are given a special mandate while providing for a cardinal act to lay down detailed rules.

[7] 'Closing and Miscellaneous Provisions', and the *Postambulum*

62. It is strange that the last chapter of the Constitution has changed the most in recent years. For example, the constitution-maker inserted a provision declaring retroactively the constitutional ranking of the Transitional Provisions.

63. The closing provisions ordered different dates of entry into force of some Articles of the new Constitution as exceptions to the principal rule according to which the Fundamental Law takes effect on 1 January 2012. These provisions introduced new designations of some constitutional organs and based the legitimacy of the new Fundamental Law on the fact that it was adopted pursuant to the rules of the old Constitution on constitution-making.

64. Interestingly, the Fundamental Law has a so-called *postambulum*, a closing remark wishing 'May there be peace, freedom and accord' – which is a reference to one of the demands of the Revolution of 1848.

[C] The Constituent Power

[1] The Content of the Constituent Power

65. In Hungarian constitutional law, the National Assembly is the constituent power. Although Parliament also exercises legislative power, these two powers are separated from each other. So, for example, the National Assembly may not amend the Fundamental Law by an ordinary, or even a cardinal act, but only as a constituent power. So, it is an essential requirement that Parliament may act explicitly in this capacity during the constitutional process. The constituent power differs from that of the legislative in the applicable procedural rules, including majority requirements.

66. Parliament's constituent power is full and exclusive. While a number of countries observe a distinction between the constituent (*pouvoir constituant*) and the amending (or constituted) power (*pouvoir constitué*), the Fundamental Law does not recognize this differentiation: both powers are exercised by the National Assembly, mostly under the same procedure.

[2] The Problem of Unconstitutional Constitutional Amendments

67. The issue of constitutionality of constitutional amendments was raised in the practice of the Constitutional Court already in the 1990s, but the Court consistently rejected the possibility of reviewing constitutional amendments, either formally or substantially. According to the Court, constitutional review of constitutional provisions is conceptually impossible.[27] All the provisions of the Constitution are legally equivalent, so there is no legal hierarchy between the Constitution's own norms.[28]

68. As a matter of fact, this question became the focus of public attention only after 2010, following the reorganization by a two-thirds majority of the public law

27. László Sólyom, *Az alkotmánybíráskodás kezdetei Magyarországon* (Osiris Kiadó 2001) 276–277.
28. *See* Decisions 23/1994. (IV. 29.), 293/B/1994. and 1260/B/1997. of the Constitutional Court.

system, as the new government (using its constitution-making parliamentary majority) began to change a number of principles and rules that were previously considered to be well-embedded constitutional values. And, as the political technique became used more frequently whereby legal provisions previously declared unconstitutional by the Constitutional Court were then incorporated into the Fundamental Law by means of constitutional amendments (thus avoiding the possibility of constitutional review), the need was also expressed that basic constitutional values and principles should be protected by the Constitutional Court in such a way as to allow review of constitutional amendments. The concept and permissibility of unconstitutional constitutional amendments were also debated in the literature.[29] However, the Fourth Amendment to the Fundamental Law in 2013 ended the disputes over jurisdiction in this regard, clarifying that the Constitutional Court could only examine the formal regularity of the constitution-making process but not the content of constitutional amendments.

[3] Procedural Rules of Constitution-Making

69. As said above, both the adoption of a new constitution and the amendment of the Fundamental Law may take place under the same procedural rules. According to Article S) of the Fundamental Law, the President of the Republic, the government, any parliamentary committee or any member of the National Assembly may initiate such a procedure. The Fundamental Law contains no specific provisions for parliamentary debates on such matters; in practice, the rules of the normal legislative procedure are applied in these cases. For the adoption of a new constitution or for the amendment of the Fundamental Law, the votes of two-thirds of the MPs are required. Once the proposal has been approved by the necessary majority, the Speaker of the National Assembly signs the text so adopted within five days and sends it to the President of the Republic. The Head of State has to sign it also within five days of receipt and order its promulgation in the official gazette. However, if the President of the Republic finds that any procedural requirement laid down in the Fundamental Law has not been met, he or she will request the Constitutional Court to examine the issue. Should the examination by the Constitutional Court not establish a violation of such requirements, the President of the Republic has to sign immediately and promulgate the new Constitution or amendment.

[4] The Amendments of the Fundamental Law of 2011

70. Despite Prime Minister Viktor Orbán once saying (in a frequently quoted statement) in 2012 that the Fundamental Law was 'as firm as granite', the Hungarian Constitution of 2011 is probably the most flexible constitution in the world.

29. *See* a collection of the relevant studies in *Alkotmányozás és alkotmányjogi változások Európában és Magyarországon* (Fruzsina Gárdos-Orosz and Zoltán Szente eds., NKE Közigazgatás-tudományi Kar 2014).

[a] The First Amendment

71. The first important change took place immediately at the time of the entry into force of the Fundamental Law, when two days earlier the Parliament passed the Transitional Provisions of the Hungarian Fundamental Law and which came into effect in parallel with the new constitutional text itself. The Transitional Provisions were adopted by Parliament on the basis of the authorization of the Closing Provisions of the Fundamental Law, with the aim of ensuring smooth transition from the old to the new constitutional text. By adopting these provisional rules, the constitution-maker chose a new, previously unknown solution abdicating the unity of the constitutional text. Nonetheless, the Commissioner of Fundamental Rights turned to the Constitutional Court to declare unconstitutional the Transitional Provisions. The major constitutional concern here was that this document did not contain only technical rules for the Fundamental Law entering into force, but it included also a political manifesto condemning – among others – the communist period of the country, and making the Hungarian Socialist Party, the largest opposition party of that time, responsible for the communist dictatorship as the legal successor of the old state party. In addition, the legal nature of the Transitional Provisions and their place in the hierarchy of legal sources were not clear. However, in order to avoid constitutional review of the document, the government parties, using their constitution-making majority in Parliament, got a constitutional amendment through the National Assembly in June 2012 stating that the Transitional Provisions belong to the Fundamental Law, and as such, they have constitutional status. Besides that, the modification also encompassed some other provisions for current policy purposes (like increasing the allowances of the former heads of state, rewarding in this way Pál Schmitt, a close political ally of the government, who was involved in a plagiarism scandal, and resigned from office for that reason).

[b] The Second Amendment

72. According to the Second Amendment to the Fundamental Law adopted in the autumn of 2012 (formally modifying the Transitional Provisions), the right to vote may be exercised only if voters register for the electoral roll at least fifteen days before general elections or national referendum. However, the Constitutional Court in December 2012 heard a petition filed by the Commissioner of Fundamental Rights, and, due to formal reasons, annulled most parts of the Transitional Provisions, including these new rules on the voters' obligation to request registration.[30]

[c] The Third Amendment

73. On the initiative of the government, a third amendment to the Fundamental Law took place in December 2012. On this occasion, Parliament has authorized itself to lay down statutory rules in the cardinal act for the acquisition and exploitation of fields and forests, as well as for 'integrated agricultural production and

30. Decision 45/2012. (XII. 29.) of the Constitutional Court.

farming'. The purpose of the amendment was to provide special protection for the sectoral policy of the government majority which aimed to prevent lands and forests from becoming foreign property.

[d] The Fourth Amendment

74. The Fourth Amendment of the new Constitution, which entered into force on 1 April 2013, was the most extensive change, not only modifying a number of provisions but also adding some new constitutional rules to the text. The explanation of the amending proposal argued for the constitutionality of the Transitional Provisions emphasizing that the constitution-making power also extended to divide the constitutional text into two parts in a way that the first part contained the main text of the Constitution, while the second part encompassed transitional provisions, and that Parliament had duly complied with formal requirements when it had done so. Notwithstanding this and noting the Constitutional Court's decision to repeal the Transitional Provisions, the constitution-maker expressed its will 'to include not only the nullified provisions, but the full content of the Transitional Provisions' in the (unified) text of the Fundamental Law. Accordingly, the political statement originally included in the Transitional Provisions – with only minor changes – was incorporated into the chapter 'Foundation' of the Fundamental Law, and the Closing Provisions were completed with some new rules.

75. Furthermore, the Fourth Amendment incorporated into the constitutional text a number of other provisions which had been enacted by Parliament after 2010, but were declared unconstitutional by the Constitutional Court. Thus, it inserted the definition of marriage and family into the Fundamental Law in a form that had been previously invalidated by the Court when it had declared the relevant Family Protection Act null and void.[31] According to the new constitutional definition, the 'family' is based on marriage and a parent–child relationship, thus explicitly favouring the traditional family model as compared to any other (such as cohabitation) relationship.

76. Other new rules regulated in detail the procedure of constitutional amendments, making it clear that the Constitutional Court may only review them from a procedural point of view. Although in the past there was no constitutional basis for the Court to override the will of the constitution-making power,[32] this theoretical possibility was raised in some Constitutional Court's rulings after 2010 as a minority opinion,[33] and it was advocated by some constitutional scholars too.[34]

31. Decision 43/2012. (XII. 20.) of the Constitutional Court.
32. Decisions 293/B/1994., 23/1994. (IV. 29.), 290/B/2002. of the Constitutional Court.
33. For example, 61/2011. (VII. 13.) of the Constitutional Court.
34. *See supra* n. 29.

77. After the Constitutional Court had annulled the provisions of the Act on the Freedom of Conscience and Religion and the Status of Churches, which had governed the procedure for the registration of churches,[35] the Fourth Amendment to the Fundamental Law authorized Parliament to regulate the conditions of recognition of church status in a cardinal law. Another amendment reversed the Constitutional Court's decision which had repealed the provisions of the Electoral Procedure Act restricting political campaigns. Since the provisions of the law allowing media service providers to announce political advertisements only free of charge and banning such advertisements in campaign periods had also been invalidated by the Court,[36] the repealed rules were also included in the text of this constitutional amendment, changing the former constitutional requirements in this way.

78. As to the freedom of expression, Parliament also reversed the previous jurisprudence of the Constitutional Court on hate speech when it stated in the Fundamental Law that 'the right of the freedom of expression may not be exercised with the aim of violating the dignity of the Hungarian nation or of any national, ethnic, racial or religious community', and has established judicial protection against any expression that violates these communities (Article IX section (5)). Another provision of the Fourth Amendment, according to which State-funded university education may be linked to a fixed-term employment contract or to the pursuit of an entrepreneurial activity in order to keep graduates in Hungary, has also neutralized a former decision of the Constitutional Court in which the Court annulled a government decree of similar content (even if only for procedural reasons).[37] The constitution-maker also superseded a Constitutional Court ruling[38] when it allowed Parliament and local authorities to ban homeless people from public spaces.

79. In addition, the Fourth Amendment to the Fundamental Law included several new provisions as well, like the constitutional authorization given to the government to determine, within the limits of the law, the management rules of higher education institutions and to supervise their financial management. Some of the procedural conditions for recognition as a nationality were also included in these modifications of the constitutional text. The powers of the Speaker of the National Assembly have been confirmed, in particular his or her disciplinary powers, and his/her commanding power over the Parliamentary Guard was recognized in the Fundamental Law. As a further novelty, this amendment regulated the legal status of the President of the National Office of Judiciary, and as a part of it, his or her power to transfer individual cases from a competent court to another court. As was already noted, the Fourth Amendment explicitly stated that the Constitutional Court may only examine proposed new constitutions or constitutional amendments for compliance with formalities. For the constitutional review procedure, it prescribed that the Court's examination may not go beyond the framework of the petitioner's request, and set down some other new procedural rules. The former restriction imposed on

35. Decision 164/2011. (XII. 20.) of the Constitutional Court.
36. Decision 1/2013. (I. 7.) of the Constitutional Court.
37. Decision 32/2012. (VII. 4.) of the Constitutional Court.
38. Decision 38/2012. (XI. 14.) of the Constitutional Court.

constitutional review of public finance legislation has been expanded by declaring that laws issued at a time when the amount of public debt exceeded 50% of GDP could not be abolished for this period even if the limitations on the Constitutional Court's jurisdiction would disappear. Another significant provision of this amendment was to repeal the decisions of the Constitutional Court made prior to the entry into force of the Fundamental Law.

80. A further rule – on a provisional basis, until the public debt exceeds half of the GDP – authorized Parliament to impose extraordinary financial contributions in the event where a payment obligation of the State would arise from a decision of the Constitutional Court, the Court of Justice of the European Union, or any other court or executive body that is not covered by the state budget. The position of Parliament against the Constitutional Court was reinforced by the rule which authorized the legislature to determine the method of calculating the public debt and the GDP. The Fourth Amendment has reaffirmed the termination of the mandate of the President of the Supreme Court, the President and members of the National Judicial Council, and the Data Protection Commissioner by the earlier legislation.

81. The Fourth Amendment to the Fundamental Law once again intensified the debates on the Hungarian situation of the rule of law, both domestically and abroad.[39] Many scholars considered it as the 'final blow' for constitutionalism.[40] The Commissioner for Fundamental Rights turned to the Constitutional Court to declare the amendment unconstitutional for formal reasons, but the Court rejected the petition.[41]

[e] The Fifth Amendment

82. The next modification of the Constitution was partly inspired by the heavy international criticisms of the Fourth Amendment. According to the explanatory memorandum of this new proposal, 'as a result of the Constitutional Court's decision on the Fourth Amendment, the controversies over the new Fundamental Law were closed in Hungary', yet the new amendments were necessary to ensure that 'some constitutional issues can no longer serve as an excuse for attacks against Hungary'. For this purpose, the Fifth Amendment to the Fundamental Law, on the one hand, reaffirmed Parliament's power to define the organizational form of religious communities in a cardinal act as well as the constitutional authorization to differentiate between various religious communities by introducing the concept of 'established churches', for which 'the State grants specific rights'. As a result of

39. For example, Venice Commission, Opinion on the Fourth Amendment to the Fundamental Law of Hungary, CDL-AD(2013)012, Opinion 720/2013. See also Katalin Kelemen, *The New Hungarian Constitution: Legal Critiques from Europe,* 42 Review of Central and East European Law (2017) 26-30.
40. Imre Vörös, *The Constitutional Landscape after the Fourth and Fifth Amendments of Hungarian Fundamental Law*, 55(1) Act. Juridica Hun. 1–20 (2014); Zoltán Szente, *The Political Orientation of the Members of the Hungarian Constitutional Court between 2010 and 2014*, 1(1) Const. Stud. 123, 133 (2016).
41. Decision 45/2012. (XII. 29.) of the Constitutional Court.

international protests and criticisms of the Fourth Amendment, this constitutional change has allowed in an implicit way the commercial media to broadcast political advertisements during election campaign periods maintaining however the limitation that political ads can be published only free of charge and under the conditions laid down by law.

83. It was also a consequence of international criticisms that the special power of the President of the National Office of Judiciary to transfer individual cases from the competent court to another court has been abolished. The constitutional authorization for imposing extraordinary financial contributions in the case where a decision of an international court or the Constitutional Court would jeopardize the balance of the state budget has also been abrogated. Finally, the Fifth Amendment provided an opportunity for the fusion of the Hungarian National Bank and the Hungarian Financial Supervisory Authority which took place quite soon thereafter.

[f] The Sixth Amendment

84. After a long government-sponsored anti-migration campaign which argued that migration enhances the threat of terrorism, inland security and the 'Christian culture' of Hungary, the Sixth Amendment to the Fundamental Law in June 2016 added a new type of special legal order to the already existing five. According to the new rules, 'in the event of a significant and direct threat of a terrorist attack', or if such an attack occurred, the National Assembly, on the initiative of the government, may declare 'a state of terrorist threat' for a fixed period of time, and may simultaneously authorize the government 'to introduce extraordinary measures laid down in a cardinal act'. The period of that state of terrorist threat may also be extended.

[g] The Seventh Amendment

85. The Seventh Amendment to the Fundamental Law was also linked to a long-running and current policy campaign of the government. After the Council of the European Union had decided that Member States should share the burden of the migrant crisis by relocating asylum seekers from the front-line States (Greece and Italy) among all other Member States, the Hungarian government initiated a national referendum in February 2016 against this controversial quota system. However, the turnout did not reach the validity threshold set by law (more than half of all voters) since only 40.32% of voters cast valid votes.[42] Nevertheless, the government proposed a constitutional amendment adding a new sentence to the so-called EU clause, stating that the joint exercise of competences by EU institutions and the Hungarian authorities must 'comply with the fundamental rights and freedoms provided for in the Fundamental Law', and it may 'not limit the inalienable right of Hungary to determine its territorial unity, population, form of government and state structure' (Article E) section (2)). In connection with this provision, the amendment

42. Zoltán Szente, *The Controversial Anti-Migrant Referendum in Hungary Is Invalid*, https://constitutional-change.com/the-controversial-anti-migrant-referendum-in-hungary-is-invalid/.

filled a lacuna in police powers, now empowering the police to participate in the prevention of illegal migration (Article 46 section (1)).

86. Another new provision explicitly prohibits the settlement of 'foreign population' in Hungary. In order to exclude the competence of EU institutions to settle non-Hungarians in the country, the amendment specifies that any 'foreign national' who does not have the right to free movement and residence 'may only live in the territory of Hungary under an application individually examined by the Hungarian authorities' (Article XIV section (1)). The apparent purpose of these rules was to provide a legal tool for the government to oppose the relevant EU policy by referring to the constitutional prohibition on the settlement of 'alien populations' in Hungary.

87. This issue was linked to the introduction of the bases of constitutional identity into the text of the Fundamental Law. After the reference in the Preamble to the honour of the historical constitution and the Holy Crown, a new statement was inserted expressing that '[w]e hold that the protection of our identity rooted in our historic[al] constitution is a fundamental obligation of the State'. Accordingly, Article R) section (4) was added with the imposition of a new obligation of all public authorities to protect 'the constitutional identity and Christian culture of Hungary'.

88. Another change has affected the scope of privacy at the expense of the freedom of expression and the right of assembly, emphasizing that the exercise of the latter rights may not impair private and family life and the home of others, and the State has to 'provide legal protection for the tranquillity of homes' (Article VI sections (1)–(2)).

89. Article XXII section (3) was also modified, empowering public authorities to prohibit the use of public space 'as a habitual dwelling', opening the way for punishing the homeless, which has been balanced only by declaring that the State must 'strive to ensure decent housing conditions and access to public services for everyone' (Article XXII section (1)).

90. This constitutional amendment has also created the possibility of separating administrative courts from the organizational system of ordinary courts (Article 25 sections (1)–(3)).

91. Finally, the constitution-makers wanted to narrow the interpretative room of courts specifying the rules of purposive legal interpretation. According to the new constitutional guideline, in the course of identifying the purpose of law, the preamble and the official statement (explanatory memorandum) of the law must be taken into account (Article 28).

[h] The Eighth Amendment

92. After the local elections of October 2019, in which the ruling parties suffered heavy losses in the larger cities, the government announced that it would refrain from establishing a high administrative court in order to avoid further international criticism. For this purpose, the Parliament removed all constitutional provisions referring to the new system of administrative courts. Thus, these amendments, adopted in December 2019, were only of technical nature, eliminating the provisions introduced by the Seventh Amendment on administrative courts.

[i] The Ninth Amendment

93. In late autumn 2020, the government submitted to Parliament a new amendment to the Fundamental Law. This time too, the constitutional amendment served specific political purposes of the governing parties, and targeted reactions to some recent political conflicts, which again underscores the instrumental nature of the Constitution. Thus, for example, one of the changes has supplemented Article L) of the Fundamental Law by stating that '[t]he mother is female, the father is male', which was in line with the government's political campaign and policy that recognizes only the traditional (Christian) family model as legitimate. This article has already ruled out same-sex marriage, but the new rules, together with a newly adopted legislation providing that only married couples will be allowed to adopt children, aim at excluding same-sex couples from adoption.

94. Another has a similar spirit stating that 'Hungary shall protect the right of children to a self-identity corresponding to their sex by birth, and shall ensure an upbringing for them that is in accordance with the values based on the constitutional identity and Christian culture of our country.' Gender studies have previously been banned from public universities, and this new constitutional provision would recognize only the sex by birth as a part of personal identity.

95. Another amendment has given Parliament broad powers to transfer public assets to public interest foundations over which the government has no control. It is to be noted that many political scandals in recent years have resulted from the fact that the government transferred state ownership and budget subsidies free of charge to public foundations, over which state control has been formally abolished. These mechanisms seem to be constitutionally recognized by the new amendment stating that 'the establishment, operation and termination of public trust funds performing a public task as well as the performance of such public tasks by the public trust fund shall be regulated in a cardinal law'.

96. The amendment simplified the constitutional rules governing the special legal regime by replacing the previous six different states of emergency with three – a state of war, a state of emergency, a state of danger – and by extending the powers of the government, whereby the government is granted exceptional powers to govern by decree in each of the states of emergency.

[j] The Tenth Amendment

97. This amendment to the Fundamental Law, adopted in May 2022, extended the possible scope of the state of danger to cases of 'armed conflict, war or humanitarian disaster in a neighbouring country', allowing the government to retain its exceptional powers after a health emergency caused by the Covid-19 pandemic.

[k] The Eleventh Amendment

98. The Eleventh Amendment was adopted in July 2022, and it ensures that local elections are held at the same time as elections to the European Parliament. The amendment also renamed the counties as 'castle-counties', in order to revive the pre-World War II constitutional traditions.

[l] The Twelfth Amendment

99. The government initiated the latest amendment to the Fundamental Law in November 2023, which once again aligned the constitutional text with the government's current policy objectives. The amendment, adopted on 12 December 2023, stipulated that 'in order to protect the constitutional identity', an independent public authority should be established by a cardinal law. According to the official explanation of the amendment, this public body should be set up to investigate foreign interference in political decision-making and elections. This was motivated by the fact that an opposition movement had received a significant amount of foreign support before the previous parliamentary elections. Although this was not illegal, the government majority wanted to cut off the opposition from this source of funding.

100. Under another provision, the state will provide everyone with a unique digital identifier and has also authorized the government to issue a decree specifying what data the state can collect for the purpose of digital administration.

101. A further provision prohibited the establishment and operation of trade unions in the Hungarian Defence Forces and authorised the government to regulate the status of professional soldiers by decree.

[m] Other Attempts

102. It is to be noted that since the Fundamental Law has entered into force, dozens of unsuccessful attempts to amend the Constitution have been made, proposed mainly by opposition parties, but none of them have received sufficient support in the National Assembly.

[D] The Constitutional Principles and Methods of Constitutional and Legal Interpretation

103. Despite the old Constitution (of 1949/1989), the Fundamental Law of 2011 defines the major methods of constitutional interpretation. The relevant guidance is scattered in the constitutional text without any hierarchy among the different interpretive principles.

104. Article N) section (1) declares that Hungary enforces 'the principle of balanced, transparent and sustainable budget management', while section (3) makes respect of this principle the duty of – among others – the Constitutional Court. This is an unusual provision having unclear and obscure content, for it is questionable which constitutional requirements should be preferred if the issue of constitutionality is confronted with economic rationality (like balanced budgets). In practice, although the Constitutional Court sometimes refers to these principles in very general form, no relevant jurisprudence has evolved so far.

105. According to Article R) section (3), the provisions of the Fundamental Law must be interpreted: (a) 'in accordance with their purposes', (b) 'with the Avowal of National Faith', and 'with the achievements of our historical constitution'. The first reference relates to the objective teleological (or purposive) method of constitutional interpretation. It is to be noted that the Fundamental Law prescribes a similar interpretive rule also for the ordinary courts (Article 28), and since most part of the Constitutional Court's case law deals with constitutional complaints – namely, the review of individual judicial decisions – this specific type of legal interpretation is used in this context. In other words, in the course of the constitutional review of judicial decisions, the Constitutional Court checks whether the court properly considered the objective purpose of the legal norms it had to apply in the specific case. This 'objective purpose' means the social aim that the lawmaker wanted to achieve by the legal act, rather than the subjective and original intent of those who took part in the lawmaking process.

106. Since the preambles of legal norms, like the National Avowal, did not have normative power in Hungarian legal traditions, the making of the constitutional preamble into a sub-principle of interpretation stands as a real innovation. Given that the Preamble contains very abstract values, solemn phrases and historical references, its real effect on the case law is fairly limited. The role of the 'achievements of the historical constitution' is quite similar. Since the new Constitution's entry into force, there has been great discussion about the content of this provision in Hungarian legal literature.[43] The content of the unwritten, historical constitution was inherently ever-changing, and there is no guidance to determine which period or state of the historical constitution should be applied. The Fundamental Law only records that the self-determination of the Hungarian State was lost on 19 March

43. *See supra* n. 24.

1944 when Nazi Germany occupied the country. Presumably, this date is the endpoint of the historical constitution. However, because of the war rules or the anti-Jewish laws that were in force in 1944, this state of the historical constitution can hardly be assumed or followed. In reality, the Constitutional Court occasionally selects certain rules or customs in historical Hungarian public law; that is, it considers the historical constitution as a sort of menu. However, in the course of constitutional interpretation, the use of the historical constitution does not have any jurisprudential basis, and the frequent references to it usually represent only decorative elements to the Constitutional Court's rulings.

Chapter 3: State Territory

107. The state territory of Hungary is determined and internationally guaranteed by the Peace Treaty of Paris signed on 10 February 1947 which was adopted by the Allied Powers and Hungary. The Treaty – which was promulgated in Hungary by the Act XVIII of 1947 – has restored the state boundaries in accordance with the situation of 1 January 1938, depriving the country of her territorial gains under the First and Second Vienna Awards in 1938 and 1940.[44] In fact, the state borders largely correspond to those laid down in the Trianon Peace Treaty of 1920.

108. Hungary is located in Central Europe; Hungarian authorities often claim that Europe's geometric centre can be found in the Hungarian village of Tállya, although this issue is highly controversial.

109. The state territory has an area of 93,030 square kilometres; the length of its borders is 2,215 kilometres. The country has seven neighbours: Slovakia to the north, Ukraine to the north-east, Romania to the east, Serbia, Croatia and Slovenia to the south, and Austria to the west. Hungary is a border country of the European Union to Ukraine and Serbia, as well as a border country of the Schengen Area to Croatia and Romania (*see* Figure 1).

110. According to the Fundamental Law, the territory of Hungary is comprised of the capital (*főváros*), its districts (*kerületek*), the counties (*megyék*), the cities (*városok*) and communities (*községek*).

111. The powers of territorial division of the country are shared between Parliament and the Head of State along the logic that while the relevant competences relating to the capital city, its districts and the counties (including to establish, abolish, amalgamate or separate them) are conferred on the National Assembly, all jurisdiction concerning the legal and administrative status of the municipalities fall within the scope of responsibility of the President of the Republic (notably, as regards these competences of the Head of State, his/her decisions need the proposal and the countersignature of the Minister of the Interior).

44. After Hungary lost about two-thirds of its state territory as the historical Hungarian Kingdom under the Trianon Peace Treaty of 1920 after the First World War, the primary aim of Hungarian foreign policy was the revision of that Treaty. For that purpose, the country formed an alliance with Nazi Germany and Fascist Italy. As a result of this alliance, these countries, as arbitration powers, awarded certain territories with largely Magyar-populations to Hungary. The two Vienna Awards (named after the relevant decisions made in Vienna, at the Belvedere Palace) were declared null and void by the Peace Treaty of Paris in 1947.

Figure 1 Map of Hungary

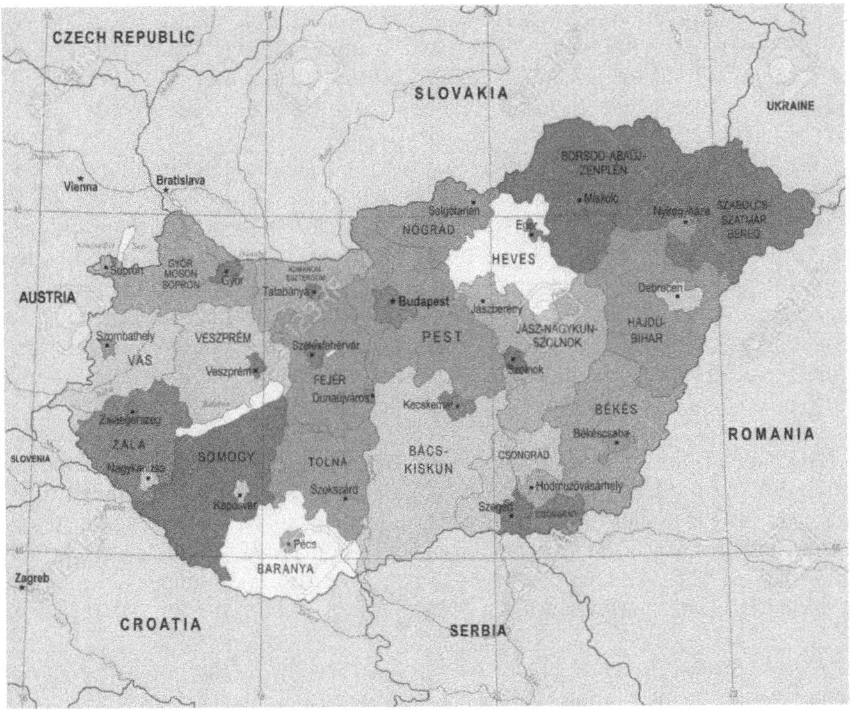

Chapter 4: Population and Demographics

112. The population of Hungary as of 2022 was approximately 9,603,000 (about 1,076 women per 1,000 men).[45] The average age of the population was 43.1 years (41 for men and 45 for women). Life expectancy at birth was 72.55 years for men and 79.05 years for women (2022).[46] Population density is 103 per km^2.

113. The country's demographic situation is constantly deteriorating. On the one hand, there is a continuous decline in population and, on the other hand, the average age of society is growing. While the number of live births per thousand people is 9.1, the number of deaths is 14.1 (2022). The total fertility rate is 1.52, whereas according to most accepted expert assessments, 2.1 would be needed to maintain the population. A further problem in terms of population decline is that, since 2010, according to estimates, 300–500,000 Hungarians left the country, mainly from the younger age group, while the restrictive immigration policy of the country does not allow it to supplement this loss from external sources.

114. Due to the permissive regulation of citizenship which grants Hungarian nationality to the people of Hungarian origin all over the world, the number of Hungarian citizens is higher than that of the country's population. Although there are no official statistics, since the introduction of the new citizenship regime allowing Hungarians living abroad to acquire Hungarian citizenship, the number of citizens has increased by more than one million.

115. At the last national census held in 2022, 84.2% of the population declared themselves to be Hungarian, 13.7% did not answer their nationality question and 4% declared themselves to be of another nationality. The real proportion of nationalities is obviously much higher: the number of the largest ethnic minority, the Gypsy population, for example, is estimated at 400,000–800,000.

116. There are also only expert estimates about the religious affiliation of the population, based on the 2022 census data and the number of 1% tax donations from those who have paid personal income tax. According to the national census of 2022, for example, most people declared themselves Roman Catholic (27.5%), followed by Calvinists (9.83%), Lutherans (1.84%), and Greek Catholics (1.72%), while 16.1% of the respondents said they were non-denominational and 40.1% did not answer the question about their religion. Compared to the previous census in 2011, the number of adherents of the major historic churches has fallen sharply.

45. Source: National Statistical Office, https://www.ksh.hu/stadat_files/nep/hu/nep0001.html.
46. Source: National Statistical Office, https://www.ksh.hu/stadat_files/nep/hu/nep0001.html.

Chapter 5: Popular Sovereignty

117. The principle of popular sovereignty is a relatively young tenet of Hungarian constitutional law. According to the traditional approach, all sovereign power was vested in the Holy Crown (*Iurisdictio Sacrae Coronae*) which was the exclusive source and possessor of state sovereignty.[47] The main reason for the long life of this peculiar sovereignty doctrine of medieval origin was that, for most part of its history, a foreign (non-Hungarian) ruler was sitting on the throne of Hungary, and the Hungarian Estates were always reluctant to recognize the full sovereignty of a foreign ruler.

118. The people's sovereignty was constitutionally recognized only after the Second World War, even though during the decades of the socialist regime this doctrine did not have real significance. The constitutional revision of 1989 reformulated the sovereignty clause stating that the 'supreme power is vested in the people', rather than 'in the working people', as the original constitutional text said, and completing this provision with a reference to the direct exercise of this power (which was missing beforehand). The Fundamental Law changed even this formula, saying that the 'source of public power' is the people.

119. So today, popular sovereignty or sovereignty of the people is one of the fundamental principles of the Hungarian constitutional law. Article B) section (3) of the Fundamental Law declares that the people are '[t]he source of power'. This clause expresses the exercise of public authority to derive from the people. Some claim that it means primarily the constitution-making power of the citizens,[48] but this view might be correct at least indirectly, since this power is vested in Parliament (Article S) of the Fundamental Law, the organ of popular representation. It can be more plausibly said that all public power must be traceable to popular will.

120. But it is only the most abstract formulation of this principle. The Constitution goes further saying also that the people are not only the source of public authority but also participate in exercising it. Section (4) of the same article provides that the people exercise 'their power through their elected representatives, and also directly in exceptional cases'. In this way, there are two basic forms of citizen participation. First, the usual way of exercising public power is indirect democracy when the people take part in it through its representative bodies, like the National Assembly and regional and local governments. The representative bodies exercise that power in an indirect way, in so far as they are directly elected bodies and decide public affairs in the name and interest of, and are empowered by, the people. Moreover, citizens 'in exceptional cases' may exercise their power directly when they decide themselves in constitutional frameworks (through referendums).

47. Szente, *supra* n. 22.
48. József Petrétei, *Magyarország alkotmányjoga I: Alapvetés, alkotmányos intézmények* (Kodifikátor Alapítvány 2013) 72.

121. The concept of 'people' in this context means only eligible citizens having the political right to vote and to participate in referendums.

122. There is a delicate relationship between direct and indirect forms of the exercise of public power. An earlier landmark decision of the Constitutional Court declared that although the referendum as an instrument of expressing public will is exceptional in its nature, it is the primary version of exercising public power.[49] Presumably, this means that when the citizens decide on a public matter, their decision is binding on the national representative body. However, this form of public power has also its own limits, inasmuch as a national referendum may be held, as a major rule, only in cases falling within the scope of responsibilities of the National Assembly. Indeed, there are exceptions to this rule, and there are some parliamentary competences which are prohibited subjects for national referendum.

123. Moreover, in respect of popular sovereignty, public power may be exercised only on the basis of democratic legitimacy. According to this precept, all public law acts must be traceable to popular sovereignty.[50]

124. The Twelfth Amendment to the Fundamental Law established the so-called Sovereignty Protection Office 'to counter attempts to interfere with Hungary's sovereignty'.[51] The Office's task is to investigate and detect activities that threaten sovereignty.[52] The Office is an autonomous state administrative body, its President is appointed by the Head of State on the recommendation of the Prime Minister for a six-year term, but can be re-elected several times. The Office conducts investigative and analytical activities, the results of which it may make public, but it determines itself what it considers to be a threat to state sovereignty, and it also establishes its own procedural rules. It can request data from any institution and manage personal data. There are no legal remedies against its decisions.

---

49. Decision 52/1997. (X. 14.) of the Constitutional Court.
50. Decision 30/1998. (VI. 25.) of the Constitutional Court.
51. *See supra* Part I, Chapter 2, §2.02 [C] [4] [l].
52. Act LXXXVIII of 2023.

Chapter 6: Republican Form of Government

125. The republican form of State had an important symbolic significance for a long time after the transition process to democracy in 1989/1990. Notably, the proclamation of the new republic took place on the same day, on 23 October 1989, when the landmark constitutional revision was promulgated.

126. As the form of the People's Republic in the Communist Constitution of 1949 symbolized the rupture of the Western-type democracies, the return to the republican form of government in 1989 sought to demonstrate a break with the communist past. Thus, the official name of Hungary became the Republic of Hungary. However, the Fundamental Law of 2011 has changed this name, dropping the reference to that form of State, and renaming the country simply 'Hungary'. Although this was explained by the fact that the official name of most States is simply the common denomination of the country, it was in fact intended to mark the end of the period since the regime change in 1989–1990 and the beginning of a new political era. It is to be noted that after 1989–1990, republicanism has never become a definite political ideology, but critics of the new constitutional regime have tried to use the republican form of government as a symbol of the claim to restore the 'republican constitution' of 1989 (i.e., the Constitution of 1949 in its 1989 version).[53]

53. *Harcz az Alkotmányért* (László Majtényi and Virág Zsugyó eds. Kalligram 2019).

Chapter 7: National Symbols

127. The national symbols are included in the first chapter 'Foundation' of the Fundamental Law. The Constitution recognizes three emblems, describing in detail their forms or content. These are the coat of arms, the flag and the national anthem.

128. The coat of arms (*see* Figure 2) can be traced back to the symbol of the State's founding family (the House of Árpád) seeing as it contains eight horizontal bars of red and silver portrayed on the shield. The double cross also has medieval roots: it was originally a Christian symbol but later symbolized the independence of the Hungarian Kingdom. At the top of the shield, there is a picture of the Holy Crown. This has been the coat of arms since 1990, when a constitutional law, as a symbolic act of the democratization process, replaced the old one that had been introduced by the first written constitution in 1949.

129. With regard to the republican form of government of the country, the appearance of the crown – a basic symbol of monarchies – may be surprising, but the dominant view is that the Holy Crown has symbolized statehood in Hungarian history, rather than the monarchy. Although during the actual period of the historical constitution (i.e., before the Second World War) interpreting it with this kind of differentiation would be hard, the appearance and symbolism of the coat of arms are no longer disputed.[54]

Figure 2 The Coat of Arms

54. The alternative to the 'crowned' coat of arms during the debates in 1989 and 1990 was the so-called Kossuth coat of arms that was used in the Revolution of 1956, but this proposal was not adopted. For these debates, *see* Iván Halász and Gábor Schweitzer, *Szimbolika és közjog: Az állami és nemzeti jelképek helye a magyar alkotmányos rendszerben* (Kalligram 2010) 48–63.

130. The flag of Hungary contains three horizontal bands of equal width, coloured red, white and green from top to bottom 'as the symbols of strength, fidelity and hope' respectively (*see* Figure 3).[55] The colours of the tricolour were fixed in the nineteenth century, although this colour scheme follows the basic colours of the coat of arms. The association of the colours with the high values of strength, fidelity and hope is also rooted in the nineteenth century.

Figure 3 The Flag of Hungary

131. The national anthem is the poem 'Hymn' of Ferenc Kölcsey, written in 1823, set to music by Ferenc Erkel. Its musical version was first performed in an official ceremony in 1844. Notably, the first line of the anthem is put above the Preamble of the Fundamental Law like a motto.

132. The Fundamental Law allows that the coat of arms and the flag 'may also be used in other historically developed forms'. Nevertheless, the detailed rules for the use of the national symbols are laid down in a cardinal act. This law[56] provides for the use of the coat of arms (and its variants) and the state badges of honour.

133. It is to be noted also that the national symbols are protected by criminal law, as the Penal Code of 2012[57] determines the violation of the national emblem as a crime. According to this law, 'those who publicly use offensive or degrading expressions for the Anthem, Flag, Coat of Arms or the Holy Crown, or otherwise dishonour them, is punishable by a term of imprisonment for a term of one year'.[58] It is worth noting that the Penal Code also punishes the violation of the symbol of the Holy Crown, although it does not belong to the national symbols.

134. The Fundamental Law defines the national holidays, specifying also the content of official commemorations (Article J) sections (1)–(2)). Thus:

- on 15 March, the revolution and independence war of 1848–1849 are celebrated;
- 20 August is the day of memory for the foundation of the State and of King Saint Stephen, the State Founder; and
- 23 October is the day of commemoration of the 1956 Revolution and war of independence.

55. Art. I) s. (2) of the Fundamental Law.
56. Act CCII of 2011.
57. Act C of 2012.
58. Art. 334 of the Penal Code.

135. In addition, the official State holiday is 20 August.

Chapter 8: Democracy

136. Article B) section (1) of the Fundamental Law states that Hungary is a 'democratic rule-of-law State'. While the jurisprudence of the Constitutional Court relating to the expression of 'democratic rule of law' entrenched in Article 2 of the Constitution of 1949/1989 between 1990 and 2011 aimed primarily at evolving and extending the content of the rule of law principle, the meaning of the democracy principle which is implied also by the same clause was much less sophisticated. It is meaningful because the text of Article B) section (1) of the Fundamental Law corresponds to that of the former Constitution.

137. The particular form of democracy is determined by the various provisions of the Fundamental Law. Its basic content is that the exercise of public power is bound to constitutional rules; that is, the protection of individual rights and minorities limits the exclusive effect of the majority principle. Nonetheless, it is still based on popular sovereignty, and it has been frequently discussed and cited in connection with the direct and indirect forms of exercising public power. Section (3) of the same article declares that the source of public power is the people, while the next paragraph explicitly refers to the representative and direct ways of exercising power.

138. The Constitutional Court has never defined the concept of democracy in terms of constitutional law, and in its case law, this principle did not appear as such a constitutional value like the rule of law or human dignity, whose violation could in itself be the basis for declaring a legal norm unconstitutional. Instead, the Court primarily used the principle of democracy as a justification for interpreting other constitutional values, like freedom of expression or direct citizens' participation. Beyond the very abstract attributes of the exercise of public authority, the democratic character of state power is often associated with the parliamentary form of government, free elections, pluralism, multiparty system and the constitutional protection of basic rights.

139. While the dominant view in the interpretation of the principle of democracy between 1990 and 2010 was that this term should be understood as 'constitutional democracy',[59] since 2010 this concept has faded, at least in government communications which, on the basis of several statements made by Prime Minister Orbán, refers to it as an 'illiberal democracy'. This concept seeks to express a political ideology that defends 'Christian freedom' against liberalism. Although it does not appear in statutory law, this ideology is used to justify moving away from several fundamental principles and values of constitutional democracy.

140. In this respect, it should be mentioned that constitutional democracy has been criticized by a number of international organizations since 2010, claiming that its level has declined significantly and continuously. There are many doubts that, as a consequence of partly the new constitutional rules serving unilateral political

59. Petrétei, *supra* n. 49, 83.

interests and partly political practice, the democratic institutional system has been eroded to such a great extent that it can hardly be imagined that the ruling coalition government could be overthrown by democratic elections. The European Parliament declared in September 2022 that 'there is increasing consensus' that 'Hungary is no longer a democracy', and it 'has become the EU's first ever authoritarian Member State'.[60]

60. European Parliament resolution of 15 Sep. 2022, P9_TA(2022)0324 Existence of a clear risk of a serious breach by Hungary of the values on which the Union is founded. https://www.europarl.europa.eu/doceo/document/TA-9-2022-0324_EN.pdf.

Chapter 9: The Principle of the Rule of Law

§9.01 The Constitutional Requirements of the Rule of Law

141. Article B) paragraph (1) of the Fundamental Law declares the principle of the rule of law without defining it. Its content is specified primarily by different provisions of the Constitution. The relevant values have been arranged under the concept of the rule of law by the Constitutional Court's jurisprudence. Such subprinciples, as explicitly expressed by the constitutional text, are the recognition and protection of fundamental rights (Article I) section (1)), the division of powers (Article C) section (1)), the independence of judges (Article 26 section (1)) and rights to a fair trial (Article XXIV section (1)).

142. The Fundamental Law refers to this principle in its Article U) that was inserted into the constitutional text by the Fourth Amendment in 2013. In some respects, this article looks like a political manifesto that, for example, stigmatizes the largest opposition party at the time of the constitutional amendment as a legal successor of the Hungarian Socialist Workers' Party (the Communist Party of the previous dictatorship) that shares the responsibility of its predecessor as beneficiary of its unlawfully accumulated assets. Section (1) of the article specifies the beginning of the new era of the rule of law counting it from the first free elections held in 1990, and sharply separating it from the 'previous communist dictatorship'.

143. In the 1990s, the Constitutional Court played a prominent role in establishing the detailed content of the principle. In those years, the Court took on the task of determining the constitutional requirements of the rule of law from case to case. The starting point of the Court's interpretation was that the very general and abstract principles of the Constitution are not only declarations but autonomous legal norms, and the violation of such values itself provides enough reason for establishing the unconstitutionality of a legal rule.[61] Although the Court has never given a consolidated concept of the rule of law, it enunciated very early on that 'the rule of law is realized by the fact that the Constitution is indeed and definitely prevails'.[62] Nevertheless, developing the substance of this tenet, the Court went far beyond the constitutional text, and took several extra-textual considerations into account.

144. In the first years after the system change (i.e., the transition to democracy in 1989–1990), a particularly important constitutional issue was how to handle the legal consequences of the Communist era in accordance with the rule of law. The Court took the view that the aspects of natural justice could not overcome the requirements of the rule of law. Although the Court acknowledged that it had always taken 'historical circumstances' into account, it nevertheless declared that the system change took place on the ground of legality – an important component of the rule of law. The principle of legality requires that the foundational rules of the legal

61. Decision 9/1992. (I. 30.) of the Constitutional Court.
62. Decision 11/1992. (III. 5.) of the Constitutional Court.

system should unconditionally be given effect. Moreover, all legal norms, regardless of the time of their adoption, must comply with the rules of the Constitution.

145. One of the relevant landmark cases of the Court was to annul the 'Zétényi-Takács Act', a law which would reopen culpability for crimes committed before the system change but which had not been pursued by the State for political reasons, even if the limitation period had already lapsed. As the Court argued, the reopening of the limitation period would entail retroactive legislation, which was incompatible with the principle of rule of law. In this way, the tenets of *nullum crimen sine lege* and *nulla poena sine lege* were recognized and became parts of the rule of law principle.[63] It is to be noted, however, that the Court decided the opposite the following year when it upheld new legislation proposed by the government with more or less the same content and referring to the 'generally accepted principles of international law' which would allow ex post facto legislation in case of war crimes and genocide.[64] In this manner, the Court indirectly recognized that certain acts of bloody suppression during the Revolution of 1956 were war crimes, thus opening the way for criminal proceedings. That said, however, the prohibition of retroactive criminal legislation is no longer valid in its original form because Article U) sections (6)–(7) of the Fundamental Law of 2011 declares that '[s]erious criminal offences laid down in an Act which were committed against Hungary or persons under the communist dictatorship in the name or in the interest of, or in agreement with the party-state and which were left unprosecuted for political reasons by ignoring the Act on criminal law in force at the time of commission, shall not be considered as time-barred', and provides that the limitation periods for such crimes must be calculated as of the day of the entry into force of the Fundamental Law.

146. Another crucial requirement of the rule of law is legal certainty. According to this principle, it is the responsibility of the State – and above all the legislator – to ensure that the law as a whole and individual pieces of legislation are clear, unambiguous and knowable to their addressees. Moreover, also included is that formalized procedural rules must be complied with to create valid legal norms.[65] Legal certainty requires not only the clarity of legal rules but also the predictability of the operation of constitutional institutions.[66] It is true, however, that the Court has never reached the recognition and protection of legitimate expectations, even though it evolved the doctrine of the moderate protection of 'acquired rights', which stipulates that closed legal relations may be changed only exceptionally for other constitutional purposes. The concept of acquired rights emerged in the domain of social policy concerning legal entitlements for particular social services provided by law. 'Legal certainty requires, among other things, the protection of the acquired rights, the intactness of completed or closed legal relationships, and the constitutional limitation of the changeability of long-term legal relations originating in the past.'[67]

63. Decision 11/1992. (III. 5.) of the Constitutional Court.
64. Decision 53/1993. (X. 13.) of the Constitutional Court.
65. Decision 9/1992. (I. 30.) of the Constitutional Court.
66. Decision 75/1995. (XII. 21.) of the Constitutional Court.
67. Decision 11/1992. (III. 5.) of the Constitutional Court ABH 1992, 81.

However, this principle does not establish an absolute rule or protection.[68] The rights and entitlements provided by law may be reduced or even abolished if needed for attaining a legitimate aim, provided that the underlying public interest exceeds the importance of the protection of acquired rights.[69] As to the level of constitutional protection of acquired rights, the Court developed a distinction between so-called *ex gratia* entitlements, and 'purchased rights'. While the first group of the acquired rights is based exclusively on the social policy of the government, which has a wide discretion to provide them, purchased rights are legal entitlements for which the citizens (as service users or 'entitled persons') have paid (like pension or basic health services). Noteworthy is that, in 1995, the Court extended constitutional protection of property rights to this class of acquired rights.[70] However, the whole construction of acquired rights has been destroyed by wide-ranging social and economic legislation since 2010, in which legal measures have been upheld by the Constitutional Court referring to the changed constitutional text[71] or to its lack of jurisdiction.

147. Another fundamental requirement of the rule of law is that public authorities should operate within the limits of their organizational framework and procedural rules set by law.[72] Since all state bodies are subject to law, the legality of their actions must be controlled by the courts. Article XXVIII section (7) states consequently that everyone has 'the right to seek legal remedies against any court, authority or other administrative decision which violates his or her rights or legitimate interests'. It also follows from the Constitution that public authorities must exercise their powers in good faith and in cooperation with each other.[73]

148. During the 1990s the Constitutional Court deduced the most important standards of lawmaking from the principle of rule of law, which were incorporated later in statutory law. Thus, legislation should have regulatory content that is clear to its recipients. The date of entry into force of the law has to be established in a way that sufficient time should be available to prepare for the application of the law.[74]

149. The earlier jurisprudence of the Constitutional Court found that it can be an abuse of legislative power if an individual decision emerges in the form of (normative) legal regulation[75] because it might exclude the opportunity for a legal

68. Decisions 515/B/1997., 1011/B/1999., 495/B/2001. of the Constitutional Court.
69. Decisions 43/1995. (VI. 30.), 62/1993. (XI. 29.), 16/1996. (V. 3.), 142/2010. (VII. 14.), 3062/2012. (VII. 26.) of the Constitutional Court.
70. *See* the Decisions 43/1995. (VI. 30.) and 45/1995. (VI. 30.) of the Constitutional Court.
71. Decision 23/2013. (IX. 25.) of the Constitutional Court.
72. Decision 56/1991. (XI. 8.) of the Constitutional Court.
73. Decision 8/1992. (I. 30.) of the Constitutional Court.
74. Art. 2 s. (1) and (3) of Act CXXX of 2010 on the Law Making.
75. Decision 5/2007. (II. 27.) of the Constitutional Court.

remedy for individuals.[76] In spite of these prior decisions, in practice, personalized legislation and lawmaking for specific cases have become quite frequent in the last few years.

§9.02 The Decline of the Rule of Law after 2010

150. In fact, the principle of the rule of law has definitely lost its central position in constitutional jurisprudence in the last few years. The Constitutional Court refers to this principle much less frequently than before, and it is doubtful that the Court maintains its original starting point that the abstract breach of the rule of law (without violating any other constitutional rule) would in itself justify the declaration of unconstitutionality of a specific law or legal provision. While in the 1990s the Court derived a whole series of unenumerated rights from the principle of the rule of law, it has long since abandoned this practice. It is also significant that since 2010, when the Conservative government coalition of Fidesz and the Christian Democrats came to power and began to transform the whole legal system, more and more criticisms have been raised by supranational institutions, human rights organizations and other NGOs about the continually worsening situation of the rule of law in Hungary. These critics have mostly adverted to the demolishing of judicial independence, political influence over all neutral institutions, from the Constitutional Court to the National Election Commission, and limitations on fundamental rights, especially the freedom of religion and the freedom of the press. In some cases, non-compliance procedures were launched, even if only a few of them were referred to the European Court of Justice by the European Commission.[77] In September 2018, the European Parliament, for the first time in its history, triggered the procedure under Article 7 of the Treaty on the European Union for investigating whether the rule of law was systematically threatened in this Member State. The European Parliament expressed in its resolution that it found 'the existence of a clear risk of a serious breach by Hungary of the values on which the Union is founded'. The resolution based on several different fact-finding missions and reports prepared by the Venice Commission, the European Parliament, the European Commission, the Organization for Security and Co-operation in Europe, the UN Human Rights Committee, as well as some judgments of the Court of Justice of the European Union and the European Court of Human Rights, specified 'the main concerns related to the functioning of the constitutional and electoral system, the independence of the judiciary and of other institutions, the rights of judges, corruption and conflicts of interest, privacy and data protection, freedom of expression, academic freedom, freedom of religion, freedom of association, the right to equal treatment,

76. Decisions 6/1994. (II. 18.) and 45/1997. (IX. 19.) of the Constitutional Court.
77. Zoltán Szente, *Challenging the Basic Values? Problems in the Rule of Law in Hungary and the Failure of the EU to Tackle Them*, in *The Enforcement of EU Law and Values: Ensuring Member States' Compliance* 456–475 (András Jakab & Dimitry Kochenov eds., Oxford University Press 2017).

the rights of persons belonging to minorities, including Roma and Jews, and protection against hateful statements against such minorities, the fundamental rights of migrants, asylum seekers and refugees, and economic and social rights'.[78]

151. As a matter of fact, all independent international rule of law indices have shown serious backsliding in the rule of law in Hungary in recent years.[79] In fact, among the EU Member States, the situation of democracy under the rule of law is the worst in Hungary.

152. The assessment of the recent constitutional developments in Hungary, including the situation of the rule of law, has deeply divided the domestic scholarly community. While the majority of Hungarian constitutional scholars have condemned the trends of the past few years,[80] some apologists have tried to justify the contemporary constitutional changes.[81]

153. The extent of corruption is a serious and persistent rule of law problem. According to independent surveys, the corruption situation in Hungary has significantly deteriorated in recent years. According to the global scores of the Corruption Perceptions Index, in 2009, Hungary was the 46th least corrupt country in the world, whereas in 2022 it only ranks 77th in the same list.[82] In particular, the Prosecution Service is reluctant to take action against political corruption, often not even when

---

78. European Parliament, P8_TA-PROV(2018)0340, *The Situation in Hungary.* European Parliament resolution of 12 Sept. 2018 on a proposal calling on the Council to determine, pursuant to Art. 7(1) of the Treaty on European Union, the existence of a clear risk of a serious breach by Hungary of the values on which the Union is founded (2017/2131(INL)).
79. *See*, e.g., Freedom House, Democracy in Retreat. Freedom in the World 2019, https://freedomhouse.org/report/freedom-world/freedom-world-2019/democracy-in-retreat; World Justice Project Rule of Law Index 2019, https://worldjusticeproject.org/sites/default/files/documents/WJP-ROLI-2019-Single%20Page%20View-Reduced_0.pdf; Bertelsmann Stiftung Transformation Index BTI, https://www.bti-project.org/en/reports/country-reports/detail/itc/HUN/; András Jakab & György Gajduschek, *The Rule of Law, Legal Consciousness and Compliance,* in *Social Report [of Hungary]* 277–294 (István György Tóth ed., 2019).
80. *See,* e.g., Kriszta Kovács and Gábor Attila Tóth, *Hungary's Constitutional Transformation*, 7 European Constitutional Law Review 183–203 (2011), *Constitution for a Disunited Nation: On Hungary's 2011 Fundamental Law* (Attila Tóth Gábor ed., Central European University Press 2012); Nóra Chronowski and Márton Varju, *Constitutional Backsliding in Hungary,* 6(3) Tijdschrift voor Constitutioneel Recht, 3 296–310 (2015); Szente, *supra* n. 78; Gábor Halmai, *Illiberal Constitutionalism? The Hungarian Constitution in a European Perspective*, in *Verfassungskrisen in der Europäischen Union* 84–103 (Stefan Kadelbach ed., Nomos 2018); Márton Varju, Nóra Chronowski, Gábor Sulyok and Petra Bárd, *Hungary: Constitutional Evolution or Regression?,* in *The Role of National Constitutions in European and Global Governance. National Reports* 1–41 (Anneli Albi & Samo Bardutzky eds., T.M.C. Asser Press 2019).
81. *The Basic Law of Hungary: A First Commentary* (Lóránt Csink, Balázs Schanda & András Varga Zs eds., Clarus Press–National Institute of Public Administration 2012); László Trócsányi, *The Dilemmas of Drafting the Hungarian Fundamental Law: Constitutional Identity and European Integration* (Schenk 2016).
82. Source: https://www.transparency.org/.

the European Anti-Fraud Office (OLAF) encourages it to do so.[83] Hungary often emerges in the academic literature as an example of centralized corruption and state capture.[84]

154. The situation of the rule of law in Hungary has entered international dimension after the European Parliament triggered the Article 7 TEU procedure against Hungary in September 2018. In addition, in early 2022, the European Commission launched the 'rule of law conditionality' procedure against Hungary, a mechanism that has been in force in EU law since January 2021. As a result of this procedure, the EC suspended the payment of Hungary's share of the recovery fund and other EU funds at the end of 2022 until Hungary meets the EU's conditions for restoring the rule of law. The European Commission, in the protection of the EU funds, has made the payments conditional on the fulfilment of the so-called horizontal enabling conditions and 27 so-called milestones, mainly related to anti-corruption measures, public procurement and judicial reform which Hungary must meet during 2023.[85]

---

83. In the best-known case, the *Elios* case, the Prime Minister's son-in-law was also involved in a street lighting scandal.
84. *See,* e.g., Mihály Fazekas and István János Tóth, *From Corruption to State Capture: A New Analytical Framework with Empirical Applications from Hungary*, 69(2) Pol. Res. Q. 320–334 (2016).
85. For details *see* Beáta Bakó, *Challenges to EU Values in Hungary – How the European Union Misunderstood the Government of Viktor Orbán* (Routledge, 2023) 39–46; and László Detre, András Jakab & Tamás Lukácsi, *Comparing Three Financial Conditionality Regimes and their Application to Hungary: The Conditionality Regulation, the Recovery and Resilience Facility Regulation, and the Common Provisions Regulation,* Max Planck Institute for Comparative Public Law & International Law (MPIL) Research Paper No. 2023/23.

Chapter 10: The Principle of the Separation of Powers

155. After 1949, during the Communist era, socialist state law was based on the principle of unity of state power. In formal terms, the National Assembly exercised the supreme power to which all other public bodies were subordinate. In practice, in the period of the Party-State, Parliament had no real power, and the centralized and undivided political power was in the hands of the Communist Party.

156. When the communist system collapsed, it was self-evident that the new constitutional architecture must be built upon the principle of the separation of powers. The 1989 constitutional revision really enforced this tenet, but without *expressis verbis* appearance of this principle in the renewed constitutional text. However, the Constitutional Court has frequently referred to the separation of powers as a fundamental constitutional requirement in the institutional structure of public power.[86] According to this approach, '[t]he principle of separation of powers means not merely that one branch of power cannot deprive another one of its jurisdiction, but also signifies: there is no unlimited power in a democratic State under the rule of law, and to this end, certain branches of power necessarily limit the jurisdiction of other branches'.[87]

157. While the Constitutional Court established the principle of separation of powers only through a contextual interpretation of the previous constitutional text, the Fundamental Law already explicitly included it stating that '[t]hat the functioning of the Hungarian State shall be based on the principle of the division of powers' (Article C) section (1)).

158. Constitutional jurisprudence, however, has been uncertain in this respect, in particular in recent years. For example, the Constitutional Court upheld the Nullity Act of 2011,[88] declaring null and void all non-appealable judicial decisions of previous years which, in the context of the street riots in the autumn of 2006, were based solely on police reports and testimony. Although the Act was a politically motivated encroachment into the sphere of judicial power, the Court did find that the legislator had the power to adopt special laws for doing justice in order to achieve its political goals, and the contested Act was not unconstitutional because it had quashed judicial decisions in favour of those convicted.[89]

159. Some scholars refer to the 'temporal' division of power as one of the types of power-sharing, whereby the same person may hold public office for a limited period of time, and the possibility of re-election is also limited.[90] It should be noted, however, that there are no such restrictions for positions of political nature.

86. Decisions 31/1990. (XII. 18.) and 38/1993. (VI. 11.) of the Constitutional Court.
87. Decision 28/1995. (V. 19.) of the Constitutional Court.
88. Act XVI of 2011.
89. Decision 24/2013. (X. 4.) of the Constitutional Court.
90. Petrétei, *supra* n. 49, 92.

160. In constitutional terms, there is no hierarchy between the major power branches. Still, as usually, the case in parliamentary systems, the Executive Branch has the greatest political power. It has been true in Hungary since the system change of 1989–1990, but this trend has been more pronounced since 2010, for the government, relying on its frequent constitution-making majority, successfully neutralized the crucial institutional counterbalances of the executive power, with the National Assembly becoming a rubber-stamp Parliament. The importance of the legislature has been further diminished by the continuing special legal order, during which the government has issued more than 800 emergency decrees by the end of 2022, many of which suspended or amended laws under the authorization of the Fundamental Law.

161. Although the Fundamental Law brought about only little institutional change in the system of the separation of powers, the government has packed the most powerful organs, and it was able to appoint its close political allies to almost every independent institution, including the Constitutional Court, the National Judicial Office, the State Audit Office, the Prosecution Service, the Budget Council, the National Election Commission, the Hungarian National Bank and the National Media Council.[91] As a result, the separation of powers has lost the significance that it had since the democratic transition after the collapse of the communist regime.

91. For details, *see* Szente, *supra* n. 78, 467.

Chapter 11: Forms of Direct Democracy

§11.01 The National Referendum

162. The first referendum in the history of Hungary took place in December 1921, when Sopron, a border town in Western Hungary, and the surrounding settlements voted on whether they belonged to Austria or Hungary (the people voted in favour of Hungary). Nevertheless, the referendum did not become a well-accepted institution in Hungarian public law. Although the Constitution of 1949 made reference to referendums (empowering the collective body of the Head of State, the Presidential Council to hold a referendum on matters of national importance), it was inconsistent with the doctrine that the Parliament exercises all rights deriving from popular sovereignty.

163. The forms of direct democracy were made permanent parts of Hungarian constitutional law by the Act XVII of 1989 on the Referendum and Popular Initiative. That statute made it possible to hold a referendum on a large scale: subject to a few exceptions, all issues falling within the scope of responsibility of Parliament could be subject to a national referendum. The procedural issues were laid down in Act C of 1997 on the Election Procedure.

164. The Fundamental Law and the Act on the Referendum Initiative and Procedures Act[92] introduced several changes to the previous legislative framework. They eliminated the institutions of consultative referendums (a popular vote that did not bind the legislature) and popular initiative (which obligated the Parliament to put an issue on its agenda and to discuss it), but these procedures were never of practical importance. The new rules re-introduced the threshold for validity to the level before the 1997 constitutional amendment (i.e., only if more than half of eligible voters cast valid votes), which made it very difficult for referendum initiatives to succeed.

165. A national referendum may be initiated by any Hungarian citizen having the right to vote, a party or a private law association (if its charter covers the subject of the referendum). The organizer must submit the proposed referendum question to the National Election Commission (NEC) for authentication before commencing the collection of supporting signatures. The referendum question must be worded in such a way that it be clear not only to the voters but also to Parliament in the sense of what kind of legislation is to be passed on the basis of the referendum outcome. Once the question has been approved by the NEC, the organizers may collect signatures in support of the referendum within forty days. If the NEC refuses authentication of the question, the organizers may appeal the decision to the *Kúria*. The Supreme Court must decide the case (against which no further legal remedy is available) within ninety days.

92. Act CCXXXVIII of 2013. However, the general procedural rules are provided by the Act XXXVI of 2013 on the Election Procedure.

166. A referendum is mandatory if it is initiated by at least 200,000 voters; in all other cases, it is optional. The mandatory nature of the referendum means that the popular vote must take place within 180 days. The initiating signatures have to be submitted to the NEC for checking if they are genuine.

167. If there are more than 100,000 but less than 200,000 signatures, Parliament will decide whether to hold the referendum. The same parliamentary decision is necessary if the national referendum is proposed by the President of the Republic or the government. However, if a national referendum is held, its decision is always binding on the legislature, which means that the National Assembly is obliged to enact the result of the referendum and cannot legislate otherwise for three years. It should be noted, however, that the referendum only binds Parliament as a legislative – but not as a constitution-making – power.[93]

168. In all cases, even when the requirements for a national referendum have been met, Parliament decides whether a national referendum will be held or not. Its decision may be appealed to the Constitutional Court. If the National Assembly approves the holding of a referendum, the date of the popular vote is set by the President of the Republic. No national referendum may take place on the day of general elections for Members of Parliament, members of the European Parliament or local authorities and mayors, nor forty-one days preceding or following such elections.

169. As a general rule, a national referendum may be held on matters falling within Parliament's competence. However, the Constitution specifies a number of public matters about which no referendum may be held even though they belong to the jurisdiction of the National Assembly (Article 8 section (3)). Thus, it is not possible to hold a referendum on:

- any matter aimed at the amendment of the Fundamental Law;
- an annual budget law, or the implementation of the central budget;
- central taxes, duties, contributions, customs, duties or the central conditions for local taxes;
- the law on elections of Members of Parliament, members of the European Parliament, local government representatives and mayors;
- any obligation arising from international treaties;
- person- and organization-related matters falling within the competence of the National Assembly;
- the dissolution of Parliament;
- the dissolution of a local government representative body;
- the declaration of war, state of national crisis and state of emergency;
- the declaration and extension of a state of preventive defence or any matter related to participation in military operations;
- the granting of amnesty.

93. Decision 2/1993. (I. 22.) of the Constitutional Court.

170. A national referendum is valid if more than half of all voters have cast valid votes, and it is conclusive if more than half of those voting validly have given the same answer to the question asked. All Hungarian citizens who have the right to vote may participate in a popular vote because it is a fundamental political right which is constitutionally protected.[94]

§11.02 THE NATIONAL REFERENDUMS IN HUNGARY SINCE 1989

171. The national referendum held at the dawn of the system change in autumn 1989 was the first electoral test of the reborn Hungarian democracy. This referendum was still an important part of the democratic transition process initiated by some opposition movements in order to break the vantage point of the state party and secure a peaceful change of power before the first free elections. The result of the referendum on all four questions raised supported the opposition's standpoint and contributed significantly to the transition to democracy.

172. In 1990, a referendum held on the question of whether the President of the Republic should be directly elected by the people was unsuccessful.

173. In 1997, a national referendum on NATO accession was held. In order to ensure the success of this national referendum, Parliament changed the relevant rules, providing that the referendum would be valid if at least 25% of the voters gave the same answer to the referendum question. As it turned out, this was necessary because less than half (49%) of voters participated. The vote brought a decisive victory for supporters of NATO membership, with 85% of votes in favour.

174. A few years later, in 2003, Hungary's accession to the European Union was the subject of a referendum in which the overwhelming majority (83.76%) voted in favour of EU membership. However, the very low turnout was disappointing (45.62% of voters).

175. In 2004, at the initiative of Fidesz, the major opposition party of that time, a referendum was held on whether Hungarians living beyond the state borders could, at their request, obtain Hungarian citizenship by preferential naturalization. Although participation did not reach the validity threshold, the referendum question was socially extremely divisive and poisoned even more the relationship between advocates and opponents of the idea of extending citizenship to Hungarians not living in the country.

176. The next referendum was held in 2008 on a number of public policy issues. The popular vote, initiated again by opposition parties, rejected by a large majority the introduction of tuition fee and healthcare charges.

94. Decision 52/1997. (X. 14.) of the Constitutional Court.

177. The Hungarian government launched a national referendum in February 2016 against the controversial quota system proposed by the EU for resettling migrants among the Member States. According to this plan, Member States would share the burdens of the migrant crisis by relocating asylum seekers from the front-line States (Greece and Italy) among themselves. The Hungarian government, led by Viktor Orbán, held an anti-immigration stance from the very beginning of the migrant crisis. The government's intention was to reject the EU migration policy in a referendum. However, the turnout did not reach the threshold set by law for validity, with only 40.32% casting valid votes.

178. In summer 2021, the government submitted five referendum initiatives to confirm certain provisions of the Child Protection Act.[95] At the same time, a leading opposition politician submitted five proposals for a national referendum on different issues. Among the initiatives, four of the five referendum questions proposed by the government were put to referendum on the same day as the parliamentary elections. However, the national referendum held in April 2022 was invalid on all questions (which concerned a ban on sex education for minors) due to low turnout. It is to be noted that contrary to the government's referendum proposals, the *Kúria* and the Constitutional Court declared all the opposition-initiated referendums unlawful and rejected.

179. Besides these referendums, there have been a number of unsuccessful referendum initiatives not being held due to the decision of the NEC or the Supreme Court. Thus, several attempts have been made to hold a referendum for the direct election of the President of the Republic, but the Constitutional Court repeatedly rejected this issue as having an illegitimate purpose to amend constitutional text. Some other referendum initiatives failed several times due to their unconstitutional nature, aimed at restoring the monarchical form of state, or reintroducing the death penalty.

§11.03 Local Referendum

180. The representative body of local government may hold a local referendum on a matter falling within its own competences. However, no local referendum may be held on the budget and final accounts of the local government, local taxes, personal and organizational decisions falling into the scope of responsibility of the local council, or the dissolution of the representative body.

181. As a general rule, the representative body may hold a local referendum on matters where required by law or by local government decree. In the latter case, at least one-quarter of the local councillors must support the referendum, whereas it is required by law to call a local referendum on changing the administrative status of the municipality (e.g., in case of amalgamation or dissolution of municipalities). In

95. *See infra* n. 382.

addition, a local referendum may also be initiated by a committee of the representative body, a group of local voters whose required number is specified in a local government decree, which may not be less than 10% and not more than 25% of the electorate.

182. The referendum question and the supporting signatures are certified by the local electoral committee. These decisions may be challenged in court which must review such cases within thirty days.

183. Local residents may vote in a local referendum, which is valid if more than half of eligible voters cast valid votes, and successful if more than half of the valid votes answered the question in the same way. If the outcome of the local referendum imposes an obligation on the representative body of the local government to make a decision (i.e., to issue a local decree or an individual resolution), it has to do so within 180 days.

184. In theory, a referendum may be held at county and capital levels, subject to the provisions governing the local referendum, but such a referendum has not yet taken place.

§11.04 Other Forms of Citizens' Participation

185. The Act on the national referendums refers only very briefly to the European Citizens' Initiative since the primary regulation of this institution is part of EU law.

186. According to the Local Government Act,[96] the representative body of local government has to hold public hearings at least once a year to inform the local population and to get their opinions about local public affairs.

187. It is worth noting that the Conservative government has used a new form of citizens' participation named 'national consultation' since 2011. The first occasion of asking the opinion of citizens occurred in 2011 on some issues of the new constitutional regulation. Since then, thirteen 'national consultations' have been held on specific public policy issues, like particular measures of social policy and family protection, taxation, immigration, and so on. Nevertheless, this form of public consultation is not institutionalized, but it is much rather a tool of political propaganda for the governing parties, one that seeks to support government policy with popular, easy-to-answer, directed, leading questions that actually replace the national referendum without legal consequences.

---

96. Act CLXXXIX of 2011.

§11.05 Constitutional Practice

188. Interestingly, the democratic enthusiasm of the 1989–1990 system change did not lead to the rise of direct democracy. Although the constitutional foundations and statutory rules of the referendum and the people's initiative were already created in 1989, an early ruling of the Constitutional Court, presumably in defence of the constitutional structure that had just been established, prevented the holding of a national referendum on the dissolution of Parliament in 1993 (at that time the Court had jurisdiction to review the constitutionality of referendum questions). The ruling stated that a referendum could not even be implicitly aimed at amending the Constitution.[97] This decision had long-term consequences for direct democracy in Hungary. On the one hand, the judgment prevented constitutional issues from being decided by national referendums, thereby diverting the institution of referendum to public policy issues, and, on the other hand, from then on, the electoral bodies and the courts interpreted the statutory conditions of national referendums in a very restrictive way.

189. For example, the prohibition of referendums on budget laws has generally been interpreted as prohibiting all referendums that affect the state budget in any way. But it is easy to see that virtually every referendum has budgetary implications. The clarity of the referendum question, which could be answered in the affirmative or in the negative, has also served as a basis for strict, restrictive interpretations, as was the rule that no referendum could be held on obligations under an international treaty. As a result, between 2010 and 2013, less than 0.1% of referendum initiatives were approved by the National Election Commission. Since the renewal of the composition of the NEC, it has steadfastly refused initiatives which were not supported by the government. Thus, in 2014 and 2015, it rejected twenty-three referendum initiatives for lifting the Sunday shopping ban, except the one that aimed at upholding the ban.

190. The constitutional requirements for national referendums are interpreted inconsistently by the NEC and the *Kúria,* which often gives rise to suspicions of political influence. Thus, in the case of the EU migrant quota referendum noted above, it did not relate to the powers and duties of Parliament, but its subject was a particular policy measure of the European Union. Furthermore, since the Constitution's EU clause declares that the competences arising from the Fundamental Law are exercised by EU institutions 'under an international agreement', no referendum could constitutionally be held on obligations deriving from EU membership. Finally, the question was deceptive because there was no EU regulation which would require 'mandatory settlement of non-Hungarian citizens in Hungary', as the referendum question suggested.[98] Nevertheless, in this case, the NEC and the high courts spectacularly deviated from their previous practice and found the referendum question lawful. Interestingly, shortly after the referendum, the NEC returned to its

97. Decision 2/1993. (I. 22.) of the Constitutional Court.

98. *See*, in detail, Szente, *supra* n. 42; and Gábor Halmai, *The Invalid Anti-Migrant Referendum in Hungary* (2016), https://verfassungsblog.de/hungarys-anti-european-immigration-laws/.

'normal' practice. It refused the initiative on the referendum on Hungary's plan to organize the Olympic Games in 2024, although the proposed question met all legal requirements: it was unambiguous and belonged to Parliament's competence, as it was submitted to annul the relevant law of Parliament.

191. In the case of the government's 2021 referendum initiatives, the *Kúria* has departed spectacularly from its previous practice, approving the type of questions it had considered ambiguous and unlawful in other cases while refusing to put opposition referendum questions to popular vote (except for one, which was rejected by the Constitutional Court). In the latter case, the Constitutional Court declared the opposition-initiated referendum question unconstitutional, although this jurisdiction was abolished in 2012 (and taken over by the *Kúria*).

Chapter 12: The Relationship Between the International and the Domestic Law

§12.01 THE CONSTITUTIONAL FUNDAMENTALS

192. The first constitutional provision about the relationship between international and domestic law emerged in 1989 when a constitutional amendment inserted a new rule as Article 7 section (1) in the constitutional text saying that Hungary 'accepts the generally recognized rules of international law' and ensures 'harmony between obligations assumed under international law and domestic law'. This clause was frequently criticized for its blurred meaning, so not surprisingly, the Constitutional Court had to give an authoritative interpretation of the text,[99] according to which the generally recognized principles of international law are parts of domestic law, while international treaties need special transformation for becoming enforceable in Hungary.[100] This ruling reflected more or less a dualist approach to the relationship between international and domestic law, which means that most international law requires special transposition into domestic law to be binding and applicable. The former Constitution also imposed implicitly the obligation on the competent public authorities to ensure harmony between domestic law and international law.

193. The Fundamental Law contains a very similar wording, rephrasing and modestly completing the former constitutional text. Article Q) section (2) declares that '[i]n order to comply with its obligations under international law, Hungary shall ensure that Hungarian law is in conformity with international law'. The mostly dualist approach has also remained seeing as section (3) of the same article continues to comprise the acceptance of 'the generally recognized rules of international law', while the next sentence provides that 'other sources of international law will become of the Hungarian legal system by promulgation in laws'.

194. In this wording, the phrase 'generally recognized rules' probably encompasses the norms of universal customary law, the general principles of law recognized by the international community and the peremptory norms of international law.[101] As to the place of these pieces of international law in the hierarchy of legal norms, the generally recognized rules are situated below the Fundamental Law, but they have precedence over any other legal acts of domestic law.

195. Although the Fundamental Law does not specify what the 'other sources' of international law are, presumably, all international treaties and binding decisions of international organizations that impose international obligations on Hungary fall within this category. The constitutional command prescribing obligations of the

---

99. Gábor Sulyok, *Incorporation of International Law into Domestic Law under the Fundamental Law of Hungary*, in The Transformation of the Hungarian Legal System 2010–2013 33 (Péter Smuk ed., Complex 2013).
100. Decision 53/1993. (X. 13.) of the Constitutional Court.
101. Sulyok, *supra* n. 100, 35.

competent state authorities to ensure the harmonization between domestic and international law is traditionally interpreted as having no legal norms of the domestic legal order in opposition to norms of the latter.

§12.02 Treaty-Making Power

196. The Fundamental Law does not contain any detailed provisions on treaty-making powers. It only states in the chapter on the Parliament that the National Assembly authorizes 'the expression of consent to be bound by international treaties falling within its functions and powers'. The detailed rules are defined by Law L of 2005 on the Procedure relating to International Treaties. According to this Act, the binding effect of an international treaty can be recognized if the text of the treaty is known and the competent public body has authorized it to be so. If the subject matter of an international treaty falls within the competence of the Parliament (or, in other words, it affects the scope of parliamentary legislation), this authorization must be given by the National Assembly, in any other case, by the government. In the case where Parliament gave such an authorization, the international treaty must be promulgated by legislation, while in all other cases, it should be promulgated by government decree.

197. The coherence of the legal system and the compatibility between domestic and international law is guaranteed by the Constitutional Court which, on the proposal of one-fourth of the Members of Parliament, the government, the Commissioner of Fundamental Rights, the President of the *Kúria* or the Public Prosecutor, may annul any legislative act if it is in opposition with the international law. Judges may also initiate this review if they perceive that a legal regulation they are bound to apply is contrary to an international treaty. Moreover, the President of the Republic may initiate an *ex ante* constitutional review of the international treaty before its promulgation.

198. The constitutional rule according to which no national referendum can be held on any obligation arising from international treaties (Article 8 section (2) point d)) is another safeguard for the harmony between the two bodies of law.

§12.03 The Relationship Between the EU Law and the Domestic Law

199. During and after the democratic transition in 1988–1990, there was a wide-ranging political consensus that Hungary should join the European Communities (EC), but this needed a long process of harmonizing national law (influx itself in that time) with Community law. In December 1991, Hungary signed the Association Agreement with the EC. The application for European Union membership was formally submitted on 1 April 1994, and the direct accession negotiations began in 1998 with their successful conclusion at the end of 2002. In the meantime, the Hungarian Parliament had adopted an amendment to the Constitution creating the legal conditions for accession. This was clear and indispensable after the Constitutional

Court had decided in 1998 that the obligations arising from the Association Agreement could not be fulfilled without constitutional authorization. It is also required for the direct effect and applicability of EC law in Hungary.[102]

200. Accession was put to a national referendum which resulted in impressive support for membership: 83.75% of voters were in favour of accession (the voter turnout was, however, fairly low, at 45.62%).

201. Hungary signed the Accession Treaty together with nine other candidate countries in April 2003 which entered into force on 1 May 2004.

202. A detailed analysis of the EU clause of the Fundamental Law is found in Chapter 18, §18.04.

102. Decision 30/1998. (VI. 25.) of the Constitutional Court.

Chapter 13: Lawmaking and the Hierarchy of Legal Sources

§13.01 The Constitutional Fundamentals

203. The concept of legal sources is used in two different ways in Hungarian law. According to the most widespread understanding, legal norms are the sources of law (external legal sources), while the alternative view considers that lawmaking bodies are the legal sources (internal legal sources).[103] Under the first meaning, legal sources can be understood in a wider and a narrower sense. First, this concept embraces all legal acts, which are called 'normative acts governing public organizations', while in the narrower sense, it implies only generally binding legal norms ('legal rules', in the words of the Fundamental Law).[104]

204. The Hungarian legal system, rooted in civil law culture, prefers statutory law to judge-made law. The Fundamental Law classifies itself as the foundation of the entire legal system (Article R) section (1)) which determines all legal acts and enumerates the lawmaking organs. The Constitution also refers to the law of the European Union which may, under certain conditions, lay down generally binding rules of conduct.

205. The Constitution explicitly specifies certain conditions for the validity of legal norms. Thus, it determines the principle of the hierarchy of legal sources defining the relationships among the various legal norms. This principle means, on the one hand, the primacy of the Fundamental Law and, on the other hand, that the various legal acts belong to a hierarchical order in which no legal rule may conflict with legal norms of higher levels. Besides that, the Fundamental Law declares that, apart from the Constitution itself, 'generally binding rules of conduct may be laid down' only in legal rules 'adopted by an organ having legislative competence and specified in the Fundamental Law' (Article T) section (1)). Then, only those legal acts are valid which have been promulgated in the Official State Gazette (*Magyar Közlöny*).

206. The detailed rules on the fundamental requirements for the lawmaking process, the preparation, modification and effectivity of legal norms are all determined by the Act on the Lawmaking.[105]

§13.02 The Principle of Hierarchy of Legal Norms

207. As noted above, the legal system is based on the principle of the hierarchy of legal norms. The main function of this tenet is to ensure the unity and coherence

---

103. Miklós Szabó, *A jogforrás*, in *Bevezetés a jog- és államtudományokba* (Miklós Szabó ed., Bíbor Kiadó 1997) 34.
104. Following the general use of terminology, in this monograph we understand the legal sources in this narrower sense.
105. Act CXXX of 2010.

of the system of legal norms, requiring that no contradiction may occur among the various legal acts. According to this principle, the lower-level legal acts cannot be in conflict with those placed at a higher level in the hierarchy. In fact, this relationship defines the priority of the higher-level legislation in the event of norm conflicts.

208. The Constitution lists the generally binding legal norms and assigns them a place in the hierarchy of the norms. These are:

- acts of Parliament;
- government decrees;
- decrees of the President of the National Bank of Hungary;
- prime ministerial decrees;
- ministerial decrees;
- decrees of the heads of autonomous regulatory organs; and
- local government decrees.[106]

209. It is to be noted that the legal acts of EU law are not classified in the hierarchy of the legal acts, even though they are binding on Hungary. All these legal acts have special relations with the legal regulations specified by the Fundamental Law in a separate chapter on the special legal orders and in Article E) section (3) on the constitutional empowerment of Hungary's EU membership.

210. Finally, the hierarchy of legal norms does not include so-called public law regulatory instruments and other legal instruments of state administration because they are not considered legal acts which may establish rights and impose obligations on the citizens.

211. Although the Constitution does not qualify itself as a legal norm, it ensures that the legal system of Hungary is based on the Fundamental Law which is at the top of the hierarchy of legal norms. As a matter of fact, any other legal norms trump all lower-level regulations. A breach of the ranking of legal acts as set by the Fundamental Law is itself unconstitutional.

212. It follows from the principle of the hierarchy of legal norms that higher-level legislation may modify or abrogate lower-level legal acts. This is, however, only the main rule; not every higher-level legal norm may amend lower-level regulations since the legislative powers of the various lawmaking organs do not overlap each other. For example, even though a ministerial decree is at higher level in the hierarchy of legal norms than local government ordinances, Ministers have no legislative power to regulate local relations.

106. Art. T) s. (2) of the Fundamental Law.

213. The principle of the hierarchy of legal norms is applied not only to the relationships of the various kinds of legal regulations, but it holds also that the normative acts governing public organizations may not be in conflict with the legal norms enumerated in Article T) section (2) of the Constitution.[107]

§13.03 THE LEGAL SOURCES OF DOMESTIC LAW

[A] Acts of Parliament

214. Acts of Parliament are the highest level legal norms adopted in a special legislative procedure by the National Assembly which regulates basic social relations.[108] The Fundamental Law does not define exhaustively what social conditions are to be regulated by acts of Parliament. Nevertheless, the Constitution stipulates that certain matters must be regulated by an act of Parliament. It contains a full list of the cardinal acts and determines some other matters subject to regulation (like defining crimes and their sanctions) to be regulated by Act. These are called the 'exclusive legislative subjects', which means that they may be regulated only by acts of Parliament.[109] In addition, the National Assembly has a universal legislative power, which means that Parliament, within the framework of the Fundamental Law, may regulate any subject. Acts of Parliament may be adopted only in a legislative procedure defined in the Constitution, the Act on Lawmaking, and in the parliamentary standing orders.

215. The 'cardinal acts' form a special group of acts of Parliament. The adoption or amendment of this kind of law requires the votes of two-thirds of the members of the National Assembly present. Even at the time of the democratic transition in 1989, so-called constitutional laws were introduced into the legal system to regulate some of the most important constitutional issues[110] which could be adopted only with a two-thirds majority of all Members of Parliament. The purpose of this legal institution was to settle the issues that had not been regulated by the Constitution of 1949/1989. This was closely related to the fact that no new constitution was adopted at the time of the system change, and the arrangement of certain controversial issues was left to these special laws. As a matter of fact, the constitutional laws served for a while as a sort of constitutional 'supplement'. The original idea was that the two-thirds majority requirement should promote the creation of a consensus among the government and opposition parties of the day on matters which concerned the fundamental issues of the legal system. It is worth noting that the procedural requirement was eased fairly soon when a constitutional amendment reduced the majority

---

107. Art. 24 s. (1) of the Act CXXX of 2010.
108. Jakab and Szente, *supra* n. 16, 597.
109. Zoltán Szente, *A törvénykezdeményezési jog*, in *Az Alkotmány kommentárja: I. kötet* (András Jakab ed., Századvég Kiadó 2009) 848.
110. Act XXXI of 1989.

requirement to the two-thirds majority of MPs present (and the adjective 'constitutional' was abandoned).[111] The Fundamental Law of 2011 has not changed this procedural requirement despite some criticism of the consensus requirement for a special part of parliamentary legislation,[112] but has renamed this type of act of Parliament as 'cardinal act'. This was due to the new historicism of the constitution-makers trying to find links with the historical constitution. Nevertheless, this terminology is incorrect because in the unwritten, historical Hungarian constitution, cardinal acts did not have any special procedural requirement compared to the other acts of Parliament. Indeed, the cardinal acts were not formalized, and those acts were considered as 'cardinal' that regulated outstanding constitutional issues.[113] It has been a notable change since the Fundamental Law entered into force on 1 January 2012 that not only complete laws could be ranked as cardinal acts, but also provisions within ordinary laws.[114] The constitutionality of this practice is questionable, however, as the Fundamental Law refers in all cases to 'cardinal acts', not 'cardinal provisions'.

216. As regards the subject matter of this qualified majority legislation, there has been a significant change since the new Constitution came into force. While the original function of these laws was to relieve pressure on the Constitution[115] by regulating the most important issues of state organization and the fundamental laws based on the consideration that broad political consensus is needed on these issues,[116] since 2012, the structure of the objects of cardinal acts has changed. Whereas detailed regulation of several fundamental rights was excluded from these special majority statutes, some policy issues require a qualified majority for legislation, like the tax and pension system, the protection of families, the legal status of churches, the preservation, protection and property rights of arable lands and forests, and the protection of national assets.

217. Nevertheless, the recent jurisprudence of the Constitutional Court has confirmed previous practice,[117] including the approach that the main purpose of cardinal acts is to secure broad consensus among the members of the National Assembly.[118]

---

111. Act XI of 1990.
112. Arguing that in these cases the political responsibility for lawmaking blurs the line between the government and opposition parties. *See*, e.g., Herbert Küpper, *A kétharmados/sarkalatos törvények jelensége a magyar jogrendszerben* MTA Law Working Papers (2014) 5.
113. Gábor Schweitzer, *A magar királyi köztársaságtól a Magyar Köztársaságig: Közjog- és tudománytörténeti tanulmányok* (Publikon Kiadó, 2017) 149.
114. András Jakab and Emese Szilágyi, *Sarkalatos törvények a magyar jogrendben*, in *A magyar jogrendszer állapota* (András Jakab & György Gajduschek eds., MTA TK JTI 2016) 246.
115. Géza Kilényi, *Az alkotmányozás és a 'kétharmados' törvények* 49 Jogtudományi Közlöny (1994) 201–209.
116. Attila, Tóth Gábor, *A jogok törvénye: Értekezések az alkotmányos szabadságról* (Gondolat 2014) 244.
117. Decision 43/2012. (XII. 20.) of the Constitutional Court.
118. Decision 17/2013. (VI. 26.) of the Constitutional Court.

[B] Government Decrees

218. In the hierarchy of sources of law, decrees issued by the government are located directly below the level of parliamentary legislation. The constitutional authorization of the government applies to two types of government decrees.[119] First, acting within its scope of responsibility, the government may adopt decrees in matters not regulated by an act of Parliament. In academic literature, this is usually called an 'autonomous' or 'original' lawmaking power. However, the other kind of government decree is issued much more frequently. These government decrees are adopted on the basis of authorization by act of Parliament in order to lay down more detailed rules under that act. In fact, these are executive orders.

219. The making of government decrees is the competence of the government as a collegiate organ, and accordingly may be adopted in government meetings. The decrees adopted are signed by the Prime Minister immediately after the decision of the government.

220. The Minister for Justice is responsible for the government's legislative activity. This means that he or she has to review any draft regulations in terms of their compatibility with the Constitution and European Union law.

[C] The Decrees of the Governor of the Hungarian National Bank

221. The Fundamental Law authorizes the Governor of the Hungarian National Bank (MNB) to issue decrees within his or her function as laid down in a cardinal act.[120] These are executive orders since the Governor may issue decrees only on the basis of authorization of an act of Parliament. On issuing such decrees, the Governor may be substituted by the Deputy Governor he or she designated in a decree.

222. In formal sense, these decrees are at the same level of the hierarchy of legal sources as government decrees. In principle, however, this may not lead to a conflict of laws, for the Governor of the MNB has the power to issue decrees within the scope strictly defined by the Act referred to above.

[D] The Decrees of the Members of the Government

223. The Constitution confers lawmaking power not only on the government as a body but also on its members. These can only be executive orders (i.e., they may be issued under the authorization of an act of Parliament or a government decree). Each member of the government may only issue such decrees clearly within his or

119. Art. 15 s. (3) of the Fundamental Law.
120. Act CXXXIX of 2013 on the legal status of the Hungarian National Bank.

her scope of responsibility. Among these decrees as a whole, decrees issued by the Prime Minister have the highest legal ranking; decrees issued by other Ministers are of equal standing to one another.

224. It is to be noted that the lawmaking competence of a Minister may not be taken over by another member of the government. When the competent Minister is prevented from acting, his or her political Secretary of State is responsible for acting in substitution in lawmaking activity. If the subject of a decree covers the portfolio responsibilities of several Ministers, the Ministers concerned may issue a joint decree.

225. Ministerial decrees must also be reviewed in advance by the Minister of Justice, and if he or she disagrees with a draft decree from a constitutional or EU law point of view, the government will decide on the dispute.

[E] The Decrees of the Heads of Independent Regulatory Authorities

226. The reasons for the organizational autonomy of independent regulatory authorities also justify the autonomous lawmaking power of these bodies. Thus, the heads of the National Media and Info-communications Authority, the Hungarian Energy and Public Utility Regulatory Authority, the Supervisory Authority for Regulated Activities and the Hungarian Atomic Energy Authority on the basis of authorization by act of Parliament and in their range of functions may issue decrees which cannot be in conflict with any parliamentary legislation, government decree, Prime Minister's decree, ministerial decree or decree of the Governor of the Hungarian National Bank. In the issuing of decrees, the head of an independent regulatory organ may be substituted by the deputy he or she has designated. These are regulations of markets and should be free from direct political influence.

[F] Local Government Decrees

227. The independent regulation of local public affairs by democratically elected local bodies is a crucial element of local self-government. Accordingly, the Fundamental Law grants lawmaking power to local and county councils. The Local Government Act[121] and some sectoral laws determine the subjects which must be regulated by local government decree. Local governments may regulate, *inter alia*, their own organizational and procedural rules, the municipal budget, the imposition and rates of local taxes, social benefits provided by the local authority, the operation of certain public services, the local building requirements and the order of the use of public spaces. In a number of cases, local authorities are not only empowered to issue local decrees, but are obliged to do so.

---

121. Act CLXXXIX of 2011.

228. It is a special feature of local government decrees that they have restricted territorial effect in so far as they are binding only on the administrative territory of the given municipality or county. In addition to this, their personal scope extends only to their own inhabitants, and to those who are in some way connected with the town or county (e.g., those who have real estate there, companies operating in their territory).

229. Local decrees may not be in conflict with any other legal norm. They have to be promulgated in a way that is usual in the respective municipality or county.

[G] Special Legal Sources

230. The system of legal sources contains some specific norms. Their speciality is that normally, they may not be adopted at all.

231. Legislative decrees were issued between 1949 and 1989 by the Presidential Council, a collective body exercising the power of the Head of State before the transition to democracy. These statutory rules could replace missing laws or amend or repeal acts of Parliament, which was necessary because, during the Communist era, there was only a façade parliament that met a few days a year and adopted only a few laws. Although no such legislation can be enacted since 1989, some legislative decrees are still in force.

232. The ordinances that can only be issued during a special legal order may be classified also in the group of special legal sources. In the extraordinary situations defined by the Constitution, for the protection of the constitutional order of the country or the safety of life and property of citizens, or the prevention of threats thereto, government by decree is provisionally allowed. The special ordinances issued under such circumstances may suspend or modify ordinary laws temporarily, within a specified period of time. It is to be noted, however, that during the successive 'states of danger' declared since March 2020, the government has issued hundreds of such emergency decrees.

233. Beyond the provisional nature of these decrees, there are other constitutional limitations on these extraordinary lawmaking powers for the protection of constitutional democracy. Thus, the effect and application of the Fundamental Law cannot be suspended even under special legal orders, and the operation of the Constitutional Court cannot be restricted. It is also an essential provision that, although fundamental rights may be restricted or suspended in a special way during these periods, certain rights are inviolable even under a special legal order. These are the right to life and human dignity, the prohibition of torture, inhuman and degrading treatment, the prohibition of slavery and human trafficking, and the prohibition of carrying out a medical or scientific experiment without voluntary consent. As well, some criminal law safeguards are also untouchable, such as the presumption of innocence, the right to a fair hearing and the principle of *nullum crimen sine lege*.

[H] The Public Law Regulatory Instruments and Other Legal Instruments

234. The Act on Lawmaking has established a special group of legal norms, the public law regulatory instruments for those laws, which are issued by public authorities for the operation of their own or their subordinate organs, but may not contain binding rules on third persons (i.e., natural persons, or organizations with or without legal personality).

235. These instruments are of two types. The collegiate bodies, the National Assembly, the government and other organs of central government, the Constitutional Court, the Budget Council and the representative bodies of local governments may issue 'normative resolutions' on their own organization and operation, activities and action programmes. 'Normative instructions' may be used by the President of the Republic, the Prime Minister, the heads of central administrative bodies, the President of the National Office of Judiciary, the Prosecutor General, the Commissioner for Fundamental Rights, the Governor of the National Bank of Hungary, the President of the State Audit Office, the heads of the capital and county government offices, mayors, the chairmen of the county assemblies and chief administrators of local governments for regulating the organization, operation and supervision of those entities under their management.

236. In addition, there are other legal instruments which, although not normative (i.e., having a regulatory character), still impact on the application of the law. As a matter of fact, 'uniformity resolutions', which are issued by the *Kúria* are halfway between lawmaking and law application. Although the Supreme Court does not have any regulatory power, these decisions, which are issued for ensuring the unity of judicial practice, are binding on the ordinary courts.

237. The judgments of the Constitutional Court have an *erga omnes* effect in the sense that the constitutional interpretations of the Court are generally binding and, in particular, before 2010, the jurisprudence of the Court had a great impact on the whole domain of the law.

238. In many areas of the legal system, soft law, including legal practice and certain precedent decisions, is also of paramount importance.

§13.04 The Personal, Territorial and Temporal Effect of Legal Norms

239. The effect of legal norms determines the scope of application of the various pieces of law. The personal effect of legal acts answers the question of who the addressees of a particular legal norm are or who are bound by it. The personal scope of Hungarian legal acts includes all natural persons and organizations with or without legal personality who are in the territory of Hungary, as well as Hungarian citizens outside the country. In the case of local government decrees, the personal effect is limited to those who live or work in the administrative area of the given local authority.

240. The territorial scope of Hungarian legal acts extends over the territory of Hungary, whereas in the case of local government decrees it covers only the administrative territory of the local authority concerned.

241. As to the temporal effect of the legal norms, each legal act has to specify the date of its entry into force, which may be a day after that act has been promulgated (*pro future* effect). If the date cannot be precisely determined, the date of entry into force may be linked to the occurrence of a future condition. Unless the purpose of the regulation is otherwise achievable, the date of entry into force may be the day of promulgation (*ex nunc* effect). Exceptionally, a legal norm may have a retroactive (*ex tunc*) effect, but it is subject to strict conditions. In the case of criminal law, this is only possible if the change is in favour of the accused, either in the substance of the law or in respect of procedure. As far as civil legislation is concerned, retroactive lawmaking is prohibited if it would impose new obligations or make an existing obligation more severe, or, possibly, it would declare an act or behaviour illegal ex post facto.

§13.05 Validity and Applicability of Legal Rules

242. As has been said above, some conditions for the validity of legal norms are determined by the Fundamental Law, and certain other requirements are set out by the Act on Lawmaking. According to these rules, legal norms are valid only if:

(a) they have been issued by a public authority which has proper (relating to the adoption or issuance of the particular norm) lawmaking powers;
(b) they have been made by complying with the relevant procedural rules;
(c) they are not contrary to any higher-level regulation (i.e., the principle of hierarchy of legal norms is respected); and
(d) they have been promulgated in a regular way.

243. It is to be noted that these are conjunctive conditions, so all of them must be applied to the lawmaking process.

244. As for lawmaking authority, it is important to know that such empowerment may come only from the Constitution. The importance of the procedural rules has been emphasized sometimes in the jurisprudence of the Constitutional Court, even if the rigidity of the relevant practice has been moderated in the meantime. In the 1990s, the Court recurrently held that only the regular lawmaking process, in which all procedural requirements have been met, may produce valid legal norms.[122]

122. *See*, e.g., Decision 11/1992. (III. 5.) of the Constitutional Court.

245. In the later jurisprudence of the Court, however, this requirement has been softened such that not just any procedural breach would lead to the unconstitutionality of the particular legal act, but only those errors which follow directly from the Constitution. Thus, a failure to involve stakeholders in the lawmaking process or an omission of an impact assessment of the designed regulation was insufficient to find unconstitutionality, even though those obligations were required by the then Act on Lawmaking.[123]

§13.06 OTHER REQUIREMENTS OF LAWMAKING

246. Beyond the primary conditions of validity of legal acts, the Act on Lawmaking determines some other requirements for codifying law. Thus, legislation should have a regulatory content that can be clearly understood by its addressees.[124] The Constitutional Court derived this requirement from the principle of the rule of law in a way that the Court found legal certainty as an essential component of this tenet. According to this sub-principle, the State has a duty to ensure that the law as a whole, as well as individual legal acts, are clear, unambiguous, and comprehensible for their addressees.[125]

247. Another requirement of lawmaking is the prohibition of the retrospective legislation. This requirement follows also from the principle of legal certainty. In the wording of a landmark decision of the Constitutional Court, '[l]egal certainty requires, inter alia, the protection of acquired rights, the maintenance of closed or otherwise permanently terminated legal relationships, and the limitation of changeability of permanent legal relationships created in the past through constitutional rules'.[126] This principle appears both in civil law and in criminal law, but imposes different requirements in each. In civil law, it means that no legal act may impose an obligation, or may render any liability more burdensome for a period prior to its entry into force, and it may not undermine or restrict a right or make any conduct unlawful retroactively.[127] In criminal law, the prohibition covers mainly the sub-principles of *nullum crimen sine lege* and *nulla poena sine lege*. Since the system change, several attempts have been made to ensure the punishability of crimes committed during the Communist dictatorship (between 1949 and 1989) but not pursued for political reasons, even if they were not considered crimes at the time when they were committed or if the limitations period for these acts had already expired. The Constitutional Court had declared in 1992 that it was unconstitutional to make crimes punishable again if the limitation period for those crimes had already expired or to extend the statutory limitation period for crimes which had not yet expired.[128] In this way, the Court, repealing a private bill aiming at reviving the punishability of statute-barred crimes in an ex ante constitutional review process, categorically

123. *See*, e.g., Decision 50/1998. (XI. 27.) of the Constitutional Court.
124. Art. 2 s. (1) of Act on Law Making.
125. Decisions 9/1992. (I. 30.) and 26/1992. (IV. 30.) of the Constitutional Court.
126. Decision 11/1992. (III. 5.) of the Constitutional Court.
127. Art. 2 s. (2) of Act on Law Making; Decision 25/1992. (IV. 30.) of the Constitutional Court.
128. Decision 11/1992. (III. 5.) of the Constitutional Court.

prohibited any retroactive criminal legislation. Nevertheless, barely a year later, when the government attempted to get through Parliament a very similar bill using a different legal basis, the Constitutional Court spectacularly changed its mind and upheld the new law allowing the re-evaluation of these crimes to be punished as war crimes and crimes against humanity.[129] As a matter of fact, there were only a few criminal trials on this legal ground during the 1990s. When the Fidesz government came to power in 2010, these efforts received new impetus. The Fundamental Law of 2011 reopened the criminalization of so-called communist crimes, obliterating their statute of limitations retroactively. In 2011, Parliament adopted a law on the punishability of and the exclusion of the statute of limitations for crimes against humanity and certain crimes committed under the Communist dictatorship.[130] The latter was person-targeted legislation ('lex Biszku') aiming at bringing Béla Biszku, a former Communist Party leader to trial.[131]

248. It is also a guarantee of the rule of law that the date of entry into force of legal rules must be set by the lawmaker in such a way as to allow sufficient time for the addressees to prepare for their application.

249. In addition, all legal norms must comply not only with the substantive and formal requirements of the Fundamental Law but also with Hungary's obligations under international law and European Union law.

250. Further, there are some technical requirements of codification, such as ensuring that the new legal norm does not contain unnecessary provisions; does not repeat constitutional or legislative rules, and does not contain any provision without normative (i.e., regulatory) content. Moreover, the same or similar life conditions must be regulated in the same or similar way and preferably in the same legislation.

251. There are special rules for governmental lawmaking procedures. It means that if a legislative bill or a draft government or ministerial decree is under preparation, the initiator must prepare a prior impact assessment on the expected social, legal, economic and environmental effects of the proposed legislation. Explanatory memoranda must be provided for all legislative drafts.

252. According to the Act on Lawmaking, there are several conditions for amending legislation. Thus, only valid laws may be amended, and only the lawmaking body having the appropriate legislative powers may modify a particular legal act. For example, a government decree may be modified by another government decree, or an act of Parliament. The amending legislation has to mark explicitly the modified legal norm.

129. Decision 53/1993. (X. 13.) of the Constitutional Court.
130. Act CCX of 2011.
131. As a result of this law, Béla Biszku was prosecuted in 2012 and sentenced at first instance to imprisonment, but in 2016 the criminal trial was terminated due to Biszku's death.

§13.07 CONFLICT OF LEGAL NORMS

253. As was pointed out above, conflicts of legal norms can be resolved generally by the principle of hierarchy of legal acts. When it is not possible (because there is a contradiction between legal norms of the same level), two major rules are used. Noteworthy, these are not explicitly predicated by the Constitution or any other legal regulation, but they are considered as internal, logical rules of law.

254. First, a special regulation must be applied instead of a general rule among the different legal acts relating to the same things (*lex specialis derogate legi generali*). Another conventional rule is *lex posterior derogate legi priori* which means that if there are two conflicting rules at the same level on the same subject, the legal norm adopted later should prevail.

Chapter 14: Citizenship and the Legal Status of Non-citizen Persons

255. Although the idea of legal regulation of Hungarian citizenship arose in the first half of the nineteenth century, the first citizenship law was passed in 1879.[132] Before that time, according to the historical constitution, the bond between the State and its inhabitants was expressed by membership of the 'Holy Crown' which included all the citizens of the country since the 1848 revolution (i.e., not only members of privileged orders as beforehand), despite the fact that in the twentieth century, due to the frequent changes to the borders of the country (the territorial losses and acquisitions of state territory having raised many problems of citizenship), the 1879 statute remained in force until new legislation in 1948.[133] Citizenship was subject to new legislation again in 1957.[134] The law now in force (Citizenship Act) was adopted in 1993,[135] but has been amended several times since then.

§14.01 The Constitutional Foundations and the Principles of Citizenship Law

256. The Fundamental Law devotes an article to citizenship in the chapter 'Foundation', among some other provisions relating to sovereignty. The Constitution refers only to the most usual way of acquiring Hungarian citizenship, stating that the child of a Hungarian citizen is a Hungarian citizen by birth, but at the same time, it authorizes the Parliament to specify other instances of original or acquired Hungarian citizenship in a cardinal act (Article G) sections (1) and (4)).

257. The constitutional provision declaring that no one may be deprived of Hungarian citizenship through birth or acquired in a lawful manner is an obvious reaction to the socialist era when those who emigrated from Hungary without permission (termed 'dissidents' in that period) were deprived of their nationality.

258. Finally, the Constitution declares that Hungary protects its citizens. But, the principle of equal citizenship is not applied fully since those Hungarian nationals who live outside the state borders and have two nationalities do not have the same rights in many areas as their peers living in Hungary (*see* below).

259. The Citizenship Act contains several other principles. Thus, no distinction may be made between citizens of Hungary on the basis of the source of citizenship (birth or acquisition). The right to change nationality cannot be arbitrarily restricted. And, finally, the Citizenship Act has no retroactive effect. Hungarian citizenship is governed by the laws in force at the time of the facts or events affecting nationality.

132. Act L of 1879.
133. Act LX of 1948.
134. Act V of 1957.
135. Act LV of 1993.

§14.02 The Content of Citizenship

260. In a political sense, the community of Hungarian citizens coincides with the political nation of Hungary, regardless of the national or ethnic origins of its inhabitants. In legal terms, citizenship is a legal relationship between the State and its residents. Its content is made up of the rights and obligations deriving from it. The most important citizenship rights are defined by the chapter 'Freedom and Responsibility' of the Fundamental Law, but this does not include a complete list of these rights. Citizens' rights enshrined in the Constitution are the right to education (Article XI), the prohibition of expulsion and the right to return from abroad at any time (Article XIV section (2)), social and welfare rights provided by the State on the basis of Article XIX which formulates social security of citizens as a 'State's aim', the right to vote, the right to hold public office (Article XXIII sections (7)–(8)), and the right to consular protection (Article XXVII section (2)). In practice, citizens' rights are the most widespread in the field of public services, especially in social and healthcare.

261. As to the other side of the citizenship, although the Fundamental Law formulates most duties as general ones which relate to 'everyone', in practice, most of them oblige Hungarian citizens or are enforceable only against them. These are the parents' obligation to take care of their minor children, including the provision of schooling for them and, conversely, the adult children's obligation to take care of their parents if they are in need (Article XVI sections (3)–(4)). Everyone, including each citizen, is obliged to protect and maintain natural resources (Article P) section (1)).

§14.03 The Creation, Acquisition and Termination of Hungarian Citizenship

262. Hungarian citizenship law is based on the principle of *ius sanguinis*, which means that most Hungarians acquire Hungarian citizenship by descent, by birth, if at least one of their parents is a Hungarian citizen.

263. A non-Hungarian citizen may acquire Hungarian citizenship by naturalization if he or she so requests; has been living in Hungary continuously at least for eight years preceding the application; does not have a criminal record in Hungary or is not subject to criminal proceedings before a Hungarian court; his/her subsistence and place of residence is provided in Hungary; his or her residence in the country does not violate Hungary's public and national security, and, finally, he or she has passed an exam in the Hungarian language.

264. However, under certain conditions, the Citizenship Act provides for a number of benefits and exemptions from the aforementioned conditions, such as requiring a shorter stay in Hungary for a person who has been married for at least three years to a Hungarian citizen or whose marriage has ended by the death of a spouse, if his or her minor child is a Hungarian citizen, if he/she was born in Hungary, or if the applicant has refugee status or is stateless in Hungary.

265. The conservative government coalition that came to power in 2010 – using its two-thirds parliamentary majority – amended the Citizenship Act in 2010 to provide Hungarian citizenship to Hungarians living abroad under preferential conditions. Thus, on their application, those non-Hungarians whose ancestor was a Hungarian citizen or likely to have Hungarian origin and are able to prove their Hungarian-language proficiency may be granted preferential naturalization. In this case, they are not required to live in Hungary or to take a citizenship exam. The extension of Hungarian citizenship to those Hungarians who live in neighbouring countries generated long and bitter political debates. Since citizenship embodies a legal bond between a State and the citizens, it was feared that granting it to Hungarians living abroad would lead to conflicts with neighbouring countries. This did occur later to an extent, especially in Slovakia and Ukraine, where domestic law does not permit dual citizenship. The opposition parties accused the government majority of extending citizenship only for political reasons since citizenship includes the right to vote in Hungarian general elections. The extension of the right to vote was criticized arguing that the Hungarians who live abroad do not contribute to public burdens and are not affected by the decisions of the Hungarian National Assembly. It is certain that in the parliamentary elections of 2014, the government parties received about 95% of the votes of Hungarians living in neighbouring countries. According to some analyses, in 2014, these votes were necessary for the conservative coalition to gain a two-thirds majority in Parliament. In fact, already in 2001, a law was adopted which provided a so-called Hungarian card for those Hungarians who lived abroad. The card certified the Hungarian nationality of its owner and provided a number of cultural, travel and educational benefits in Hungary.

266. At the same time, it is also to be noted that Hungarians who have dual citizenship and live in neighbouring countries do not have all the rights enjoyed by citizens living in Hungary. The Fundamental Law itself allows an exception to equal citizenship when it authorizes the legislature to provide in a cardinal act that 'only persons with a domicile in Hungary may be granted the right or the full right to vote and to be voted for'. As a matter of fact, Hungarian citizens who live outside the national borders have only one vote: they may vote only for the party lists but not for candidates in individual constituencies. Nor may they claim consular services outside of Hungary since they are not entitled to a whole range of social and welfare services which are provided for those citizens who live in the country.

267. A special form of naturalization is repatriation. This is a legal way of acquiring Hungarian citizenship for those people who were already citizens in the past but lost it for certain reasons. This can be the case when a person had left the country without permission during the Communist regime and was therefore deprived of his/her nationality in punishment, or if his or her citizenship ceased because the area where he/she lived had become the territory of another State.

268. Hungarian citizenship can be terminated for two reasons: resignation and withdrawal. A Hungarian citizen may, by a declaration addressed to the President of the Republic, waive nationality if he/she resides abroad and holds citizenship in another country (or is likely to have it). The objective of avoiding statelessness lies behind the rule that a person who has not acquired foreign citizenship within three years of accepting his or her resignation may request restoration of his/her Hungarian citizenship from the President of the Republic.

269. Hungarian citizenship can be withdrawn from a person who has acquired Hungarian citizenship illegally by misleading the public authorities, in particular by giving false information or concealing data or facts necessary for their decision. There is no possibility of revocation after twenty years from the date of acquiring citizenship.

270. Formally, the President of the Republic decides on all citizenship matters, including naturalization, repatriation and withdrawal, on the basis of a proposal by the competent Minister (now the Minister of the Interior).

§14.04 The Legal Status of Foreigners Residing in Hungary

271. Hungary signed and ratified the 1951 Refugee Convention of Geneva in 1967, and the detailed rules on the right of asylum are entrenched in an act of Parliament (the Asylum Law).[136] In line with this international agreement, according to the Fundamental Law, Hungary will 'upon request, grant asylum to non-Hungarian nationals who are persecuted in their country or in the country of their habitual residence for reasons of race, nationality, the membership of a particular social group, religious or political beliefs, or have a well-founded reason to fear direct persecution if they do not receive protection from their country of origin, nor from any other country' (Article XIV section (4)). This statement of the constitutional text of 2011 was completed by the Seventh Amendment to the Fundamental Law with a restrictive provision saying that a non-Hungarian national is not entitled to asylum 'if he or she arrived in the territory of Hungary through any country where he or she was not persecuted or directly threatened with persecution'. It is worth noting that this addition was attached to the text at the peak of the anti-migrant government campaign in 2018, the government opposing continuously since 2015 the migrant policy of the European Union and conveying the central political message that 'Hungary wants to decide with whom it wants to live with'. Notably, another provision was attached to this article stating that '[n]o foreign population shall be settled in Hungary', and any 'foreign national (not including persons who have the right to free movement and residence), may only live in the territory of Hungary under an application individually examined by the Hungarian authorities' (Article XIV section (1)). At the same time, the traditional institution of refugee protection, the principle of non-*refoulement*, has remained in the Constitution in a form that no one can be

136. Act LXXX of 2007.

'expelled or extradited to a State where there is a risk that he or she would be sentenced to death, tortured or subjected to other inhuman treatment or punishment' (Article XIV section (3)).

272. According to the Asylum Law, asylum seekers are entitled to stay, care, support and accommodation in the territory of Hungary, but they are obliged to cooperate with the asylum authority, in particular by giving credible data and information necessary to conduct the asylum procedure.

273. Since 2016, Hungarian authorities have often been subject to international and domestic criticism for their unfair treatment of asylum seekers and strict asylum practice. In particular, the institution of asylum custody has been heavily criticized, mainly because of the length and the circumstances of detention. Asylum custody can be ordered for a number of reasons, and, although normally it can last only up to seventy-two hours, the length of detention may be extended several times, with a maximum duration of six months.

274. As a general rule, if refugee status has been granted to the asylum seeker, he or she has the same rights and obligations as citizens, with the exception that they do not have the right to vote in general elections (they may, however, vote at local elections and referendums), and they cannot be public office-holders.

275. It is to be noted that the Asylum Law defines certain other types of legal status for foreigners whose life or security is threatened in their country of origin, but who do not meet the conditions for obtaining refugee status, or who need only for temporary protection. Their status, with certain limitations, is similar to that of the refugees.

Chapter 15: Political Parties

276. The legal status of political parties was first regulated in 1989, during the transition period to democracy. Through the recognition of the right to form political parties, they became constitutional institutions. By and large, the bases of this regulation have remained unchanged since 1989.

§15.01 Constitutional Status of Political Parties

277. The constitutional cornerstones of political party pluralism are laid down by the Fundamental Law in its chapter 'Freedom and Responsibility' that is found among the basic rights. According to Article VIII section (3), political parties may be formed and may operate freely on the basis of the right to association. By virtue of this provision, party formation enjoys fundamental rights protection.

278. But political parties are not only manifestations of a basic right. The Fundamental Law, taking over the former constitutional rules, attributes certain constitutional functions to them, declaring that political parties 'participate in the formation and expression of the will of the people'. This means that these organizations are intermediary entities between the citizens and representative bodies. The constitutional text clearly distinguishes political parties from state authorities, prescribing that they may not exercise public power directly. This rule is obviously rooted in the experiences of the one-party system of the Communist era when public authorities existed under the strong and direct control of the ruling Communist Party. This separation is mirrored by many conflict of interest rules entrenched in the Fundamental Law and the empowerment of the legislature to determine further public offices which may not be held by members or officials of political parties.

279. Under the truce agreement of 1945, through Act V of 1945, there is a ban on Fascist and Hungarist[137] parties.

280. Having regard to the constitutional importance of political parties – both as manifestations of a basic right and as having constitutional functions – the Fundamental Law prescribes that detailed rules for the operation and management of political parties must be laid down in a cardinal act.

§15.02 The Basic Rules on Party Organizations

281. The Act on Political Parties[138] was adopted in 1989, and it has – as a rare exception – remained in effect until today. This legislation is, however, a *lex*

137. 'Hungarism' was a Hungarian national socialist ideology and political movement from 1930 to 1945. The political party of this movement, the Nazi friendly 'Arrow Cross Party' came to power in the autumn of 1944, and was swept away by the Soviet occupation in the spring of 1945.
138. Law XXXIII of 1989.

specialis compared to the Civil Code of 2013,[139] which means that the latter must be enforced unless the 1989 Act prescribes otherwise. In addition, some other statutes contain rules concerning political parties too, like the electoral laws governing the parties' participation in elections and their campaign activities.

282. A party may be formed under the right to association in the same way as private law associations. It means that at least ten people may establish a party for promoting political aims. Parties must apply for registration and be registered by the court.

283. Political parties cannot establish or operate units at workplaces and educational institutions. Only those who have the right to vote may found a party and fill a leading position in it. The general membership may be natural persons only.

284. According to the Act on Political Parties, the property of a party can consist of fees paid by its members, subsidies from the central budget, real estate provided free of charge by the State, contributions of natural persons of Hungarian nationality, bequests of natural persons, or its business, commercial activities. However, a party may not accept financial contributions from a foreign State or foreign organization, regardless of its legal status, or from a natural person who is not a Hungarian citizen. It is prohibited to accept anonymous donations.

285. Parties that obtained at least 1% of votes at the last general elections are entitled to budgetary support. The total sum of subsidies is determined by the annual Budget Act, 25% of which amount is allocated to these parties. The remaining 75% of budgetary support is paid to the parliamentary parties in proportion to their election results. In addition, parliamentary parties can have a foundation which is also entitled to get financial grants from the state budget for the purpose of pursuing scientific, educational and research activities in order to develop a political culture. The legality of the financial management of parties is controlled by the State Audit Office.

286. The legal control of the parties' activities is exercised by the Prosecution Service. In the event of a party's violation of law, the prosecutor may bring the party before the courts. The court may be asked to abolish the party if it is functioning in an unconstitutional or illegal way or dissolve the party if it has ceased activity and has not disposed of its property. In this regard, a party is deemed to have ceased functioning if it has failed to nominate any candidates for two successive general parliamentary elections.

§15.03 Party Pluralism in Hungary

287. In Hungary since 1990, there has been a multiparty system. In 2022, when the day of parliamentary elections was settled, 267 parties had been registered by

139. Law V of 2013.

courts,[140] while 44 parties have registered with the National Election Office for the 2022 parliamentary elections. The party system has always been in flux; for example, 30 new parties were registered in 2018 and 70 in 2017. A total of 116 parties were registered between 2014 and 2018, and 51 parties between 2010 and 2014. A similar wave of party formation took place in the first half of the 1990s. Although most of them have disappeared since then, three of the parties that came to Parliament as a result of the 1990 parliamentary elections are still represented in the National Assembly.

288. Despite the fact that formally there are many parties, there is a dominant party system in Hungary which means that the ruling party coalition is in a predominant power position, and the government composed of the party alliance between Fidesz and its satellite party, the Christian Democratic Party, can hardly be overthrown in parliamentary elections. This is not only due to the fragmentation of the opposition but also due to the fact that almost all state organs and public institutions have been packed by the government parties which, on the one hand, effectively support government policy and, on the other hand, provide them with a huge competitive advantage in all elections.[141] The almost unlimited financial resources available to the government parties and their active and open support by the public media have seriously distorted equal opportunities among the parties in the last two parliamentary elections.

289. The operation of the business and fake (or bogus) parties create another constitutional (and political) problem in Hungary. Business parties nominate candidates only for siphoning away budgetary subsidies, while bogus parties are those established to draw away voter support at the expense of (mostly opposition) parties. It is a common feature of business and fake parties that they do not engage in any real activity outside the election campaign period; that is, they are established only for specific purposes during the election period. Such parties participated for the first time in the 2014 elections. In 2017, the Campaign Funding Act[142] was amended so that if a party receiving state campaign support fails to achieve 1% of votes at the parliamentary election, it is required to repay campaign money received from the state budget.[143] Nonetheless, a number of bogus parties launched in the 2018 elections later failed to pay back state subsidies, and the Prosecution Service has acted only selectively against the organizers of such parties.

140. Source: National Office of Judiciary.
141. It is a typical example that before the 2018 parliamentary elections the State Audit Office imposed heavy fines on some opposition parties in controversial circumstances. *See* the relevant reports of the Organization for Security and Co-operation in Europe, *infra* nn. 246-248.
142. Act LXXXVII of 2013.
143. Act CLX of 2017.

Chapter 16: Principles of Economic Constitutionalism

§16.01 CONSTITUTIONAL DEFINITION AND PRINCIPLES OF NATIONAL ECONOMY

290. Although the Fundamental Law does not contain a separate chapter on economic or financial constitution(alism), the constitutional text comprises dispersedly a number of provisions related to the economic order of Hungary. The relevant principles and rules can be organized into three groups of norms, namely: (1) the general principles of national economic system; (2) budgetary rules including the 'debt-brake' rules; and (3) economic rights.

291. The constitutional determination of the national economic system can be traced back to the period of democratic transition when it was important to go beyond the former socialist planned economy and to provide a constitutional guarantee for a market economy. This ambition was expressed by the Preamble of the renewed Constitution from 1989 declaring that 'in order to facilitate a peaceful political transition to a constitutional state', the Parliament as the constitution-making power established 'a social market economy'. Notwithstanding that the Fundamental Law did not take over this provision, it can be deduced indirectly from several constitutional provisions that the country's economy is based on the market economy.[144] In the most general terms, Article M) section (1) of the Fundamental Law refers to the country's economic order, according to which '[t]he economy of Hungary shall be based on work which creates value and freedom of enterprise'. The next section seems to define certain state functions which are necessary to achieve these constitutional aims and values. Thus, the State has to 'ensure the conditions for fair economic competition', to prevent any abuse of economic dominance, and to defend the rights of consumers. Notably, perhaps owing to the strong restriction of the Constitutional Court's power to review public finance laws, there is no new constitutional jurisprudence around the new formation of the national economic system.

292. The constitutional rules on state budgets entail a particularly important area of the 'financial constitution'. The Fundamental Law determines basic budgetary principles, specifying also the primary responsibility for the implementation of these tenets. Thus, budget management must be 'balanced, transparent and sustainable' for which Parliament and the government are primarily responsible. Besides them, other public authorities also have responsibilities in this field. The Constitutional Court, the ordinary courts, the local governments and other state organs, 'in the course of performing their duties', are obliged to respect the above-mentioned budgetary principles.[145] Although this is not clear on the basis of the text, presumably, the budgetary responsibility of state organs extends only to their own budgets,

---

144. This view is shared also by the Constitutional Court. *See*, e.g., Decision 3001/2016. (I. 15.) of the Constitutional Court.
145. Art. N) s. (1)–(3) of the Fundamental Law.

rather than the state budget as a whole because budgetary interests obviously cannot overrule the requirement of legality whose respect is indispensable for all public authorities.

§16.02 The Principles and Rules of State Budget

293. The Fundamental Law contains the most important jurisdictional rules of the state budget. The government has the exclusionary power and duty to submit to Parliament a state budget bill with implementation by the statutory deadline. The latter point implies that legislation on the state budget must be adopted in special legislative proceedings. Thus, Parliament has the power to adopt the budget law and to approve its implementation (Article 1 section (2) point b)). Both laws have to be enacted every year (Article 36 section (1)). In constitutional terms, the annual budget is the plan for public finance over a year, which authorizes public bodies to collect public revenues and to dispense public expenditures. While the law on the state budget is a financial plan by nature, after the budgetary year, Parliament has to approve the implementation of the law on the state budget by a further law (Appropriation Act). Since Parliament is the supreme people's representative body and has the strongest democratic legitimacy, it is the most appropriate body to adopt these laws of decisive importance for the State's organization.[146] As a result of the logic of the parliamentary form of government, both the state budget law and the Act on its implementation must be adopted by a simple majority of the Members of Parliament present (rather than by a cardinal act).

294. The Fundamental Law determines only the basic content of the state budget law. According to the relevant provisions, it must 'contain all State expenditures and revenues in the same structure, in a transparent manner and in reasonable detail'. The structure of both the annual budget law and the Act on its implementation are defined by law.[147]

295. Since 2006, it was a constitutional requirement that the annual state budget must be adopted by Parliament in a special law separate from other matters. This standard was defined by the Constitutional Court based on the former Constitution which required that a Budget Act has to be adopted by an autonomous statute.[148] This ruling intended to stop the adoption of so-called salad laws, namely the legislative practice of amending a lot of other statutes in a specific Act which amendments do not relate to the subject of the latter Act passed. Despite this attempt of the Court, this practice became popular again in the past few years without being further objected to by the Constitutional Court. A single piece of law in 2012, for example, amended forty-five previous acts of Parliament having different subjects,[149] while another one, adopted in 2019, modified seventy-eight statutes.[150]

146. Jakab and Szente, *supra* n. 16, 603.
147. Act CXCV of 2011 on State Budget.
148. Decision 4/2006. (II. 15.) of the Constitutional Court.
149. Act CCVIII of 2012.

296. One of the novelties of the Fundamental Law was that, in accordance with European trends, it also includes so-called debt-brake rules. The Constitution provides that Parliament may not adopt a state budget law which allows the state debt to exceed half of GDP. This provision has been, however, a dead letter since its birth. Although the amount of the State's debt declined for years after the entry into force of the new Constitution, it never shrank to below half of GDP so as to activate this provision. The next paragraph says that '[a]s long as State debt exceeds half of the Gross Domestic Product, Parliament may only adopt a State Budget Act which contains state debt reduction in proportion to the Gross Domestic Product' (Article 36 section (5)). The most plausible interpretation of reading these two provisions is that decreasing the level of state debt by the annual Budget Acts is a permanent obligation of Parliament as far as its proportion will be less than a half of the GDP. It is to be added that the same paragraph permits a deviation from these debt-ceiling rules only for special legal orders in order to mitigate the consequences of the causes, and 'if there is a significant and enduring national economic recession, to the extent required for restoring the balance of the national economy'. However, the debt-ceiling rules of the Fundamental Law have so far proved unsuccessful that is shown by the facts that public debt has increased in successive years, for example, from 65.3% in 2019 to 79.3% in 2020.[151]

297. The Fundamental Law imposes debt-reducing obligations not only on Parliament but also on the government too, ordering that in the implementation of the annual budget laws, 'no debt or financial obligation may be assumed which allows the State debt to exceed one half of the Gross Domestic Product', with the exceptions of special legal order as described in the preceding paragraph. Article 37 contains an even stricter obligation prescribing that as long as the state debt exceeds one-half of GDP, no financial obligation may be assumed as a result of which the debt ratio would be higher than in the previous year (Article 37 sections (2)–(3)).

298. It is a common deficiency in these debt-ceiling rules that no constitutional control is provided by the Fundamental Law regarding their implementation, as Article 37 section (4) has eliminated the Constitutional Court as the institutional guarantee for financial constitutionalism. This provision has suspended constitutional review of all public finance legislation (laws on the state budget and its implementation, central taxes, duties, pensions and healthcare contributions, customs and the central conditions for local taxes), unless the right to life and human dignity, the right to the protection of personal data, freedom of thought, conscience and religion, and rights related to Hungarian citizenship are violated by such laws.[152] Although this restriction is only provisional, inasmuch as the Fundamental Law has

150. Act CXXVII of 2019.
151. *Source*: Eurostat, https://ec.europa.eu/eurostat/web/products-euro-indicators/w/2-23102023-bp#:~:text=At%20the%20end%20of%20the,from%2083.4%25%20to%2083.1%25.
152. This limitation of constitutional review was introduced by an amendment of the former Constitution in 2010 by Act CXIX of 2010.

imposed it as long as state debt exceeds one-half of GDP, having regard to the fact that the ratio of GDP-debt is significantly over 50%, this jurisdictional limitation is expected to prevail for a long time.

299. Although the restriction was justified by the negative effects of the world economic crisis, the elimination of constitutional review as a guarantee for all public finance issues, even only for a deemed transitional period, brings up the assumption that constitutional constraints on legislative power can be put aside in economically difficult times.[153] It deserves attention that this limitation has not been lifted after the country successfully overcame the economic depression. But whatever the reasons for this crude limitation of the Constitutional Court's review power, the condition of the revival of full-scale constitutional review (i.e., the reduction of state debt below one-half of GDP) is unjustified and a hardly defensible argument because the level of rights protection should not depend on economic indicators.

300. The Constitution also requires that a government has to implement the annual Budget Act 'in a lawful and expedient manner, with efficient management of public funds' (Article 37 section (1)). Some constitutional provisions seek to achieve these goals. Thus, any financial support or contractual payments from the central budget may only be granted to such organizations in which the ownership structure, organization and activity are transparent. Above and beyond this, every organization managing public funds is obliged to account publicly for its financial management. According to another rule, all data relating to public funds and national assets are to be considered as data of public interest, which implies that these data must be public. Practice shows, however, that these general declarations do not have any real significance, and no constitutional judicature is built on them. The quality of freedom of information, for example, has dropped considerably in the last few years. Thus, the institutional protection of this right was significantly reduced after this function was taken over from a parliamentary ombudsman by an administrative authority, the data of some large-scale public investments were made secret, and the provision of public interest information became a paid public service.

301. When Hungary joined the European Union in 2004, it undertook the introduction of the euro as soon as possible. At that time, the first target date of the conversion to this currency was 2008, but the world financial crisis swept away this plan. After the radical change of economic policy (known as an 'unorthodox' one) which began in 2010, accession to the Eurozone was removed from the political agenda. It is well illustrated by the fact that the *forint* as the 'official currency of Hungary' was incorporated into the Fundamental Law of 2011 (Article K)) which means that the introduction of the euro would need a constitutional amendment. However, conversion to the euro is not expected in the near future, even though most of its conditions, called the 'Maastricht criteria', have been met by Hungary.

153. Zoltán Szente, *Breaking and Making Constitutional Rules: The Constitutional Effects of Financial Crisis*, in *Hungary, in Constitution in the Global Financial Crisis: A Comparative Analysis* 242 (Xenophon Contiades ed., Ashgate 2013).

§16.03 CONSTITUTIONAL RULES OF NATIONAL ASSETS

302. A separate set of constitutional provisions deals with the protection of national assets. Article 38 section (1) of the Fundamental Law lists state property, with the property of local governments also under this category, and adding as well that the management and protection of national assets aim at 'serving the public interest, meeting common needs and preserving natural resources, as well as at taking into account the needs of future generations'. It is an additional formal requirement that Parliament must adopt a cardinal act on the responsible management of national assets. The protection of public property falling within the group of national assets must meet certain further requirements. Thus, these assets may only be transferred for purposes specified by an act of Parliament, 'taking into account the requirement of proportionate value'. Moreover, any contract for transfer (sale and purchase) or utilization (lease, usufructuary lease or use) of national assets may be concluded only with organizations of which the ownership structure, the organization and the activity aimed at the management of the national assets transferred or assigned for utilization (i.e., handover to property management) is transparent. Although the Fundamental Law does not provide for the institutional guarantee of these principles or the way in which they have to be controlled, it should be noted that the Prosecution Service has the responsibility of protecting the public interest and has powers appropriate to enforce these constitutional provisions (*see* outlined *infra* in Part II, Chapter 8, §8.02, [B]). Although the press in recent years has revealed a number of cases concerning the disposal of properties belonging to national assets to foreign offshore companies, there is little evidence in practice that the Prosecution Service has exercised its duties of protecting the public interest in such matters.

303. In the domain of national assets, the Constitution empowers the legislature to determine the scope of exclusive state property and assets of outstanding importance for the national economy in a cardinal act, as well as limitations on and conditions of alienation of national assets of outstanding importance for the national economy. In addition, the same act may establish a state monopoly for certain economic activities (Article 38 section (2)). The first category includes the Holy Crown and the other royal badges; the Parliament building; mineral resources, natural waters and certain water utilities; national roads and their infrastructure; the national core network of railways and accessory infrastructure; the state-owned international commercial airport, its associated aeronautical telecommunications, air traffic control services; caves, and so on.[154] The range of exclusive economic activity of the State has considerably broadened as the State's economic engagement has become more and more extensive in recent years. These activities include, among others, the transport and storage of pipeline products, mining, the production and distribution of radioactive materials, the establishment and operation of broadcasting channels, state-owned water utilities and regional public utilities, gambling, tobacco trade,

154. Act CXCVI of 2011 on National Assets.

public transport, the establishment and operation of national roads and their infrastructure, the national core network railway track and the infrastructure it comprises. However, the state and the local government may grant the provisional right to pursue these activities to private enterprises by way of concession, as provided for in separate laws. The takeover of certain economic activities into a state monopoly and then subsequently licensing them to private parties through concessions (such as in case of gambling and the tobacco trade) has caused a number of legal conflicts after 2010. On the basis of recent experience, it can be said that the standards of the protection of property rights provided by the European Court of Human Rights are stronger than those of the Hungarian Constitutional Court.[155] While the Constitutional Court did not object to the establishment of a state monopoly over tobacco retailing and the cancelling of the then-extant state concessions and the redistributing of them through a highly debated application system,[156] the ECtHR held that the withdrawal of prior licences by law without compensation was a breach of the property rights of the holders affected.[157]

304. The constitutional rules for the protection of national wealth were to a large extent undermined by the Ninth Amendment to the Fundamental Law, which stated that 'public funds shall be the revenues, expenditures and claims of the State'. The context of the constitutional amendment was that, from 2020, most public universities and a significant amount of public assets were placed under the management of so-called public interest foundations, thus removing these assets from the direct control of the state, while they were subject to the political control of the governing parties through their Boards of Trustees.

305. Economic rights such as the right to property or the freedom of enterprise can also be included in the economic constitution, but they will be discussed separately, in the chapter on constitutional rights (*see* in details *infra* in Part III, Chapter 11).

155. Zoltán Szente and Fruzsina Gárdos-Orosz, *Judicial Deference or Political Loyalty? The Hungarian Constitutional Court's Role in Tackling Crisis Situations*, in *New Challenges to Constitutional Adjudication in Europe: A Comparative Perspective* 96–97 (Zoltán Szente & Fruzsina Gárdos-Orosz eds., Routledge 2018).
156. Decision 3194/2014. (VII. 15.) of the Constitutional Court.
157. ECHR Case of *Vékony v. Hungary*, Application No. 65681/13 (2015).

Chapter 17: Emergency Powers: The Special Legal Orders

306. The Fundamental Law recognizes three types of special legal order: a state of war, a state of emergency and a state of danger. Although the enforcement of a special legal order is closely linked to state sovereignty, the relevant rules are contained in a separate chapter of the Fundamental Law at the end of the constitutional text (just before the closing and miscellaneous provisions). The particular types of special legal order have been defined and circumscribed for reason that they jeopardize the normal functioning of the legal system. It is common ground, however, that in certain situations endangering the constitutional order, the integrity of the country or the property or life of its citizens, the government is granted with exceptional powers to address the emergency.

§17.01 Common Rules for Special Legal Orders

307. The Constitution contains several common rules on special legal orders (Articles 52 and 53). One of them is that the extent of extraordinary power is subject to the rule that the exercise of fundamental rights may be suspended or may be restricted beyond the extent allowed by the general rule of rights-limitations (i.e., the necessity-proportionality rule as defined in Article I) section (3)). Nevertheless, certain fundamental rights may not be suspended or restricted even under a special legal order. These are the right to human dignity and life, the prohibition on torture, inhuman or degrading treatment or punishment and servitude. The most important constitutional guarantees in criminal law, like a fair trial, the presumption of innocence, a right to defence, and the principles of *nullum crimen sine lege* or double jeopardy, are also untouchable even in emergency situations. Furthermore, the application of the Fundamental Law may not be suspended, and the operation of the Constitutional Court may not be restricted under special legal orders. Under the Constitution, the exercise of the exceptional powers granted to the government during the period of the special legal order is also subject to scrutiny by Parliament in so far as the National Assembly may repeal a decree adopted by the government during such a period. Nevertheless, the government may re-enact the repealed decree with identical contents if it 'is justified by a substantial change in circumstances' (Article 53 section (3)).

308. It is also a constitutional safeguard that a special order must be terminated by the organ entitled to introduce it if the conditions for its declaration no longer exist. Finally, the Fundamental Law provides that the detailed rules to be applied under a special legal order are laid down in a cardinal act.[158]

158. Act CXIII of 2011.

§17.02 The Types of Special Legal Orders

[A] The State of War

309. The National Assembly may declare a state of war in the event of the declaration of a war or in the event of the danger of war, in the event of external armed attack or its imminent danger, and in the event of the fulfilment of an alliance commitment regarding collective defence. Such a decision needs the votes of two-thirds of MPs. If the National Assembly is prevented from taking such decisions, the President of the Republic has the right (and duty) to do so. According to the Fundamental Law, Parliament is deemed to be prevented from acting if it is not in session and convening it is made impossible by insurmountable obstacles caused by shortage of time or the events of war, a state of national crisis or state of emergency. It must be unanimously decided by the Speaker of the National Assembly, the President of the Constitutional Court and the Prime Minister whether these circumstances exist, that is, whether the National Assembly is prevented from acting.

310. In all events, if the President of the Republic has declared a state of war because the National Assembly was prevented from acting, as soon as it is able to sit, Parliament must review without delay whether the declaration of the national crisis was justified, and decide on the legality of the measures adopted. These decisions also require a two-thirds majority of MPs.

311. During a state of war, the National Assembly may not dissolve itself and may not be dissolved, and no general elections may be called or held. In such a case, a new National Assembly must be elected within ninety days of the termination of the state of national emergency. In a surprising rule, however, a newly elected National Assembly is prohibited from being formed in a state of war. Instead, the old National Assembly may be convened again by the President of the Republic, even if it has already dissolved itself or has been dissolved. The Head of State may then convene the constitutive sitting of the new Parliament on a date within thirty days of the termination of the state of national crisis.

312. Once the state of war has been announced, the government exercises the powers delegated to it by the National Assembly. Within the scope of its responsibilities, it may decide on the deployment of the Hungarian Defence Forces abroad or within Hungary, on their participation in peacekeeping and humanitarian missions in a foreign operations area, or on stationing them abroad, on the deployment of foreign armed forces in Hungary or their departing from the territory of Hungary, or on stationing them in Hungary and, finally, on the introduction of extraordinary measures laid down in a cardinal act. The government may adopt decrees by means of which it may suspend application of certain legislation, derogate from the provisions of such acts and take other extraordinary measures. Upon the termination of the state of national crisis, such decrees of the government cease to have effect.

[B] The State of Emergency

313. A state of emergency may be declared in the event of an act aimed at overthrowing or subverting the constitutional order or at acquiring exclusive power, or 'a serious unlawful act massively endangering life and property' (Article 50 section (1)). Proclamation here is similar to that of the state of war: it is primarily the right of the Parliament, but in case the National Assembly is prevented from acting, the President of the Republic must declare it. All the above-mentioned rules relating to the Parliament during the state of war are to be followed during a state of emergency as well. The state of emergency may be declared for thirty days, but the National Assembly may extend it by thirty days if the circumstances serving as grounds for it continue to exist.

314. In the period of a state of emergency, the government has the same law-making powers as in a state of war.

[C] The State of Danger

315. If an armed conflict, war situation, humanitarian catastrophe in a neighbouring country, or a serious incident endangers life and property, in particular a natural disaster or industrial accident, or their consequences must be eliminated, the government may declare a state of danger and may introduce extraordinary measures set out in a cardinal act in order to avert the danger. This kind of special legal order may be declared for thirty days. Parliament may authorize the government to extend the state of danger if the circumstances of its original declaration exist. In this situation, the government can exercise the same exceptional powers as in the other two special legal orders, i.e., may suspend the application of certain acts of Parliament, derogate from the provisions of acts and take other extraordinary measures.

§17.03 Constitutional Practice

316. Although the Fundamental Law does not specify the 'mass immigration crisis', in reality, this is a new form of special legal order that was introduced by the Parliament in September 2015 with a package of ten amending laws[159] contained in the Asylum Law.[160] In accordance with this legislation, the government has been given broad authorization to declare a mass migration crisis by government decree throughout the country or part of it for up to six months, which period may be

159. The Act CXL of 2015 has modified some other laws (such as the Police Act and the Act on National Defence) adjusting them to the rules of mass migration crisis.
160. Art. 80/A.–80/G of Act LXXX of 2007.

extended by the government. Such a crisis situation can be qualified as an extraordinary legal order since, among other things, it provides special administrative measures, exemptions from a number of procedural rules, the application of specific criminal law provisions, and authorization for special use of police and law enforcement services.

317. Notwithstanding this, because the Fundamental Law lists exhaustively all types of special legal orders (since the authorization for suspending the legal effects of acts and exercising extraordinary public powers have inherent constitutional implications) without granting the power to Parliament to establish new forms of them, the constitutionality of the 'mass immigration crisis' can be put in question. It is particularly worrying that the effect of the mass migration crisis has been continuously prolonged by the government in certain areas of the country since 2015, even though its legal conditions have not existed for years. Another type of quasi-special legal order was introduced in 2020 by amending the 1997 Act on Public Health[161] when the government terminated the state of danger declared for the COVID-19 pandemic. The amendment of that pre-existing 'health emergency situation' allowed the government to introduce almost the same legal restrictions without parliamentary authorization that it could only apply under special legal order.

318. A special legal order was declared for the first time since the Fundamental Law came into effect in March 2020, when the government introduced a state of danger due to the COVID-19 pandemic 'in order to protect the health and lives of Hungarian citizens and to prevent the negative consequences' caused by the COVID-19 pandemic as a 'human epidemic causing mass illness endangering the safety of life and property'.[162] The declaration of the state of danger attracted considerable international attention and led to heated political debates in Hungary as well, due to the allegedly unlimited powers it had granted to the government. In addition, it raised serious constitutional concerns because in Hungarian law a human epidemic does not fall within the conceptual scope of a natural disaster, nor can it be interpreted as an industrial catastrophe, whereas the Fundamental Law allows the introduction of such kind of special legal order only in these two cases. The declaration of state of danger was based on the cardinal act specified in the Fundamental Law for the implementation of a state of danger, the Disaster Protection Act which, besides natural disasters and industrial catastrophes, also defines a 'human epidemic causing mass illness' and the 'epidemic threat' as 'events' that can serve as a basis for declaring such an emergency situation. However, the Constitution, as it has been said above, allows the state of danger only for the cases of natural disaster and industrial catastrophe, and a cardinal act cannot, of course, supplement the exhaustive list set out in the Constitution.[163]

---

161. Act CLIV of 1997.
162. Government Decree 40/2020. (III. 11.).
163. Csaba Győry & Nyasha Weinberg, *Emergency powers in a hybrid regime: the case of Hungary*, The Theory and Practice of Legislation, 8(3) (2020); Zoltán Szente & Fruzsina Gárdos-Orosz, *Using Emergency Powers in Hungary: Against the Pandemic and/or Democracy?* in Pandemocracy in Europe: Power, Parliaments and People in Times of COVID-19 (Matthias C. Kettemann and Konrad Lachmayer eds., Hart 2021).

319. This type of state of danger was declared on two further occasions. During this period, Parliament passed several 'authorization acts' confirming all the emergency decrees previously issued by the government, and even consenting to all decrees to be issued later. By these laws, Parliament committed a kind of 'suicide' by waiving in advance its power of *ex post* control of emergency decrees, and thus made the exceptional power of the government unlimited. All these legislative provisions were questionable from a constitutional point of view, not only because Parliament waived its constitutional obligation to control continuously every emergency decree but also because Parliament did not cease to work under the special legal order, and passed a total of fifty-two laws.

320. When the pandemic situation no longer justified the maintenance of the state of danger, the government pushed through Parliament the Tenth Amendment to the Fundamental Law to extend its scope to 'armed conflict, war or humanitarian disaster in a neighbouring country' and immediately declared a new state of danger referring to the Russia-Ukraine war in May 2022. The government extended the state of danger in October 2022[164] until May 2024; so apart from a short period, since March 2020, Hungary has been under a continuous special legal order.

321. The government has engaged in very intense lawmaking activity during successive emergencies. Until the end of 2023, more than 750 emergency decrees invoked the special legal order. In doing so, it has been criticized for using its exceptional powers for political purposes that were often unrelated to the health crisis caused by the COVID-19 pandemic or the Russia-Ukraine war. For example, it took over the management of some strategically important private companies and changed their leadership, reduced revenues of opposition-led municipalities and the budgetary support of political parties, and severely and controversially restricted a number of fundamental rights such as right to assembly, freedom of information or right to strike. However, the Constitutional Court has always shown deference to the government's exceptional powers, upholding all the emergency decrees that had been challenged.

164. Government Decree 424/2022. (X. 28.).

Chapter 18: Other Sovereignty Issues

§18.01 State Independence and Constitutional Identity

322. Pursuant to Article B) section (1) of the Fundamental Law, Hungary is 'an independent and democratic State under the rule of law'.

323. Independence was for a long time a neglected principle around which no special constitutional jurisprudence had been established. In very recent times, this value and national sovereignty have become more appreciated as basic elements of the 'constitutional identity' of Hungary. The independent nature of the State signifies both 'internal' sovereignty, meaning the entirety of constitutional power of the State, and 'external' sovereignty, postulating the country's international recognition as a sovereign State. After forty years of Communist rule (when Soviet troops were stationed in the country), when state sovereignty was restricted, this clause has had significance as a constitutional barrier against any new-born dependence.

324. National sovereignty, together with constitutional identity, has gained particular emphasis only in recent years,[165] especially as part of the Hungarian government's actions against the European Union, especially against its migration policy. The 'fight against Brussels' has had some constitutional implications, for example, with the Commissioner for Fundamental Rights petitioning the Constitutional Court for an abstract constitutional interpretation to declare that the settlement of groups of foreigners in Hungary is incompatible with the Fundamental Law. In the relevant decision, the Court reserved the power to consider whether the joint exercise of powers between Hungary and the EU institutions violates, among others, Hungary's sovereignty and self-identity based on its 'historical constitution'. The Court said that for this purpose, it may carry out a so-called sovereignty control on the one hand and an identity control on the other hand. [166] In 2021, the Constitutional Court went even further: at the initiative of the Minister of Justice, in an abstract constitutional interpretation procedure, it stated that 'where the exercise of joint competences with the [European] Union is incomplete, Hungary shall be entitled, in accordance with the presumption of reserved sovereignty, to exercise the relevant non-exclusive field of competence of the EU, until the institutions of the European Union take the measures necessary to ensure the effectiveness of the joint exercise of competences'.[167]

325. The references to constitutional identity were incorporated in the constitutional text by the Seventh Amendment in May 2018, postulating it as rooted in the historical constitution and establishing the duty of all state organs to protect it

165. For details, *see* Fruzsina Gárdos-Orosz, *The Reference to Constitutional Traditions in Populist Constitutionalism – The Case of Hungary,* 61(1) Hungarian Journal of Legal Studies (2020); and Zoltán Szente, *Constitutional Identity as a Normative Constitutional Concept,* 63(1) Hungarian Journal of Legal Studies (2022).
166. Decision 22/2016. (XII. 5.) of the Constitutional Court.
167. Decision 32/2021. (XII. 22.) of the Constitutional Court.

together with 'the Christian culture of Hungary' (*see* outlined *supra* in Part I, Chapter §2.02, [C] [4] [g]).[168] In parallel, Article E of the Fundamental Law was complemented by a constitutional stipulation providing that the joint exercises of competences together with the EU institutions must 'comply with the fundamental rights and freedoms provided for in the Fundamental Law', and it may 'not limit the inalienable right of Hungary to determine its territorial unity, population, form of government and state structure'.

326. The National Avowal, namely the preamble to the Fundamental Law, unusually in terms of sovereignty classifies the epochs of recent Hungarian history, expressing the view that the country lost its self-determination on 19 March 1944 and regained its sovereignty only on 'the second day of May 1990, when the first freely elected organ of popular representation was formed'. The latter date is seen by the Constitution as 'the beginning of our country's new democracy and constitutional order'.

327. Obviously, it is problematic if the constitution-making power takes a full stand on controversial historical issues (there is no consensus in Hungary that the German occupation of the country in 1944 was a real turning point in the history of Hungary), though this part of the Preamble seems only a solemn declaration without any constitutional effect.

§18.02 State Monopoly of the Use of Coercion

328. It is the sovereign right of the State to maintain exclusive power to use legitimate violence. This power, however, is limited insofar as even the State may use coercion legitimately only for specific purposes, namely in order to enforce the Fundamental Law and laws (Article C) section (3)). This article provides constitutional authority for state organizations to use force, like the police or the Hungarian Defence Forces using weapons within the limits of the law.

329. In accordance with the monopoly on the use of coercion, all actions which aim at acquiring or exercising power by force, and of exclusively possessing it, are unconstitutional per se. Beyond the public authorities' duty to protect the constitutional order from such actions, the Fundamental Law grants the right to and imposes the obligation on everyone to resist such attempts in a lawful way (Article C) sections (2) and (3)). The latter provision, however, hardly has any real significance or normative content: so far, there are no precedents for its application, and it has not afforded any effective protection against the authoritarian tendencies of recent years.

168. See also the role of the Sovereignty Protection Office (*supra* Part I, Ch. 5), established by the Twelfth Amendment to the Fundamental Law (*see supra* Part I, Ch. 2, §2.02[C][4][l]).

§18.03 Responsibility for Hungarians Beyond the State Borders

330. In Hungary, since the system change, there has always been a consensus among the political parties about the moral and political commitment of the State to support Hungarian minorities living outside the state borders. Accordingly, the Fundamental Law states that Hungary bears responsibility for the fate of Hungarians living beyond its borders, facilitates the survival and development of their communities, supports their efforts to preserve their Hungarian identity, the effective use of their individual and collective rights, the establishment of their community self-government, their prosperity in their resident country, and promotes their cooperation with each other and with Hungary (Article D)). A similar declaration can also be read in the first sentence of the Preamble of the Constitution saying '[w]e, the members of the Hungarian nation …, with a sense of responsibility for every Hungarian' (proclaim the Constitution).

331. The Constitution tries to provide a sort of moral foundation for this commitment by declaring that 'there is one single Hungarian nation that belongs together' and, further, several provisions of the National Avowal refer to the foundations of the unity of the Hungarian national community.

332. Yet the form of this support has led to political hostilities and endless debates among the parties ever since Hungarians beyond the border have been able to gain Hungarian citizenship in a preferential way and have been given the right to vote. It is worth noting that the Fundamental Law only opened the way to extend the suffrage to them, but did not make it mandatory.[169]

333. In practice, the Hungarian parties and NGOs existing in the neighbouring countries receive financial support from Hungary every year, the constitutional basis of which is provided by this provision.

§18.04 Membership of the European Union

334. As EU membership requires the transfer of sovereign rights of the Member States to EU institutions, membership itself needs constitutional authorization. This is given by the 'EU clause' of the Fundamental Law which determines the purpose and conditions of the transfer of public powers. According to this provision, the creation of European unity is a constitutional objective to which Hungary must contribute 'in order to enhance the liberty, well-being and security of the people of Europe' (Article E) section (1)). As the following paragraphs set out the conditions of Hungary's membership, it is a rational conclusion that Hungary pursues this constitutional aim by way of its participation in the EU as a Member State.

169. 'A cardinal act may provide that only persons with domicile in Hungary may be granted the right or the full right to vote and to be voted for, and may specify further requirements for the eligibility to be voted for.' Art. XXIII, s. (4) of the Fundamental Law.

335. The precise content of this constitutional authorization is that Hungary may exercise some of its competences arising from the Fundamental Law (i.e., sovereign rights) jointly with other Member States or through EU institutions. The acknowledgement of the primacy of EU law is associated with this authorization, stating that legitimate EU law may lay down generally binding rules of conduct.

336. The Constitution sets conditions for this way of exercising transferred jurisdictions. One of them is the basis of an international treaty. Apparently, this is Hungary's accession treaty which was signed in 2003 and promulgated by law in the next year.[170] In fact, this law was only the legal vehicle of the founding treaties of the European Union which were promulgated by this act of Parliament. In this way, every obligation of membership derives evidently from international treaties. Although the wording of the EU clause would seem to suggest that only the founding treaties can impose obligations on Hungary, this narrow interpretation would apparently be wrong, for these treaties authorize EU institutions to adopt EU laws. Whatever international treaty is implied in this provision, authorization to express consent requires the votes of two-thirds of the Members of Parliament.

337. The Constitution specifies the objective and extent of the transfer of public powers to EU institutions as it aims to participate in the EU as a Member State. Accordingly, these powers may be transferred only to the extent necessary to exercise the rights and fulfil the obligations following from that membership. Beyond the latter requirement, there are other constitutional limits to the delegation of sovereign rights to the institutions of the EU, namely that the exercise of transferred competences must comply with the fundamental rights and freedoms provided for in the Fundamental Law and may not limit the inalienable right of Hungary to determine its territorial unity, population, form of government and state structure.[171]

§18.05 Official Language

338. Article H) of the Fundamental Law provides that Hungarian is the official language of the country and must be protected. In addition to this, Hungarian Sign Language, as a part of Hungarian culture, is also protected by the Constitution. Pursuant to this provision, public authorities use Hungarian in their operation. Nevertheless, it does not entail the exclusive use of Hungarian since the right to use one's mother tongue is implied by the right to privacy, while it is widely recognized by procedural rules in judicial and administrative proceedings.

§18.06 National Currency

339. Although successive Hungarian governments were pushing for a long time to join the Eurozone, this is no longer an official goal for a few years now. That was

170. Act XXX of 2004.
171. For the constitutional practice, *see supra* Part I, Ch. 18, §18.01.

the reason for defining the *forint* as the official currency of Hungary (Article K)). Self-evidently, this currency is the account basis for a number of public functions of monetary and budgetary policy.

Part II: The Exercise of State Power

Chapter 1: The National Assembly

§1.01 Historical Sketch of the Hungarian Parliament

340. Although a medieval chronicle reported that already in the second half of the ninth century a National Assembly (*Országgyűlés*)[172] had been held, there is a consensus that the institution of the general assembly is rooted in the annual occasions during which the king judged personally in Fehérvár, the medieval seat of the kingdom. For these events, the king usually invited not only the members of the King's Council but also the greatest lords and high priests of the country and often discussed with them not only grievances and complaints but also the most important national affairs.

341. The National Assembly was established by the end of the thirteenth century, and besides legislation and taxation, the judicial function of the assembly has remained for centuries. These were early estate assemblies which convened the privileged orders, the high priests (*praelati*), barons (*barones*) and nobles (*nobiles*). However, the fully developed feudal state evolved only by the mid-fifteenth century (when some boroughs' deputies were summoned). Until then, the composition of Parliament was not permanent. The nobles from the very beginning had the privilege of personal appearance, and even in the fifteenth century some crowded estate assemblies were held in the open air. Nevertheless, when the composition of the National Assembly was fixed by law in 1608, the representation of the nobility by elected deputies (*nobiles electi*) became exclusive. This law divided Parliament into two 'tables' (chambers), but it was really only the institutionalization of a long-standing practice. The composition of the National Assembly reflected the social structure of the privileged classes in which four estates were represented in the general assembly. The lower chamber was composed of the deputies of nobility – to which house the county assemblies of nobility elected their delegates – and royal towns, while the great landowners or lords (barons and magnates) and high priests of the Catholic Church, complemented by high dignitaries of the Kingdom, sat in the upper house.

172. In Hungary, the earliest written source of the term 'parliament' (parlamentum publicum, parlamentum generale) dates back to the late 13th century. Zoltán Szente, *A parlamentek története: A korai rendi gyűlések kialakulásától a modern népképviseleti törvényhozásokig* (Országház Könyvkiadó 2018) 119.

342. The powers and duties of the medieval and early modern Parliament were not fixed or recognized by law. In spite of this, the National Assembly was considered to represent the entire country, dealing with matters concerning the liberties of the whole kingdom (*universarum regnicolarum libertatem*). From the early sixteenth century, the most important parliamentary functions were participation in lawmaking and taxation. Remarkably, the National Assembly as a typical estate assembly, apart from short interruptions, has been operating continuously for centuries.

343. The principle of popular representation was achieved in the lower House in 1848 as a result of the revolution of that year (the upper House preserved its old structure), and after the fall of the war of independence against the Habsburg Empire, it was revived by the Great Compromise of 1867 when Hungary became equal with the other half of the Empire within the framework of the Austro-Hungarian Monarchy. The bicameral system of Parliament also remained unchanged after the disintegration of the Monarchy and the revolutionary movements of 1918–1919, as the continuity of the historical constitution was partly restored. The upper House was reorganized in 1926, and became a corporative chamber. At the end of the Second World War, a unicameral Temporary National Assembly was founded in 1944, and the history of the 'thousand-year' constitution ended.

344. Historical Hungarian public law defined the concept of Parliament primarily on the basis of its constitutional position and functions. Thus, the legislature expresses the sovereign will of the State: its purpose is to legislate in general terms[173] (together with the other constituent of 'the legislature', the king).[174] Other ancient conceptualizations focused on the public power of Parliament. On these views, Parliament was considered to be the 'supreme, legally unlimited and irresponsible, that is sovereign' organ of the State.[175] In other words, the historical constitution was formally based on the principle of parliamentary supremacy.

345. Interestingly, though in a completely different political and legal context, this approach to legislative power continued when the Communist Party seized power. However, in structural terms, the first written Hungarian Constitution in 1949 broke up the centuries-old tradition, and a one-chamber National Assembly was established. Despite the fact that according to official Communist ideology all public power was in the hands of the National Assembly embodying popular sovereignty, in reality, the one-party parliament played a subordinate role in the decades of the 'existing Socialism'. After the collapse of the Communist system in 1989, in the period of transition to democracy, the old bicameral structure of Parliament was not restored, but the National Assembly rapidly became a pluralist, multiparty legislature in a new system of parliamentary government.

---

173. Ernő Nagy, *Magyar közjog* (3d ed. 1890) 197, 235.
174. Móric Tomcsányi, *Magyarország közjoga* (Királyi Magyar Egyetemi Nyomda, 5th ed. 1943) 455.
175. Kálmán Molnár, *Magyar közjog* (Danubia 3d ed. 1929) 390; and Tomcsányi, *supra* n. 176, 455–456.

§1.02 Constitutional Concept of National Assembly

346. The Fundamental Law defines the National Assembly as the supreme organ of popular representation. This concept refers equally to the way of creating the mandate of Parliament and the source of its power. Although Parliament is a continuously functioning body, its legitimacy must be regularly renewed by elections. However, its representative nature means not only that its mandate is created by general elections but implies also that the National Assembly exercises powers delegated by the people, so its competences derive from popular sovereignty. According to the jurisprudence of the Constitutional Court, the operation of representative bodies is the primary way of exercising public power. Nevertheless, it means only that it is a usual way of public decision-making, compared to direct participation of voters, which is only exceptional.

347. The constitutional concept of National Assembly incorporates also the presumption that Parliament must exercise its powers on behalf of the people. This provision is the source of the free mandate of Members of Parliament, which exempts them from voters' instructions and other legal constraints.

348. In Hungary, the legislative power is not divided: the unicameral National Assembly has a monopoly on enacting laws. It is worth noting that Hungarian judicial practice does not acknowledge Parliament's legal responsibility for damages caused by legislation.[176]

§1.03 Parliamentary Functions and Duties

349. The unicameral National Assembly exercises the legislative power in Hungary. The Fundamental Law does not specify the major constitutional functions of Parliament, but the academic literature usually identifies legislation and the control of government as the two primary parliamentary functions.

350. Article 1 section (2) of the Fundamental Law enumerates the most important competences of Parliament. This list contains different types of responsibilities and duties, between which sometimes no clear distinction can be made. Most of these competences, like constitution-making, the adoption of acts, the approval of the state budget, or general amnesty, are exclusive parliamentary powers, while some other competences, most typically the treaty power, are shared with other organs. Then, although the Constitution specifies the adoption of the central budget and the approval of its implementation, these decisions are made in the legal form of statutes, so these powers could be implied in the lawmaking power. There are some tasks that the Parliament has to exercise on a regular basis, like the adoption of the annual budget, or the election of certain high officials (if their position is vacant).

176. Jakab and Szente, *supra* n. 16, 545.

351. The powers of the National Assembly, as enshrined in the Fundamental Law, are exclusive powers in the sense that they may not, in principle, be transferred by Parliament to another body. Although the President of the Republic may exercise certain parliamentary powers during special legal orders, and the government is obliged to take immediate action to replace acts falling within the competence of Parliament in the same situation, these cannot be regarded as the exercise of delegated powers because all these actions may be done only if Parliament is prevented from holding a session and exercising its own powers.

352. It is to be added that most parliamentary powers specified in the Constitution are also mandatory ones or constitutional obligations of the National Assembly because under certain conditions, the legislature is bound to exercise them. In such cases, Parliament's discretionary power is limited to deciding only how it exercises its rights. These powers are, in particular, fulfilling legislative obligations, approving the annual state budget, and electing the high officials stipulated by the Fundamental Law. However, Parliament cannot be sanctioned for failing to exercise its jurisdiction, except in the specific cases when the President of the Republic may dissolve the National Assembly.

353. The enumeration of the tasks and powers of Parliament is not exclusive, but it contains only the most important competences. Specific laws comprise a number of other parliamentary functions. The number of these responsibilities has increased considerably since 1990 and amounts, today, to almost five hundred.

[A] Constitution-Making

354. According to the Fundamental Law, Parliament has exclusive constituent power in Hungary. The content of this power is to adopt a new constitution or to amend the existing one. Thus, the constitution-making power of the Parliament is exclusive and unlimited in the constitutional sense. Consequently, there is no constitutional way to review the duly declared constitutional will (*see supra* Part I, Chapter 2, §2.02, [C] [2]).

355. Although both functions are performed exclusively by Parliament, the Fundamental Law draws a difference between constitution-making and legislative power. When the National Assembly exercises the former, it must make clear that the ongoing procedure aims at adopting or modifying the Fundamental Law, since Parliament must comply with special formal procedural rules.

356. The Hungarian legal system does not know the institution of unconstitutional constitutional amendment, so the expression of constitution-making power cannot be conceptually unconstitutional. The Constitutional Court, already in the 1990s, faced the problem of how to adjudge constitutional amendments that contradict other parts of the constitutional text that were not directly addressed by the amendment. Since 1949, the *Országgyűlés* has always exercised its constitutional power in the form of acts of Parliament, a custom surviving the 1989 constitutional revision. While the fusion of the constitution-making and the legislative power was due to unlimited parliamentary sovereignty before 1989, the maintenance of this way of constitutional amendments was, however, hardly justifiable after the democratic transition and within the framework of the rule of law. Yet, the Constitutional Court never objected the legal form of the constitutional amendment acts, but it took the view instead that such laws have a double character: those provisions which introduce a change into the constitutional text are parts of the constitution-making will, whereas those rules which are not formally incorporated into the Constitution are acts (of legislative power). Still, the Court has always refrained from reviewing such constitutional amendment acts, arguing that even their 'statutory provisions' are so closely connected to the constitution-making power that the Court may not examine their constitutionality 'because it would also mean that the Constitutional Court, which is institutionalized for constitutional protection, would take over the competence of the constitution-making power'.[177] Although the theoretical possibility of constitutional review of constitutional amendments caused an academic debate in the early 2010s,[178] the Fourth Amendment of the Fundamental Law affirmed the earlier approach explicitly by stating that the Constitutional Court, at the proposal of the President of the Republic, may review only whether or not the procedural requirements laid down in the Fundamental Law with respect to adoption of a new constitution or the amendment of the Fundamental Law have been met (Article S) section (3)).

357. Direct democracy can also limit the legislative power, forasmuch as the Parliament is bound to the decision of a national referendum. However, since the first major ruling of the Constitutional Court on the relationship between direct and indirect exercises of public power, it has been a dominant view and a constitutional rule that the Constitution may not be amended by a referendum because the constitution-making procedure is exhaustively regulated by the Constitution (today the Fundamental Law), so any constitutional change brought about a popular vote would mean a de facto withdrawal of the constitution-making power from the Parliament.[179]

[B] Legislation

[1] The Scope of Legislative Power

358. The most classical function of the National Assembly is to make laws. The acts of Parliament are normative legal rules regulating basic social relations, and they are enacted by the National Assembly according to special legislative procedures. It is also a monopoly power, even if other public authorities are also empowered to issue legal rules. The lawmaking power of the National Assembly covers the enactment of new laws and the amendment or the invalidation of existing laws. In

177. Decision 1260/B/1997. of the Constitutional Court.
178. *See supra* n. 29.
179. Decision 2/1993. (I. 22.) of the Constitutional Court.

spite of the historical constitution though, the Fundamental Law does not recognize the power of authentic interpretation of laws (*interpretatio authentica*) by Parliament because the courts are bound only to the promulgated legal texts.

359. The scope of parliamentary legislation is not determined precisely by the Fundamental Law. In most general terms, by enacting laws, the National Assembly may confer rights upon citizens and assign them certain obligations. Nevertheless, the Constitution stipulates certain subject matters which may be regulated only by laws. Only an act of Parliament may specify the annual state budget and its implementation,[180] the calculation method of the state debt,[181] or the list of Ministries.[182] Matters exclusively for legislation may be specified only by the Constitution.[183]

360. In addition, some of these exclusively legislative matters fall within the category of cardinal acts which may be passed by a two-thirds majority vote of the MPs present. The Hungarian constitutional system has applied the qualified majority requirement to certain subject areas since 1989, but until the entry into force of the Fundamental Law in 2012, the laws relating to fundamental rights and the legal status of public authorities belonged primarily to this category. In spite of this clear delineation, the new Constitution has renamed and restructured this special sort of legislation inasmuch as some traditional public policy areas like 'the protection of families', 'the organization of integrated agricultural production' and 'family farms and other agricultural holdings', the performance of military service, and so on have also been taken up into the group of the cardinal acts (the new archaistic name of these acts of Parliament).

361. More than thirty of these legislative items are specified by the Constitution. Some cardinal acts concern state sovereignty like the Act on Citizenship,[184] or the legislation on the use of the coat of arms and the flag,[185] on the parliamentary elections[186] and on the electoral procedure,[187] while others determine the detailed rules for certain fundamental rights, such as the law on the independent authority responsible for personal data protection and the freedom of information,[188] on the organizational forms of religious communities,[189] on the operation and economic management of political parties,[190] on the freedom of the press,[191] and on the rights of nationalities.[192] A separate set of cardinal acts regulate the legal status and the operation of the most important public bodies, like the legislation on the National

180. Art. 36 s. (1) of the Fundamental Law.
181. Art. 37 s. (6) of the Fundamental Law; Act CXCIV of 2011.
182. Art. 17 s. (1) of the Fundamental Law.
183. Decision 121/2009. (XII. 17.) of the Constitutional Court.
184. Act LV of 1993.
185. Act CCII of 2011.
186. Act CCIII of 2011.
187. Act XXXVI of 2013.
188. Act CXII of 2011.
189. Act CCVI of 2011.
190. Act XXXIII of 1989.
191. Act CIV of 2010.
192. Act CLXXIX of 2011.

Assembly,[193] on the President of the Republic,[194] on the Constitutional Court,[195] on the organization and administration of courts[196] and the Public Prosecution Service,[197] on the legal status of judges[198] and the Prosecutor General and the prosecutors,[199] on local governments,[200] on the National Bank, on the State Audit Office,[201] on the Hungarian Defence Forces,[202] and on the Police[203] and the national security services.[204] Finally, as it was referred to above, the Fundamental Law requests cardinal acts in the field of public policy, namely, among others, on the protection of families,[205] on the preservation and management of national assets,[206] or on the pension system.[207]

362. Since the Fundamental Law specifies only subject matters, there are more cardinal acts than topics for which the qualified parliamentary majority is required. In addition, cardinal acts may be amended by ordinary acts of Parliament in special cases.[208] Apart from these cases, cardinal acts may not be invalidated or amended by a normal act of Parliament (to be adopted by a simple majority), and from a legislative point of view, according to the jurisprudence of the Constitutional Court, there is no difference between ordinary and cardinal acts.[209] This position has triggered criticism in academic literature, arguing that both the importance of the affected legislative matter and the more stringent procedural requirements impart a privileged position on cardinal acts compared to ordinary acts of Parliament.[210]

[2] The Limits of Legislative Power

[a] Substantial Limits

363. Due to the constitutional command of the hierarchy of legal sources, acts of Parliament, including both ordinary and cardinal acts, may not contravene the Fundamental Law. More generally, fundamental rights as entrenched in the Constitution delimit the scope of legislative power. It can also be noted that, following

193. Act XXXVI of 2012.
194. Act CX of 2011.
195. Act CLI of 2011.
196. Act CLXI of 2011.
197. Act CLXIII of 2011.
198. Act CLXII of 2011.
199. Act CLXIV of 2011.
200. Act CLXXXIX of 2011.
201. Act LXVI of 2011.
202. Act CXIII of 2011.
203. Act XXXIV of 1994.
204. Act CXXV of 1995.
205. Act CCXI of 2011.
206. Act CXCVI of 2011.
207. Act LXXXI of 1997.
208. Art. 17 s. (4) of the Fundamental Law allows that 'provisions of a cardinal act regarding the designation of Ministries, Ministers or organs of the public administration may be amended by an act'.
209. Decision 43/2012. (XII. 20.) of the Constitutional Court.
210. *See*, e.g., András Jakab and Péter Cserne, *A kétharmados törvények helye a magyar jogforrási hierarchiában*, 5 Fundamentum (2001) 40–49.

German constitutional theory, the jurisprudence of the Constitutional Court (backed up by some constitutional scholars[211]) claims that beyond the enumerated constitutional rights, the right to human dignity and self-determination also have a core area which is untouchable by the legislature – even without a more precise textual basis.[212]

364. Parliamentary lawmaking is restricted also by the competences of other public bodies; the legislative power cannot be unlimited within the scope of state activity either. It is obvious, for example, that Parliament cannot take over the role of the courts. In relation to this, since the Constitutional Court's rulings are binding on everyone, the legislator is bound also by the constitutional interpretation of the Court. Nevertheless, the separation of jurisdiction among the various public authorities is not always clear. For example, when Parliament ordered the courts through the controversial Nullity Act[213] to render specific judgments in the cases relating to the street riots of 2006, many thought that it interfered with the domain of the judicial power. However, in the concrete constitutional review procedure initiated by some judges, the Constitutional Court found the law constitutional.[214]

365. Moreover, the legislation of the European Union also limits the legislative power of the National Assembly since Hungary, as a member of the EU, has transferred some of its legislative power to the institutions of the European Union. However, Article E) section (3) circumscribes the scope of the waiving of legislative power, setting certain conditions for it. The Constitutional Court has also reserved its own power to review whether the delegation of powers does not violate Hungary's sovereignty or constitutional identity.[215] The National Assembly is indirectly involved also in the lawmaking procedures of EU institutions, and the government must cooperate with Parliament to develop Hungary's position in respect of draft EU legislation. According to the Act on the National Assembly, the legislature and the government have to cooperate with each other in matters relating to the EU.

366. In addition, *ius cogens* and the generally recognized rules of international law, as well as the international legal obligations of Hungary, also restrict the scope of legislative authority of Parliament.

367. According to the former practice of the Constitutional Court, the means of regulating something is unconstitutional in those cases where the legal rule does not have a normative (regulatory) character but contains an individual decision because it deprives the affected party of the right to a legal remedy.[216] The constitutional

---

211. Attila Tóth Gábor, *Az emberi méltósághoz való jog és az élethez való jog* in Emberi jogok (Gábor Halmai and Attila Tóth Gábor eds., Osiris Kiadó 2003) 268; Albert Takács & Ildikó Kmetty, *Az eutanáziához való jog: Indítvány az Alkotmánybírósághoz* 7 Fundamentum (2003) 128, 131; Sólyom, *supra* n. 27, 459.
212. Decision 64/1991. (XII. 17.) of the Constitutional Court.
213. Act XVI of 2011.
214. Decision 24/2013. (X. 4.) of the Constitutional Court.
215. Decisions 22/2016. (XII. 5.) and 32/2021. (XII. 20.) of the Constitutional Court.
216. Decision 45/1997. (IX. 19.) of the Constitutional Court.

guarantees of the protection of the property rights, for example, apply even if the property is expropriated by an act of Parliament.[217] In spite of these well-known concerns, however, since 2010, this legislative tool has become quite often, especially in the form of laws tailored to specific individuals to provide them with special exemptions and benefits. These laws often serve to remove legal obstacles to the appointment of government party trustees to public office, to extend their term of office, or to provide them with material benefits. In some cases, however, this method was also used against certain individuals (such as a 2011 law that allowed a former communist party leader to be prosecuted[218]).

[b] Procedural Limits

368. Besides the substantial requirements of parliamentary lawmaking, the legislature may only enact laws by observing the rules of legislative procedure. These rules are constitutional guarantees that ensure the legality and controllability of the decision-making procedure of the National Assembly and the legitimacy of the acts of Parliament. The most important formal requirements are laid down by the Constitution, while the detailed rules of procedure are set by Parliament itself, partly acting in its legislative capacity, and partly in the scope of its autonomy, namely Parliamentary Standing Orders.

369. The jurisprudence of the Constitutional Court refers to the requirement of compliance with the formal conditions for validity – or procedural constitutionality – of the laws. While in the early 1990s, the Court took a strict stance in this issue, insisting on full compliance with procedural rules in the course of lawmaking, its jurisprudence later became much more moderate, declaring that only a serious procedural defect could result in the unconstitutionality of a law. It means that not all procedural irregularities lead to 'public law invalidity', but only a violation of a procedural requirement which arises directly from the Constitution.[219] The indulgent practice of the Constitutional Court, which tolerates less serious procedural irregularities, has continued after the Fundamental Law of 2011 came into force.[220]

370. Although an invalidated act of Parliament should be regarded as not having been created at all, and it should therefore be annulled with retroactive effect to the date of its promulgation, the Constitutional Court Act allows the Court, accounting for the interests of legal certainty or the particular interests of the petitioner, to declare such a law null and void with *ex nunc* effect.

217. Decision 21/1990. (X. 4.) of the Constitutional Court.
218. *See supra* n. 129.
219. Decisions 29/1997. (IV. 29.), 52/1997. (X. 14.), 66/1997. (XII. 29.), 1/1999. (II. 24.), 39/1999. (XII. 21.) of the Constitutional Court.
220. *See* Decision II/258/2019. of the Constitutional Court.

[C] Budgetary Power

371. The National Assembly adopts the annual central budget and approves its implementation. In theory, this power provides a decisive influence for Parliament in public policy-making. Besides, this is also a constitutional guarantee ensuring that the national representative body determines how public money is spent and the authorizing of the executive power to collect public revenues and to dispense public expenditures (appropriation).[221] In this way, it is a primary parliamentary device to control the activity of the Executive Branch.

372. In a constitutional respect, the state budget is 'the annual plan of the State's financial management'[222] which is composed of the respective budgets of:

(a) the central government;
(b) social security;
(c) special budgetary funds, and
(d) the local government fund.

373. In the normal case, the annual budgetary plan relates to the public finance of the state budget for the following year. The implementation of the annual budget must also be approved by Parliament in a law on the appropriation account. Thus, the National Assembly has to adopt such a law always after the budgetary year.

374. While the adoption of the annual state budget was a full and exclusive power of Parliament after 1990, the Fundamental Law has severely restricted it in different ways. First, its Article N) declares the principle of balanced, transparent and sustainable budget management. The National Assembly (and the government) has a primary responsibility for complying with this principle (Article N) section (2)). Other limitations on the Parliament's budgetary power are set in the constitutional chapter on Public Finances, ordering that the National Assembly may not adopt the central budget as a result of which the state debt would exceed half of GDP. Furthermore, as long as that debt exceeds half of GDP, Parliament may only adopt a central budget which provides for debt reduction in proportion to the GDP. Apart from these debt-brake rules, the Constitution contains also a procedural restriction when it binds the validity of the state budget act to the approval of the Budget Council.

375. The Parliament's budgetary power is not only a right but also an obligation: if the National Assembly is unable to approve the annual budget in due time, it may have consequences for its entire mandate. If Parliament does not adopt the Budget Act for the year in question by 31 March, the President of the Republic may dissolve Parliament (Article 3 section (3) point b)).

---

221. Jakab and Szente, *supra* n. 16, 603.
222. Decision 4/2006. (II. 15.) of the Constitutional Court.

[D] Treaty Power

376. The Fundamental Law states that Parliament may authorize recognition of the binding force of an international treaty if its subject matter falls within the duties and competences of the National Assembly (Article 1 section (2) point d)). According to the relevant act of Parliament,[223] international treaties belong to the scope of responsibility of the National Assembly when they relate to matters subject to legislation as provided by the Fundamental Law, or to other issues within the competence of Parliament. Having regard to the fact that the Hungarian legal system is a dualist one as to the relationship between domestic and international law, such international treaties have to be promulgated by acts of Parliament. It means that an international obligation becomes part of the Hungarian legal system only through its transformation by way of a domestic legal source.

377. In order to ensure the compatibility between international treaties and obligations and the Fundamental Law, the Constitutional Court has the power of reviewing the conformity of an international treaty or its provisions with the Fundamental Law prior to its ratification. Such an *a priori* constitutional review may be initiated by the President of the Republic or the government and one-quarter of the Members of Parliament, depending on who is entitled to recognize the binding effect of the international treaty.

[E] Election of High Public Officials

378. The Fundamental Law confers jurisdiction on Parliament to elect some 'public law dignitaries' (*legfőbb közjogi méltóságok*). Article 1 section (2) point e) establishes the most important appointment powers of the National Assembly. According to this provision, Parliament elects the President of the Republic, the Prime Minister, the members and President of the Constitutional Court, the President of the *Kúria* (Supreme Court), the Prosecutor General, the Commissioner and Deputy Commissioners for Fundamental Rights, and the President of the State Audit Office. The Constitution does not include all appointment powers of Parliament since a statute may also delegate to Parliament the right to elect other high officials. Election by Parliament lends strong public and political legitimacy to these dignitaries. However, this method of creating the mandates of those various public law officials does not establish any subordinate relationship between Parliament and the relevant dignitaries. Parliament has a monopoly power to elect the public officials listed by the Fundamental Law, which means that their positions cannot be filled in any other way.

223. Act L of 2005.

[F] Declaration of War and Peace

379. Although the declaration of war and peace is a traditional power of Parliament, when Hungary declared war last time (on the side of Germany against the Soviet Union in 1941), it occurred on false legal grounds with the circumvention of Parliament (only with the subsequent approval of the National Assembly).

380. The Fundamental Law defines neither the form nor the procedure of such decisions.

[G] Declaration of Special Legal Orders

381. In theory, the National Assembly has a crucial role in declaring special legal orders. Because under such conditions, the government or provisional bodies have extraordinary powers, it is justified that the exercise of such a huge range of power should be subject to the approval of the body with the highest democratic legitimacy.

382. According to Article 49 of the Fundamental Law, Parliament has the power to declare a state of war in the event of the declaration of a state of war or the imminent danger of armed attack by a foreign power (danger of war) or in the case of external armed attack or its danger, or under the collective defence obligation arising from NATO membership. The state of emergency may be proclaimed also by the National Assembly in the event of armed actions aimed at overthrowing or subverting the constitutional order or at exclusively acquiring power, in the case of serious unlawful act of violence massively endangering life and property. The legislature may take these decisions only with the votes of two-thirds of MPs.

383. If the state of war or the state of emergency has been declared by the President of the Republic because the National Assembly was prevented from making such decisions, Parliament, as soon as it can act again, reviews at its first sitting whether the Head of State's act was justified, and decides on the legality of the measures adopted.

384. During a state of war or a state of emergency, the National Assembly may not dissolve itself and may not be dissolved since no general elections may be called or held in such period. If the mandate of the National Assembly expires in such a situation, the new Parliament must be elected within ninety days of the termination of the state of national crisis or state of emergency.

[H] General Amnesty

385. The general amnesty means a legal exemption from punishment for a crime which falls within a specified category of crimes or criminals. The National Assembly may grant general amnesty by law, usually extending it to minor crimes only.

386. Since the system change, Parliament has granted a general amnesty only once, when in 1991 it renounced criminal prosecutions for the less serious crimes committed during the 'taxi blockade'. This was a mass demonstration of taxi drivers that erupted as a protest movement against the rise of gasoline prices. The Act on the Exercise of General Amnesty[224] was adopted at the proposal of Árpád Göncz, the first President of the Republic after the collapse of the communist regime. Until now, in Hungary, since 1990, this has been the only bill submitted by the Head of State to Parliament.

[I] Other Powers and Duties

387. Beyond the most important tasks and powers entrenched in the Fundamental Law, the Hungarian National Assembly has a number of other responsibilities. While some of them are mentioned in the constitutional text, like the dissolution of local government representative bodies operating in contravention of the Fundamental Law or allowing the Hungarian Defence Forces to take part in military operations, many others are determined by statutes, such as the adoption of the annual reports of certain state bodies, or the election of leading government officials.

§1.04 Organizational Structure of National Assembly

[A] Plenum

388. In Hungary, the legislative power is exercised by the unicameral National Assembly. The main decision-making body of Parliament is its plenum, that is, the joint meeting of all elected Members of Parliament. Each deputy is entitled to participate in the parliamentary debates, and any of them may be excluded from plenary sittings only exceptionally and temporarily for disciplinary reasons.

[B] The Parliamentary Officers

389. The leading officials of the National Assembly are the President (Speaker) of the Parliament, the Deputy Speakers, the Principal of the National Assembly and the notaries of the Parliament.

390. The Speaker convokes the parliamentary sessions and sittings, except the inaugural meeting of the Parliament which is convened by the President of the Republic. He or she chairs the meetings and ensures compliance with the Standing Orders. The Speaker is responsible for upholding the dignity of the National Assembly. For this purpose, he or she exercises law enforcement and disciplinary powers to ensure the uninterrupted operation of Parliament. The President of the National

224. Act V of 1991.

Assembly represents the Parliament before other public bodies and in international relations. In the scope of his or her administrative tasks, the Speaker manages the Office of the National Assembly and the Parliamentary Guard and appoints their leaders.

391. Besides his or her parliamentary functions, the Speaker – subject to certain restrictions – exercises the powers of the President of the Republic if the Head of State is prevented from acting or if the term of office of the President is terminated for any reason, and until the new President of the Republic takes up his duties.

392. The main function of Deputy Speakers is to stand in for the Speaker, especially chairing the plenary sittings by rotation. The Principal of the National Assembly is appointed by the Speaker who determines his or her tasks.

393. The parliamentary notaries provide technical assistance to the Speaker and Deputy Speakers in presiding over floor debates, certifying parliamentary minutes, counting votes, and so on.

394. The National Assembly elects the Speaker, Deputy Speakers and notaries by simple majority with more than one-half of the MPs present. According to the custom established since 1990, the President of the National Assembly is always one of the members of the party constituting the largest parliamentary faction, while the Deputy Speakers and notaries are divided among the nominees of the government and opposition groups.

[C] Parliamentary Committees

395. Parliamentary committees are the advisory, consultative and controlling bodies of the National Assembly which, in the cases specified by law, exercise certain decision-making powers. The main task of the committees is to assist the main decision-making body of the Parliament, namely, the joint meeting of the deputies.

396. There are two types of committees in the Hungarian Parliament: standing and temporary committees. While the National Assembly is legally obliged to set up certain standing committees, it may also form temporary committees for specific purposes. The operation of the standing committees is linked to the mandate of the National Assembly: they operate continuously during the parliamentary term, but every new Parliament re-establishes its committee system. Conversely, temporary committees are set up by Parliament for a specific task, on an occasional basis, and their operation lasts until the task assigned to them is performed. However, the principle of discontinuity applies to both types of committees; that is, their mandate is limited to the term of office of the National Assembly that created them.

[1] Standing Committees

397. The standing committees play a pre-eminent role in both the legislative process and the parliamentary control of executive power. They conduct the second reading of all bills and prepare them for the final vote of the plenary meeting. Furthermore, they hear the Minister candidates and advise on their nomination.

398. The National Assembly forms the system of its standing committees at its constituent sitting and elects the presiding officers of the committees. With the exception of 2010, since 1990, the Parliament has always been able to establish its standing committees on the basis of compromise between the political parties represented in the National Assembly. The members and officers of the committees are elected by the National Assembly based on the nomination of the parliamentary factions. The parties are represented in the committees in proportion to their parliamentary seats, so membership of standing committees reflects the composition of the plenum of the Parliament. In this way, a majority of MPs representing the government parties is provided for in the standing committees too. The only exception is the Committee on Immunity, Incompatibility, Discipline and Mandate Control (whose composition is based on the principle of parity), and the Housing Committee into which each parliamentary faction sends one member. The Committee Representing the Nationalities is the only standing committee in which not only MPs but also non-MPs (the 'nationality advocates') may be members.

399. Although Parliament is basically free to decide how many and what committees it establishes, the Act on the National Assembly lays down the requirement to form standing committees on immunity, incompatibility, disciplinary cases and validation of mandates; constitutional affairs; the state budget; foreign affairs; defence; European Union affairs; national security, and, more recently, Hungarian communities abroad. Furthermore, according to a previous decision of the Constitutional Court, in the course of the establishment of parliamentary committees, it must be ensured that all members have at least one committee membership.[225] However, this constitutional requirement has never been fully respected, and its validity has been doubtful since all rulings of the Constitutional Court were repealed by the Fourth Amendment of the Fundamental Law (even if it would have been easier to meet this requirement since the number of MPs was reduced to 199).

400. Before 2010, the scope and responsibility of standing committees roughly followed the government structure, but since 2010, when some big, 'peak ministries' were established, this tradition was broken (*see* Table 1).

Table 1 The Number of Standing Committees by Election Cycles

1990–1994	1994–1998	1998–2002	2002–2006	2006–2010	2010–2014	2014–2018	2018–2022	2022–
14–18	17–19	22	25	18	20	14	17	17

225. Decision 27/1998. (VI. 16.) of the Constitutional Court.

401. In addition, some committees deal with Parliament's internal affairs, like the Immunity Committee (being responsible for immunity, incompatibility, disciplinary and mandate control cases) or the House Committee. Now (in the parliamentary cycle of 2022–2026), the following parliamentary standing committees are at work:

- House Committee;
- Legislative Committee;
- European Affairs Committee;
- Sustainable Development Committee;
- Economic Committee;
- Defence and Law Enforcement Committee;
- Justice Committee;
- Budget Committee;
- Culture Committee;
- Foreign Affairs Committee;
- Immunity Committee;
- Agriculture Committee;
- National Security Committee;
- National Cohesion Committee;
- Social Welfare Committee;
- Business Development Committee;
- Committee Representing Nationalities.

402. The committee responsible for the nomination of the members of the Constitutional Court is in a special situation because, while its term of office extends over the whole parliamentary cycle, it does not work continuously but only holds meetings if a new constitutional judge must be nominated.

403. Some committees have real decision-making competences. The Standing Orders grant such authority to the European Affairs Committee in matters relating to the European Union inasmuch as this Committee takes a stand on the government's position in EU affairs. In some cases, Parliament delegates specific decision-making power beyond traditional parliamentary functions to parliamentary committees as well, even though the parliamentary machinery is often not transparent or even scandal-ridden in such cases. Thus, the Economic Committee was empowered between 2013 and 2017 by law to license private corporations to market government bonds for settlement rights in Hungary.

404. The House Committee has a leading role in designing the continuous flow of parliamentary work. This Committee has been operating since 1990. It is chaired by the President of the Parliament (Speaker), while its membership consists of the Deputy Speakers, and the leaders of the parliamentary factions. Yet only the faction leaders have the right to vote in this Committee. The representative of the government may participate with consultative rights in its meetings.

405. The House Committee is the scene of the cooperation between the parliamentary factions in order to ensure the smooth operation of Parliament, especially by settling disputes arising from day-by-day operations, and determining the work schedule of the plenary meetings. One of the major tasks of the House Committee is to propose the agenda for the National Assembly which includes the subjects for consideration and the manner in which submissions are discussed. The Committee may take decisions only unanimously: if the parliamentary factions fail to reach a compromise on matters under discussion, the Speaker tables a proposal on the agenda for the plenary session and the continuation of parliamentary debate.

406. The Legislative Committee has been in a dominant position in the parliamentary lawmaking process, especially since second reading (the detailed parliamentary debate) of the bills has taken place in the committees rather than in the plenary meetings. This Committee, through deciding on proposed amendments submitted by other committees and compiling the amendments consented to into a summary version, finalizes the legislative texts and submits them for final vote in the National Assembly.

407. The Budget Committee plays a crucial role in the legislative process of the annual state budget, for it coordinates with all other committees discussing their relevant parts of the budget proposal, and submits the final version of this bill to the plenary meeting.

[2] Temporary Committees

408. In principle, Parliament may set up a temporary or ad hoc committee to investigate any issue. The right of enquiry is an authority of Parliament as a legislative body for the purpose of obtaining appropriate information on specific issues related to the operation of executive power or any other public affair, and, in this way, it is a device for controlling the government and raising questions of political responsibility.

409. The parliamentary groups for the governing and opposition parties can delegate an equal number of members to committees of enquiry.

Table 2 The Number of Enquiry Committees by Election Cycles

1990–1994	1994–1998	1998–2002	2002–2006	2006–2010	2010–2014	2014–2018	2018–2022	2022–
1	7	6	15	8	7	0	0	0

410. The functioning of enquiry (or investigative) committees has not been a success story so far. Since 2010, for instance, no enquiry committee has been set up at the initiation of the opposition parties, although in theory the operation of these committees is an important instrument of the parliamentary opposition to control executive power (*see* Table 2). In the short history of investigative committees since the regime change, such committees have usually been set up by government parties to investigate the controversial activities of previous governments and, due to the composition of parity of these committees, the enquiry committees were able only rarely to complete their work successfully.

[D] Party Factions

411. The Fundamental Law provides that Members of Parliament may establish parliamentary factions (groups) for coordinating their activities in accordance with the Standing Orders (Article 5 section (4)). The parliamentary rules of procedure explicitly prefer the creation and functioning of party groups in the legislature since they provide effective frameworks for the individual MPs to cooperate with each other and to express their views collectively, thereby enhancing the effectiveness of parliamentary debates. Thus, parliamentary groups may appoint a principal speaker for each item on the agenda; they are entitled to a time allotment in legislative debates; they may nominate committee members and propose items for the parliamentary agenda; their leaders have the right to take the floor before the agenda, and such like. Besides that, all factions are entitled to receive monthly financial support in proportion to their size to cover their operating costs, as well as staff employed by the Office of the National Assembly. The parliamentary groups can, free of charge, use offices and basic supplies provided by the Office of the Parliament. It is worth noting that parliamentary group leaders also have certain constitutional functions specified by the Fundamental Law. They may express their opinion to the President of the Republic prior to the dissolution of the National Assembly (Article 3 section (4)).

412. Parliamentary factions may be formed by the MPs belonging to the same party. At least three deputies may form a group if they all were elected from the same national party list during the last general elections; otherwise, at least five MPs are required to establish a faction. No Member of Parliament may join more than one parliamentary faction. If an MP loses his or her membership in a parliamentary faction, he/she will become an independent deputy and be excluded from joining any other group for a period of six months.

§1.05 The Operation of Parliament

[A] The Rules of Parliamentary Procedures

413. The legal framework for legislative activity is provided for by the Act on the National Assembly[226] and a parliamentary resolution on the rules of procedure[227] of the Parliament. It means that the standing orders of Parliament are divided into an Act and a normative resolution of the legislature adopted within the scope of its autonomy. Although parliamentary procedural rules had been adopted

226. Act XXXVI of 2012.
227. Resolution of the National Assembly 10/2014 (II. 24.).

traditionally under the rubric of the self-government of Parliament from the revolution and independence fight of 1848, this tradition was interrupted in 2012. The reason for the new, divided regulation was that the standing orders contain rules prescribing obligations for non-parliamentarians (like visitors or participants without a parliamentary mandate in meetings), and that requires statutory regulation.

[B] The Constituent Sitting of the National Assembly

414. According to the Fundamental Law, '[t]he general elections of the Members of the National Assembly shall be held in the month of April or May of the fourth year following the election of the previous National Assembly, except for elections held due to the National Assembly dissolving itself or to it being dissolved' (Article 2 section (3)). In the latter cases, a new Parliament must be elected within three months of the dissolution.

415. The operation of the newly elected Parliament begins with its constituent sitting, which is convened by the President of the Republic within a month following the general elections. This sitting has multiple functions, from the verification of the members' mandates to the election of the officers of the National Assembly. Parliament usually already sets up its standing committees at its inaugural meeting (but in 1998 and 2006 it did so only at its subsequent sitting). It is a constitutional practice that the parliamentary parties prior to this meeting agree on the distribution of leading positions in the chamber, and the list and composition of the standing committees. This is the occasion also when the President of the Republic proposes to Parliament a new Prime Minister (as the mandate of the government automatically terminates at the constituent sitting of the new Parliament).

[C] Sessions and Sittings

416. The National Assembly holds two ordinary sessions each year. The 'spring session' lasts from 1 February to 15 June, while the 'autumn session' begins on 1 September and ends on 15 December. During these legislative sessions, Parliament holds sittings. Each sitting – except the inaugural meeting – is convened by the President of the National Assembly. During sessions, Parliament holds sittings every week. This practice meets the constitutional requirement for the continuous operation of the National Assembly.[228]

417. During the legislative break, an extraordinary session or sitting may only be convened upon the motion of the President of the Republic, the government or one-fifth of MPs. All such initiatives must specify the subject matter of the proposed session or meeting.

228. Decision 4/1999. (III. 31.) of the Constitutional Court.

418. The orders of the day, together with the special debate rules to be applied, are adopted by Parliament at the recommendation of the House Committee. If the parliamentary groups fail to reach an agreement in this committee, the Speaker will propose the orders of the day for a sitting.

[D] Quorum and Majority Requirements

419. The National Assembly is able to take decisions only if more than half of the deputies are present (parliamentary quorum). A quorum is a necessary, but not sufficient, condition to pass a valid parliamentary decision; it may in fact require a special majority. In general, Parliament adopts its decisions by a majority vote of those present at the sitting. However, the legislature may only pass cardinal acts with a two-thirds majority of the votes of the deputies in attendance, while constitutional amendments or the election of a number of public officials need an even greater majority: a two-thirds majority of all MPs elected. In addition, the Parliament Act and the Standing Orders of Parliamentary Resolution also require a special majority for a number of procedural decisions.

[E] Debate Rules

420. The plenary debates are prepared by the House Committee which may propose the agenda of the sittings and the method of debate to Parliament. Nevertheless, if no consensus has evolved, the Speaker makes these proposals. In practice, the government has the greatest, albeit informal, agenda-setting power through the President of the National Assembly.

421. Although the official language of parliamentary debates is Hungarian, those MPs who acquired their mandates from a nationality list and the nationality advocates may all use their mother tongue when taking the floor, provided that they indicate this intention beforehand.

422. The procedural rules set speaking times given to the parliamentary factions and the individual MPs, as well as the legal entitlement for taking the floor. During debate, the Speaker gives the floor, and he or she ensures an orderly parliamentary debate. Parliament frequently discusses the agenda items in a predefined time frame.

423. The National Assembly may decide to hold a sitting *in camera* at the request of any MP supported by a two-thirds majority vote of MPs.

424. Under certain conditions, at the initiative of at least five MPs, Parliament may close the debate (*cloture*). The President of the Republic may adjourn a sitting of Parliament for a maximum of thirty days but only once per parliamentary session (prorogation).

425. As to the legal forms of parliamentary decisions, the National Assembly may adopt amendments to the Fundamental Law, cardinal and ordinary acts, resolutions (mainly on individual matters) and political manifestos (in general, on political or policy issues).

426. During plenary sittings, in determined periods, MPs may submit interpellations or questions to the government or any of its members on any matter within their competence. Deputies may put questions to the Commissioner for Fundamental Rights, the President of the State Audit Office, the Prosecutor General and the President of the National Bank on any matter within their respective competences (Article 7 section (1) of the Fundamental Law).

427. Members of Parliament have a disciplinary responsibility for preserving the dignity of the National Assembly and for complying with parliamentary procedural rules. Basically, it is the Speaker's duty to uphold the order of parliamentary sittings and to preserve the dignity of Parliament. However, Parliament as a whole may decide on the imposition of the most severe disciplinary sanctions. After the ECtHR objected to parliamentary disciplinary rules for lack of legal remedy,[229] Parliament ensured that MPs submit an objection to the Immunity Committee (now Committee on Immunity, Conflict of Interest, Discipline and Mandate Control) if the Speaker (or his/her deputy when presiding) has imposed a disciplinary sanction against them.

428. It is to be noted that in 2012, the Parliament Act introduced parliamentary disciplinary rules that are stricter than before. While the new disciplinary order retained certain penalties, it introduced new sanctions, such as fines or, for the most serious parliamentary offences, the provisional expulsion of the offending MP or suspension of the member's rights.

[F] Special Parliamentary Procedures

[1] Legislative Process

429. Legislative process is the most typical decision-making procedure of the Parliament. The Fundamental Law and the Act on Lawmaking[230] include the basic rules of the parliamentary process of lawmaking, but the detailed provisions are enshrined in the Parliamentary Resolution on Standing Orders. The Constitution reserves the right to propose legislation for the President of the Republic, the government, parliamentary committees and any Member of Parliament. The legislative proposal must contain the title, the draft text and a reasoning of the bill. The right to submit draft legislation does not guarantee that the bill will actually be debated; it depends on political support for the proposal. Once the proposal has been

229. ECHR Case of *Karácsony and Others v. Hungary*, Applications Nos 42461/13 (2014) and 44357/13 (2016).
230. Act CXXX of 2010.

accepted by Parliament for negotiation, the bill is subject to a general debate on the necessity and regulatory principles of the proposal in plenary sitting at least five days after its submission. It is a legal requirement to publish such legislative initiatives on the website of the National Assembly. After the general debate on the bill in plenary meeting, Parliament designates the standing committee which will proceed with detailed debates beginning in the week following. It is a real speciality of the legislative process in Hungary that the plenary sitting does not have the power to discuss bills in detail (i.e., paragraph by paragraph). After the committee stage, the draft law is processed by the Legislative Committee, which draws up a single package of all preferred amending motions as well as the consolidated text of the bill (combined with the supported modifications) and submits them to the plenary session of Parliament. The plenum may vote on this proposal only as a whole (block vote), so Parliament does not have any opportunity to select among the various amending proposals.

430. While the ordinary laws need a simple majority vote, cardinal acts may be adopted only by a two-thirds majority vote of the MPs present. It is to be noted that, after a final vote, Parliament, at the proposal of the initiator of the act, the Speaker, or the government may initiate *ex ante* constitutional review of the act prior to submitting it to the Head of State to be signed and promulgated.

431. Once the National Assembly has adopted the law, the Speaker must sign it within five days and send it to the President of the Republic for signature and promulgation. The Head of State has also a five-day-period to sign and promulgate it. Otherwise, he or she may send the adopted law to the Constitutional Court for an *ex ante* review, or, if he/she has political objections, the Head of State may send it back to Parliament for reconsideration. In fact, both possible ways provide a suspensive veto power for the President: in both cases, when the Constitutional Court finds the law constitutional or the Parliament readopts the law, he or she must sign and promulgate it without delay.

[2] Budgetary Process

432. Although the annual budget must be adopted by law, special rules are applied to the budgetary process. One of the most important differences is that the budget bill is discussed by all standing committees. Then, this bill is debated in two rounds which have different functions. In the first in-depth debate, Parliament discusses amendments that propose transfers between different budget chapters. The National Assembly then votes on the amending proposals (until 30 November in each year), deciding on the main amounts for each chapter and the whole budget, including the total amount of revenues and expenditures. In the subsequent debate, only amendments proposing transfers within each budget chapter may be tabled and may therefore no longer affect the general amounts adopted. In the process of drafting the budget law, the Budget Council received important powers of scrutiny (in some cases, veto power) (*see* details *infra* in Part II, Chapter 10, §10.03).

433. According to the Fundamental Law, the President of the Republic may dissolve the Parliament if it is not able to approve the annual budget by 31 March.

[3] Other Special Procedures

434. Besides general proceedings, certain parliamentary proceedings may demand special debate rules. There is a very wide range of such procedures, from special legislative processes (like debating an appropriation bill) to a no-confidence vote. In most cases, these regulations contain a special set of rules or a combination of otherwise normal rules. The relevant procedural provisions are tailored to the specialities of the particular proceedings, and intend to be exceptions to general working methods.

435. These procedures may be special because of their content or procedural aspects. As to the former, the importance of the parliamentary decision justifies the application of rules that are different from the general provisions of the standing orders. The constitution-making process, the adoption of an annual budget, or the vote of no-confidence are such procedures. Other special procedures aim at speeding up the legislative process, like the urgent and extraordinary procedures.

[G] The Termination of the Parliament's Mandate

436. The mandate of Parliament terminates when its four-year period expires. In the legal sense, the parliamentary cycles of consecutive legislatures adjoin with each other, as the parliamentary term ends with the founding sitting of the new Parliament. Parliament may also be dissolved prematurely, with the President of the Republic setting the date for new general elections, if the National Assembly, when the mandate of the government terminates, fails to elect the person proposed by the President for Prime Minister within forty days of presentation of the first proposal, or if the legislature fails to adopt the central budget for the year in question by 31 March. Before doing so, the Head of State has to seek the opinion of the Prime Minister, the Speaker of the Parliament, and the leaders of the parliamentary factions (Article 3 section (3) points a)–b)). In addition, Parliament may dissolve itself at any time during its term of mandate by a simple majority vote.

§1.06 The Legal Status of Members of the National Assembly

[A] The Basic Principles of the Mandate of MPs

437. The legal status of Members of Parliament is based on two principles. The principle of free mandate means that each MP represents the whole people.[231] In

231. It is to be noted that before the system change, until 1990, the MPs had imperative mandates and they could be recalled by the voters of their constituency.

legal terms, once elected, MPs are independent of their electors. They are subject only to laws, so they may be instructed neither by their voters nor their parties or any other organizations. They are free to shape their views and to decide how they exercise their rights as Members of Parliament. This freedom is guaranteed by law in that they are elected for a fixed term of four years, and they cannot be held politically accountable during this term of office, nor can they be recalled from office because of their actions or the way they vote. The relationship between MPs and their votes is political by nature. The deputies are politically accountable to their electors only in the sense that the voters may assess their MPs' performance in that they have the opportunity to renew the composition of Parliament at subsequent parliamentary elections.

438. The greatest challenge to the principle of the free mandate is traditionally the relationship of MPs to their parties, as the vast majority of deputies obtain their mandate with the support of a political party, and they exercise their rights as members of a party's parliamentary faction. The parties always try to bind their elected representatives themselves by different means. For example, there have been several occasions in the past where the parties signed a contract with their candidates obliging them to pay a large amount of compensation if they subsequently left the party or, in other cases, the parties requested a blank resignation form of their candidates for the case where the latter would leave their factions. Political practice shows that most MPs are usually disciplined in representing the policies of their parties, who sometimes instruct their members how to vote or impose fines on them for not following the party's directive. However, the bond that connects parties with their parliamentarians is not a legal one but political in nature. The contractual obligations infringing the principle of free mandate are legally invalid and cannot be enforced before a court. The MPs follow the political direction of their parties only for political reasons. If an MP does not follow the party whip in his or her parliamentary work, his or her party only has political tools to sanction this behaviour, such as expelling him/her from the faction or not supporting him or her in the next general elections.

439. The other basic principle of the legal status of MPs is the equality of their mandates. It means that all MPs' rights and obligations are identical regardless of how their mandate was created, whether in an individual constituency or as candidates on a list nominated by a party or a nationality. This principle is a consequence not only of the equal right to hold public office but also of the free mandate, for all MPs represent the abstract will of the whole people. Nevertheless, the equal rights of MPs should be interpreted as an equal opportunity for the deputies to be part of the majority: the standing orders differentiate between MPs in a number of ways, depending on their party affiliation or whether they belong to the majority or to the minority (e.g., in respect of the speaking time, or the right to table a motion).

[B] The Creation and Termination of Parliamentary Mandate

440. The mandate of the Members of Parliament originates from elections since they are elected by direct and secret ballot by citizens eligible to vote, based on universal and equal suffrage in elections which guarantee the free expression of the voters' will. Although the mandate of an MP begins when he or she is elected, his or her legal status becomes complete only when this fact is certified by Parliament, and the oath is taken on the floor, whereupon the MP may exercise all his or her rights and privileges as a Member of Parliament.[232]

441. The mandate of the members of the National Assembly may cease, on the one hand, for subjective as well as objective reasons, and, on the other hand, for normal or extraordinary reasons. For objective reasons, the mandates of the representatives are automatically terminated if the term of office of the whole Parliament is terminated, regardless of its reason. It is the case if the term of office of the legislature expires, where the Parliament is dissolved by the Head of State or the National Assembly dissolves itself. Subjective reasons are linked to the person of the MP. Thus, the parliamentary mandate terminates in the event of his or her death, resignation, loss of the right to vote or because of a conflict of interest.

442. The legally recognized thirteen nationalities may get a preferential parliamentary mandate (max. one mandate for each nationality) or, if they fail to win such a mandate, they are represented in the National Assembly by a nationality advocate. For the first time, the German nationality was able to get a nationality mandate in the general elections of 2018. The nationality advocates may take the floor at sittings of the National Assembly if, according to the House Committee, the item on the agenda affects the interests and rights of nationalities. They have no right to vote in Parliament.

[C] The Rights and Obligations of MPs

443. The rights of the Members of Parliament can be classified in different ways. They may exercise their rights personally or (exceptionally) by proxy, individually or collectively, and they enjoy participatory and so-called status rights.

[1] The Way of Exercising MPs' Rights and Individual Versus Collective Rights

444. The Members of Parliament exercise their rights personally, except that committee members may participate in committee meetings personally or by proxy. They exercise their rights usually individually (like the right to propose legislation, the right to speak in debates or the right to interpellation), but there are certain rights that deputies may only exercise collectively (e.g., to form or join a parliamentary

232. Zoltán Szente, *Az Országgyűlés tagjainak jogállása*, in *Az Alkotmány kommentárja: I. kötet* (András Jakab ed., Századvég 2009) 680–681.

faction or to propose closure). In Hungarian parliamentary law, with some exceptions, a standard threshold for collective rights is one-fifth of the elected MPs, like in the case of a motion of no-confidence, to initiate a committee of enquiry or to propose the convening of an extraordinary session. In certain cases, the law specifies how many MPs are needed to exercise special rights. Thus, a minimum of five (in exceptional cases, three) deputies may form a parliamentary faction. Besides these, because Parliament is a collegiate body, MPs do not exercise individual public authority, but only joint, in a duly convened plenary sitting.

[2] Participatory Rights

445. Participatory rights include the rights to:

- attend and participate in parliamentary sittings;
- speak at the plenary sittings and committee meetings and the freedom of parliamentary speech;
- information necessary for their representative functions (with the obligation of public institutions to support MPs in performing their duties and to supply them with the information they require);
- make proposals (including the right to submit legislative bills);
- raise interpellations and questions;
- be elected as a parliamentary officer;
- participate in forming a parliamentary faction and in its operation; and
- vote in parliamentary voting.

446. All these rights may be legitimately restricted in cases laid down in the Parliament Act or in the Standing Orders of Parliamentary Resolution. Thus, for example, the right of MPs to participate in plenary sittings may be temporarily suspended by a disciplinary sanction; the right to speak is limited by the procedural rules for a number of reasons; the right to submit legislative proposal means only to set the parliamentary process in motion, but it does not guarantee the parliamentary debate of the private member's bills, and so on.

[3] Status Rights

447. A special set of MPs' rights relate to their legal status in order to protect the integrity of Parliament or to enable the members of the National Assembly to perform their duties effectively.

[a] Parliamentary Immunity

448. The function of parliamentary immunity is to protect the autonomy and independence of Parliament through the protection of integrity of its members because the decisions of the legislative powers can be considered legitimate only if they have been taken as a result of a free decision-making process. For this purpose, parliamentary immunity guarantees the personal freedom of MPs by protecting them from unauthorized interference and harassment. In other words, it provides protection for the deputies against unjustified official persecution or other harassing procedures of public authorities.

449. Parliamentary immunity has two forms. The non-accountability (or immunity, in narrow sense) grants impunity to MPs insofar as they cannot be held legally liable for their speeches given or votes cast in plenary or committee sittings. Freedom of speech and vote are warranted by the prohibition of any punitive procedure against MPs for their views expressed in function of their mandate while they are members of the National Assembly. This protection is absolute in the sense that the protected activities as such are not criminal offences, and, moreover, that protection extends beyond the term of the MP's mandate. In other words, they can never be held criminally or otherwise liable for what they said or how they voted in Parliament. This immunity privilege of MPs for their spoken words and votes cast does not cover certain sorts of speech determined by law. Thus the incitement to violence against a religious, ethnic, national, or similar community, offences against national symbols, of public denial of National Socialist (Nazi) and Communist crimes, and the abuse of confidential data do not fall within the scope of this kind of protection.

450. It is to be noted that the Constitutional Court has always acknowledged the freedom of speech of Members of Parliament as a special form of the fundamental right of expression, even though the MPs' freedom of speech has been continuously recognized by constitutional text as an immunity.[233] The Court has never clarified why it classified this right as a fundamental human right rather than as a parliamentary privilege, which originates in a special status and only applies to parliamentarians.[234]

451. The other type of parliamentary immunity is the inviolability of the person. It means that Members of Parliament cannot be detained unless caught in the act of committing a crime; no criminal and no infraction[235] proceedings may be brought against them, and finally, their personal freedom cannot be restrained by measures of force under the Act on Criminal Proceeding without the prior approval of the National Assembly. All these procedures and actions against an MP need a prior suspension of immunity in the particular case(s).

452. Members of Parliament may not waive their right to immunity unless subject to proceedings for a minor offence. This also shows that the institution of immunity protects the autonomy of the whole legislature. At the request of the Prosecutor

233. Decision 34/2004. (IX. 28.) of the Constitutional Court.
234. Later, however, this domestic interpretative practice was confirmed by the ECtHR. *See* ECHR Case of *Szél and Others v. Hungary*, Application No. 44357/13 (2014); ECHR Case of *Karácsony and Others v. Hungary*, Applications Nos 42461/13 (2014) and 44357/13 (2016).
235. The acts falling within this category are sometimes called 'minor', 'bagatelle' or 'administrative' crimes to which a specific Code and procedures apply.

General, or (in judicial process) the court, Parliament may, after an investigation and at the proposal of the Immunity Committee, suspend the immunity of an MP, provided that a two-thirds majority of MPs present vote in favour.

[b] Conflict of Interest Rules

453. The mandate of a Member of Parliament is incompatible with any other office or post in state or local government, except for those specified by law. This kind of public law incompatibility follows from the principle of separation of powers. Nevertheless, membership in the government itself is not incompatible with a parliamentary mandate, which is justified by the parliamentary form of government of Hungary. The only restriction imposed on those MPs who are elected or appointed as Prime Minister or other members of the government is that they may not be elected an officer of the National Assembly or a member of a parliamentary committee.

454. Concerning economic or financial conflicts of interest, a Member of Parliament may not be, among other things, a sole or majority owner or a senior officer or senior executive in a financial institution operating in the financial sector, or a member or shareholder with an ownership interest in any business organization not classified as a 'transparent organization' by act of Parliament. Besides, there are some restrictions on the MPs even after the expiry of their mandates, inasmuch as they may not conclude an agreement to acquire a stake in a business organization controlled directly or indirectly by the Hungarian or a foreign state or a local government.

455. An MP may not be employed in another paid job, nor accept remuneration under a contract of employment other than as a researcher, teacher, artist, proofreader or editor or for activities subject to intellectual property rights.

456. The termination of an MP's mandate due to a conflict of interest may be declared by a two-thirds majority of the Members of Parliament present.

457. It is not only an ethical expectation but also a legal principle that Members of Parliament may not use their privileges and rights for their own personal gains. Thus, an MP may not refer to his or her capacity as Member of Parliament in professional or business affairs since he or she may not obtain unauthorized access to information with reference to his/her parliamentary mandate. Moreover, MPs may not accept gifts or other free benefits tied to their mandates that have a value higher than the member's current monthly remuneration.

458. The transparency of Parliament's work is served by the rules which require Members of Parliament to file a declaration on their property and income for each year and then a final declaration within thirty days after the expiry of their mandates. In addition, deputies must keep a record of gifts and free benefits valued at above one-twelfth of the stipend paid to an MP. It is to be noted, however, that while the failure of an MP to end a conflict of interest may lead to the termination of his or her mandate, an omission to comply with the obligation to make statements on their property, income and gifts does not carry any legal sanction.

[c] Financial Independence of Members of Parliament

459. The financial independence of Members of Parliament is ensured by law regulating their remuneration and other benefits. The monthly stipend payable to an MP is determined by law, and extra allowance is to be paid for committee membership, housing benefit, and fuel cards for transport. The Office of the National Assembly must provide each member with a properly equipped office (in or outside Budapest).

[4] The Obligations of Members of the National Assembly

460. While the Fundamental Law and the Act on the National Assembly provide wide-ranging rights and privileges for Members of Parliament, only a few – and abstract – obligations are imposed on them by law or standing orders. The Act requires MPs to play an active role in the work of the Parliament and to promote its operation. They are expected to attend parliamentary sittings and meetings of the committee of which they are a member. Members of Parliament must be present when Parliament votes. If MPs do not attend at least one-third of the votes, their remuneration may be reduced in proportion to their absence. Deputies must, of course, comply with standing orders and the debate rules of Parliament, subject otherwise to disciplinary sanction.

461. Members of Parliament are expected, in general terms, to keep regular contact with their voters in order to know their opinions. But this applies in practice only to MPs elected in individual constituencies; otherwise, failure to do so will not result in any sanction.

§1.07 CONSTITUTIONAL PRACTICE

462. The functioning of the Hungarian Parliament is characterized by stability. Since 1990, all legislatures have completed their four-year cycles (*see* Table 3).

Table 3 Parliamentary Cycles since the System Change

1	1990–1994
2	1994–1998
3	1998–2002
4	2002–2006
5	2006–2010

6	2010–2014
7	2014–2018
8	2018–2022
9	2022–

463. Parliament has functioned as a kind of 'law factory' since the regime change. Legislative activity was an inevitable consequence of the democratic transition in the 1990s. As the whole process took place in an evolutionary (and not revolutionary) way, the legal system of the former dictatorship had consequently to be fundamentally changed. The reason for similarly active parliamentary lawmaking in the 2010s was, on the one hand, the need for a new transition – towards authoritarianism this time – in the political and legal system, and, on the other hand, the need for frequent corrections to rapid legislation. In recent years, Parliament has adopted much more than 100 laws every year (except the election year 2022): 223 in 2012; 252 in 2013; 113 in 2014, 230 in 2015; 190 in 2016; 208 in 2017; 139 in 2018; 128 in 2019; 129 in 2020; 151 in 2021; 81 in 2022; and 121 in 2023.

464. At first glance, both the structure and political character of the Hungarian National Assembly are very typical compared to other European legislatures: its major functions are lawmaking and control of executive power. It is a multiparty Parliament where intense debates take place, and the opposition MPs can freely criticize the government.

465. However, the practice and performance of this legislature are significantly different from other national parliaments in Europe. The institutional changes introduced by the new Fundamental Law may have only moderately adjusted the look of the National Assembly since the only new institution that has been established is the Budget Council, 'an organ supporting Parliament's legislative activities and examining feasibility of the State Budget'. But this is not a purely advisory body. Its prior consent is required for the adoption of the state budget by Parliament. If the Council does not approve the annual budget by 31 March of the year running, the President of the Republic may dissolve Parliament. Although the Council may refuse to give its consent only in specified cases (e.g., if the budget bill would allow state debt to exceed half of GDP), its decision may not be reviewed or annulled, so it has a real veto right – which is an exceptional restriction on Parliament's budgetary power. This absolute veto power of a non-elected body over the budgetary power of the popular representation is unprecedented in constitutional democracies.

466. Despite moderate institutional changes, massive parliamentary reforms have been achieved since 2010.[236] The purpose of these reforms was to facilitate

236. For a detailed description of the pre-2010 period of parliamentary law, *see* Zoltán Szente, *Verfassung und Verfassungsmäßigkeit im ungarischen Parlamentsrecht* 50 Jahrbuch für Ostrecht (2009) 95; and Dezső et al., *supra* n. 1, 118–124.

the transformation of the government's intentions into law. To this end, the legislative process has been extremely accelerated and simplified. For example, it was possible to get a new law through Parliament in two days. This 'extraordinary urgent procedure', introduced in 2011, allowed the enactment of a new law the day following its introduction in Parliament. Likewise, any bill could be amended fundamentally right up to the final vote; that is, after closure of the plenary debate. Although these parliamentary contrivances were abolished in 2014, some new procedures were established in their place, such as dispensing with the second reading of bills (holding it in the designated standing committee), depriving thus Parliament of the opportunity to debate the details of the legislative proposals. Another significant measure was the introduction of the 'block vote' in 2014. This means that Parliament may not vote on the amendment proposals, or choose among them, but is obliged to vote *en bloc* on the whole summary, and then the last version of every bill prepared by the Committee on Legislation. As a consequence, Parliament may not choose among the various amendment proposals for the bills and thereby, as a body, is unable to realize on its own preferences.

467. There have been many other significant changes in parliamentary lawmaking practice in recent years as well. For example, there has been an increase in the number of legislative bills submitted by individual government party MPs, even though prepared by the central government, in order to avoid the otherwise compulsory coordination process. Legislation directed uniquely at particular individuals has also become a practice, although this has raised some constitutional concerns. These personalized statutes often provide privileges, exemptions or special entitlements for certain persons (usually politicians), creating loopholes in and exceptions to the general rules. Offering special advantages, relief or rewards for selected people on a political basis, these acts offend the normative character of law. This legislative device has been used when the desired goal cannot be reached in the normal way (e.g., by an individual administrative act) but only by the intervention of Parliament. 'Omnibus legislation' (enacting 'salad laws') has also become a frequently used technique of lawmaking. Here, a statute will cover a number of diverse and unrelated legal provisions, often amending many other laws. Frequently, these laws are large-size legal packages combining highly different subjects, which make the whole legislative process opaque and difficult.

468. As a result of these recent developments, the role of Parliament has been dramatically reduced since 2010.[237] Parliament does not have autonomous policy-making capacity, and there is a strong degree of political discipline within the parliamentary factions of the centralized government parties. In addition, opposition rights have been significantly weakened under the Fidesz–KDNP government. Parliamentary politics has traditionally been determined by the hostile relationship between the government parties and the opposition parties and the lack of cooperation between them in Hungary.

---

237. Zoltán Szente, *The Twilight of Parliament – Parliamentary Law and Practice in Hungary in Populist Times*, 1 International Journal of Parliamentary Studies (2021).

469. Since 2010, the frequent two-thirds parliamentary majority of the government has led to significant restrictions on opposition rights. Parliamentary disciplinary sanctions are usually only applied to opposition MPs in the current Hungarian Parliament. In particular, the imposition of fines occurs frequently against opposition MPs, punishing their political demonstrations on the chamber floor. The curtailment of MPs' rights was most spectacular in an event in December 2018, when some opposition MPs were removed by force from the building of the public television broadcaster by security guards, even though MPs have the right to enter or stay in any public institution. However, in spite of a clear violation of MPs' rights, the Prosecution Service did not initiate criminal proceedings against the security guard members, but rather against the opposition MPs who were involved in the incident, invoking their violent action. Following the indoor and outdoor political actions of some opposition MPs in December 2019, Parliament significantly restricted the rights of members of the National Assembly and tightened parliamentary disciplinary rules. While previously MPs could freely enter any public institution in the exercise of their functions, the new regulation now allows them to request information only after prior consultation with the head of public authorities.[238] The range of disciplinary offences has been extended and disciplinary sanctions have been tightened. In the most serious case, when an MP uses physical violence or threatens to do so, he or she may be banned from Parliament for a maximum of twenty-four sitting days or sixty calendar days, while the most severe penalty may amount to the six-monthly salary of an MP.[239]

470. Since 2020, a major constraint on legislative power has been the exceptional powers of the government which were granted by five consecutive states of danger (announced by the government itself) until the end of May 2024. During this period, the government issued more than eight hundred emergency decrees, amending or suspending more than fifty acts of Parliament. At the end of 2022, the government even rewrote the Budget Act by decree (subsequently confirmed by Parliament) – unprecedented in the past.

238. Act XVIII of 2019.
239. Act CVIII of 2019.

Chapter 2: Electoral System

471. The Fundamental Law does not provide for the manner in which MPs or local government representatives are elected. The Constitution only defines the principle of popular sovereignty, stating that '[t]he source of public power shall be the people', and the power is exercised by the people 'through elected representatives or, in exceptional cases, directly' (Article B) sections (3)–(4)). Thus, the detailed rules for both national and local electoral systems are set out in cardinal acts, all of which were adopted after 2010,[240] except the law regarding the election of members of the European Parliament.[241]

472. Despite the fact that the cornerstones of the electoral system have remained untouched, significant changes were made in recent years to the detailed rules and electoral procedural rules, as a result of the fact that the conservative government coalition has had most of the time since 2010 a two-thirds majority in Parliament, and thus has been able to shape freely the relevant laws.

§2.01 The Election System of the Members of Parliament

473. In 2010, the number of MPs was reduced by a constitutional amendment, providing that it may not be more than 200. Based on this, the new electoral law adopted in 2011 (hereinafter 'Election Law') reduced the number of MPs to 199 from the previous 386 (according to which a smaller Parliament was first elected in 2014). All this did not change the nature of the mixed electoral system (i.e., the combination of the elements of the majority and proportional systems), but many other changes were made to the detailed rules in 2011. For example, parliamentary elections had only one round, and territorial lists were abolished. This means that since 2014, voting for parties only proceeds on a national list. Moreover, as a real innovation since 2014, not only the votes cast for losing candidates in the individual constituencies but also the surplus votes of the winner are taken into account when the list votes are counted (the so-called winner's compensation). Another significant change was that the Hungarians who live abroad have received the right to vote, and they can cast their votes on the national lists. The Election Law has abolished the participation threshold, which means that voters' turnout no longer has to exceed 50%.

---

240. These laws are:

- Act CCIII of 2011 on the Election of the Members of Parliament;
- Act L of 2010 on the Election of the Members of Local Self-Governments and Mayors;
- Act CLXXIX on the Right of Nationalities; and
- Act XXXVI of 2013 on Electoral Procedure.

241. Act CXIII of 2003.

474. General elections are held in a one-round, two-vote system. The latter means that each voter – except those who do not have a residence in Hungary – has two votes, one of which can be cast for candidates in individual constituencies and the other for the national party lists.

475. The Hungarian electoral system is a 'mixed' one, combining elements of the majority (first-past-the-post) system and the proportional election system. Of the 199 MPs, 106 are elected in individual constituencies covering the whole territory of the country by direct election, in a relative majority system. The remaining ninety-three members are elected from national party lists (*see* figure below). The number of seats available for national party lists is reduced by the number of representatives of nationalities who have been granted a privileged mandate:[242]

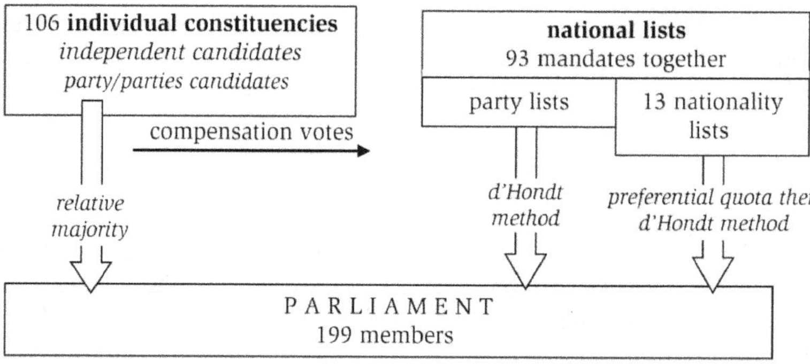

476. In the individual constituencies, a candidate becoming an MP will have received the most valid votes. If there is a tie, by-elections must be held. The remaining ninety-three seats (possibly reduced by the number of preferential mandates won by election from the nationality lists) are distributed among the candidates of the parties in proportion to the votes cast for the respective party lists based on the d'Hondt method. In distributing these mandates, a threshold of 5% is applied, which means that a party may get parliamentary seats only if it has got at least 5% of all valid votes cast for party lists (the threshold is 10% or 15% for a common list of two or more parties respectively).

§2.02 THE ELECTION SYSTEM OF THE MEMBERS OF THE EUROPEAN PARLIAMENT

477. For the European Parliament, Hungary has twenty-one seats of the total 751 (which will be reduced when the United Kingdom finally leaves the EU). The election of MEPs takes place every five years in a one-round proportional system. On this particular occasion, the whole country is considered a single constituency. Votes

242. *See supra*, Part II Ch. 1, §1.06, [B].

can be cast only for the lists of those parties which have met the requirements of presenting a national list, namely having collected 20,000 valid nominations from the voters. The twenty-one MEP mandates are distributed among the party lists reaching at least 5% of votes cast.

478. Any citizen of an EU Member State residing in Hungary may participate in EU elections for MEPs.

§2.03 Election Procedural Rules

479. The relevant law[243] contains the principles of election procedure. These are the protection of the fairness of elections, voluntary participation in the electoral process, equal opportunities between candidates and nominating organizations, the promotion of the exercise of the rights of voters with disabilities, good faith and lawfulness in the exercise of the right to vote, and the publicity of the election procedure.

[A] Electoral Bodies

480. All elections are prepared, administered and arranged by the election bodies, being the electoral committees and electoral offices. Electoral committees are independent bodies whose primary task is to determine election results, to ensure the fairness and legitimacy of elections, to enforce impartiality, and, if necessary, to restore the legal order of elections. They exist at regional (county) and local levels, as well as in each individual constituency. 'Vote counting committees' are also considered as electoral committees. The final results of the general elections are officially set and announced by the National Election Commission. It is composed of seven members and three deputy members who, on nomination of the President of the Republic, are elected for a term of nine years by the Parliament on a two-thirds majority vote.

481. Registration of voters and other administrative tasks related to the elections are carried out by electoral offices whose organizational order is parallel to that of the electoral committees. The National Election Office is an autonomous administrative body. It keeps the central electronic registry of voters, prepares and implements the decisions of the National Election Commission. Its President is appointed for a term of nine years by the President, at the nomination of the Prime Minister, from among eligible Hungarian citizens who have a higher education qualification.

---

243. Act XXXVI of 2013 on electoral procedure (hereinafter 'Election Procedural Law').

[B] Elections

482. The procedure of electing Members of Parliament can be divided into different stages.

483. The date of the parliamentary elections is of constitutional importance, which can guarantee a regular renewal of the composition of National Assembly. This is the reason why the Fundamental Law contains detailed provisions on when general elections have to be held.

484. In the normal case, general elections must be held in April or May of the fourth year following the election of the previous National Assembly. If, however, the Parliament has dissolved itself or has been dissolved, the next parliamentary election must be held within ninety days after dissolution (Article 2 section (3) and Article 3 section (6)). Special rules are applied during a state of national crisis or a state of emergency because in these periods the National Assembly may not dissolve itself nor may be dissolved, and, furthermore, no general elections may be called or held. In such cases, a new National Assembly must be elected within ninety days of the termination of the state of national crisis or state of emergency (Article 48 section (7)).

485. The Election Procedural Law comprises more specific rules as well. Thus, the election day must be announced at most ninety days, but not later than seventy days before the day of the election, and must be held on a Sunday. Election day may not be a day of rest determined by the Labour Code, or Easter Sunday, or Pentecost Sunday (Whitsun).

486. If a mandate becomes vacant, a by-election must be held within 120 days to fill the parliamentary seat, but no by-election can be held in the next election year.

[C] Nomination

487. Any eligible Hungarian citizen can be an individual candidate in parliamentary elections if they have been validly nominated by at least 500 voters (each voter may recommend only one candidate for the election). Individual candidates may represent a single party, may be a joint candidate (having more parties' support) or be a party-independent one.

488. As to the proportional element of the election system, the parties who are entitled to set a national party list must have at least seventy-one individual candidates from individual constituencies representing at least fourteen counties and one of the individual constituencies of Budapest. All thirteen registered nationalities have the right to set their own national list by their national minority self-government.

[D] Election Campaign Rules

489. While the detailed rules on election campaigns are determined by the Election Procedural Law, the Fundamental Law contains a restrictive provision in its freedom of expression clause ordering that 'during the electoral campaign period for the formation of democratic public opinion, political advertisements may only be published in media services free of charge, under the conditions guaranteeing equal opportunities, laid down in a cardinal act' (Article IX section (3)).

490. The specific rules of election campaigns define the campaign period, during which campaign activity can be continued, and which lasts from the fiftieth day before the day of the vote until the end of the election day. The most important campaign tools are posters, electoral gatherings, and political advertisements, subject to special rules. According to a special provision of the Election Procedural Law, the activities of public bodies within their jurisdiction are not considered campaign activities, which in turn provides a huge advantage for political decision-making bodies because they may freely express their opinion or support in a manner that is not subject to restrictions on political campaigning.

[E] Voting

491. Voters may cast their votes in polling stations on election day from 6.00 a.m. until 7.00 p.m. Ballots are counted by teller committees, with the election returns determined by the competent election committees.

[F] Legal Remedies

492. Candidates, voters, and nominating organizations concerned may appeal the electoral committees' first instance decisions. It is not possible to appeal against their second instance decisions or the resolutions of the National Election Commission. Appeals must be examined and decided on by the third day after filing, at the latest. If the right of appeal has already been exhausted or no appeal was available to the claimants, the final decisions of the electoral committees can be brought before the courts.

493. Judicial review is conducted by the court of competent jurisdiction according to the seat of the electoral committee which passed the decision of second instance. The resolutions of the National Election Commission are reviewed by the *Kúria* (i.e., the Supreme Court). The Court has to decide the case in non-litigious proceedings with a panel of three professional judges no later than on the third day after filing. In such proceedings, the provisions of the Code of Civil Procedure relating to administrative lawsuits must be applied properly.

§2.04 CONSTITUTIONAL PRACTICE

494. According to a frequently mentioned cliché, 'general elections are celebrations of democracy'. Certainly, in Hungary, after decades of Communist rule, parliamentary elections began to be significant and really democratic events only from 1990.

Table 4 Voters' Turnout in Parliamentary Elections in Percentages of Voters (1990–2018)

	First Round	*Second Round*
1990	65.11	45.54
1994	68.92	55.12
1998	56.26	57.01
2002	70.53	73.51
2006	67.83	64.39
2010	64.20	46.64
2014	61.24	–
2018	70.22	–
2022	70.21	–

495. However, the last three general elections (in 2014, 2018 and 2022, *see* Table 4) were assessed by the OSCE/ODIHR (Office for Democratic Institutions and Human Rights) as only partly fair because, although the organization of the general elections was effective, '[t]he main governing party enjoyed an undue advantage' for several reasons,[244] there was 'a pervasive overlap between state and ruling party resources, undermining contestants' ability to compete on an equal basis',[245] and the absence of a level playing field was characteristic[246] in these elections.

496. The Hungarian electoral system is particularly disproportionate, which has not only ensured the stability of every government since 1990, but has led in some cases (indeed all three times since 2010) to the constitutional omnipotence of the governing parties, having acquired a constitution-making parliamentary majority. In 2010, for example, the major governing party, Fidesz, acquired 52.73% of the votes which was transformed into 68.13% of parliamentary mandates (66.83% in 2014).

244. Hungary. Parliamentary elections 6 April 2014 OSCE/ODIHR Limited Election Observation Mission Final Report, OSCE Office for Democratic Institutions and Human Rights, Warszaw, 11 July 2014. 1.
245. Hungary. Parliamentary elections 8 April 2018 OSCE/ODIHR Limited Election Observation Mission Final Report, OSCE Office for Democratic Institutions and Human Rights, Warszaw, 27 June 2018. 1.
246. Hungary. Parliamentary elections and referendum 3 Apr. 2022 OSCE/ODIHR Election Observation Mission Final Report, Warszaw, 29 Jul. 2022.

497. However, while the victory of the conservative parties resulting in a two-thirds parliamentary majority in the 2010 elections was due to the great disproportionality of the election system, the same majority achieved in the next three general elections had other origins too.

498. The election rules had been rewritten a number of times since 2010. The changes were usually favourable for the government parties which have always unscrupulously exploited their two-thirds parliamentary majority necessary for amending these rules. Still, some of these amendments are not objectionable from a constitutional point of view. One of them, for example, introduced a one-round method instead of the earlier two-turn voting system. This served well the interests of the ruling government coalition that had successfully integrated the moderate right-wing parties in the preceding years, while the opposition was (and has remained) hopelessly fragmented. The absence of a second round has deprived the left-liberal opposition parties of the opportunity for withdrawing their own nominees for the odds-on opposition candidates in the various constituencies. However, in constitutional sense, the number of election rounds is only a technical, neutral thing.

499. Other changes raised constitutional controversies, like the discriminatory election rules relating to the exercise of the right to vote by those voters who were staying abroad on the election day. According to the rules objected to, while Hungarian citizens who live beyond the borders may cast their votes by correspondence, the law excludes the same way of voting for those who are abroad on the day of the general election, but live in Hungary anyway.

500. The unequal financial conditions of the government and the opposition parties have also generated long-standing legal debates. In particular, the publicly funded government political campaigns and advertisements produced a crossfire of controversy with political content that was the same or similar to the political advertisements of government parties. This has provided a huge advantage for the governing parties since public information campaigns of general interest issued by the government are not subject to restrictions on political advertising. In this way, as the government can make unlimited use of public resources to promote its own message, there is a huge difference in the financial resources available to the government side and opposition parties during election campaigns. It has also meant a serious harm to equal opportunity in that public media have been tools of government propaganda, public advertisements have been distributed on a party-political basis among the various media platforms, and a large part of the written and electronic media came into the hands of businessmen close to the government which also support the government parties.

501. Beyond that, the political contest has also been distorted by certain restrictions on political campaigns. In 2013, for example, the government majority adopted legislation that allowed only public media to publish political advertisements. The reason for the change was likely that, by then, the government had managed to put the public media under its full political control, so by restricting political advertisements in the commercial media, it could have gained significant dominance in election campaigns. But, the Constitutional Court abolished this provision in *ex ante* constitutional review at the initiative of the President of the Republic because the Court found it to be a disproportionate restriction on the freedom of expression.[247] Nonetheless, this ruling was superseded by the Fourth Amendment to the Fundamental Law, and the same restriction was inscribed into constitutional text. Yet, as a result of international protest,[248] the Fifth Amendment did abolish the monopoly of public media in this field, but has preserved the constitutional order for free publicity of political advertisements. The predominance of government parties in the media has thus remained since commercial channels only exceptionally publish political advertisements for free.

502. Another recurrent criticism relates to alleged gerrymandering. According to a Constitutional Court ruling, since the right to equal voting is significantly influenced by the electoral system, its rules should be settled by law or even by cardinal acts, and it therefore found the delimitation of constituencies by government decree, and the legal authorization for this practice, to be unconstitutional.[249]

503. As a consequence of this Constitutional Court's ruling of 2005 (declaring that the difference in the number of voters in individual constituencies should be as small as possible), the constituencies had to be redrawn in a way to include a similar number of voters in each of them (Decision 22/2005 (VI. 17.)). In the general election of 2010, for instance (when still individual candidates in 176 constituencies were elected), there were already significant differences in the size of each constituency: the difference between the population of the smallest and the largest district, for example, was a factor of 2.5. The boundaries of the constituencies were redrawn by the government majority in a way that the new constituency map strongly favours the governing parties.[250]

504. Another problem affecting the fairness of general elections is the often politically biased operation of some public bodies that should otherwise be neutral in political terms. After 2010, the leaders of these bodies were replaced by politically loyal people. In 2010, for example, the new Parliament adopted a law which allowed the replacement of those five members of the National Election Commission who were not delegated by the parliamentary parties. Until that time, these members were elected by the outgoing Parliament still before the general elections for the next parliamentary cycle. In its new composition, the National Election Commission has followed a practice beneficial for the government parties. The State Audit Office, led by a former MP of the Fidesz who was elected in 2010 for twelve years, just shortly before the general elections of 2018 imposed huge fines on the parliamentary opposition parties, depriving them of a substantial portion of their

247. Decision 1/2013. (I. 7.) of the Constitutional Court.
248. *See*, e.g., Venice Commission, *supra* n. 39, 10–12.
249. Decision 193/2010. (XII. 08.) of the Constitutional Court.
250. Csaba Molnár and Róbert László, *Hány szavazó kell az Összefogásnak a parlamenti többséghez?*, http://www.valasztasirendszer.hu/?p=1942632&_ga=2.225841500.751485544.1561494981-851406330.1561494981; Majtényi and Zsugyó, *supra* n. 54, 24.

financial resources, while the financial management of the government parties was not investigated in the election year at all.

505. All these circumstances are problematic in themselves, but their overall effects put the fairness and trustworthiness of the whole system of general elections into question.

Chapter 3: The President of the Republic

§3.01 INTRODUCTION

506. In the greater part of Hungary's constitutional history, the country was a monarchy and its Head of State was the monarch. Hungary had a total of sixty kings crowned, but at some points, it had two rival monarchs. During the long history of the country, when the king was a minor, he was held captive or otherwise obstructed in his reign, or in case of an *interregnum*, a regent exercised the powers of the Head of State. A few times (during the revolutions) saw the dethronement of the ruling Habsburg dynasty proclaimed, like in 1707, 1849 and 1918, but the kingdom was always restored after the revolt was suppressed. After the First World War and the collapse of the Austro-Hungarian monarchy, the *entente* powers did not consent to the return of the king last crowned, Charles IV Habsburg, to the Hungarian throne, and the provisional Hungarian Diet elected Miklós Horthy as governor (or regent). This post was originally intended to be temporary until the question of succession was definitively decided. The state of the 'kingdom without a king', however, remained unchanged until the Nazi occupation of the country in 1944, when a German-friendly puppet government was established. The form of State was decided in 1946 when the republican model was introduced by law, and a President of the Republic was elected. The Communist Constitution of 1949 changed that state structure from a republic to a 'people's republic', and the powers and duties of the Head of State were conferred on a 21-member body, the Presidium of the People's Republic. The republican structure and the position of the President of the Republic were restored only by the general revision of the Constitution in October 1989. Although the idea of the transition to a presidential form of government arose during the constitution-making process, it was eventually rejected for 'historical and legal reasons',[251] and the Fundamental Law of 2011 did not make any significant changes to the status of President of the Republic.

§3.02 POWERS AND DUTIES OF THE PRESIDENT OF THE REPUBLIC

507. The status of the President of the Republic is laid down in Articles 9–14 of the Fundamental Law, while detailed rules are set out in Cardinal Act CX of 2011.

508. The Fundamental Law defines the constitutional functions of the Head of State in the same way as the former Constitution did. According to this definition, he or she embodies 'the unity of the nation', and is 'the guardian of the democratic functioning of the state organization'. The next section declares that the President of the Republic is the Commander-in-Chief of the Hungarian Defence Forces (Article 9 sections (1)–(2)).

251. This was revealed by an interview with the Prime Minister in 2012. http://www.origo.hu/itthon/20120403-orban-viktor-a-prezidencialis-rendszerrol-is-beszelt-a-kurian.html#.

509. In principle, the Fundamental Law particularizes these functions by enumerating the most important competences of the Head of State. Yet these responsibilities link with the constitutional functions of the President only accidentally and incoherently. The embodiment of the national unity is apparently only a symbolic function. The Head of State is generally considered as the 'primary public law dignitary' who should stand above the political parties. Although he or she 'represents Hungary', this only means performing mostly ceremonial tasks and duties since the determination of foreign policy falls within the competence of the government. Moreover, the President of the Republic has barely effective powers by which he or she could really guard the democratic functioning of the State. If the Head of State has constitutional concerns with a law that was adopted by the Parliament, he or she may send it to the Constitutional Court, initiating its preliminary constitutional review instead of signing and promulgating the law. In the cases specified by law, the President may dissolve the Parliament and simultaneously call for new general elections. Beyond these, the Fundamental Law provides that the Head of State, within his/her scope of responsibility, must refuse to appoint or nominate the candidates if the conditions required by the law are not met or if 'he or she has well-founded reasons to conclude that it would lead to a serious disorder in the democratic functioning of the state organization'. By the same token, the President may deny an award to an honouree nominated by the government 'if it would violate the values enshrined in the Fundamental Law' (Article 9 sections (6)–(7)). Both of these latter rules have incorporated the essence of earlier Constitutional Court rulings into the constitutional text. However, the President of the Republic may not supersede the decisions of any other public authority, and may not give instructions to them, so he or she has only weak powers to ensure the democratic functioning of the state organization. One might think that this constitutional function may be carried out by the symbolic power and personal authority of the Head of State. But in reality, although incumbent Presidents are usually one of the most popular politicians, this position is traditionally a part of the political spoils system on the one hand, and on the other, the Head of State does not play any meaningful political role.

510. The title of Chief Commander of the Defence Forces does not have any meaningful content. According to the long-standing practice of the Constitutional Court, the President is not the commander of the army: he or she does not have any political responsibility; therefore, he/she may not exercise any real power interrelated to the army. An early decision of the Court surprisingly concluded that no specific powers can be derived from the presidential functions since they are not rules of jurisdiction – yet denying thus the logical argument that general functions can be performed by fulfilling the tasks corresponding to them. The Court argued that the Head of State stands out with the organization of the army, and the government should manage the Defence Forces. Using contra-textual argumentation, the Constitutional Court held that the constitutional significance of the relevant Article of the Constitution is nothing else than a declaration that 'the President of the Republic must be authorized to exert at least one traditional commanding power'.[252] Although this ruling of the Court was only a part of the political struggle between the President of the Republic and the government in the early 1990s, this approach has remained dominant until today.

511. The constitutional competences of the President of the Republic can be divided into two groups, depending on whether the acts of the Head of State need the countersignature of a member of the government or not. Since the President is not accountable in a political sense, the government must take political responsibility for the President's actions. This occurs with the countersignature of the President's decisions by the member of the government whose scope of responsibility is affected by the action. According to the Constitutional Court's jurisprudence, owing to the absence of political accountability, the President of the Republic has only a narrow margin of discretion in these areas, with the unexplained exception of awarding honours (the latter exception can be traced back to a concrete claim of President László Sólyom, who was also the first President of that Court, that he refused an honour for the socialist Prime Minister Gyula Horn alluding to 'moral considerations').[253] For example, the President may not deny honours to those proposed by the government, unless he/she 'reasonably concludes that the implementation of the proposal would seriously undermine the democratic functioning of the state organization'.[254]

512. The countersignature of the competent member of the government is necessary for most of the appointments made by the President. Hence, the Head of State, at the proposal of the Prime Minister, will appoint Ministers, the Governor and Deputy Governors of the Hungarian National Bank, and the heads of independent regulatory organs. At the recommendation of the competent Minister, he or she accredits and receives ambassadors and envoys, appoints university professors, assigns university rectors, and appoints and promotes generals. It is to be noted, however, that no countersignature is needed for certain appointment decisions of the President, like nominating the Prime Minister, the President of the *Kúria*, the President of the National Office for the Judiciary, the Prosecutor General, the President of the Budget Council, and the Commissioner for Fundamental Rights to the National Assembly. In this respect, the appointment of professional judges is a special competence which is exercised on the basis of the proposal of the President of the National Office for the Judiciary, but the appointments themselves do not require the countersignature of a government member, and likewise the confirmation of the President of the Hungarian Academy of Sciences and the President of the Hungarian Academy of Arts in his or her office.

513. On the proposal of the government, the President of the Republic bestows awards, decorations, prizes and titles (as specified in an act of Parliament), and

252. Decision 48/1991. (IX. 26.) of the Constitutional Court.
253. Decision 47/2007. (VII. 3.) of the Constitutional Court.
254. Decision 36/1992. (VI. 10.) of the Constitutional Court.

authorizes the use of foreign state decorations. In addition, members of the government submit proposals and subsequently countersign the President's decisions on:

- granting individual pardons;
- matters of territorial organization (related to the changes of the administrative status of the municipalities);
- matters related to the acquisition or termination of citizenship (in case of naturalization, repatriation, and withdrawal and resignation of the citizenship).

514. In practice, the President exercises these powers at different frequencies: while individual pardons, which may be granted on the basis of the proposal of the Minister of Justice, occur only rarely, the administrative status of municipalities changes relatively often at the initiative of the Minister of the Interior because it embraces all the amalgamations, partitionings, and establishment of communities. Similarly, there are many citizenship cases, for which the same Minister makes proposals, and he/she countersigns such decisions.

515. Moreover, the President of the Republic, on the basis of authorization by the National Assembly, expresses consent to be bound by international treaties.

516. Nevertheless, the President's decisions on the date of general elections for members of the National Assembly, local government representatives and mayors, as well as European Parliament elections and national referendums, are autonomous actions of the Head of State which do not require the countersignature of the government. The same applies to the dissolution of the National Assembly, though he or she may dissolve Parliament only in cases determined by the Fundamental Law. The President convenes the constitutive sitting of the National Assembly in an autonomous way, and no countersignature is required for the actions of the Head of State made in the legislative process. Thus, he or she may attend the sittings of the National Assembly, may address the chamber, and may submit bills to Parliament. As a matter of fact, the President only occasionally takes part in parliamentary meetings, and since 1990, the Head of State has submitted a bill to Parliament only once. Notwithstanding this, the Head of State may influence the political agenda in another way as well, seeing as he or she may initiate national referendums.

517. The President of the Republic has only a relatively weak veto power in political decision-making processes. The laws adopted by Parliament have to be sent to the Head of State for signature and promulgation. If the President has constitutional concerns about the law passed by Parliament, he/she may send the Act to the Constitutional Court to examine its conformity with the Fundamental Law (constitutional veto). In case of a new constitutional text or a constitutional amendment, the President may initiate only a procedural review with the Constitutional Court. If only political concerns are at issue, the Head of State may send the law adopted back to Parliament for reconsideration (political veto).

518. The President of the Republic has some powers in relation to special legal orders. In cases defined by the Fundamental Law, he or she may proclaim a state of war and a state of emergency, if the National Assembly is prevented from making such decisions.

§3.03 The Election of the Head of State and the Termination of His/Her Mandate

519. The Fundamental Law sets only mild conditions to attain the office of President of the Republic: any Hungarian citizen who has reached the age of thirty-five years may be elected Head of State.

520. During the process of the democratic transition in 1988–1990, there was much debate about how the Head of State should be elected. In 1989, at the initiation of the opposition movements, a successful referendum was held deciding that the President of the Republic would be elected only after the first democratic general elections (reducing the chances of the Communist Party candidate being elected), while an invalid national referendum was held on the election method of the President in the next year. The constitutional revision of 1989 provided that the Head of State is elected for five years by the National Assembly and may be re-elected only once. The same rules were applied by the Fundamental Law. In order to ensure the continuity of office-holding, the Constitution prescribes that the President of the Republic has to be elected no sooner than sixty, but no later than thirty, days before the expiry of the mandate of the previous Head of State, or, if his or her mandate ended prematurely, within thirty days of that termination. The National Assembly elects the President by secret ballot.

521. Since the President of the Republic is elected by the Parliament, the candidates may be nominated only by the Members of Parliament. At least one-fifth of the MPs may submit a written recommendation to the National Assembly. Every MP may recommend only one candidate (otherwise, all his/her recommendations are invalid). That candidate who receives the two-thirds votes of the Members of Parliament will be elected President of the Republic. If no candidate acquires the necessary votes, a second round must be held in which votes may be cast for the two candidates receiving the highest and the second highest numbers of votes in the first round. In this round, a simple majority of votes cast is enough for election regardless of the number of those participating in the vote. The voting procedure does not involve any floor debate, and it must be completed within no more than two consecutive days. The President-elect takes office upon the expiry of the mandate of the previous President of the Republic or, if his or her mandate ended prematurely, on the eighth day after the announcement of the result of the election. Prior to taking office, the President-elect must take an oath before the National Assembly.

522. The mandate of the President of the Republic terminates upon the expiry of his or her five-year term of office. Beyond this, if he or she becomes incapable of performing his or her functions for more than ninety days, or if the conditions required for his or her election no longer exist, or in case of a conflict of interest, his/her mandate will also be terminated. Parliament decides by a two-thirds majority whether or not these circumstances exist in such cases. The Head of State may resign from his/her office and, under the conditions set by the Fundamental Law, may be removed from office (*see* below). So far, this took place only once (Pál Schmitt, in 2012).

§3.04 Incompatibility and Accountability of the Head of State

523. The President of the Republic may not hold any other state, social, economic or political office, and may not pursue any other gainful occupation, and may not receive remuneration for any other activity, except for activities falling under copyright protection.

524. Following Hungarian public law traditions, the Fundamental Law guarantees the inviolability of the person of the Head of State. This means, on the one hand, that his or her person receives enhanced criminal protection. On the other hand, the President enjoys immunity against any criminal or disciplinary procedures. The latter means that criminal proceedings against the Head of State may be instituted only after the termination of his or her mandate. During his/her term of office, any prosecution is subject to special rules entrenched in the Fundamental Law. According to these rules, the President of the Republic may be liable for prosecution only if he or she intentionally violates the Fundamental Law or, in connection with performing his or her office, any act of Parliament, or if he or she commits an intentional criminal offence, provided that one-fifth of the members of the Parliament propose impeachment proceedings in order to remove the President from office. The plenary body of the National Assembly decides on this initiative with a two-thirds majority vote held by secret ballot. If Parliament votes in favour of impeachment, the President of the Republic may not exercise his or her powers until the impeachment proceedings are concluded. The impeachment procedure is conducted by the Constitutional Court. If the Court, as a result, establishes the responsibility of the Head of State, it may remove him/her from office. In case of a criminal offence, the President's removal opens the way for normal criminal proceedings before an ordinary court.

525. The Head of State does not have a deputy; the position of Vice President does not exist. However, if the President of the Republic is temporarily prevented from acting, or if his or her mandate terminates for any reason, the Speaker of Parliament may exercise the functions and powers of the Head of State until he or she is no longer prevented from acting, or until the new President of the Republic takes office, respectively. The fact of temporal incapacity of the President may be established by Parliament at the initiative of the President of the Republic, the government or any MP. During substitution, the Speaker of the National Assembly may not exercise his or her rights as an MP, and he or she must also be substituted by a Deputy Speaker in Parliament.

§3.05 The Position of the Head of State in the Constitutional Life

526. In the period of the democratic transition and in the early 1990s, the constitutional status of the Head of State was a controversial issue in political and public law discourse. First, the acquiring of this position could have ensured the political survival of the reformist wing of the former state party, and the division of political power between that Communist Party and the new opposition movements. However, the advancement of the system change quickly moved beyond this idea. A little bit later, there were political tensions between the conservative government led by József Antall and the President, Árpád Göncz, who belonged to the largest opposition party – which have been manifested in constitutional controversies as well. In this debate, the Constitutional Court supported the government's position in several rulings declaring, for example, that in the parliamentary system, such as the form of government in Hungary, the government embodies and possesses 'solely the executive power'; consequently, 'the President of the Republic is outside the executive power'. The Constitutional Court drew this conclusion from the principle of the inviolability of the Head of State and the lack of political responsibility.[255] Since 2010, however, the political neutrality of the President of the Republic has appeared illusory, and the Constitutional Court's decisions taken before the entry of the Fundamental Law on 1 January 2012 have been repealed by the Fourth Amendment to the Fundamental Law.

527. Since the democratic transition in 1989–1990, a total of six people have held this position. Árpád Göncz was the first democratically elected President of the Republic from 1990 (re-elected in 1995). He was followed by Ferenc Mádl (2000–2005), László Sólyom (2005–2010), Pál Schmidt (2010–2012), János Áder (2012–2022) and Katalin Novák (2022–). Until now, two Presidents have been re-elected and all of them have completed their term of office, except Mr Pál Schmidt, who resigned after it turned out that he had obtained a doctoral degree tainted with plagiarism. While the Presidents of the first two decades of constitutional democracy had performed their functions more or less in a politically neutral way, and gained certain prestige for the presidential office, the two presidents elected after 2010 willingly served the government's ambitions and goals. It has been particularly noticeable that they have not acted in any way against the increasingly authoritarian political decision-making and the dismantling of the rule of law.

528. Overall, the Head of State does not play a meaningful political role, but he or she has mostly ceremonial and representative functions, avoiding political conflicts with the incumbent governments.

255. Decision 48/1991. (IX. 26.) of the Constitutional Court.

Chapter 4: The Government

529. The main body of executive power is the government, which is a central, corporate body exercising general public authority. The legal status of the government is determined by the Fundamental Law (Articles 15–22), while the detailed rules on its organization and operation are laid down in Act XLIII of 2010, addressing the central public authorities and the legal status of the members of government and state secretaries. The rules governing the operation of the government are set by the body themselves in a government decree.[256] Besides these, in the area of executive power, the Fundamental Law also prescribes that the list of Ministries and the legal status of government officials are to be regulated by acts of Parliament.

§4.01 Tasks and Functions of the Government

530. According to the traditional approach to the constitutional role of the government, it is the top organization of executive power empowered to execute laws. In doing so, the government has a dual nature in a functional sense: the Executive Branch embraces both governance and public administration. Broadly speaking, the former comprises political decision-making (or policy-making), while the latter refers to the administrative implementation (enforcement) of policy decisions. It is to be noted that this is just an analytical conceptualization; the constitutional text simply defines the government as 'the general organ of executive power', which is 'the principal organ of public administration' (Article 15 sections (1)–(2)).

531. The general executive competence of the government is expressed by the constitutional text in a negative way, stating that the body exercises all the functions and powers which are not expressly conferred by the Constitution or any law on another organ. This extremely broad jurisdiction is specified more precisely only in two respects. First, the Fundamental Law empowers the government to establish organs of state administration within the limits of the law. This stipulation excludes the setup or change of ministerial structure since those may be determined only by an act of Parliament. Second, the government may issue a law, called a 'government decree', of which there are two types. The first sort issues from within its scope of responsibility, unless the subject matter is otherwise regulated by an act. The second sort of government decree is the more usual: such regulations are issued on the basis of authorization of an act of Parliament. From a legal point of view, however, no distinction may be made between the two forms of government decree, which are ranked below acts of Parliament but above all other legal rules in the hierarchy of legal norms.

256. Government Decree 1144/2010. (VII. 7.).

§4.02 THE ESTABLISHMENT AND COMPOSITION OF THE GOVERNMENT

532. As has been said above, the Prime Minister and the Ministers are the members of the government. Although there is no formal Deputy Prime Minister, the PM may designate, by means of a decree, one or more Deputy Prime Minister(s) from among the Ministers. Albeit considered for a long time that the PM was only *primus inter pares*, in fact his or her mandate is created in a different way from that of the Ministers.

533. In the normal case, the first step in the formation of a government is that the President of the Republic presents to the National Assembly in due course his or her proposal for the premiership. This happens in the constitutive sitting of the new National Assembly when the previous government's term of office expires. According to common parlance, after the general elections, the President will assign the government formation to the leader of the party which won the parliamentary elections, or to the politician who, based on the election results, is most likely to be able to set up a government with a parliamentary majority. In fact, this is only an informal phase of government formation; in legal terms, the President submits a proposal for the new Prime Minister to Parliament at its inaugural session. Yet, since 1990, the Head of State has always nominated the leader of the party winning the general elections, so this practice can be seen as a constitutional convention. In other cases, the Head of State will nominate the Prime Minister within fifteen days if the mandate of the former PM has ceased for any other reason unless it has ended due to a successful motion of censure. In contrast to the former constitutional rule being in effect before 2012, the candidate PM does not have to announce his/her government's programme before the plenary meeting of the Parliament. The National Assembly, without debate, only votes on whether or not it accepts the person proposed by the President to be the Prime Minister. The election occurs on the basis of an absolute majority of the members of the Parliament, and this support can ensure the continuity of governance.

534. If the National Assembly fails to elect the person proposed, the President will present a new candidate within fifteen days. However, the President is not obliged to recommend other candidates; the Head of State may retain the first nomination.

535. The PM-elect takes office in the plenary session of Parliament. The next stage of government formation is the nomination of Ministers by the newly elected PM. The candidates must be heard by the competent standing committee of the National Assembly, but the statement of the committee on the aptitude of the candidate does not bind the President of the Republic who, on the proposal of the PM, appoints the Ministers and State Secretaries (the latter are not formally members of the government). In theory, according to constitutional practice, the Head of State may refuse to appoint the candidates only if the person nominated does not meet the constitutional requirements of government membership or he or she reasonably thinks that the appointment could jeopardize the democratic functioning of the state organization.

536. After the Head of State has appointed the Ministers, the government takes an oath before the National Assembly. However, this is merely a ceremonial act, as the Fundamental Law states that the government is established upon the appointment of the Ministers just before taking the oath before Parliament.

§4.03 THE MEMBERS OF THE GOVERNMENT

537. The government consists of the Prime Minister and Ministers. The Hungarian form of government is sometimes called 'Prime Ministerial' or 'Chancellor-type', referring to the strong position of the Prime Minister. He or she is indisputably a central figure of the government. The PM's powerful position is based partly on the fact that he/she is the only member of the government who is elected by Parliament, while in practice, he or she chooses the other members of the collegiate body. Beyond that, the constructive motion of no-confidence also strengthens his or her constitutional (and political) status.

538. The scope of responsibility of the Prime Minister is not specified by the Fundamental Law. The Constitution points out the lawmaking power by which the PM may issue decrees. Apart from this, the Constitution says only that he/she defines the general policy of the government.

539. Only a Hungarian citizen without a criminal record and who has the right to vote can be elected Prime Minister. Although the Constitution does not refer to the term of office of the PM, the government's mandate terminates upon the formation of the newly elected National Assembly – which means also that the term of office of the Prime Minister may not be longer than that of the Parliament (i.e., it may not exceed four years). The Prime Minister's mandate also terminates if the National Assembly adopts a motion of no-confidence, electing a new Prime Minister at the same time or if Parliament does not pass a confidence vote moved by the Prime Minister. Until now, Parliament has voted only once on a constructive motion of censure (in 2009). The mandate of the Prime Minister also terminates if the acting PM resigns or dies. This has only happened once so far, in 2004, when Péter Medgyessy resigned. József Antall, the first PM after the system change, died in 1992. The mandate of the PM also ends if he or she fails to eliminate a conflict of interest, or if the conditions required for his or her election no longer exist. The National Assembly may decide to declare such an incompatibility or to establish the absence of the conditions required for the election of the Prime Minister on a two-thirds majority vote of the MPs present.

540. The termination of the Prime Minister's mandate automatically terminates the mandate of the whole government, in accordance with the logic of parliamentary government. So far, the Prime Minister has always come from the largest government party (*see* Table 5 for the list of PMs).

Table 5 The List of Prime Ministers since 1990

József Antall	(1990–1993)	MDF
Péter Boross	(1993–1994)	MDF
Gyula Horn	(1994–1998)	MSZP
Viktor Orbán	(1998–2002)	Fidesz
Péter Medgyessy	(2002–2004)	MSZP
Ferenc Gyurcsány	(2004–2009)	MSZP
Gordon Bajnai	(2009–2010)	MSZP
Viktor Orbán	(2010–)	Fidesz

541. As has been said above, the Prime Minister has no permanent deputy, but he or she may appoint one or more deputy PMs from among the Ministers.

542. The other members of the government are the Ministers. There are two types of Minister: those who lead a Ministry and those Ministers without a portfolio. Traditionally, the Ministries are listed by an act of Parliament, but because the relevant law requires a simple majority in the National Assembly, normally the government may determine the ministerial structure, based on its parliamentary support.

543. In 2023, the government consisted of sixteen members, the Prime Minister, a deputy Prime Minister, and fourteen Ministers in charge of Ministries.

544. According to the Constitution, the Ministers in charge of a Ministry control autonomously those sectors of state administration and the subordinated organs within their mandate, while Ministers without portfolio perform those functions determined by the government or the Prime Minister. As a matter of course, all Ministries may act within the framework of the general policy set by the government. Like in the case of the Prime Minister, the Fundamental Law is reticent about the precise scope of responsibility for Ministers. It states only that the members of the government, within their functions, may issue decrees, either autonomously or in agreement with one or more other Ministers, which laws may not conflict with any act of Parliament, government decree or a decree of the Governor of the Hungarian National Bank. Ministers may issue ministerial decrees only on the basis of an authorization by an act of Parliament or a government decree; thus, they can only be executive ordinances.

545. As was said above, Ministers are appointed by the President of the Republic on the proposal of the Prime Minister. The candidates of the PM are heard by the appropriate committee of the National Assembly, but the committee's view made on the aptitude of the nominee is not binding on the Head of State. Only those Hungarian citizens who have no criminal record and have a right to vote are eligible to be appointed as Minister. Ministers have to take an oath before Parliament.

546. The term of office of Ministers ends upon the termination of the government's mandate, or by resignation, death, losing the right to vote, or conflict of interest. Apart from this, Ministers may be discharged at the proposal of the Prime Minister by the Head of State.

§4.04 Government in Action

547. The detailed rules for the operation of the government are determined by a government decree.[257] According to these rules, the government fulfils its tasks and exercises its powers at government meetings as a body, under the leadership of the Prime Minister. The government holds meetings on a weekly basis (usually on Wednesdays), with the exception of the summer holidays. The meetings of the government are prepared by the Conference of Administrative State Secretaries of the Ministries, which prepares all the matters to be submitted to the government for discussion and decision.

548. In a formal sense, there are two kinds of documents which may be tabled in government meetings. Reports only inform the government, while proposals are motions requiring a decision by the government. Proposals have specific content elements (e.g., they should contain draft text). In the first stage of governmental decision-making, proposals and draft ministerial decrees must be sent to all Ministries and government departments concerned for their opinion. As a rule, government bodies involved in the decision-making process are obliged to render their opinion within five working days. The aim of the preparatory process is to build a compromise on the proposal among the Ministries and other government agencies.

549. From a legal point of view, the government may issue decrees, resolutions, directives or policy statements. While government decrees are legal acts fitting into the hierarchy of legal norms, the other types of decisions are addressed to government agencies which exist as subordinates to the government. The latter may set objectives and goals, or contain general guidelines or instructions to government bodies.

550. The rules of procedure of the government do not provide for the precise method for taking decisions, but in practice, final decisions are declared by the PM after discussions. The decisions of the government include a summary, which is made immediately after the government meeting. With the permission of the Prime Minister, it is also possible to make an audio recording of the meeting, but in practice, this likely occurs only exceptionally.

551. The constitutional provisions tie the term of office of the government to that of the National Assembly, by which the constitution-maker tried to eliminate the situation where no government having full authority would exist. Still, in some

---

257. *See supra* n. 258.

cases, it is inevitable that the mandate of the government will end without the establishing of a new one. This is the case if the mandate of the Prime Minister ceases for any reason other than a constructive vote of no-confidence. The general rule for such cases is that a caretaker government works until the formation of the new government. The caretaker government exercises full powers of the government, except that it may not express consent to be bound by international treaties, and may adopt decrees only on the basis of authorization by act of Parliament in cases of urgency. If the government's mandate has ended by virtue of the resignation of the Prime Minister, the PM may exercise his or her powers until the election of the new Prime Minister, save that he or she may not propose the dismissal of Ministers or the appointment of new Ministers, and may issue decrees only on the basis of authorization by an act of Parliament in cases of urgency. If the mandate of the PM has terminated upon his or her death, the declaration of a conflict of interest, a failure to fulfil the conditions required for his or her election or because the National Assembly has expressed its lack of confidence in the Prime Minister in a confidence vote, the powers of the PM are exercised by his or her deputy (if there are more deputies, the acting PM has to designate a first deputy Prime Minister) under the aforementioned limitations. Quite similar rules are applied to the Ministers of the caretaker governments, who exercise ministerial responsibilities until a new Minister is appointed or another member of the new government is assigned to perform temporarily the ministerial functions, and may adopt decrees only in cases of urgency.

§4.05 The Parliamentary Responsibility of the Government

552. It is an old controversy among Hungarian constitutional historians whether there has ever been a parliamentary government in Hungary before the system change in 1989–1990. Some scholars claim that the 1848 revolution introduced parliamentarianism in Hungary, which was consummated after the Great Compromise between Austria and Hungary in 1867, while others suggest that it was the country's form of government in the interwar period. But even if the conditions for parliamentary governance were provided for in principle, the logic of parliamentary government did not prevail in practice. The greatest chance for parliamentarianism to take root was probably after the Second World War, during the so-called coalition period between 1946 and 1949. But this attempt was overshadowed by the fact that the country was under Soviet occupation, and a Soviet-type dictatorship was then introduced, institutionalized by the 1949 Communist Constitution.

553. In spite of the uncertainty over those historical traditions, it was not disputed during the regime change that a Western-type parliamentary democracy should be built up in Hungary. The most important institutional feature of this form of government is the political responsibility of the government to Parliament, which was included in the constitutional text during the general constitutional revision in October 1989. However, in the summer of 1990, the Constitution was amended on the basis of a political pact of the largest government and opposition parties (between the conservative Hungarian Democratic Forum and the liberal Alliance of

Free Democrats), and a constructive version of the motion of censure was institutionalized by a constitutional amendment,[258] primarily on the basis of the German pattern. The Fundamental Law of 2011 has preserved this kind of parliamentary responsibility under unchanged procedural rules. This process may begin with a written motion of no-confidence submitted to the Parliament by one-fifth of MPs against the Prime Minister. The motion must include a proposed new Prime Minister. The National Assembly may decide on the motion after three but no later than eight days following the submission of the motion of no-confidence. However, the Constitution does not provide whether, under this 'cooling-off' period, Parliament should debate the motion or not. What is certain is that if the National Assembly supports the motion of no-confidence, it thereby expresses its lack of confidence in the Prime Minister and simultaneously elects the person proposed in the motion. In accordance with the majority requirement of the election of the Prime Minister, the adoption of the motion of censure requires the votes of more than half of the MPs.

554. Apart from the motion of censure, the Prime Minister also has the power to move Parliament to vote on its confidence in the government. However, if more than half of the deputies do not support the Prime Minister in that confidence vote, it is considered an expression of Parliament's lack of confidence in the PM. After such a vote, Parliament must elect a new prime minister. The same procedure applies to the special form of confidence vote, as the Prime Minister may connect it with a proposal (most likely with a bill) submitted by the government.

555. When the Fundamental Law states that the government is accountable to the National Assembly (Article 15 section (1)), it not only refers to the procedures of the motion of censure and confidence but also embraces other mechanisms through which the legislature may control the activity of the government. Thus, the Constitution specifies that the members of the government are also accountable to Parliament, even though Hungarian constitutional law does not know individual ministerial responsibility. On this point, ministerial accountability means that they are obliged to report on their actions to the National Assembly and to attend the sittings of parliamentary committees if they so wish.

556. Within the scope of the government's general parliamentary responsibility, the government, through the Prime Minister, is obliged to report regularly to Parliament on its work, at least once a year. Ministers are also required to appear and report to the parliamentary committee(s) that heard them before their appointment, at least on an annual basis. It should also be mentioned here that MPs may interpellate and question the members of the government in the plenary sittings of Parliament.

557. As to EU affairs, the National Assembly may request information from the government on its position to be represented in the decision-making procedures of EU intergovernmental institutions and may take a position on the drafts placed on

258. Act XL of 1990.

the agenda in those proceedings. In the course of the decision-making by the EU, the government must act on the basis of the position taken by the National Assembly.

§4.06 Administrative Bodies Assisting the Work of the Government

558. The work of the government is supported by a variety of bodies, including ministerial cabinets, government committees, government commissioners, and commissioners of the Prime Ministers and the Ministers.

559. Among these, cabinets have the most important role. Their task is to prepare the government's decision on issues that affect the responsibilities of several Ministries and other central administrative agencies. According to the existing rules, the government may set up cabinets for preparing draft government statements prior to government meetings in matters of social policy, economic policy and national security. At the moment, there are four cabinets established for strategic and family policy, economic matters, national security affairs and national policy. The members of the cabinet are the Ministers involved in their duties and the persons appointed by the Prime Minister. A government decree may designate other persons permanently invited to cabinet meetings. The cabinets may, exceptionally, take decisions in matters within the competence of the government.

560. The government may set up government committees to manage coordinated solutions for significant tasks falling within the scope of its competence, affecting the responsibilities of several Ministers. The members of the government committees are the relevant Ministers concerned. A government decree may list persons permanently invited to the meetings of these committees.

561. The government may appoint a Government Commissioner to carry out tasks within the scope of its responsibility, or other priority tasks. The activities of the Government Commissioner are managed by the Prime Minister and the Minister appointed by the government.

562. The Prime Minister and the Ministers may also appoint commissioners who perform tasks falling within their own competence.

§4.07 Constitutional Practice

563. The constitutional amendment of 1990 reached its goal inasmuch as it aimed at consolidating the position of the government of the day. The executive power has been characterized by stability after the constructive motion of no-confidence was introduced in the summer of that year. It means that the governing parties have always filled their term of office, even though the person of the

Prime Minister has sometimes changed due to death (József Antall, in 1993), resignation (Péter Medgyessy, in 2006) and a vote of no-confidence (Ferenc Gyurcsány, in 2009) (*see* Table 6). Although formally the whole period after the system change can be characterized by coalition government, since 2010 only a façade coalition or a quasi-one-party government has been operating, as the Christian Democratic People's Party has participated in general elections on a joint list with the major government party, Fidesz.

564. In spite of the government stability during the parliamentary cycles, prior to 2010, the incumbent government, with only one exception (in 2006), was always overthrown in successive parliamentary elections; that is, general elections resulted in a change of government every time.

Table 6 The Governments of Hungary since the First Democratic Parliamentary Elections after the System Change (1990–2022)

Prime Minister	*Term of Office*		*Party Composition*
József Antall (MDF)	23 May 1990	12 December 1993	MDF–FKGP*–KDNP
Péter Boross (MDF)	12 December 1993	21 December 1993	MDF–FKGP–KDNP
21 December 1993	15 July 1994	MDF–EKGP–KDNP	
Gyula Horn (MSZP)	15 July 1994	6 July 1998	MSZP–SZDSZ
Viktor Orbán (Fidesz) I.	6 July 1998	27 May 2002	Fidesz–FKGP–MDF
Péter Medgyessy (Independent)	27 May 2002	29 September 2004	MSZP–SZDSZ
Ferenc Gyurcsány (MSZP) I.	29 September 2004	9 June 2006	MSZP–SZDSZ
Ferenc Gyurcsány (MSZP) II.	9 June 2006	14 April 2009	MSZP–SZDSZ**
Gordon Bajnai (Independent)	14 April 2009	29 May 2010	MSZP***
Viktor Orbán (Fidesz) II.	29 May 2010	10 May 2014	Fidesz–KDNP
Viktor Orbán (Fidesz) III.	10 May 2014	10 May 2018	Fidesz–KDNP
Viktor Orbán (Fidesz) IV.	10 May 2018	24 May 2022	Fidesz–KDNP
Viktor Orbán (Fidesz) V.	24 May 2022	incumbent	Fidesz–KDNP

*In February 1992, FKGP split into two parts, one of which remained in the coalition government, while the other part went into opposition.

**SZDSZ left the government in April 1998.

***The government was supported externally by SZDSZ.

MDF = Hungarian Democratic Forum

FKGP = Independent Shareholders' Party

KDNP = Christian Democratic People's Party

MSZP = Hungarian Socialist Party

SZDSZ = Alliance of Free Democrats

Fidesz = Originally, it was an acronym of the Alliance of Young Democrats; later this name has been left.

565. Until now, a vote of constructive no-confidence occurred only once in the Hungarian Parliament, under special circumstances. In fact, the procedure was proposed by the incumbent socialist Prime Minister, Ferenc Gyurcsány, to his own parliamentary faction, electing Gordon Bajnai as the new PM at the same time. Accordingly, 92 Members of Parliament, all representing the Socialist party (the then major government party), submitted a motion of constructive no-confidence and elected their own candidate. This procedure has been heavily criticized by many, claiming that this process was not in harmony with the spirit of the Constitution. They argued that by the institution of constructive censure, the Constitution wanted to provide an effective tool for the parliamentary opposition of the day to change governments, so it was not intended to help the government parties to replace their own PM so as to avoid parliamentary elections. Nevertheless, on 14 April 2009, Parliament voted in favour of the motion with a solid majority, and elected the new candidate of the government parties, Gordon Bajnai, as the next Prime Minister.

566. So far, there has been only one example of the operation of a caretaker government, when, in 1993, after the death of Prime Minister József Antall, such a government was formed under the leadership of Péter Boross, the former Minister of Interior (and the next PM).

567. The parliamentary elections of 2010 figured as a milestone not only in a political but also in a constitutional sense. The conservative government established as a result of these elections, taking advantage of its constitution-making majority in Parliament, began a strong centralization policy, leading to a gradual submission by the previously independent public authorities to the central government. As a consequence, the Constitutional Court, the National Judicial Office, the Prosecution Service, the Commissioner of the Fundamental Rights, the State Audit Office, the National Election Commission and the National Office of Judiciary are under the strong political control of the Executive Branch. Seeing as the government has successfully occupied the leading positions of the controlling public authorities, it is not surprising that the autonomous agencies of executive power, which should in theory be independent of direct governmental control (like the autonomous regulatory agencies), are also under strong political influence.

568. The government is not only the centrepiece of political power, but the entire political system is dominated by executive power. In the beginning, as a legacy of the politico-administrative approach of the socialist era, the corporate nature of the government was stressed, where the Prime Minister was seen only as a *primus inter pares* who could not instruct the other members of the body. Today, the Prime Minister is clearly in a leading and decisive position. This phenomenon is sometimes portrayed as 'the presidentialization' of government,[259] whereas the political character of governance in the recent past is typified as a 'plebiscitary leader democracy'.[260]

569. The government has exercised exceptional powers in constitutional terms since March 2020, when it declared a state of danger due to COVID-19 pandemic. Since then, with a brief interruption of four and a half months, Hungary has been continuously under a special legal order (the fifth in a row), which gives the government the power to suspend or amend laws, take extraordinary measures, or restrict fundamental rights more extensively than the Constitution normally allows.

259. András Körösényi, *Parlamentáris, vagy 'elnöki' kormányzás? Az Orbán-kormány összehasonlító perspektívából* 6 Századvég (2001) 3–38.
260. Gábor Illés, András Körösényi and Rudolf Metz, *Broadening the Limits of Reconstructive Leadership: Constructivist Elements of Viktor Orbán's Regime-Building Politics*, 20(4) The Brit. J. Pol. Intl. Rel. 790–808 (2018).

Chapter 5: The System of State Administration

570. As already noted, the government, as the supreme body of executive power, is not only the political decision-maker but also the highest organ of public administration.

571. The Hungarian public administration embraces two large spheres: the state administration, in the first place, is a hierarchically structured organizational system under the management of the government. The system of local self-government, in the second, consists of democratically elected county (capital) and municipal governments, over which the government exercises legal supervision.

572. The organizational system of the state administration exists basically at two tiers, at central and county levels; however, in certain administrative fields, its subnational bodies operate at different (regional, district or local) levels, or their activities cover different areas.

§5.01 The Central Administrative Bodies

573. The most important rules for the state administrative bodies are determined by the Fundamental Law, the Government Administration Act,[261] the Act on the Central Administrative Bodies and the Legal Status of the Members of Government and State Secretaries.[262]

574. There are more than one hundred central-level government bodies which form a hierarchically structured, complex organizational system. The different types of organs are classified primarily into groups according to the nature of their activities and the extent of their autonomy. These are:

- independent regulatory bodies;
- bodies of the central government administration;
- autonomous state administrative agencies; and
- law enforcement agencies and the national security services.

[A] The Independent Regulatory Authorities

575. One group of central administrative bodies is composed of two organs having their own constitutional status. These are the autonomous regulatory bodies which may be established by act of Parliament to perform and exercise certain functions and powers belonging to the Executive Branch. The head of an autonomous regulatory organ is appointed by the Prime Minister or, on the proposal of the Prime Minister, by the President of the Republic for the term specified in a cardinal act.

261. Act CXXV of 2018.
262. Act XLIII of 2010.

The lawmaking authority and the extent of autonomy distinguish this kind of central agency from other central government bodies. The head of an autonomous regulatory organ may issue decrees within his or her jurisdiction and acting on the basis of authorization by legislation. He or she must report annually to the National Assembly on the activities of the autonomous regulatory organ.

576. Today, the National Media and Infocommunications Authority, the Hungarian Energy and Public Utility Regulatory Authority, the Authority for the Supervision of Regulated Activities, and the Hungarian Atomic Energy Authority are granted this administrative status.

[B] The Bodies of the Central Government Administration

577. At the highest level of central government exist the government and those other bodies which are directly subject to the government. These latter comprise the Prime Minister's Office, the Ministries, the government offices and the central offices.

578. The Prime Minister's Office is a central state administration body with special authority as the Prime Minister's administrative organization led by an administrative State Secretary. In fact, this is the administrative secretary of the PM.

579. The Ministries are central governmental bodies with special tasks and functions under the government's control, acting as the Ministers' work organizations. In Hungarian public law, only members of the government (the Ministers) have direct jurisdiction; their Ministries act with only delegated power as administrative bodies. The list of Ministries is defined by law[263] in accordance with the Fundamental Law. In 2010, the second Orbán government reduced the number of Ministries, establishing some so-called top ministries integrating several different administrative branches. From 1 January 2024, the following Ministries exist:

- Ministry of Agriculture
- Ministry of Construction and Transport
- Ministry of Culture and Innovation
- Ministry of Defence
- Ministry of Energy
- Ministry of European Union Affairs
- Ministry of Finance
- Ministry of Foreign Affairs and Trade
- Ministry of the Interior
- Ministry of Justice
- Ministry of National Economy
- Prime Minister's Cabinet Office
- Prime Minister's Office

263. Act II of 2022.

– Ministry of Public Administration and Regional Development.

580. The Prime Minister's Office plays a crucial role in the Hungarian parliamentary government, expressing the leading position of the Prime Minister. According to the official duties of the Prime Minister's Office, it provides general political coordination for the government. The Minister of the Prime Minister's Cabinet Office organizes and manages government propaganda and is referred to in day-by-day speech as 'a propaganda ministry'. He also oversees the civilian national security services.

581. The Ministers are members of the government, and they manage their own Ministries. Ministerial staff is headed by an administrative state secretary, while a political state secretary is responsible for the political representation of the Ministry. The various administrative areas belonging to the scope of responsibility of the Minister are supervised by state secretaries.

582. Ministers without portfolios do not manage separate Ministries; according to the Fundamental Law, they may be appointed to perform specific tasks determined by the government. Their work is assisted by a Ministry specified by law or by the Prime Minister's Office. At the moment, only the deputy Prime Minister is seen as such a minister, responsible for national, nationality and church policy.

583. The government offices are the Central Statistical Office and the National Intellectual Property Office. These offices are central government administrative organs having specific competences established by law and managed by the government. The direct supervision of the particular government offices is exercised by the Minister designated by the government in the relevant decree.

584. The central offices are also central government administrative bodies with special authority established by law or government decree under the authority of a Minister. There are a number of central offices performing several different tasks and functions, from market supervision to service delivery. For example, the National Research, Development and Innovation Office or the Education Authority operates in this form.

[C] The Autonomous State Administrative Agencies

585. A special group of central public administration bodies consists of the 'autonomous state administrative bodies'. In principle, their autonomous legal status reflects the intention to exempt them from the direct political control of the government; that is, to depoliticize their executive activity, for otherwise the State would gain too much influence in the management of market conditions. For this purpose, these agencies are established by law, even though they are integral parts of executive power. According to the laws establishing these authorities, they should be independent, subordinated only to the law. They cannot be instructed in their function, so they perform their tasks separately from other bodies without any external influence. Only an act of Parliament may assign a task to autonomous state administrative organs. With the exception of the Public Procurement Authority, their heads are appointed by the President of the Republic on the proposal of the Prime Minister. The autonomous state administrative agencies are the Competition Authority, the Directorate General for Audit of European Funds, the Integrity Authority, the National Authority for Data Protection and Freedom of Information, the National Election Office, the Public Procurement Authority, and the Sovereignty Protection Authority.

[D] The Law Enforcement Agencies and the National Security Services

586. For a detailed description of these organs, *see infra* in Part II, Chapters 12 and 13.

§5.02 The Territorial and Local Administrative Bodies

587. Although no administrative regions exist in Hungary, there are government offices of general competence at the county level and in the capital city, which more or less integrate the state administration bodies operating at subnational tiers. They are headed by government commissioners[264] who are appointed by the Prime Minister. Government offices exercise a number of administrative authorities at first and second instance; coordinate the operation of the various state administrative organs at territorial level; and exercise legal supervision of local authorities.

588. In the 1990s, prior to the establishment of the local government system, the previous 'unified state administration' was fragmented. The functions that were not transferred to the local authorities remained within the responsibility of the state administration, with 'deconcentrated organs' working at a territorial level and subordinate to the various line Ministries. In the 2000s, however, in parallel with the gradual weakening of democratic county self-government, the territorial state administration was integrated into the government offices working at the county level and the capital city. Nonetheless, a number of state administrative powers and duties were delegated by law to local authorities for economic and efficiency reasons. As a result of the new wave of public administration reforms after 2010, however, most of these powers have been withdrawn from local governments by state administrative organs, shifting the centre of gravity of territorial and local administration to the sphere of state administration.

589. The county government offices have 174 district-level sub-offices, and the Government Office of the capital city, Budapest, has such organs in all its twenty-three districts.

264. In 2022, the official Hungarian name of the post was changed to a pre-World War II name (*főispán*, *comes supremus* in Latin), which has no English equivalent.

590. Since the territorial integration of the subnational state administrative bodies, the various organizational units of the government offices have been under double management. For structural issues, they are led by the government commissioners, while their professional activities are directed by the relevant line Ministry.

591. Nonetheless, there are some territorial deconcentrated bodies that are not integrated into government offices. These include law enforcement agencies (police, disaster management, the territorial offices of the National Tax and Customs Office), and organs that carry out their activities in a specific geographical area (Mining Authority; Environment, Nature Protection and Water Management Supervision) which are managed directly by a line Ministry.

§5.03 The Personnel of State Administration

592. After the system change, in the course of the reorganization of the Hungarian public administration, there was a broad consensus between the new political parties on the need to establish a unified civil service system in personnel policy, the stability of which is ensured by the separation of political and administrative positions. This effort was reflected by the detachment of the political and administrative secretaries of state in the ministerial structure, and the differentiation between the political position of the mayor and the chief administrator within local governments. The original concept, on which the regulation of the civil service was based in 1992, aimed at developing a life-career model for civil servants that provides certain additional rights, pre-eminently employment security, for those who undertake extra burdens that permanent service of the state demands.

593. Although the necessity of separating political and professional positions is, in principle, still recognized by Hungarian public service law, this separation has faded in many respects in recent years. It means, on the one hand, that more and more political positions have been established which belong to the civil service in legal sense, and on the other hand, in recent years more and more administrative positions have been involved in the political spoils system, both in state administration and local government. The idea of a life-long career in the civil service was also destroyed when the conservative government came to power in 2010 and began to get significant changes in administrative staff through, chiefly in the central government bodies. When legislation permitted employers to fire any civil servant without providing reasons, the Constitutional Court quashed the law.[265] However, the Court failed to provide effective legal protection for civil servants against arbitrary dismissal, since the legislator has prescribed a mere 'loss of confidence' as a standard reason for dismissal.

594. According to the rules in force,[266] officials of the central government administration may be in a political service relationship and a government service

265. Decision 8/2011. (II. 18.) of the Constitutional Court.

266. Act CXXV of 2018. The detailed rules of the civil servants are laid down in Act CXCIX of 2011.

relationship. Under this classification, the Prime Minister, the members of the government, the State Secretaries, the commissioners of the government, the Prime Minister and the Ministers, as well as the political advisers and the cabinet chiefs are all considered political positions. The administrative state secretaries, the deputy state secretaries, the government officials of the central and territorial state administrative bodies stand in a government service relationship.

Chapter 6: The Constitutional Court

595. In theory, the Constitutional Court is the principal organ for the protection of the Fundamental Law. Most frequently, it is considered as a separate branch of power, with the major function to seek a balance among public law institutions and to preserve the rule of law. Its name is a little bit misleading. Although since the constitution-making process in 2011, the basic law has not been called a 'constitution' anymore, this organ has retained its original name. Moreover, it is not a real juridical tribunal because it is not integrated into the Judicial Branch, and a number of the usual guarantees for judicial bodies are not applied to its existence and procedures.

596. The Court belongs to the 'Kelsenian' type of constitutional tribunal, as the single judicial body of constitutional review of legal acts. The legal status of the body is defined by the Fundamental Law in its chapter on the 'State', under a separate title (Article 24) and by the Cardinal Act CLI of 2011 on the Constitutional Court (hereinafter 'the CCL').

597. The Court is seated in Budapest. It forms a separate chapter within the structure of the central budget. It is a safeguard of its financial autonomy that the Court prepares its own budgetary proposal, and the government submits it to Parliament without changes as part of the bill on the annual state budget. Moreover, the budget of the Constitutional Court may not be less than in the previous year.

§6.01 A Short History of the Court

598. Before 1990, constitutional review had no tradition in Hungary. Although a 'Council of Constitutional Law' was set up in 1983, it had no power to annul unconstitutional statutes. The Constitutional Court was one of the new institutions established by the constitutional amendment of 1989. During the roundtable negotiations, both sides saw it as a guarantee for democracy, and since then, nomination to it has always been a complicated political bargaining process.

599. Distrust of judges by the 'Communist Party-State' and political mistrust between the negotiating parties during the transition period led to establishing an independent constitutional court with wide-ranging responsibilities. Basically, the Court was established on the pattern of the German *Bundesverfassungsgericht,* [267] establishing a 'European' model of a centralized system of constitutional review. Thus, the main task of the Constitutional Court was the *ex post* judicial review of legal rules. The regulation opened the way for everybody to lodge any case before the Court, as all petitions were filed without any personal interest or time limit

267. Gábor Halmai, *The Hungarian Approach to Constitutional Review: The End of Activism? The First Decade of the Hungarian Constitutional Court,* in Constitutional Justice, East and West. Democratic Legitimacy and Constitutional Courts in Post-Communist Europe in a Comparative Perspective 195–208 (Wojciech Sadurski ed., Kluwer Law International 2002).

(*actio popularis*). Owing to this unlimited access to the Court, sooner or later virtually all important laws landed before this body. In certain areas, *ex ante* examination of the constitutionality of legal acts (e.g., international treaties) also fell within the competence of the Court, which was also empowered to investigate conflicts between international treaties and national law. 'Abstract constitutional interpretation' was also a specific competence of the Court, by which the body, on the proposal of the Head of State or the government, could explain in detail and with *erga omnes* effect the meaning and the constitutional requirements of any provision of the basic law. The Court decided on jurisdictional disputes between public authorities and on individual constitutional complaints too; but in fact, the latter represented an indirect judicial review of statutes on which individual judicial decisions were based. Similarly, any ordinary court could turn to the Constitutional Court, initiating a concrete constitutional review of the legal rules relevant to the case before them.

600. After the landslide victory of Fidesz and its satellite coalition partner, the Christian Democrats, in the general elections of 2010, the new government coalition, based on its constitution-making parliamentary majority, changed significantly the operation of the Constitutional Court. One of the most important changes was to transform the way of nominating members of the Court. Since 1990, this system was based on parity between the government and opposition parties, so each candidate had to gain the support of both sides. According to the new rules, a parliamentary committee, composed in proportion to the members of the parties represented in Parliament, now proposes candidates who are elected by Parliament with a qualified majority of two-thirds of MPs. In this way, the Fidesz government, enjoying a parliamentary majority since autumn of 2010 (with only one short interruption), has been able to appoint solely its own people to the Constitutional Court. The number of constitutional judges was increased from eleven to fifteen. The term of office of the judges has been extended from nine to twelve years, but in parallel, the possibility of their re-election has been abolished. In addition, the Fundamental Law has empowered Parliament to elect the President of the Court (before that, he or she was elected by the judges themselves).

601. Besides these changes, the jurisdiction of the Court was also transformed. After the Constitutional Court had declared unconstitutional and annulled a law that imposed with retroactive effect a 98% tax on extremely high severance payments,[268] the government majority immediately curtailed the Court's most important power of constitutional review. Since then, the Court has been able to review and annul public finance legislation only in exceptional cases. Although this is theoretically only a provisional restriction of the Court's power, since it lasts only as long as the state debt exceeds half of GDP, this jurisdictional hurdle will hardly be overcome in the foreseeable future. In addition, the *actio popularis* (everybody's right, even without any personal interest, to turn to the Court to review the constitutionality of a statute) has been abolished, though it was the most effective tool to launch judicial review proceedings in constitutionally controversial cases for a long

268. Decision 184/2010. (X. 28.) of the Constitutional Court.

time. Nevertheless, the Constitutional Court has been compensated to a degree for the loss of its fundamental power: the new Constitution, following the German model, introduced the politically neutral institution of individual constitutional complaint. Finally, the Fourth Amendment to the Fundamental Law in March 2013 repealed all Constitutional Court rulings prior to the entry into force of the new Fundamental Law.[269]

§6.02 THE ORGANIZATION OF THE COURT

602. The Constitutional Court consists of fifteen members. According to the CCL, the members of the Court are 'independent, subordinated only to the Fundamental Law and acts'. Constitutional judges may be elected from those citizens who have no criminal record and have the right to vote in general elections. The CCL also requires professional qualifications for the membership. Thus, a member of the Court must have a law degree, and must be an outstanding academic or practising lawyer. While the former condition is met by full university professors or doctors of the Hungarian Academy of Sciences, the latter is satisfied by those lawyers who have at least twenty years of professional work experience. At the time of their election, the judges have to be at least 45 years old, but not more than 70 years of age. Nevertheless, in contrast with earlier regulations, they may complete the remainder of their term of office after reaching the age of 70 years. It is to be noted that in some cases, mainly after 2010, lack of the desired professional work experience did not prevent certain candidates from being elected.

603. The judges are nominated by a parliamentary committee, the composition of which reflects the parliamentary representation of the parties. The members of the Constitutional Court, proposed by the nomination committee, are elected by a two-thirds majority in the National Assembly. After 2010, the government parties unscrupulously exploited their qualified parliamentary majority: all constitutional judges have been selected – except three judges whose candidature was supported by an opposition party in 2016 – and elected by the votes of their party MPs. The change in the nomination system has deeply affected the composition of the Court in the sense that admittedly politically involved persons – e.g., former MPs and ministers – could get appointed to the body.

604. The term of office of constitutional judges is twelve years. After the expiry of this time, they may not be re-elected. In practice, the term of office of individual judges expires at different times. Pursuant to the CCL, Parliament must elect a new member of the Court within thirty days prior to the expiry of the term of office of his/her predecessor in order to ensure the continuity of the body.

269. For details, *see* Fruzsina Gárdos-Orosz & Kinga Zakariás, Organisational, Functional and Procedural Changes of the Hungarian Constitutional Court 1990–2020, in *The Main Lines of the Jurisprudence of the Hungarian Constitutional Court. 30 Case Studies from the 30 Years of the Constitutional Court (1990 to 2020)* (Fruzsina Gárdos-Orosz and Kinga Zakariás eds, Nomos 2022).

605. The independence of judges and the integrity of the Court are protected by wide-ranging conflict of interest rules and immunity. The members of government, the party leaders or those who are leading state officials may become constitutional judges only four years after leaving office.

606. The membership of the Court is incompatible with any other position or mandate with public authorities, social organizations, or any political or economic position, and with any other paid activity, with the exception of scientific, educational and artistic activities.

607. The personal integrity of constitutional judges is also protected by an immunity. The members of the Court are not accountable during or after their term of office for activities carried out as constitutional judges. It means that they are exempt from any legal or administrative procedures in relation to their judicial opinions. The only exception to this rule is the 'misuse of information' (being disclosure of classified state secrets, libel, defamation, and any other civil law liability for violating personality rights).

608. Besides immunity, constitutional judges are also protected by inviolability. Criminal or infraction proceedings may only be launched against the members of the Constitutional Court with the prior consent of the Court. They may be taken into custody only if caught in the act of a criminal offence. The suspension of immunity must be requested by the Prosecutor General. If the Court suspends the immunity of a judge, this decision applies only to the case for which the motion has been submitted.

609. Membership in the Constitutional Court terminates if the term of office of the judge expires. Personal reasons, death, resignation, incompatibility, ineligibility, dismissal or exclusion may also end the mandate of a member.

610. The judge may resign by way of a written statement submitted to the President of the Court. It does not need any approval or formal acceptance.

611. The plenary session of the Court may declare the incompatibility of a member. In this case, the judge concerned must eliminate the cause of conflict of interest within ten days; otherwise, the Court may issue a decision terminating the mandate of the respective member in full session. So far, no such case has been raised; the judges concerned have resigned from membership in the Court where they were appointed or elected to another office that created a conflict of interest.

612. The Court may dismiss a member if he or she is not able to perform his/her duties for reasons that are beyond his or her control. The mandate of a member of the Court may also be terminated by exclusion if this judge fails to perform his or her duties for reasons within his or her control or has become 'unworthy' of his or her office. This is the case where a judge:

– is publicly prosecuted and held, by final judgment, to have intentionally committed a crime;
– has not participated in the work of the Constitutional Court for one year for reasons imputable to him or her; or
– has intentionally failed to meet his or her obligations to make a declaration of assets or has intentionally made a false declaration on important data or facts in his or her declaration of assets.

613. Until now, no such exclusion has occurred. It is to be noted that the constitutionality of this possibility is doubtful. There is no legal remedy against such a decision of the plenary session of the Constitutional Court.

614. If the mandate of a constitutional judge expires, the vacancy must be filled by Parliament within the deadline set by law. In the past, the replacement of the judges sometimes suffered a significant delay when the parties were unable to agree on candidates. In fact, the nomination process quite soon was over-politicized, and only a few truly consensual candidates were found. Instead, before 2010, there was a tacit agreement between the government and opposition parties that they nominate the judges alternately, and support each other's candidates in the National Assembly.

615. The President of the Constitutional Court is elected by Parliament, with a two-thirds majority of all MPs, to chair the body until the expiry of his or her term of office as a judge of the Court. Among other things, the President of the Court coordinates the activities of the Court, convokes and presides over its plenary sessions, determining the scheduling and agenda of these sessions. However, his or her most important power is to appoint rapporteurs for preparing the Court's decisions in the pending cases. The President is assisted in his or her work by a vice president who is, on the proposal of the President, elected by the plenary session of the Constitutional Court from among its own members.

§6.03 The Powers and Duties of the Constitutional Court

[A] *Ex Ante* Constitutional Review

616. The Court may carry out preliminary norm control in so far as it may examine the conformity of an act of Parliament, passed but not promulgated, at the request of Parliament or the President of the Republic. In the first case, the proponent of the original bill (even before the final vote), the government (idem), or the Speaker of Parliament (after passing the Bill) may choose to send the law to the Constitutional Court for a preliminary constitutional review. The same procedure of the Court may also be initiated by the Head of State if he or she considers the law adopted (or some of its provisions) to be contrary to the Fundamental Law.

617. The Parliamentary Resolution on Standing Orders of the National Assembly may also be reviewed by the Court at the request of the Parliament still before its promulgation, as well as international treaties (before acknowledgement of their binding force), provided that the Head of State or the government, in their scope of authority, requests the Constitutional Court to carry out a preliminary review of the conformity of the respective international treaty or of its provisions with the Fundamental Law.

618. A special kind of preliminary norm control is the *ex ante* review of a new Constitution or amendments to the Fundamental Law. After the Fourth Amendment to the Fundamental Law, long political and professional disputes began on the issue of whether there were any limitations on the National Assembly's constitutional amending power. The Fourth Amendment in 2013 closed this debate, clarifying that the Constitutional Court may review a new Constitution or amendment of the current Fundamental Law only in relation to the procedural requirements laid down in the Fundamental Law for its making and promulgation. Such examination may be initiated by the Head of State before signing and promulgating the new Constitution or the amendment of the Fundamental Law. If the Court finds that the procedural rules contained in the Fundamental Law have been violated, the National Assembly must debate again the new Constitution or constitutional amendment in an attempt to adopt it again complying with the procedural requirements. The same review may be also initiated by the government, one-fourth of MPs, the President of the *Kúria*, the Prosecutor General or the Commissioner for Fundamental Rights within thirty days of promulgation. In this case, however, if the Court declares procedural non-compliance, it annuls the new constitutional text. It is to be noted that in all these cases, the Constitutional Court has to render its decision with priority, and in any event within thirty days at the latest.

619. In all preliminary control cases, the Court must decide on the petition within thirty days.

[B] *Ex Post* Constitutional Review

620. The Constitutional Court reviews the conformity of any legal regulations with the Fundamental Law on the petition of the government, at least one-fourth of MPs, the President of the *Kúria*, the Prosecutor General or the Commissioner for Fundamental Rights.

621. However, the Constitutional Court may not review and annul the constitutionality of acts on the central budget, the implementation of the central budget, central taxes, duties and contributions, customs duties and the central conditions for local taxes, unless the procedural requirements laid down in the Fundamental Law for the making and promulgation of those acts have not been respected, or the rights to life and human dignity, to the protection of personal data, to freedom of thought, conscience and religion, or the rights related to Hungarian citizenship have been violated. The restriction is only provisional because it exists as long as the state debt exceeds half of GDP. However, having regard to the fact that the level of state debt has always significantly exceeded half of GDP since the introduction of this restriction, this kind of jurisdictional limitation seems to be long-standing.[270]

622. The withdrawal of public finance laws from constitutional control has triggered heavy criticism not only in Hungarian academic literature but also among international organizations as well, because it gives, paradoxically, constitutional empowerment to unconstitutional economic government. The budgetary and financial power of the legislature (or, in an indirect way, the government majority) is really unlimited since the method for the calculation of the state debt and GDP is determined by law (i.e., by Parliament). Moreover, unconstitutional financial legislation may not be invalidated even after that the restriction will have ceased if those acts entered into force in a period when the state debt exceeded half of GDP.

623. In all these cases, if the Constitutional Court finds that the legal rule under review is contrary to the Fundamental Law, it may repeal the norm or its unconstitutional provisions.

[C] Constitutional Complaint

624. The Fundamental Law enables any citizen and organization to submit a constitutional complaint to the Court if his or her rights have been violated. The new Constitution and the CCL have extended the possibilities of the people or organizations affected to seek redress for grievances related to their fundamental rights. A constitutional complaint may be lodged if:

- the application of a legal regulation contrary to the Fundamental Law in a judicial proceeding violates any right entrenched in the Constitution;
- by exception, due to the application of a legal provision contrary to the Fundamental Law, constitutional rights were violated directly without a judicial decision; or
- a judicial decision itself violates any rights laid down by the Fundamental Law.

625. The submission of a constitutional complaint has legal preconditions. Only those whose rights have been violated directly are entitled to pursue a complaint, and if they have exhausted all possibilities for a remedy or no legal remedy was possible at all. Exceptionally, it is possible to file a constitutional complaint if a constitutional right was violated without a judicial decision, directly by the law, or no legal remedy is provided for. Constitutional complaints may be submitted in writing, within sixty days of receipt of the contested decision, or, in case of unconstitutional legal norms, within 180 days of the entry into force of the legal regulation.

626. As to the nature of the constitutional complaint, it is not clear whether this instrument is a genuine legal remedy or not. First, the Court may conduct a preliminary admissibility review of complaints: the CCL empowers the body to refuse

270. Since the introduction of this rule, no public finance law has been reviewed by the Court.

complaints if it finds that the alleged conflict with the Fundamental Law does not affect significantly the contested judicial decision, or the case does not raise constitutional law issues of fundamental importance. Second, the Court is not bound by any deadline for its ruling, even though the CCL prescribes that it should decide on constitutional complaints 'within a reasonable time'. Despite these circumstances, the ECtHR considered the constitutional complaint as an effective legal remedy.[271]

627. In 2019, Parliament had authorized also the public bodies to submit constitutional complaints to the Court if their 'rights' or competences were violated by an unconstitutional judicial decision, but this possibility was abolished in 2023 due to the European Commission's rule of law requirements.

[D] Concrete Constitutional Review (Norm Control in Concrete Cases)

628. If a judge, in the course of adjudicating a concrete case, is bound to apply a legal regulation that he or she perceives to be contrary to the Fundamental Law, the judge may then suspend the proceedings and submit a petition to declare the unconstitutionality of that legal regulation (or a provision thereof). In such cases, the proceedings may be continued only after the decision of the Constitutional Court on the issue.

[E] Examination of Conflicts Between Domestic Law and International Treaties

629. The Fundamental Law guarantees the implementation and prevalence of generally recognized principles of international law and international obligations assumed by Hungary and their primacy over domestic law. In order to comply with these international law obligations, the Constitution orders that Hungarian law must be in conformity with international law. The institutional guarantee of this principle is the Constitutional Court.

630. The Court may examine the harmony between domestic and international law on petition or ex officio. Such a proceeding may be requested by one-quarter of MPs, the government, the President of the *Kúria*, the Prosecutor General or the Commissioner for Fundamental Rights. In addition, judges may suspend proceedings before them if, in the course of adjudicating a case, they would have to apply a legal regulation that they perceive to be contrary to an international treaty.

[F] Resolving Jurisdictional Conflicts

631. The Constitutional Court may be the arbiter of the jurisdictional disputes between public authorities. If any conflict of jurisdiction arises between state

271. ECHR Case of *Szalontay v. Hungary*, Application No. 71327/13 (2019).

organs, either party may request the Court to resolve the conflict based on the interpretation of the Fundamental Law. In this procedure, the Court determines which public authority has competence in the disputed case and appoints the organ obliged to proceed. This power does not extend to jurisdictional disputes between courts; those disputes are resolved by the *Kúria* (the Supreme Court).

[G] 'Abstract' Constitutional Interpretation

632. In contrast with the US 'decentralized' model of judicial review, the Hungarian system of constitutional control covers abstract constitutional interpretation. Acting under this authority, and at the request of the public authorities entitled, the Court may interpret constitutional provisions even without a particular legal dispute before it. In doing so, the Court determines what constitutional requirements derive from a particular constitutional provision. This proceeding may be requested by Parliament or its standing committees, the President of the Republic, the government or the Commissioner of the Fundamental Rights.

633. According to the practice of the Constitutional Court, the Court gives an authoritative interpretation of the provisions of the Fundamental Law when the petition relates to a concrete constitutional issue, provided that the interpretation can be directly deduced from the Constitution.

634. As a result of such a procedure, the Court may issue an authoritative interpretation of the constitutional text. And even if non-compliance of this kind of constitutional interpretation does not have any specific sanction, any different approach is risky since the Court will likely follow its own interpretation in the future.

[H] Other Competences

635. The Constitutional Court has some other duties and powers which are only rarely exercised, or have only little practical importance.

636. The Court is entitled to examine parliamentary resolutions ordering or dismissing a referendum with regard to its conformity with the Fundamental Law. However, this power is strictly limited, inasmuch as the Constitutional Court may not examine the constitutionality of the referendum question(s) or its authentication.

637. The Court may also investigate decisions of the National Assembly concerning the acknowledgement of established churches. This is not a full power either because the Court may examine only the procedural fairness of parliamentary decision-making, without any examination of the merits of the case.

638. The Court has the power to conduct impeachment proceedings against the Head of State. This competence may be triggered by a parliamentary resolution referring to the wilful violation of the Fundamental Law or any act of Parliament in connection with the exercise of the President's official functions or an intentional commission of a criminal offence. The Constitutional Court must examine both the procedural issues and the merits of the impeachment proceedings. In doing so, the Court considers the nature of the alleged violation under examination, by means of evidence in accordance with the provisions of the Criminal or the Civil Code. As a result of this proceeding, the Court may remove the Head of State from his or her office, or may terminate the proceedings.

639. It is to be noted that, in some cases, the Constitutional Court has only an advisory or opinion-making role. Thus, on the motion of the government, the Court must give an opinion in principle on whether the operation of the representative bodies of local governments and nationality self-governments is contrary to the Fundamental Law or not. This is a precondition for Parliament to dissolve the local government if it is operating in an unconstitutional way. Also, the Constitutional Court may opine on whether the operation of a religious community is contrary to the Constitution or not. Such a proceeding may be initiated by the government (in case of an acknowledged church) or by a court (where other religious communities are concerned).

§6.04 Legal Effects of the Constitutional Court Rulings

640. In general, the Constitutional Court's rulings are binding on everyone. The Court establishes the applicable legal consequences within the framework of the Fundamental Law. However, the Court, in particular in recent years, has failed in some important cases to determine the legal consequences of its decisions. Thus, for example, it ineffectively struck down the law which dismissed a number of judges on the basis of a forced retirement because its decision did not contain any form of legal remedy, so that the judges removed did not obtain real legal protection in this way.[272] Or when the Court found that the legislation of 2011 that severely tightened the system of disability benefits was constitutionally objectionable, it did not provide for a remedy for the people aggrieved, but merely declared a constitutional omission and ordered Parliament to supplement the missing legal guarantees within a specified period of time for the future.[273]

641. If the Court declares that one or more legislative provisions of a new law to be unconstitutional, those provisions may not be promulgated. When the Court declares a legislative omission, it calls upon Parliament to perform its legislative task, setting also a deadline until when the National Assembly has to comply with its obligation. The lawmaker's task is considered as an omission when:

– the lawmaker fails to perform a task deriving from an international treaty;

---

272. Decision 33/2012. (VII. 17.) of the Constitutional Court.
273. Decision 21/2018. (XI. 14.) of the Constitutional Court.

- a legal regulation was not adopted in spite of the fact that the lawmaker's task derives from explicit authorization by law; or
- the essential content of the legal regulation that can be derived from the Fundamental Law is incomplete.

642. In the cases when the Constitutional Court finds that an international treaty is contrary to the Fundamental Law, the binding force of the agreement may not be recognized until such conflict with the Fundamental Law is eliminated. Furthermore, the Fundamental Law or the amendment to the Fundamental Law as a result of a constitution-making process may not be promulgated if the Constitutional Court, in the framework of *ex ante* constitutional review, declares that the procedural requirements of constitution-making were not met.

643. When the Constitutional Court, as a result of a constitutional complaint procedure, invalidates final judgment in a criminal case, it orders the review of the criminal proceedings.

644. There is no remedy against the Court's decisions. Yet, because the government coalition has had a constitution-making majority in Parliament since 2010 (between 2010 and 2015, and since 2018), the legislative power has been able to supersede the Court's decisions – and in many cases it has not hesitated to do so.

§6.05 Working Rules

645. The Constitutional Court's proceedings are based on the petitions of authorized entities. The petitions must contain explicit requests. The Court only rarely proceeds ex officio examining the harmony between domestic law and international treaties.

646. The Court decides in plenary sessions, in panels, or acting through a single judge. The plenary session of the Constitutional Court consists of all members of the Court. It needs a quorum of at least two-thirds of the constitutional judges, including the President or, if the President is unavailable, the Vice President.

647. The Constitutional Court takes its decisions basically on the basis of the documents at its disposal, but may order a hearing of the petitioner in person or a third party, or may invite them to make a declaration.

648. The Court has three five-member panels which may conduct proceedings in all cases that are not assigned to the plenary session's competence by the law or by the Constitutional Court's Rules of Procedure. However, the Court must decide in plenary session on the annulment of an act of Parliament that is contrary to the Fundamental Law or to an international treaty.

649. Unless provided for otherwise by the CCL, the plenary session passes its decisions by open ballot, by a majority of votes and without abstention. In case of an equality of votes, the President has the casting vote. The Court is obliged to give detailed reasoning for its decisions. In doing so, the constitutional judges who support the merits of the Court's decision are entitled to file concurrent opinions and to attach them to the rulings, while those members who do not agree with the majority decision may prepare dissenting opinions, and also have the right to publish them together with the final decision. The Constitutional Court may order that its decision be announced in public.

650. As a primary rule, the proceedings of the Constitutional Court are free of charge, and they are not be public, unless the CCL provides otherwise.

§6.06 The Interpretative Practice of the Court

651. From 1990 on, the Constitutional Court established a rich and extensive jurisprudence; virtually, it had dealt with almost all classical issues as is usual in those Western countries which have much longer constitutional traditions. Undoubtedly, the Court reached a pre-eminent position in the Hungarian constitutional system and performed a major role in elaborating and standardizing the living constitutional law. It is a commonly shared view among scholars that, in the first nine years of its operation, the Court followed a strongly 'activist' practice, relating both to its jurisdiction and to interpretive practice. In Hungarian literature, the term 'jurisdictional activism' refers to the efforts of the Court to extend its powers, while 'interpretive activism' means the practice that relies on extra-constitutional sources in the Court's reasoning.[274] The Court regarded the Constitution as a holistic unity of principles and rules. This approach paved the way for the concept of the 'invisible constitution', even if it emerged first in a concurring opinion of the first President of the Court, László Sólyom. According to this theory, the invisible constitution embraces all the background or underlying principles that are necessary to understand the written constitution and makes a coherent body of constitutional law. It is to be noted that in the post-Sólyom era, the Court began to change its earlier activism, moving in a self-restraining direction. This image of moderate judicial behaviour was strengthened with the landmark decisions having already been rendered earlier and the Court frequently now seeking middle-of-the-road solutions in subsequent hard cases. But the body, even if in a quiet way, continued its eclectic interpretive practice and based its jurisprudence largely on earlier decisions.[275]

652. The behaviour of the Sólyom Court was basically influenced by the dispute resolution approach of constitutional review, shared by the majority of the first

274. Halmai, *supra* n. 269, 189–211; Herman Schwartz, *The Struggle for Constitutional Justice in Post-Communist Europe* 87–108 (The University of Chicago Press 2000).
275. Zoltán Szente, *The Interpretive Practice of the Hungarian Constitutional Court: A Critical View*, 14(8) Ger. L.J. (2013) 1596.

bench of the Court. According to this view, the Court should decide all constitutional controversies which were submitted to it, rather than escape from the responsibility of the ultimate decision. The Court tenaciously persisted in this view throughout its workings.

653. There is good reason to think that this activism was, to a degree, unavoidable; just as every attempt between 1990 and 2011 to make a new constitution proved to be unsuccessful, the legislature was not able to resolve certain constitutional conflicts, and it failed also to correct or modernize those basic institutions the regulation of which demanded a qualified majority in Parliament. Thus, the Court was the only institution to have enough power to solve the great constitutional (and, often, political) conflicts at a time when the institutional setting was paralysed. The Court did not hesitate to play this role, since, from the very beginning of its existence, the Court has made clear that the general and abstract concepts of the Constitution are not dead letters but real and living rules, and it is the primary task of the Court to determine and set out the exact content of these provisions from case to case.

654. Although the Court's jurisprudence became more moderate or deferential from the late 1990s, the body continued to base its practice on its landmark decisions from the early 1990s. A substantial change was made by the Fundamental Law of 2011, probably based on the earlier experience of judicial activism. The ethos of the Court as a politically neutral institution has recently been questioned since the selection method of the judges changed in 2010, and since then, the government majority has been able to pack the Court. As a result, the rightist government coalition, enjoying its two-thirds parliamentary majority between 2010 and 2015 and after 2018, has been able to appoint solely its own people to the Constitutional Court. Thus, since November 2016, the Court has been composed exclusively of those members who were selected or approved by the government parties. As a consequence of this selection method, the Court is composed of constitutional judges who are loyal to the government majority. This was possible because the CCL contains a 'cooling off period' of only four years for leading officials of political parties as well as members of the government before they can be elected as judges to the Constitutional Court. But this incompatibility rule does not extend to party membership or parliamentary mandates, which means that even front-runner party politicians or backbenchers cannot be kept removed from the Court.

655. Apart from matters of composition, also the major constitutional function of the Court has changed since 2010. Originally, the major responsibility of the Constitutional Court was the constitutional review of legal norms, which competence – in different cases – extended to both *ex ante* and *ex post* control of normative acts. Since the changes in the legal status of the Court in 2011–2012, in particular as a result of the abolishment of the *action popularis* and the restriction of the review power, the focus of the Court's activity shifted from constitutional review of lawmaking to a check on the judicial power.[276]

656. As to the methods of constitutional interpretation applied, the Hungarian Constitutional Court has never elaborated a principled interpretive practice since its establishment. It has always applied different interpretive methodologies, even to cases of the same or similar nature, without any coherent legal philosophy or consistent judicial policy. The Court's jurisprudence can be characterized as an ever-changing, eclectic interpretive practice.[277] Nevertheless, while the Court quite frequently appealed to extra-constitutional sources in the 1990s, constitutional adjudication of the last decades is much more deferential to legislative intent. The focal points of constitutional interpretation have also changed.[278] Whereas in the formative years of the Constitutional Court, the values of human dignity and the rule of law had a crucial role in the course of constitutional adjudication, nowadays, the 'achievements of the historical constitution' and constitutional identity are the core values.

657. The importance of the Court has drastically reduced in the last decade, and the body nowadays has much more of a legitimizing than a counterbalancing role towards the legislative power. Although the Hungarian Constitutional Court has always operated in a highly politicized way, the fact that its composition is determined exclusively by the governing parties (which, moreover, have a constitution-making majority in Parliament) has fundamentally transformed the character of the Court from being the supreme guardian of the Constitution, the counterweight of the legislative and executive powers, to a submissive servant and legitimizer of the government's will.[279] Apart from erroneous individual decisions and the decline in the level of legal protections and constitutional standards, the most serious criticism of the Constitutional Court is that it has failed to prevent the systematic erosion of the rule of law after 2010.[280]

---

276. *See* Fruzsina Gárdos-Orosz, *The Hungarian Constitutional Court in Transition — From Actio Popularis to Constitutional Complaint,* 53(4) Acta Juridica Hun., Hun. J. Leg. Stud. 302–315 (2012).
277. Szente, *supra* n. 278, 1591.
278. Fruzsina Gárdos-Orosz, Constitutional Interpretation under the New Fundamental Law of Hungary, in *Populist Challenges to Constitutional Interpretation in Europe and Beyond* (Fruzsina Gárdos-Orosz and Zoltán Szente eds, Routledge, 2021).
279. Nóra Chronowski, *The Post-2010 'Democratic Rule of Law' Practice of the Hungarian Constitutional Court under a Rule by Law Governance,* 61(2) Acta Juridica Hun. J. Leg. Stud. (2020); Nóra Chronowski et al., *The Hungarian Constitutional Court and the Abusive Constitutionalism,* 7 MTA Law Working Papers (2022).
280. For more details, *see* Zoltán Szente, *From Guarding the Constitution to Serving Politics: The Decline of the Hungarian Constitutional Court,* in *Constitutionality of Law Without a Constitutional Court: A View from Europe* (Miroslaw Granat ed., Routledge, 2023).

Chapter 7: The Judiciary

658. The administration of justice is the monopoly of the Judicial Branch: litigation can be decided only by courts. The most important sources of the legal status of the courts are the chapter on 'Courts' (Articles 25–28) of the Fundamental Law, the Act CLXI of 2011 on the Organisation and Administration of Courts, and the Act CLXII of 2011 on the Legal Status and Remuneration of Judges. According to the Constitution, courts administer justice, deciding on criminal matters, civil disputes and other matters specified by law. Courts are the main institutions of the application of law.

659. The judiciary has traditionally been regarded as an independent branch of state power in Hungary since the courts were separated from the Executive Branch in the second half of the nineteenth century. During the socialist regime, courts were only partially independent because the influence of the state party extended to the activity of courts and to the personnel of the judiciary. The principle of the unity of state power did not recognize the judiciary as an independent branch of power, which is well expressed by the former constitutional law according to which judges could be recalled[281] (after 1972 only for reasons set by law); the President of the Supreme Court was accountable to Parliament, and the Members of Parliament could address interpellations to him or her.[282] During that whole period, the Minister of Justice was charged with the administration of courts. After the collapse of Communist rule, during the democratic transition, it was a centrepiece of institutional change and a particularly important objective to rebuild the organizational system of the judiciary and to guarantee judicial independence.

§7.01 The Principle of Judicial Independence

660. From a constitutional point of view, judicial independence is the most important principle for the functioning of the courts. Judicial independence has an institutional and a personal aspect. As to the former, the judiciary is a separate branch of government, one which is independent of the other two traditional branches, the legislative and the executive. The courts act independently; no other body can supervise their jurisprudence. Within certain limits, even individual courts are independent of each other. As for the personal independence of judges, the Fundamental Law contains only a few guarantees of this principle. Thus, Article 26 declares that judges must be independent and only subordinated to laws, and they cannot be instructed in relation to their judicial activities. In addition, '[j]udges may only be removed from office for the reasons and in a procedure specified in a cardinal act'. They may not be members of political parties or engage in political activities. Besides these, the manner of judicial appointments is also a constitutional guarantee for independence because only the President of the Republic may appoint judges as provided for by a cardinal act.

281. Art. 39 s. (1) of Act XX of 1949 (on the Constitution of the People's Republic of Hungary).
282. Art. 27 of Act I of 1972 (on the amendment of the Constitution).

661. Before 2012, when all its previous judgments were repealed, the Constitutional Court in several decisions tried to explain the content of the guarantees of judicial independence. Thus, it stressed that 'the peculiarity of the judiciary is that, against the other two "political" powers, they are permanent and neutral'.[283] In addition, it is an unconditional requirement that judicial adjudication must be independent of any external influence, and 'it is eventually under an absolute constitutional protection'.[284] However, judicial independence does not mean unlimited judicial power: courts are also subject to law.[285]

662. The exclusive power of the courts to decide litigation includes the duty of courts to provide legal protection for the parties in cases that fall under their jurisdiction.[286]

663. The courts' monopoly of adjudicating civil, criminal, administrative and labour disputes is not violated if an act of Parliament empowers the parties to agree that in case of such disputes, they may have recourse to a court abroad or arbitration.[287]

§7.02 The Organizational System of Judiciary

[A] Ordinary Courts

664. Until 1997, the judicial branch was organized as a three-tier system, with local, county-level courts (including the Metropolitan Court of Budapest) and the Supreme Court. In that year, as a part of the judicial reforms, a fourth tier was introduced at the regional level in order to ease the heavy caseload of the Supreme Court and to allow it to spend more energy on ensuring the uniformity of law application by the courts.

665. Today, the judicial system consists of ordinary courts that have four levels, which are specified by law, rather than the Constitution.

666. Most of the cases are decided at first instance by district courts (*járásbíróságok*) having a general jurisdiction. 108 such courts exist in the countryside, while there are six first-level courts in the capital city, Budapest. Each of them is led by a president of the court.

667. In total, twenty second instance courts (*törvényszékek*) work at the county level and in the capital. They are appellate courts in cases when the district courts have decided in first instance, but under certain circumstances, legal disputes may

283. Decision 38/1993. (VI. 11.) of the Constitutional Court.
284. Decision 117/1994. (III. 29.) of the Constitutional Court.
285. Decision 19/1999. (VI. 25.) of the Constitutional Court.
286. Decision 17/1994. (III. 29.) of the Constitutional Court.
287. Decision 1180/B/1990 of the Constitutional Court.

directly go to these courts, and in these cases, they act as courts of first instance. Procedural laws (the Code of Civil Procedure, the Code of Administrative Procedure and the Act on Criminal Proceeding) determine the scope of these matters due to their great importance (based on the large amounts at issue or the nature of the respective legal dispute). There are 'colleges' in all of them specialized to hear civil, criminal and economic, as well as administrative and labour cases. These courts operate in collegial bodies (in panels and sections).

668. There are also five regional courts of appeal (located in Budapest, Debrecen, Győr, Pécs and Szeged) which hear appeals from the judgments of the second instance courts; but, exceptionally, they also hear cases in the first instance where it is prescribed by law (like in electoral cases). Their area of jurisdiction embraces several counties.

669. The *Kúria* is the highest judicial body, seated in Budapest. One of its basic functions is to ensure that courts apply the law in a uniform way. For this purpose, the *Kúria* may issue so-called uniformity resolutions (*jogegységi határozat*) which are binding on all courts. The President and his or her deputy, the leaders of colleges of the regional benches, the President of the National Office for the Judiciary and the Prosecutor General may initiate the standardization procedure which can lead to the adoption of such a resolution. For the same purpose, a new institution, the so-called legal unity complaint (*jogegységi panasz*), was introduced in 2020. In this procedure, the final decisions of the *Kúria* may be challenged before a special council of the Supreme Court on the grounds that the Court in the case deviated from a previously made and published judgment of its own.

670. In order to ensure the uniform application of law, it continuously examines judicial practice. Besides that, the *Kúria* decides on the appeals filed against the judgments of the lower courts (in cases specified by law), and hears motions for extraordinary review. Since 2011, the *Kúria* is in charge of judicial review of the legality of local government decrees. This task is performed by a separate 'Local Government Council' of the Supreme Court. It is to be noted, however, that the constitutional review of local decrees has remained a competence of the Constitutional Court.

671. The *Kúria* has three departments: criminal, civil and administrative-labour law. Each department has various chambers hearing appellate cases and adopting uniformity resolutions. The President of the *Kúria* is elected by Parliament with a two-thirds majority vote on the recommendation of the President of the Republic. He or she is elected from among the judges who have been judges for at least five years.

672. It is worth noting that the Fundamental Law enables the legislature to establish a 'separate court' 'for specific groups of cases' (Article 25 section (4)). This mysterious provision originates from the original version of the Communist Constitution of 1949, and has survived all constitutional revisions. And, although there have been precedents of creating special courts for certain groups of cases (e.g., the establishment of the administrative and labour courts), these have always taken place directly by the Constitution itself.

673. Administrative disputes are resolved also by the ordinary courts. Originally, judicial review of administrative acts arose out of a Constitutional Court's ruling in which the Court in 1990 declared it unconstitutional that no judicial protection was provided against non-appealable administrative decisions.[288] As a result, the jurisdiction of ordinary courts was extended to cover judicial review of such administrative acts. Since then, all administrative decisions, contracts with public bodies and the administrative bodies' failure to act may be challenged before courts by the parties affected. In 2013, specialized administrative and labour courts were set up at county level to decide administrative disputes at first instance, but after that the reform of administrative courts had been withdrawn (*see infra* §7.03, [E] in this Chapter), these special courts were abolished, and have since been replaced in the first instance by some county-level general courts in these cases.

[B] The Administration of the Courts

674. Since the democratic transition in 1989–1990, three different judicial models have been used. Until 1997, the Minister of Justice was responsible for the administration of the judiciary. However, the judicial reforms of that year introduced a new system of court management based on judicial self-government. In this model, a 'National Judicial Council' (*Országos Igazságszolgáltatási Tanács*) was set up as the central organ of judicial administration. The Council was composed of fifteen members of which two-thirds were judges elected by the assembly of judicial delegates and chaired by the President of the Supreme Court. The rest were external members representing the political branches (the Minister of Justice and two Members of Parliament) and the legal profession (the Prosecutor General and the President of the Hungarian Bar Association). However, this model did not live up to expectations since most members of the Council were leaders of county-level courts, and they represented corporate interests at the expense of transparency and accountability of the judiciary.

675. Nevertheless, when it was decided that the central administration of courts would be transformed, the lawmaker wanted to preserve the principle of judicial self-government. The new system was introduced in 2012, interrupting the mandate of the National Judicial Council serving until 2015. The responsibilities of the Council were taken over by the President of the National Office for the Judiciary (NOJ). At the regional level, the heads of the courts have continued to perform their administrative tasks. The central administration of ordinary courts and the activity of the President of the NOJ are supervised by the National Judicial Council, members of which are elected by the colleges of the judges' delegates. The judicial collegiate bodies have a supervisory role in administrative matters also at the county and regional levels.

---

288. Decision 32/1990. (XII. 22.) of the Constitutional Court.

676. The President of the NOJ is elected from among the judges by the National Assembly by a two-thirds majority of votes, for nine years, on the proposal of the President of the Republic. He or she cannot be re-elected.

677. The President of the NOJ is in charge of all tasks and duties of the central administration of the courts, apart from the *Kúria*, where the administrative tasks are carried out by the President of *Kúria.* Among others, he or she represents courts including the preparation of annual reports to Parliament on the general situation of courts; may initiate legislation concerning courts; establishes the rules of organization and operation of the NOJ, and manages its activities. The President draws up his/her proposal concerning the budget of courts and the report on the implementation of the budget and approves the rules of organization and operation of regional courts of appeal. Other than for the *Kúria*, he or she appoints and relieves the court leaders and inspects their administrative activities. The President calls for applications for judicial postings, on the basis of the ranking made by the competent judicial councils; decides on the applications, and puts forward a proposal to the President of the Republic concerning the appointment and discharge of judges. Besides the purely administrative tasks and functions, the President of the NOJ is also in charge of some quasi-professional responsibilities as well. Thus, he or she may adopt decisions on the transfer of judges; may initiate the 'standardization procedure' proposing the *Kúria* issue a uniformity resolution; determines the criteria for the continuing professional development of judges and aptitude tests; may give orders on temporary assignments of judges to other courts without the consent of the judge concerned, and may initiate disciplinary proceeding against judges. Overall, the competences of the President of the NOJ provide an extremely strong position for him or her. For a while, referring to the uneven caseload of courts, she had also the power to designate the court in a particular case; that is, to transfer proceedings from one competent court to another court having similar jurisdiction. However, this power raised serious constitutional concerns, for it violated the right to come before the competent court, which is an important component of the right to fair trial (it was especially problematic that the Prosecutor General was vested with the same power for a time). It was, however, later abolished.

678. The activity of the NOJ is supervised by the National Judicial Council (NJC) according to the law. The NJC is composed of the President of the *Kúria* as an ex officio member and fourteen judges who have at least five-year judicial services and who have been elected by majority vote in the meeting of delegated judges. Whereas previously the Council had mostly only advisory functions related to the budget plan of the courts and the rules and recommendations issued by the President of the NOJ, due to the rule of law requirements of the EU, its powers have been strengthened to take binding opinions on a range of issues related to the administration of the justice system.

679. The new rules adopted in 2023[289] were intended to make the Council an effective counterweight to the presidents of the NOJ and the *Kúria*, after more and

289. Act X of 2023.

more conflicts have arisen between the National Judicial Council and the President of the NOJ since 2018, when the Council began to complain about the irregular practice of the President in deciding the applications for judicial positions, including the leading posts for local and regional courts. The NJC also criticized the President for ignoring the admonitions of the Council issued for the President's failure to fulfil her certain obligations. As a response to these criticisms, the President tried to block the renewal of the Council, and since not all alternate members of the Council have been elected, she declared the National Judicial Council illegitimate. In any case, the President of the NOJ, neglecting the Council's opinions and recommendations, has exercised her power without legal supervision for a long time. The conflict ended with the premature resignation of Tünde Handó, who was elected a member of the Constitutional Court by the Parliament in 2019. Later, similar conflicts took place with the president of the *Kúria* after the former constitutional judge without judicial practice, András Varga Zs., was elected president of the Supreme Court in 2021.

§7.03 THE LEGAL STATUS OF JUDGES

680. The most important feature of the judges' status is the independence of their office which is expressed and required by the Fundamental Law, stating that they are subordinated only to acts of Parliament; they may not be instructed in relation to their judicial activities, and 'judges may only be removed from office for the reasons and in a procedure specified in a cardinal act' (Article 26 section (1)).

[A] Appointment and Discharge of Judges

681. Although professional judges are appointed by the President of the Republic, the President of the NOJ has a great influence on their appointment. He or she calls for applications to fill vacant judicial posts. Only those who have reached the age of thirty years and meet the conditions set by the Act CLXII of 2011 on the Legal Status and Remuneration of Judges are eligible for appointment as a judge. These conditions comprehend Hungarian citizenship, legal capacity, qualifications in law (university law degree, professional legal examination, at least one year's experience in legal work), and passing the aptitude test. They must assume the obligation of regularly submitting declarations of interest. No person may be appointed as a judge who has a criminal record, or who is under criminal investigation, who was sentenced to compulsory psychiatric treatment, who was subject to the most serious disciplinary sanction as a legal professional, or who was banned by a court from being a lawyer.

682. The applicants are heard by the head of the relevant court, and the three best applications are ranked by the competent collegial body of judges. Notwithstanding this, the ranking of the applications does not bind the President of the NOJ, but in case of disagreement, the President must obtain the approval of the NJC or, under certain circumstances, may declare the whole application process unsuccessful. The practice of the first President of the NOJ has generated heavy criticism even within the judiciary, not only because she often ignored the opinion and ranking of the relevant judicial councils, but because sometimes she declared invalid the whole application procedure even if there were candidates who had been found otherwise eligible and capable by the competent judicial collegiate bodies.

683. In December 2019, a 'salad' act amended the Act on the Legal Status and Remuneration of Judges, allowing the members of the Constitutional Court to apply for their appointment as a judge, in which case they must be appointed by the President of the Republic as a judge for an indefinite period without a call for applications.[290]

684. Judicial office ends on death or discharge by the President of the Republic. The Head of State may dismiss a judge if he or she:

- did not pass an aptitude test;
- has resigned the office;
- has become, for health reasons, permanently unable to perform his or her duties;
- has been sentenced to imprisonment or compulsory treatment;
- did not swear an oath by a specified deadline;
- no longer fulfils the conditions for appointment;
- has been appointed or elected to an incompatible position;
- has been sentenced to loss of office as a disciplinary sanction;
- did not make a declaration of property; or
- except for the President of the *Kúria*, and the President of the NOJ, reaches the general retirement age.

[B] Incompatibility Rules

685. The incompatibility rules also serve judicial independence, but in this case, the integrity of judicial power is protected against the potential individual interests of judges and the indirect external influences which could prevail through the judges. Thus, a judge may not be a member of a political party, and may not conduct political activities. He or she may not have any other job, and, in parallel with his or her judicial service, may pursue only scientific, artistic, literary, educational and technical creative activities from which he or she has income. Besides that, a judge may not fill any leading positions in a business organization, or in any civil organization.

686. Another set of rules makes judicial service incompatible with any positions in any of the other branches of state power or with public authorities. Accordingly, a judge may not be a member of the Hungarian or the European Parliament, a

290. Art. 91 of the Act CXXVII of 2019.

mayor, a local government councillor, or senior officer in a state organ. Professional judges may not serve on a court of arbitration.

687. In the case of conflict of interest, as a major rule, the respective judge is obliged to resolve the incompatibility within thirty days; otherwise, the head of court where he or she serves initiates his/her dismissal.

[C] Promotion, Immunity, Liability and Discipline

688. According to the Act on the Legal Status and Remuneration of Judges, every judge appointed for the first time has an initial term of three years, unless he or she was previously a member of the Constitutional Court or an international court. In other cases, the appointment is for an indefinite period. The Act defines the detailed rules for the career model of judges, according to which judges can only be removed from office for reasons through procedures determined by law, and their salary depends on the length of their service.

689. The law enables the President of the NOJ to transfer a judge to another court if his or her own court is closed or its jurisdiction is reduced to such an extent that it no longer permits the employment of the judge. Judges may be dispatched by the head of a regional court to another court in the jurisdictional area of the regional bench. Beyond that, judges can also be dispatched for service reasons by the President of the NOJ to ensure an even distribution of cases among courts. In such cases, the secondment can last for a maximum of one year every three years without the consent of the respective judge.

690. The work of judges is regularly evaluated by the administrative leader of their court. The President of the NOJ has an essential role in determining the evaluation criteria. If the evaluation process results in an ineligible grade, the chair of the respective court calls upon the judge to resign within thirty days. If the judge refuses to do so, the Disciplinary Service Chamber Court decides the case which can lead to the dismissal of the judge based on his or her ineligibility. The judge may appeal to a designated council of the Disciplinary Service Chamber Court against such a decision.

691. The judge commits a disciplinary offence if he or she breaches his/her obligations in relation to his office, or violates or endangers the authority of the judicial profession by way of life or behaviour. The procedure is conducted by the Disciplinary Service Chamber Court of the relevant judicial bench. The disciplinary sanctions, in proportion to the gravity of the breach, vary from reprimands to a motion of seeking removal from office.

692. As to the civil law liability of judges, they are financially liable for any damage caused to their court by violation of their obligations arising from employment relationship. Nevertheless, the court is fully responsible for any damage caused by an unlawful act of its judges to third persons.

693. It is a part of the legal status of judges, as well as a guarantee of judicial independence, that judges enjoy immunity similar to that of the Members of Parliament. In case of the President of the *Kúria* and the National Office for the Judiciary, Parliament decides on the waiver of immunity, whereas immunity of judges may be suspended by the President of the Republic, on the proposal of the President of the NOJ. The civil assessors of courts have a limited immunity, inasmuch as they are protected from any legal procedure in relation to their involvement in the work of judiciary.

[D] The Principles of the Administration of Justice

694. In the course of judicial proceedings, everyone has the right to a fair trial (*see* outlined *infra* in Part III, Chapter 4, §4.01) which imposes obligations on the courts such as, *inter alia*, independent and impartial proceedings, reasoned judicial decisions, provision of legal representation, and the right to a remedy in law. Courts have a crucial role in guaranteeing everyone's right to equality before the law. Further, judicial activity also has to meet other constitutional and legal requirements. As a major rule, court hearings are open to the public and closed sessions can only be held in cases prescribed by law.

695. In addition, the collegiate character of the composition of courts ensures the citizens' participation in the work of judicial power, and supervision from inside the bench. As a consequence of the principle of panel courts, judicial bodies, in most cases at second instance, act in chambers, where the court is composed of a professional judge and two civil assessors. Although jury trials were introduced in 1897 for certain judicial proceedings, they were sparsely used until 1919. Today, civil assessors are elected by local authorities. Exceptionally, a single judge may also act, and according to the Fundamental Law, in certain cases, set by law, even court secretaries may also act within the powers of a single judge (Article 27 section (3)).

696. As a matter of fact, the system of constitutional review follows the centralized model in Hungary, where the Constitutional Court has exclusive power to control the constitutionality of legal acts. Nevertheless, if the ordinary courts, in the course of their proceedings, find a statute that in their opinion is in conflict with the Fundamental Law, they may stay the proceedings before them and initiate constitutional review of that act before the Constitutional Court. Courts also have a role in enforcing European Union law by seeking a preliminary ruling from the European Court of Justice in any case they think necessary (where EU law must be applied).

697. The Fundamental Law contains some provisions on how courts must interpret the law. Pursuant to Article 28, courts must 'interpret the text of laws primarily in accordance with their purposes and with the Fundamental Law'. Furthermore, in the course of legal interpretation, it must be presumed that legal norms 'serve moral and economic purposes which are in accordance with common sense and the public good', while the Seventh Amendment to the Fundamental Law in 2018 introduced new obligatory interpretative tools. Since then, in the course of legal interpretation, courts have had to take into account primarily the preambles of the legal norms and their explanatory memorandums.

698. As the latest development, in 2020, the Parliament modified the Act CLXI of 2011 on the Organization and Administration of Courts, introducing the so-called limited precedent system. According to this change, each individual decision of the *Kúria* that was published in the Collection of Judicial Decisions (i.e., in the official gazette of the *Kúria*) is binding to all courts. If, for some reason, any court in a particular case still wants to deviate from the precedents so conceived, it must expressly justify this decision.

[E] Constitutional Practice and the Recent Challenges to Judicial Independence

699. In Hungary, the principle of judicial independence has faced major challenges in recent years. The first case attracting international attention was the removal of the President of the Supreme Court on 1 January 2012. András Baka, a former judge of the European Court of Human Rights, was elected in 2009 by Parliament as President of the Supreme Court of Hungary. Due to the six-year term of his office, his mandate should have expired in 2015. However, the Transitional Provisions of the Fundamental Law (*see* outlined *supra* in Part I, Chapter 2, §2.02, [C] [4] [a]), which was adopted in December 2011, renamed the Supreme Court *Kúria*, and provided that the mandate of the President of the Supreme Court would terminate upon the entry into force of the Fundamental Law. As a consequence, President Baka's mandate was abolished about three and a half years before its normal date of expiry. In addition, new criteria were adopted for the election of the President of the *Kúria*, according to which criteria candidates were required to have at least five years' experience as a judge in Hungary. Since Baka had served on the ECtHR between 1991 and 2008, rather than on a Hungarian court, he was ineligible for the presidency of *Kúria*.

700. The case was brought to the European Court of Human Rights, which in its Grand Chamber judgment held that the premature termination of the mandate of the President of the Supreme Court violated Baka's right to access to court since he was removed by legal norms against which no judicial remedy had been provided by domestic law. Then, as the Court stated that 'there was prima facie evidence' that Baka had been dismissed because he had publicly criticized the ongoing judicial reforms, and hence his freedom of expression had been violated illegitimately.[291] Remarkably, since Parliament had in the meantime elected the President of the *Kúria*, Baka was not reinstated in his previous position.

701. In parallel with the removal of the President of the Supreme Court, the Act CLXII on the Legal Status and Remuneration of Judges, which came into force

291. ECHR Case of *Baka v. Hungary*, Application No. 20261/12 (2014).

simultaneously with the Fundamental Law on 1 January 2012, reduced the compulsory retirement age of judges from 70 to 62 prescribing that every judge must retire if he or she 'has reached the age-limit for retirement applicable to him (…) with the exception of the President of the *Kúria*' (the same rule was adopted for prosecutors and public notaries as well). In fact, the Fundamental Law empowered the National Assembly to adopt that kind of rule declaring that 'judges may remain in office until the general retirement age' (Article 26 section (2)). The official reason for reducing the compulsory age limit of judges was to end the privilege that, in contrast to other public sector employees, they could continue to work until the age of 70 (the upper age limit for judicial activity has been 70 years since 1869). Moreover, by replacing older judges with younger judges, establishing a more balanced age structure of judiciary was also given as justification for the legislation. It is to be noted that the lowering of compulsory age limits did not affect the members of the Constitutional Court and the lay assessors, who could continue to serve until the age of 70. As a result of this law, in 2012, altogether 274 judges – almost 10% of all serving judges – had to retire. The change affected court leaders even more since most of them came from the older age group of judges.

702. The Constitutional Court in 2012 invalidated the provisions of the Act CLXII on the Legal Status and Remuneration of Judges, which had reduced the compulsory age limit of judges for formal reasons, holding that such age limits can only be determined by cardinal act.[292] The Court also defined a substantive requirement for such a regulation, setting forth that the upper age limit for judicial service may be reduced only gradually, after a sufficient transitional period, without prejudice to the principle of a judge's irremovability. However, the Constitutional Court's ruling failed to give any real remedy to the judges illegally removed since it did not contain any provisions on how to reinstate or compensate them.

703. The rapid removal of a number of judges by an act of Parliament by reducing their compulsory retirement age proved to be not only unconstitutional but also breached European Union law too. The European Commission, on account of the relevant Hungarian legislation, sought a declaration from the European Court of Justice that Hungary failed to fulfil its obligations as an EU member to comply with the Council Directive 2000/78/EC establishing a general framework for equal treatment in employment and occupation. The ECJ found that the legislation which 'abruptly and significantly lowered the age-limit for compulsory retirement, without introducing transitional measures of such kind as to protect the legitimate expectations' of the judges concerned gave rise to a difference in treatment on the grounds of age which was not proportionate as regards the objectives pursued.[293]

704. As a consequence, Parliament amended the law on the legal status of judges, reducing gradually until 2023 at the latest the compulsory age limit of

292. Decision 33/2012. (VII. 17.) of the Constitutional Court.
293. *Commission v. Hungary,* Case C-286/12, 6 November 2012.

judges to 65 years. Although the new legislation did not reinstate the judges illegally removed, it offered them various forms of compensation (pecuniary compensation or other posts in the judiciary). Taking the legislative changes into account, the European Court of Human Rights refused as inadmissible the complaints of 158 judges removed to seek redress from this Court for their illegitimate dismissal. The ECtHR found that the government's interference in judicial independence 'was based on compelling grounds of the general interest', and the judges concerned received adequate compensation for their removal.[294]

705. The extremely wide-ranging powers of the President of the NOJ were subject to recurrent criticism, especially because, in several respects, these competences go far beyond administrative and management duties giving him or her thus a great influence on professional matters. The power of initiating standardization procedures, determining the criteria of performance assessments of judges, defining behavioural rules and other matters can deeply affect judges' professional activity, and can hardly be classified as administrative powers. The importance of these far-reaching powers is enhanced by the length of the President's term of office.

706. In practice, the protracted conflict between the President of the NOJ and the NJC has signalled the structural problems of the judicial system. In 2018, the NJC repeatedly objected to the President's behaviour, including her unwillingness to cooperate with the NJC. And, conversely, the President of the NOJ also questioned the legitimacy of the National Judicial Council. The conflict led the NJC to initiate in Parliament the discharge of the President of the NOJ, but the parliamentary majority rejected the proposal in 2019.

707. Another challenge to the principle of judicial independence was the attempt to separate administrative courts from the uniform system of judiciary. In 2018, the Seventh Amendment to the Fundamental Law introduced a new system of administrative courts. According to this constitutional amendment, from 1 January 2020, administrative courts should have been separated from the unified organizational system of the ordinary courts. The supreme organ in the administrative court system would have been the Administrative High Court with the responsibility to ensure the uniformity of the application of law by administrative courts. The legislative acts on the detailed rules of this reform were also adopted,[295] establishing a three-tier organizational system of administrative justice. The Administrative High Court would have had a similar status to that of the *Kúria*, including the power to issue 'uniformity resolutions', which would have been binding on all administrative courts in order to ensure the uniform law application. The Minister of Justice would

294. ECHR Case of *J.B. and Others against Hungary*, Application No. 45434/12 (2018).

295. Act CXXX of 2018 on the Administrative Courts and the Act CXXXI of 2018 on the Entering into Force of the Law on the Administrative Courts and Certain Transitional Provisions. It is to be noted that the first attempt to introduce the institutional reform of administrative courts failed in 2016, when organizational changes were incorporated into a bill on administrative procedure. However, the Constitutional Court quashed the relevant provisions, because they had been adopted by a simple majority, rather than the necessary two-thirds majority. Decision 1/2017. (I. 17.) of the Constitutional Court.

have performed the tasks and functions of central administration of administrative courts. According to the original plans, the new system of administrative courts should take effect on 1 January 2020. However, the reform plans quickly got into the crossfire of political debates. The critics of the reforms claimed that this kind of reorganization of the judiciary was unjustified: administrative proceedings have been properly administered also by ordinary courts,[296] where the specialization of judges dealing with administrative matters has already been realized. Most critics assumed that the real reason for restructuring the system of administrative courts was to outsource the most politically sensitive matters, such as freedom of information cases, legal disputes related to political rights, refugees and elections, to specialized courts under the close supervision of the government. These suspicions have been confirmed by the selection method for administrative judges, preferring those candidates who have professional experience as government officials. The judicialization of administrative disputes (i.e., the abolishment of the administrative appeal) might be the price paid for the establishment of the Supreme Administrative Court because the caseload of the administrative courts of that day would have not justified the formation of a three-level administrative justice system. Others suggested the risk of influx of new judges who were not trained and socialized in courts, but in the hierarchical system of state administration.[297] However, following the European Parliament elections of 2019, the government unexpectedly announced that, in order to avoid the expected international criticism, the reorganization of administrative justice and the introduction of the Supreme Administrative Court would be postponed.[298] In fact, the first instance administrative and labour courts were abolished from 31 March 2020, or, more exactly, they were merged with the county (capital) courts.[299]

708. Another controversy emerged when a new act allowed constitutional judges to be appointed judges at their request even if they had not previously been judges and did not meet the general conditions for judicial appointment. Under this Act, the President of the Republic appointed eight constitutional judges as judges in the summer of 2019, and one of them, András Varga Zs., who has never been a judge, was elected by the National Assembly, the President of the *Kúria* in the autumn of 2020.

709. In 2022, the European Commission made the payment to Hungary of part of the Recovery Fund and some other EU funds conditional on the government implementing substantial judicial reforms in 2023. In order to comply with these rule of law requirements, the Parliament has amended the relevant acts on judiciary on several occasions in 2023, reducing the much-criticized excessive power of the

296. *See* the EU justice scoreboard: https://ec.europa.eu/info/policies/justice-and-fundamental-rights/effective-justice/eu-justice-scoreboard_en.
297. *Blurring the Boundaries. New Laws on Administrative Courts Undermine Judicial Independence* (Hungarian Helsinki Committee 2018) 4.
298. Act LXI of 2019.
299. Act CXXVII of 2019.

President of the NOJ and the President of the *Kúria*, and changing certain operational rules (e.g., allowing ordinary courts to request a preliminary ruling from the CJEU and making the case allocation system in the *Kúria* automatic).

Chapter 8: The Prosecution Service

§8.01 CONSTITUTIONAL BASES

710. Although the institutional antecedents of the Prosecution Service are usually located back in the fifteenth century in Hungary, its first statutory regulation took place only in 1871.[300] The Royal Prosecutor's Office prosecuted criminal offences and was subordinate to the Minister of Justice. This institutional model was replaced after the Second World War by a system in which the Public Prosecutor's Office was removed from government supervision and held accountable to the National Assembly, and its main function was completed by a general legal supervisory power for the purpose of preserving the lawful order of society.[301]

711. The legal status of the prosecutor's office was significantly changed by the constitutional revision of 1989 since, besides the traditional representation of the State's claim to prosecute criminal offences, it was endowed with the function of protecting the constitutional order of the regime change.

712. The current status of the Prosecution Service is determined by the Fundamental Law of 2011. According to Article 29 section (1), the Prosecutor General and the Prosecution Service must be independent (of any other public body). Its basic constitutional function is to 'contribute to the administration of justice by exclusively enforcing the State's demand for punishment as public accuser'. For this purpose, the Prosecution Service prosecutes criminal offences, takes action against other unlawful acts and omissions, as well as contributes to the prevention of unlawful acts. As a secondary function, which is usually called the 'public interest protection function', the Prosecution Service is 'a guardian of public interest' exercising 'further functions and powers'. Detailed rules are laid down by two cardinal acts, Act LXIII on the Prosecution Service and Act CLXIV on the Legal Status of the Prosecution General, the Prosecutors and Other Prosecution Employees, and the Prosecutors' Career.

713. In a formal sense, the Prosecution Service is seen as a contributor to the administration of justice. Criminal justice is a state monopoly: law enforcement, the determination of criminal responsibility and the enforcement of punishment is the exclusive task and duty of the State, which performs these functions through the Prosecution Service.

714. The Service is an independent and autonomous constitutional organ which is subject only to law and is accountable to Parliament. This accountability, however, does not imply an organizational subordination; the Prosecution Service is not a body of Parliament. Although the Prosecutor General receives his or her mandate from Parliament, which is entitled to terminate it in the cases provided for by law,

300. Act XXXIII of 1871.
301. Legislative Decree No. 13 of 1953.

the National Assembly may make such decisions only on the proposal of the President of the Republic. Furthermore, the Prosecutor General is also obliged to report annually to Parliament on the activities of the Prosecution Service, and MPs can ask questions of the Prosecutor General on matters falling within his/her responsibility, but, on the one hand, there is no any sanction for Parliament's rejection of the annual report, and, on the other hand, the Prosecutor General has no political responsibility to Parliament. Another guarantee of the organizational independence of the Prosecution Service is that all prosecutors are appointed by the Prosecutor General, who exercises employer's rights over them (i.e., sets and controls the terms of their employment).

715. This autonomy is also expressed by the fact that the Prosecution Service forms a separate chapter in the annual budget act.

§8.02 THE POWERS AND DUTIES OF THE PROSECUTION SERVICE

[A] The Role of Prosecutors in the Criminal Proceedings

716. The Fundamental Law enumerates the most important powers and duties of the Prosecutor General and the Prosecution Service. Thus, in respect of the prosecution of criminal offences, they exercise rights in connection with criminal investigations, conduct the prosecution in court proceedings, and supervise the lawfulness of penal enforcement. It should be noted that according to Hungarian law, criminal proceedings are divided into three stages, and the Prosecution Service is involved in important functions in all three phases: criminal investigation, preparing and submitting the charges to the court, and the conduct of the actual prosecution before the court.

717. The prosecutors' tasks related to criminal investigations are as follows:

- to request investigations by other investigative authorities;
- to supervise their investigations;
- to examine and amend the decisions and actions of the investigating authority;
- to instruct the investigating authority;
- to decide on appeals against the investigation (e.g., against any investigative action or if the police refuses the investigation);
- to approve secret surveillance.

718. In certain cases specified by the Act on Criminal Proceedings[302] (in particular investigations against high officials or policemen), the Prosecution Service performs the investigation itself.

719. After the closing of criminal investigation, in the 'prosecution phase' of the criminal proceedings, the Prosecution Service decides on the charges to be laid,

302. Act XC of 2017.

which must be based on the evidence obtained during the investigation. The prosecutor prepares the indictment and submits it to the criminal court.

720. In the final stage, the Prosecution Service conducts the prosecution as the 'public accuser'. In doing so, the prosecutor has all the rights of parties in litigation, including motions for evidence, or submitting ordinary and, under circumstances set by law, extraordinary appeals against the trial court's decision. The prosecutor may withdraw the accusation at any time before the final judgment of the court.

[B] Legal Supervision of the Enforcement of Punishment and Protection of the Public Interest

721. The Prosecution Service exercises legal supervision over the enforcement of punishment. In this area, the prosecutor decides on complaints submitted against the circumstances of imprisonment.

722. Apart from the tasks of the prosecutors in the field of criminal law, a part of the Prosecution Service's activities relates to the protection of the public interest. Here the prosecutors may act in cases of environmental protection, financial management of public money, child protection, public registries, consumer's protection, and so on. For these purposes, the Prosecution Service has the right to file lawsuits and may intervene in any ongoing court proceeding; it may initiate administrative procedures and exercises general legal supervision over the administrative authorities and police bodies. The Prosecution Service may turn to the courts for the dissolution of any organization having legal personality if it ceases its activity or engages in activities that violate the Fundamental Law or laws. Thus, the so-called Hungarian Guard, an extreme-right organization, was dissolved by court on the initiative of the Prosecution Service in 2009, as its activities differed from those contained in its statute and violated the dignity of the Roma people and other groups.

§8.03 Organizational Structure of Prosecution Service

723. The most important characteristics of the prosecutorial organizational system are centralization, hierarchy and independence. The hierarchical relationship prevails throughout the organization, which means that the prosecution offices and the prosecutors are bound by the instructions of their superior prosecution offices and prosecutors. The whole Prosecution Service is led and directed by the Prosecutor General, while the prosecution offices at the various levels are under the single leadership of their heads.

724. The organizational system of the Prosecution Service is parallel to that of the courts; that is, local, county (capital) and regional prosecution offices exist under the Prosecutor General's Office. All offices are led by their heads who are appointed and dismissed by the Prosecutor General; the only exceptions are the two Deputy

Prosecutor Generals who are appointed for an indefinite period by the Head of State at the proposal of the Prosecution General from among prosecutors. One of them is responsible for criminal matters, while the 'public law deputy' oversees the prosecutorial activities outside those tasks relating to criminal proceedings.

725. Criminal investigations exclusively belonging to prosecutorial authority are conducted by a specific central unit of the Prosecution Service assigned to this task (the Central Chief Prosecution Office of Investigation) and regional offices of that central unit (Budapest Prosecution Office of Investigation, Pest Region Prosecution Office of Investigation as well as investigative prosecution offices at local level).

§8.04 The Legal Status of Prosecutor General and Prosecutors

726. The Prosecutor General is elected for nine years by the National Assembly from among the prosecutors at the proposal of the President of the Republic. He or she must be elected with the votes of two-thirds of the Members of Parliament. In spite of the unusual length of his/her mandate, the Prosecutor General can be re-elected since neither the Fundamental Law nor the relevant laws preclude the same person from being re-elected.

727. As has been said above, the Prosecutor General leads and directs the organization of the Prosecution Service. In doing so, he or she may issue circulars and individual instructions that bind all prosecution offices and prosecutors. Although the Prosecution Service conducts criminal investigations only in certain cases set by law, the Prosecutor General may take over an investigation from any investigating authority. He or she may stop any investigation or may instruct the investigating authority (in normal case, the Police) to do so. The Prosecutor General may influence the criminal law policy of the State in several ways. He or she may initiate a uniformity resolution from the *Kúria*, and may propose legislation to Parliament (without formal right to submit bills to it).

728. The mandate of the Prosecutor General is terminated by the expiry of the term of mandate, discharge, resignation, reaching 70 years of age, death, or as a result of a conflict of interest. In addition, Parliament may, on the proposal of the President of Republic, state that the Prosecutor General has lost his/her office if he or she has failed to perform the duties arising from his or her mandate through his/her own fault, or has been found guilty of committing a criminal offence pursuant to a final judgment of the courts, or has otherwise rendered unworthy in his/her post.

729. As was said above, all prosecutors are appointed by the Prosecutor General. Only those people who have legal capacity, are Hungarian citizens, and do not have a criminal record can be appointed as prosecutors. Moreover, a university law degree and a successful special legal examination, as well as at least one-year professional practice in certain legal positions, are also required for appointment. Junior prosecutors are appointed for three years after a successful application. All vacant positions in the Prosecution Service must be filled by an application process.

Within the Prosecution Service, military cases are administered by military prosecutors who have to be professional military officers too.

730. Prosecutors may not be members of a political party and may not engage in political activities. They are subject to rules on conflicts of interest similar to those of judges. Thus, any criminal process against prosecutors, with the exception of proceedings arising out of being caught *in flagrante delicto*, may only be launched with the prior approval of the Prosecutor General. It is curious that the same rule applies to the Prosecutor General himself/herself, which means that in a given case, the Prosecutor General may decide whether or not to consent to initiating or proceeding with criminal matter against himself or herself.

731. Prosecutors lose their office upon agreement, discharge, resignation, unresolved conflict of interest or death, as well as upon being sanctioned in a disciplinary procedure to the loss of office, or being sentenced in criminal proceedings to imprisonment or compulsory treatment. In addition, every prosecutor's mandate is terminated by law if he or she reaches the compulsory retirement age, which, like in the case of judges, is progressively rising to the age of 65. However, as was said above, the office of the Prosecutor General is an exception to this rule: he or she may remain in office until reaching 70 years of age.

§8.05 Constitutional Practice

732. Although the law places great emphasis on the public interest function of the Prosecution Service, there is a significant imbalance between the two main groups of its activities: the Prosecution Service acts primarily within the framework of criminal procedures, while the protection of the public interest is spectacularly neglected. For example, despite a series of corruption scandals, very few cases have been prosecuted and are even more rarely ever brought to court.

733. In a prosecutorial system, where the head of the Prosecution Service is in such a strong position like in Hungary, the choice of the Prosecutor General is particularly important because his or her leadership fundamentally influences whether the Prosecution Service acts impartially and independently of particular political and business interests. However, in 2010, when the Prosecutor General was elected, there was no consensus among the parliamentary parties, and the government parties were able to elect their own nominee, Péter Polt, a person presumably loyal to the government who was in the 1990s an MP candidate of Fidesz.[303] Since then, Polt's activity has been heavily debated, with accusations of a political bias. It is frankly general experience that in recent years, while investigative journalists have discovered a number of corruption scandals, the Prosecution Service has almost

303. Miklós Bánkuti, Gábor Halmai & Kim Lane Scheppele, *From Separation of Powers to a government without Checks: Hungary's Old and New Constitutions*, in *Constitution for a Disunited Nation: On Hungary's 2011 Fundamental Law* 264 (Gábor Attila Tóth ed., Central European University Press 2012).

always refused criminal investigations against politicians of the government parties, even in cases when the European Anti-Fraud Office (*Office européen de lutte anti-fraud*, OLAF) revealed in detailed reports what kind of abuses occurred in regard to certain EU funds. In contrast, it has launched a number of criminal investigations against opposition politicians. Notably, the Hungarian government assiduously refuses Hungary's joining the European Public Prosecutor's Office.

734. The rule of law conditions for access to EU funds have also affected the activities of the Prosecution Service. Under a 2022 salad law,[304] if the Prosecution Service or an investigating authority rejected a complaint for a major offence related to the exercise of public authority or the management of public property or terminated proceedings for such an offence, its decisions could be reviewed by a court.

304. Act XLIV of 2022.

Chapter 9: The Commissioner for Fundamental Rights

735. The establishment of the position of the Commissioner of Fundamental Rights was inspired by the constitutional enthusiasm that emerged at the time of the regime change, when the constitution-makers tried to introduce almost all the institutions of Western constitutions considered to be suitable for limiting public power. The ombudsman-type institutions did not have a tradition in Hungarian public law before the democratic transition in 1989–1990. Thus, when the general constitutional revision of 23 October 1989 established the position of the Parliamentary Commissioner for Civil Rights, it was the birth of the office of ombudsman. The legal status of the Commissioners was enacted by the Act LIX of 1993.

736. The Constitution of 1949/1989 empowered the National Assembly to establish special ombudsmen, and Parliament set up a new Commissioner for Data Protection in 1992, and another one for Ethnic and Minority Rights in 1993. In November 2007, Parliament established another ombudsman, one who was responsible for the rights of the future generations. Despite the enthusiastic beginnings, the election of the first ombudsmen encountered certain political difficulties, and the Commissioners were able to start only in 1995. Similarly, the Commissioner for the Rights of the Future Generations was elected by the National Assembly only in 2008, after several candidates of the President of the Republic were rejected by Parliament. It is true, however, that the reluctance of Parliament was not caused by its distrust of the new institution, but it had political reasons: President László Sólyom, breaking with the constitutional convention, refused to negotiate with the parliamentary parties prior to his nominations.

737. The Fundamental Law of 2011 restructured the ombudsman system, and established a single position, the 'Commissioner for Fundamental Rights'. The former special ombudsmen became his/her Deputy Commissioners, while the Parliamentary Commissioner for Data Protection has been replaced by the newly created National Agency for Data Protection and Freedom of Information.

§9.01 Constitutional Functions of the Commissioner and the Deputy Commissioners

738. The Commissioner's position is special in several respects. On the one hand, the function, the protection of fundamental rights, is unique among state bodies. On the other hand, he or she does not have any public power in the sense that he/she may not take any binding decisions. The Commissioner of Fundamental Rights cannot be classified as a branch in the system of the separation of powers. The Commissioner is frequently seen as a special controlling body of the National Assembly, although the ombudsman is not a part of the organization of Parliament, and he or she has a very independent position, even against the legislature.

739. The Fundamental Law contains only a sketchy reference to the function of the ombudsman, stating that the Commissioner performs 'fundamental rights protection activities' (Article 30 section (1)). It is slightly clarified by the preamble of Act CXI of 2011 (on the legal status of the ombudsman) by specifying that the Commissioner ensures 'the effective, coherent and most comprehensive protection of fundamental rights'. Nevertheless, the role of the institution can be better understood on the basis of its particular duties and responsibilities. Most generally, the Commissioner for Fundamental Rights enquires into violations related to fundamental rights that come to his or her knowledge, and initiates general or specific measures to remedy these grievances.

740. The Act CXI of 2011 states that the Commissioner 'pays special attention' to the protection of rights of several groups of people, like children, 'future generations', nationalities living in Hungary, and 'the most vulnerable social groups'. He or she does not have decision-making powers by which he/she could provide and specify rights and obligations for citizens. Rather, the Commissioner has only 'soft' powers and tasks, like to 'engage in social awareness raising', 'information activities', and to cooperate with organizations and national institutions 'aiming at the promotion of the protection of fundamental rights'. The Commissioner's activity is directed at public bodies, including state administrative bodies, local authorities, any other organs acting in public administration competence, law enforcement organs, the Hungarian Defence Forces, the investigation authorities of the Prosecution Service, and other organs performing public services. However, the ombudsman may not investigate the operation of the National Assembly, the President of the Republic, the government, the Constitutional Court and the courts.

741. When the second Orbán government streamlined the ombudsman system in 2011, the independence of the ombudsmen responsible for the rights of minorities and future generations respectively ceased to exist, and their duties have since been performed by deputy commissioners. They may draw the attention of the Commissioner to the threat of infringement of rights in the area of their activity; may propose to the Commissioner an ex officio investigation in particular cases; submit a petition to the Constitutional Court initiating constitutional review of a legal act, and may participate in the enquiries of the Commissioner.

§9.02 The Legal Status of the Commissioner

742. The Commissioner for Fundamental Rights and his or her deputies are elected for six years, on a two-thirds majority vote of the Members of Parliament. The President of the Republic proposes to Parliament candidates to be appointed as Commissioner, while the Deputy Commissioners are nominated by the Commissioner. After their election, the Commissioner for Fundamental Rights and his or her deputies take an oath before Parliament.

743. Any Hungarian citizen can be elected as Commissioner for Fundamental Rights or as Deputy Commissioner if he/she holds a law degree, has the right to stand as a candidate in elections of Members of Parliament, and has outstanding theoretical knowledge or at least ten years of professional experience. Furthermore, he/she must have reached the age of thirty-five years and have considerable experience in conducting or supervising proceedings concerning fundamental rights.

744. The mandate of the Commissioner and his/her deputies is incompatible with any other state, local government, social or political office. No one may become Commissioner or Deputy Commissioner if he or she was a Member of Parliament or the European Parliament, the President of the Republic, a member of the government, a mayor or local councillor, a notary, a professional member of the Hungarian Defence Forces or any law enforcement organ, or the officer or employee of a political party in the four years preceding his or her candidacy.

745. The Commissioner and his/her deputies have the right to immunity identical to that of Members of Parliament. The Commissioner for Fundamental Rights may be re-elected once.

746. As to the conflict of interest rules, the Commissioner for Fundamental Rights and his or her deputies may not be members of political parties or engage in political activities. Their position is incompatible with any other state, local government, social or political office or mandate. In addition, they may not pursue any other gainful occupation, nor accept payment for other activities, with the exception of scientific, educational, artistic activities, activities falling under copyright protection, or proof-reading or editing activities. The Commissioner and his/her deputies may not have leading positions in business organizations.

747. The mandate of the Commissioner for Fundamental Rights and that of the deputies terminate upon expiry of the mandate, death, resignation, conflict of interest, dismissal (incapacity), removal from office or if the conditions necessary for his/her election no longer exist.

748. A Commissioner may be dismissed if he or she, through no fault of his/her own, is not able to perform his or her duties for more than ninety days. A motion for dismissal may be submitted by any MP, and Parliament may decide on it by a two-thirds majority. The Commissioner may be removed from office if he or she deliberately fails to perform his/her duties for more than ninety days or does not meet his or her obligation to make a proper declaration of assets. Removal may be proposed to Parliament by its committee responsible for immunity and incompatibility and requires a two-thirds majority of votes of MPs.

749. Administration and preparatory work related to the tasks of the Commissioner and his/her deputies are performed by the Commissioner's Office.

§9.03 Procedural Rules

[A] The Initiation of the Commissioner's Procedure

750. According to Act CXI of 2011 cited above, in conducting his or her proceedings, the Commissioner for Fundamental Rights must be independent, subordinate only to legislation, and may not be given instructions on his or her activities.

751. An enquiry by the Commissioner may be requested by anyone who thinks that his or her fundamental rights have been endangered or violated by those public authorities whose activity falls within the scope of the Commissioner's responsibility. Such a petition may be submitted only if the person concerned has exhausted all available administrative legal remedies or no legal remedy is available to him or her at all. If a final administrative decision has been taken in the case, a petition may be filed with the Commissioner only within one year from notification of the decision. No procedure may be started by the Commissioner in cases which are before a court, or in which a final judicial decision has been rendered. The personal identity of the complainant must be kept secret if he or she so wishes. It is to be added that the law prescribes that no one can suffer any disadvantage on account of making a complaint to the Commissioner for Fundamental Rights. The proceedings of the Commissioner are free of charge.

752. Besides citizens' complaints, the Commissioner for Fundamental Rights may also conduct ex officio procedures as well if he or she gains notice of a mass violation of fundamental rights or the threat of thereof.

753. It is a technical rule that the Commissioner may not enquire into cases that date before the system change (more exactly, before 23 October 1989, the date of the general constitutional revision).

[B] The Commissioner's Enquiry

754. In the course of his or her enquiry, the Commissioner for Fundamental Rights may request a written explanation, declaration, information or opinion from the organization, person or employee of the organization having the obligation to cooperate. The Commissioner has relatively wide-ranging rights of enquiry. Thus, he or she may:

– request data and information from the authority subject to enquiry and request copies of the relevant documents;
– ask the head of the authority under enquiry, or the head of its supervisory authority to conduct a special investigation;
– participate in a public hearing; and
– conduct on-site inspections.

755. In the course of an on-site inspection, the Commissioner for Fundamental Rights or the members of his or her staff are authorized to enter the premises of the state body subject to enquiry; may inspect all documents which may have any relevance to the case under investigation; and may conduct a hearing of any employee of the respective authority.

756. Nevertheless, the ombudsman's investigative powers have many limitations. In the course of the enquiry affecting the Hungarian Defence Forces, for instance, the Commissioner may not inspect confidential documents of major importance to the interests of national and inland security and defence. In addition, his/her investigative powers in relation to the documents of the National Tax and Customs Authority and the Prosecution Service are also strictly restricted.

[C] The Commissioner's Actions

757. Having regard to the fact that the Commissioner may not take binding decisions over other public bodies, more specifically that he/she cannot remedy violations of fundamental rights by his or her own act, the informal actions and the personal authority of the Commissioner have great importance. Characteristically, the relevant law also emphasizes that in the course of his/her activities, the Commissioner cooperates with other public bodies and organizations aimed at promoting the protection of fundamental rights.

758. Some of the ombudsman's formalized actions are related to the body under investigation. Thus, the Commissioner may draw the attention of the competent public authority to a danger of serious infringement of fundamental rights of a larger group of persons. As a result of the investigation, the Commissioner makes a report on the enquiry he or she has conducted. The Commissioner's reports are public, but they may contain no personal and classified data, nor any secrets protected by legislation. The petitioner must be notified about the outcome of the enquiry and any measures that have been taken.

759. If, on the basis of an enquiry conducted, the Commissioner finds any abuse or infringement of fundamental rights or discovers malpractice threatening these rights, the Commissioner may initiate redress by the head of that public authority (otherwise, the ombudsman may turn directly to the supervisory authority) in order to redress the violation, and if the investigated authority is able to eliminate or terminate them within its own powers. In this case, the public body subject to the enquiry is obliged to notify the Commissioner of its response and the measures taken within thirty days. If the public authority under investigation does not agree with the findings or the recommendations of the report, the ombudsman may turn to authority's supervisory body which also has to inform the Commissioner of any developments in the case within thirty days. Eventually, if the authority subject to enquiry or its supervisory organ fails to take appropriate measures, the Commissioner may submit the case to Parliament within the framework of his or her annual report, and may ask Parliament to enquire into the matter.

760. Nonetheless, the Commissioner can seek redress from other bodies as well. Thus, he or she may initiate proceedings for the supervision of legality by the competent prosecutor through the Prosecutor General. Although the Commissioner may not investigate any case before the courts, in the course of the judicial review of an administrative decision relating to the state of the environment, he or she may participate in the proceedings as an intervener. Where appropriate, he or she may propose disciplinary proceedings, or recourse to the National Authority for Data Protection and Freedom of Information. Moreover, if as a result of his/her enquiry the Commissioner concludes that a crime has been committed, he or she may initiate criminal proceedings.

761. The Commissioner for Fundamental Rights may turn to the Constitutional Court for constitutional review of any legislation.

762. Having regard to the Commissioner's relationship with Parliament, it should be noted that he or she may give an opinion on the draft rules of law affecting his/her tasks and competences; he/she may make proposals on new or amended legislation affecting fundamental rights and/or the recognition of the binding nature of an international treaty. This is most likely to happen in his/her annual report submitted to Parliament in which the Commissioner gives information on his/her fundamental rights activities. The National Assembly debates the report during the year of its submission.

[D] Constitutional Practice

763. During the 1990s, the ombudsmen gained relatively wide recognition. According to a 1998 opinion poll surveyed by Szonda Ipsos, 79% of the population knew about the ombudsmen, and the Commissioner's Office ranked in general third on the list of the most trusted institutions (after the Constitutional Court and the President of the Republic).[305]

764. The conservative government that came to power in 2010 has significantly changed the institutional structure of ombudsmen. The institutional rank of rights protection has been reduced inasmuch as national minorities' rights and the rights of future generations are no longer guarded by independent ombudsmen, but by deputies of a single parliamentary commissioner. Beyond this, the abolishment of the position of the parliamentary ombudsman for personal data protection and freedom of information, and its replacement with a government agency generated a legal dispute because this ombudsman, who had been elected by Parliament in 2008 for a six-year term, was prematurely removed from his position on 31 December 2011 (instead of 2014), and the President of the Republic appointed a new person to the head of the newly established National Authority for Data Protection for a term of nine years.

305. http://www.jogiforum.hu/hirek/17481.

765. The European Commission launched an infringement procedure in 2013, arguing that the establishment of a new national supervisory authority violated the European Parliament and Council Directive 95/46, Article 28(1), requiring that the supervisory authorities of European Union Member States responsible for supervising the processing of personal data must enjoy an independence allowing them to perform their duties free from external influence. After the Hungarian government claimed that the premature removal of the ombudsman did not breach the institutional independence of the data protection authority, the Commission turned to the ECJ. Hungary argued before the Court that the new law on the National Authority for Data Protection met the requirements of the Directive since it provides full independence for the Authority. Moreover, if the Court found that Hungary failed to fulfil its obligations, it could lead to the compulsory resignation of the head of the new Authority before the expiry of his term of office, which would be incompatible with the principle of the independence of the data protection authority. Paradoxically, the Hungarian government itself thus acknowledged that premature removal violated the institutional independence of the supervisor of data protection. But this did not matter in the end, for the Court refused this argument, stating that a Member State cannot plead provisions prevailing in its domestic legal system to justify a failure to observe legal obligations arising under EU law. The ECJ also concluded that compulsory retirement or resignation, as a consequence of the new law, was an unlawful intervention in the independence of the former data protection authority (i.e. the parliamentary ombudsman), seeing as the previous regulation did not permit this kind of interruption of the term of office.[306] Nevertheless, the prematurely dismissed ombudsman was not re-established, and the government agency has been working smoothly since then.

766. The Fundamental Law of 2011 brought about another important constitutional change when it abolished the *actio popularis*, a tool available for every citizen to initiate without a personal interest constitutional review of any legislation before the Constitutional Court. The new Constitution did, however, leave the right of the Commissioner to initiate constitutional review of legal norms before the Court, whereby the importance of the institution increased for a while, especially after the Commissioner, Máté Szabó, petitioned the Court in some significant cases. In 2013, with the votes of the government parties, a new Commissioner was elected by Parliament, and after that the role of this office greatly diminished. The new Commissioner has been criticized frequently that he did not raise his voice either against massive violations of migrants' rights during the 2015 refugee crisis, or later against the relentless maltreatment of immigrants. In 2016, he undertook a direct political role when, in support of the government's anti-migrant campaign, he asked the Constitutional Court for an abstract interpretation of the Fundamental Law, arguing that Hungary is not obliged to admit asylum seekers who should rather be distributed among EU Member States on the basis of the asylum policy of the European Union.[307] The petition gave the opportunity to the Constitutional Court to

306. Case C-288/12, *European Commission v. Hungary*.

307. According to the controversial quota system proposed by the EU for the resettlement of migrants among the Member States (*see* Council Decision (EU) 2015/1601 of 22 Sept. 2015), the Member

declare that it stipulated its own powers to review the validity of EU law in the future in order to protect the sovereignty and constitutional identity of Hungary.[308]

767. The National Agency of Data Protection and Freedom of Information has also been often criticized, mostly by the opposition parties for its alleged political bias in favour of the government.

States should share the burden of the migrant crisis relocating the asylum seekers from the front-line States (Greece and Italy) among all the other Member States. Under this plan, Hungary would have to admit 1,294 people, out of a total of 160,000.

308. Decision 22/2016. (XII. 5.) of the Constitutional Court.

Chapter 10: The Institutions of Economic Constitutionalism

768. In relation to the State's economic activity, the Fundamental Law provides several institutions with important roles, powers and functions. While the Hungarian National Bank is responsible primarily for the monetary policy, the State Audit Office exercises supervision over public expenditure, and the Budget Council has a jurisdiction in budgetary policy.

§10.01 The Hungarian National Bank

769. The Hungarian National Bank (*Magyar Nemzeti Bank*, 'MNB') is the central bank of Hungary. It has responsibility not only for the monetary policy of the State but also for supervising the financial intermediary system, including the commercial banks, insurance companies and other financial organizations (Article 41 sections (1)–(2)). The detailed structural, operational and jurisdictional rules are determined in a cardinal act.[309]

770. The primary objective of MNB is to achieve and maintain price stability. Without prejudice to this goal, it supports the economic policy of the government using the monetary policy instruments at its disposal. Besides this, some of the other principle tasks of the MNB include holding and managing official reserves in foreign currency and gold; developing and monitoring the payment system, and having the exclusive right to issue banknotes and coins (Hungarian *forint*).

771. The Hungarian National Bank is a legal person functioning in a form of a limited liability company with its shares owned by the State (represented by the Minister of Finance). The MNB and the members of its decision-making bodies must be independent in performing their tasks and cannot take instructions from the government or – except the European Central Bank under certain circumstances – from the institutions and bodies of the European Union.

772. Its head, the Governor, is appointed (as well as the deputy governors) by the President of the Republic on the proposal of the Prime Minister for a term of six years. The same person may hold this position twice at most. The Governor is obliged to report annually to the National Assembly on the activities of the Hungarian National Bank. In addition, Members of Parliament may put questions to the Governor who is obliged to answer them. On the basis of an authorization of an act of Parliament, he or she may issue decrees on matters within his or her functions and which may not conflict with any parliamentary law.

773. The Monetary Council is the supreme decision-making body of the Bank, empowered to make strategic decisions on monetary policy. According to the MNB statute cited above, the Council consists of at least five, and at most nine members

309. Act CXXXIX of 2013.

(nine members at present). Its members are the Governor of the Bank as the chairman of the Council, the deputy governors and other members, elected by Parliament for six years.

774. The operation of the MNB is under a continuous supervision of a Supervisory Board.

775. In recent years, there have been several legal disputes concerning the operation of the Hungarian National Bank. Some of the criticism focused on the Bank's alleged indirect support for the state budget and on its broad social involvement (e.g., founding a university, buying artworks, setting up and running foundations), all financed from its operational profit.

§10.02 The State Audit Office

776. The State Audit Office is the organ of the National Assembly responsible for financial and economic audits. Its constitutional function is to control the implementation of the central budget, the administration of public finances, the use of funds from public finances and the management of national assets. The Office carries out its audits according to the criteria of lawfulness, expediency and efficiency (Article 43 section (1)). The detailed regulation of its powers and duties is laid down in a cardinal act of Parliament.[310] In fact, its jurisdiction embraces every area of financial management where public funds are spent. Basically, it exercises control over public authorities, but the State Audit Office also has the power to audit the use of budgetary subsidies for political parties, even though only in terms of the legality of the use of that budgetary support.

777. The Office has wide-ranging investigatory powers. Basically, it operates on the basis of an audit plan. In most cases, the State Audit Office acts ex officio, but it is obliged to carry out audits on the basis of a decision of the National Assembly, while it may fulfil control at the request of the government.

778. The Office prepares a report on its audits which contains the findings of its investigation and recommendations. The report is sent to the head of the body audited, who has to draw up an action plan and submit it to the State Audit Office within thirty days of receipt. If the Office does not accept the actions proposed by the body investigated, it may initiate criminal or disciplinary proceedings against the head of the audited organ or the suspension of its budgetary subsidies. In the case of the audit revealing an abusive or wasteful use of public funds or threat thereof, the President of the State Audit Office may, in order to prevent or mitigate harm, initiate with the competent authority the suspension of budgetary support and payments to the body concerned, or the seizure of assets owned or managed by the audited organ.

310. Act LXVI of 2011.

779. Although the Fundamental Law refers to the State Audit Office as a specialized organ of the National Assembly, the Office is an autonomous public authority over which Parliament does not exert any supervision or management. Nevertheless, the President of the State Audit Office must prepare an annual report on the activity of the Office and submit it to Parliament. In this report, he or she may make proposals for legislation.

780. The President of the State Audit Office is elected with the majority vote of two-thirds of the Members of Parliament for a term of twelve years. Despite this long mandate, the President may be re-elected. It is strange that, while neither the Constitution nor the Law on the State Audit Office contains any restriction about re-election, it is prescribed that if the outgoing President is not re-elected, he or she remains in office after the expiry of his/her term of office until Parliament has elected a new President. The President has the same immunity as the Members of Parliament.

781. The Vice President of the State Audit Office is appointed by the President of the Office for a term of twelve years. The Law on the State Audit Office has established specific legal status of the comptrollers who are also appointed by the President for an indefinite period.

782. It is worth noting that the activity of the State Audit Office was badly politicized when, shortly before the 2018 parliamentary elections, it imposed heavy fines on several opposition parties, while the government parties' financial management was not investigated at all. The grounds for the severe penalties were unclear, and these measures were even more worrying because the reports, findings and acts of the State Audit Office may not be challenged before a court or any other public authority. This practice was continued by the State Audit Office when it announced in December 2023 that it would significantly reduce state support for all six parties of the opposition alliance that stood in the 2022 general elections because, according to its investigation, they illegally obtained foreign financial resources before the elections. Even though the funding under review was not given to these parties but to an NGO (which is not illegal), there is no appeal against the decisions of the Office.

§10.03 THE BUDGET COUNCIL

783. One of the few new bodies introduced by the Fundamental Law is the Budget Council. In fact, the body began its activities in 2009 as an advisory body of Parliament in budgetary matters, but the Orbán government dismissed its elected members and changed its legal status.

784. The Fundamental Law defines the constitutional responsibility of the Budget Council as supporting the legislative activity of the National Assembly, and as examining the feasibility of the central budget. It takes part in the preparation of the

Budget Act (Article 44 sections (1)–(2)).[311] Its further task and duty is to give an opinion every six months on the state of implementation of the Budget Act and the expected trends in the public debt.

785. However, it is not a purely advisory body since its prior consent is required for the adoption of the state budget by Parliament. Although the Council may refuse to give consent only in specified cases (e.g., if the budget bill would allow State debt to exceed half of GDP), its decision may not be reviewed or annulled, so it has a real veto right – which is an exceptional restriction of Parliament's budgetary power. It is worth noting that under certain circumstances this veto power may have political significance because if Parliament fails to get the prior consent of the Budget Council to the state budget for the running year by 31 March, the President of the Republic may dissolve Parliament, simultaneously calling a new general election.

786. The members of the Budget Council are the President of the Council, who is appointed for six years by the President of the Republic, the acting Governor of the Hungarian National Bank and the incumbent President of the State Audit Office.

311. The detailed rules of the Budget Council are laid down in Act CXCIV of 2011 on the economic stability of Hungary.

Chapter 11: The Hungarian Defence Forces and the Constitutional Rules of Military Operations

787. The Hungarian Defence Forces are controlled by the legislature and the government, and are composed of professional soldiers. The system of general conscription was replaced by a professional army in 2004.

788. Following the termination of the Warsaw Pact in 1991, the Hungarian government began negotiations with the North Atlantic Treaty Organization on its accession to the Alliance. On 8 July 1997, NATO invited three Central European countries, Hungary, the Czech Republic and Poland. As a result of this invitation, Parliament initiated a national referendum. Because of the fear that the referendum would be unsuccessful, Parliament decided in the summer of 1997 that a national referendum would be successful if the majority of those present, but at least 25% of eligible citizens, gave the same answer to the question. In a national referendum held in November 1997, with 49.24% turnout, 85.33% of voters supported Hungary's NATO membership. In February 1998, the National Assembly adopted a resolution on the results of the referendum. Hungary, along with Poland and the Czech Republic, became a full member of NATO on 12 March 1999.

789. Since then, the constitutional and legislative rules on the Hungarian Defence Forces have been adjusted to meet NATO obligations, and the army operates as an integrated force in this alliance.

§11.01 Constitutional Rules on the Hungarian Defence Forces

790. The constitutional functions of Hungarian Defence Forces as the armed forces of Hungary are 'the military defence of the independence, territorial integrity and borders of Hungary and the performance of collective defence and peacekeeping tasks arising from international treaties, as well as carrying out humanitarian activities in accordance with the rules of international law' (Article 45 section (1)). In addition, the army takes part in the prevention of disasters and the relief and elimination of their consequences (Article 45 section (4)).

791. The Hungarian Armed Forces operate under shared management. According to the Fundamental Law, the National Assembly, the President of the Republic, the government and the Minister vested with the relevant functions and powers (of defence) have the right to direct the military forces. This provision seems to specify the laconism of the former constitutional text which comprised only that 'the President of the Republic shall be the Commander in Chief of the Hungarian Defence Forces'. While the current text contains the same provision, the Fundamental Law reflects the Constitutional Court practice of the early 1990s which divided managerial responsibilities over the army.

792. The Fundamental Law imposes similar restrictions on the political rights of members of the Hungarian Defence Forces as for members of the police and national security services. According to these limitations, professional staff members of the Hungarian Defence Forces may not be members of political parties or engage in political activities.

793. Besides these, the rules for the deployment of the army have also constitutional importance. The relevant provisions are laid down in a separate chapter of the Fundamental Law ('Decisions on participation in military operations'). These rules grant important powers to the government while trying to ensure parliamentary oversight over these decisions. The President of the Republic does not have any power in this area, which shows that the President's position as the Commander-in-Chief of the Hungarian Defence Forces is merely a symbolic title.

794. According to the Fundamental Law, while the government decides on any troop movements of the Hungarian Defence Forces and of foreign armed forces that involve crossing borders, basically, the National Assembly, with the votes of two-thirds of MPs present, decides on the deployment of the Defence Forces abroad or within the country and on stationing them abroad, as well as on the deployment or stationing of foreign armed forces in Hungary or their departing from the territory. In other cases, the government may decide on the deployment of the Hungarian Defence Forces and of foreign armed forces based on the decision of the European Union or the North Atlantic Treaty Organization and on other troop movements by them. The government, while simultaneously informing the President of the Republic, must report on all these decisions without delay to the National Assembly. This also includes authorizing the participation of the Hungarian Defence Forces in peacekeeping or other humanitarian activity in a foreign operations area.

§11.02 The Divided Management System and the Administration of the Army

795. On the basis of the Fundamental Law, the detailed rules relating to the organization, tasks, command and control, and operation of the Hungarian Defence Forces are laid down in a cardinal act.[312] As far as the management system of the army is concerned (*see* Table 7), this law partly reproduces the provisions of the Constitution and partly clarifies or specifies them.

312. Act CXIII of 2011.

Table 7 The Management System of the Hungarian Defence Forces

Parliament	*President of the Republic*	*Government*	*Minister of Defence*
Declares war and peace	Makes certain decisions concerning a specific legal order	Decides on the movement of the Hungarian Army and the foreign armed forces crossing the border	Is responsible for the implementation of the government's decisions on the country's defence and crisis management
Takes decisions concerning a specific legal order,	Appoints and promotes generals	Decides on any troop movement of the Hungarian Defence Forces and foreign armed forces crossing borders	Exercises professional control over the defence activities, and controls the operation of the army
Decides on participation in military operations	Approves the country's armed protection plan	Is responsible for the operation of the Hungarian Defence Forces	Directs the Chief Commander of the Hungarian Defence Forces
Decides on the use and the stationing of the Hungarian Army abroad or in Hungary	Appoints and dismisses the Chief of Staff of the Hungarian Defence Forces	Decides on economic mobilization	
Approves the government's decisions on the troop movements			
Accepts the long-term development directions of the army			
Provides the necessary resources for the army (in the Annual Budget Act)			

796. The day-by-day operation of the Defence Forces is managed by the Minister of Defence. The Ministry has regional bodies (military headquarters) organized at a county (capital) level. The county (capital) defence committees (consisting of the representatives of the territorial state administration bodies and local governments) contribute to the fulfilment of the military, disaster recovery and civil protection tasks. Similar committees operate at the local level as well.

§11.03 The Professional Staff of the Army

797. The professional staff of the Hungarian Defence Forces work in strict hierarchical order. The professional staff members of the army are obliged to carry out due commands in the course of their service, unless they would commit a crime by doing so. If a soldier discovers that an order is unlawful, he or she has to bring it to the attention of the commanding officer immediately. If, however, the issuer of the order maintains the order, this must be recorded in writing upon request. In this case, the commander will be solely responsible for enforcing the illegitimate order.

798. Both the current and the former law[313] on the Hungarian Defence Forces included the requirement that soldiers should, in their military oaths, undertake that they would fulfil their duties even at the risk of their lives. The Constitutional Court, reviewing the 1993 law, decided that this requirement was not unconstitutional. The Court argued that when the State ultimately requires the soldiers to sacrifice their lives in the context of their military duties, this is not a case of depriving the soldiers' lives or human dignity. The risk to soldiers' lives is strictly limited: it is requested only in the case of an armed attack against Hungary. In these cases, the life of the soldier is inescapably in danger.[314]

799. According to the Fundamental Law, the members of the professional staff of the Hungarian Defence Forces may not be members of a party or engage in political activities. Then, the Twelfth Amendment to the Fundamental Law prohibited the organization of trade unions by soldiers; that is, it is not possible to create or operate a trade union within the scope of activities of the Armed Forces (*see supra* Part I, Chapter 2, §2.02[C][4][l]). The same amendment has authorized the government to regulate the legal status of soldiers by decree.

800. The army is composed of not only professional but also voluntary military reserve soldiers and other employees. The Hungarian Army is allowed to number approx. 30,000 people (the proportion of women is approx. 20%), but there is a shortage in the personnel of the army. In spite of this (or for this reason), the Armed Forces Development Program includes a significant increase in the number of the Armed Forces by 2026, according to which it should be increased to 37,000.

313. Act CX of 1993.
314. Decision 46/1994. (X. 21.) of the Constitutional Court.

§11.04 The Defence Obligations of Citizens

801. The Fundamental Law states that all Hungarian citizens are obliged to defend the country (Article XXXI). The cardinal act on the Hungarian Defence Forces specifies the content of this obligation.

802. Although this is not fully in line with the Fundamental Law's provision which does not detail anything, the cardinal act narrows the defence obligation for citizens residing in Hungary. However, once Hungarians living in the neighbouring countries had been granted Hungarian citizenship in recent years, the reason for this narrowing is, on the one hand, that extending this obligation to foreign Hungarians could not be executed, and on the other hand, its obvious purpose was to avoid conflicts with neighbouring countries – to which these Hungarians are also bound by citizens' loyalty.

803. The armed military service obligation is imposed only on Hungarian citizens aged from 18 to 40. During military service, this obligation may be fulfilled unarmed for reasons of conscience; however, this is not a subjective right but is subject to military administrative approval. Another obligation is work connected to defence activities, which applies to all adult Hungarian men and women, having regard to their health condition and qualifications. The civil protection obligation applies to both male and female citizens between 18 and 65 years of age. It can be ordered not only in a state of emergency but also in peacetime (e.g., in a disaster situation). In addition, natural persons residing in the territory of Hungary, irrespective of their nationality, as well as legal persons, may be required to provide economic and material service (e.g., by making their property available) in order to perform defence and disaster management tasks.

Chapter 12: The Police

804. The Fundamental Law contains only a few provisions on the police in a chapter together with the national security services. As part of this, it refers to the constitutional function of the police; guarantees its control to be exercised by the government; restricts the political rights of its professional staff, and authorizes the legislature to lay down detailed organizational and operational rules in a cardinal act. These rules are determined by the Police Act of 1994.[315]

§12.01 Powers and Duties of Police

805. The Fundamental Law determines the core duties of the Hungarian police as follows:

– to prevent and investigate criminal offences;
– to protect public safety;
– to protect public order;
– to protect state borders; and
– to participate in preventing illegal immigration (Article 46 section (1)).

806. While the first three functions have always been traditional police tasks, the Border Guard was an independent armed organization between 1946 and 2007, and participation in the fight against illegal immigration became a completely new function of the police service as a result of the government's policy from 2015 onwards of closing borders and combatting immigration.

807. In addition to the tasks set out in the Fundamental Law, the Police Act assigns additional tasks to the police, like the control of border traffic, the fight against terrorism, crime prevention, criminal investigation, and certain tasks related to aliens and asylum seekers.

808. The police service carries out state administration tasks as well. It performs transport and law enforcement tasks; authorizes and supervises the activities of security guards (person and property) and private investigative activities, and so on.

809. The detailed rules relating to the use of special investigative means and techniques are laid down in the Police Act. This law defines investigative actions and authorizes the police to use coercive measures, including secret surveillance, or the use of firearms. Legal permission of the latter raised the constitutional problem of the permissibility of taking somebody's life, which led to the constitutional review of this Act. The Constitutional Court held that the constitutionality of using firearm is justified if the person concerned previously violated somebody's right to

315. Act XXXIV of 1994.

life.[316] In other words, the use of firearm is allowed against someone who took the life of another person. However, the Court declared unconstitutional the legal authorization of policemen to use firearms against fugitives because they do not present a threat to police or third parties. It means that the use of firearms is constitutionally permissible only if it is necessary to protect life.

810. Fulfilling his or her service, the police officer is obliged to perform his/her duties in accordance with statutory requirements, to obey the instructions of his or her superior, to protect public security and public order, and if necessary by risking his/her own life. In doing so, he or she has to execute the instructions of the service commander, but he or she must refuse to do so if the execution of the order would be a crime. The legal requirement that the policeman is obliged to perform his duties at the cost of his own life raised constitutional concerns as well, whether this duty violated the policeman's right to life, or not. The Constitutional Court stated that this requirement did not conflict with the right to life because police officers, when they enter into the police service, know or at least should know that such a requirement is attached to their duties, so they have voluntarily undertaken this kind of risk.

811. In addition, a long-standing constitutional dispute arose as to whether or not the faces of police officers in action should be covered in press reports. Judicial practice for a long time preferred the protection of personality rights of police officers, requiring media producers to cover the faces of acting policemen when they were featured in reports about police operations. Nevertheless, the Constitutional Court held in 2014 that because police officers perform public duties, they must tolerate the publication of their pictures without their consent.[317]

§12.02 The Organizational Structure

812. The Constitution puts the police under the direction of the government. The government performs this supervisory task through the Minister of the Interior.

813. The Hungarian police has a vertically and horizontally divided organizational structure of which the main feature is its hierarchical character. The National Police Headquarters is the central body of the police, headed by the National Police Chief Captain. The Chief Captain is appointed by the Prime Minister on the nomination of the Minister of the Interior. The Minister may manage the whole organization of the police only through his or her. The organization's territorial bodies are the county (capital) police headquarters which have separate responsibilities and powers. At the local level, there are police headquarters in towns and branch offices.

814. In addition, there are specialized bodies of the Hungarian police having far-reaching autonomy, such as the National Bureau of Investigation (established for

316. Decision 9/2004. (III. 30.) of the Constitutional Court.
317. Decision 28/2014. (IX. 29.) of the Constitutional Court.

investigating high-priority crimes), the Republican Guard (a police unit for protecting high public officials and state institutions), and the Emergency Police (a body similar to the Western European 'Gendarmerie'), the Criminal Expert and Research Institute, and the Airport Police Directorate. The Counter Terrorism Centre, which was established in 2010, has special autonomy and authority to investigate, prevent, and suppress terrorist acts and related crimes. It organizes and coordinates the activities of anti-terrorist organizations and analyses and evaluates the situation of terrorist threats in Hungary. This body provides personal protection for the Prime Minister, the Minister for Foreign Affairs and the Prosecutor General. The Centre is directly subordinate to the Minister of the Interior.

815. The police staff consists of employees of different legal status, such as professional police officers, law enforcement officials, and employees covered by the Labour Code. The Fundamental Law stipulates that the professional staff members of the police may not be members of political parties or engage in political activities.

816. According to the Eurostat, police officers numbered 383 per 100,000 citizens in 2021,[318] but the statistics, which come from the Hungarian authorities, should be carefully handled, seeing as it is well known in Hungary that the police has been badly understaffed for a number of years.

318. https://ec.europa.eu/eurostat/statistics-explained/index.php?title=Police,_court_and_prison_personnel_statistics.

Chapter 13: The National Security Services

§13.01 Constitutional and Legal Bases of Security Services

817. Similar to the constitutional regulation of the police, the Fundamental Law defines only the constitutional function of the national security services, specifying the political control over them by the government, and restricting the political engagement of the professional staff of the services. Finally, just as in the case of the police, it provides that the detailed rules must be determined by a cardinal act. This law, which was adopted in 1995 and has been modified several times since then, defines the types and tasks of the security services, their management order and the rules guiding their operation.[319]

818. In the wording of the Constitution, the core duties of the national security services are 'the protection of the independence and lawful order of Hungary, and the promotion of its national security interests' (Article 46 section (3)).

819. The Fundamental Law secures also that the national security services operate under the direction of the government. Also, similarly to the police, the Constitution provides that professional staff members of the national security services 'may not be members of political parties or engage in political activities' and authorizes Parliament to lay down the detailed rules relating to the organization and operation of the national security services and the rules for the use of special investigative means and techniques, as well as the rules concerning national security activities in a cardinal act.

820. National security services are subject to civil control. The civil national security services are under the direction of the government (by a minister), while military national security services are directed by the Minister of Defence. The civil national security services were supervised by the Minister of the Interior from 2010 to 2022, and since 2022, they have been under the authority of the Minister in charge of the Prime Minister's Office. An important element of civilian control is that the relevant committees of the National Assembly (including the National Security Committee and, in the case of military services, the Defence and Law Enforcement Committee) exercise control over national security services.

§13.02 The Types of National Security Services and Their Functions

821. The organizational system of the national security services has undergone several changes since the transition to democracy. All these changes have taken place through legislation since neither the Constitution of 1949/1989 nor the Fundamental Law has specified what services should be established and what kind of division of work and responsibility should be between them.

319. Act CXXV of 1995.

822. According to the National Security Services Law, today, there are five different national security services.

823. The Information Office is responsible for acquiring, analysing, evaluating and transmitting information which is necessary for government decisions, relevant to foreign affairs or can be utilized for national security.

824. The Constitutional Protection Office (before 2010, 'Office of National Security') is in charge of investigating and eliminating foreign intelligence efforts and activities that violate or threaten the independence, political, economic, defence or other important interests of Hungary, and of detecting and eliminating concealed attempts to alter or disrupt the lawful order of Hungary by unlawful means.

825. The National Security Service provides special services for other national security services: this body collects confidential information and uses secret information and data gathering activities. It provides special technical tools and materials for this activity based on the needs of the bodies authorized by the secret data acquirer, as well as the needs of the bodies authorized to collect confidential information.

826. The Military National Security Service is the secret service of the Hungarian Army. In its scope of responsibility, it detects attempts to attack Hungary, investigates and eliminates those efforts and activities of foreign secret services that violate or threaten Hungary's sovereignty or defence interests, and obtains, analyses and transmits information on military policy which are relevant to government decisions concerning the country's foreign or military policy.

827. The National Information Centre investigates, among others, the security and criminal situation in Hungary, in the framework of which it monitors and, on the basis of all available data, continuously analyses Hungary's national security and criminal situation, and the terrorist threats to the country. In the event of a direct terrorist threat or 'sensitive security issues', it coordinates anti-terrorist activities involving the relevant organizations.

828. All national security services work in a strict hierarchical structure. Their professional members may not be members of a party and may not engage in political activities.

§13.03 Other Police-Like Organizations

829. In Hungary, a number of specialized bodies have investigative powers. Besides the police, the National Tax and Customs Administration has such authorization in cases of tax and custom offences, while the National Defence Service controls the personal way of life and integrity of the professional members of the armed forces and the government officials having secret investigation powers.

830. Other law enforcement agencies – without investigative powers – include the Hungarian Prison Service (and its institutes), the disaster management bodies, and the Parliamentary Guard.

Chapter 14: Local Governments

§14.01 Constitutional Status of Local Governments

831. As in most European countries, the public administration consists of two great organizational schemes: it comprises the system of the centralized state administration and local government.

832. As to the latter, it is to be noted that the Fundamental Law and the cardinal act on local governments contain different definitions. While the constitutional text, focusing on these bodies as public authorities, refers to the functions of local governments as managing local public affairs and exercising local public power (Article 31 section (1)), the relevant statute conceptualizes local self-government as a political right of local communities.[320] This aspect of local government is stressed by another provision of the legislation declaring that this right belongs to the community of local voters.

§14.02 Types of Local Authorities

833. In Hungary, there is a two-tier local government system. At local level, municipal self-governments exist in the districts of the capital city (*fővárosi kerületek*), in the towns (*városok*), in the towns with county rights (*megyei jogú városok*), and in the communes (*községek*). The counties (*megyék*) represent territorial (mid-level) self-government. The capital city, Budapest, has a special administrative status, given that it is seen as both a municipal and a territorial self-government.

834. The system of Hungarian local authorities is often characterized as a fragmented one since almost all settlements have their own local self-government. In 1990, when the new local government system was founded, the basic conception was that each settlement has the right to have its own local self-government. This was a backlash against the compulsory mergers of villages during the Soviet-type council system that had existed before 1990. At the moment, there are 2,809 communes of the 3,178 municipalities (in 2023). In case of the establishment of a new commune, the amalgamation or the dissolution of existing communes, there must be a local referendum and, on the proposal of the responsible Minister, the Head of State may decide.

835. From an administrative point of view, there is only a minor difference between 'towns' and 'communes'. This differentiation has merely symbolic importance insofar as it demonstrates the development of the municipality.[321] In fact, there

320. Art. 2 s. (1) of Act CLXXXIX of 2011 (hereinafter 'Local Government Act'). Nevertheless, this law also defines the functions of local governments as they express and realize local public interest in a democratic manner in the local public affairs.
321. Ilona Pálné Kovács, *Helyi kormányzás Magyarországon* (Dialóg-Campus Kiadó 2008) 139–140.

are only loosely formulated requirements for obtaining 'town' status, and the whole process has always been essentially influenced by party politics. Since 1990, the number of towns has doubled; it has increased from 164 to 346 (*see* Table 8). After application by the respective communes, this status may be granted by the Head of State on the proposal of the Minister of the Interior. In the last few years, the pre-conditions to obtain this title became stricter (e.g., more than 10,000 inhabitants are required).

836. The category of the 'towns with county rights' is specified by the Local Government Act of 2011, comprising those towns which provide public services not only for their inhabitants but also for those who live in the surrounding area. As a matter of fact, these towns were traditionally county seats, and have more than 50,000 inhabitants because these were the formal requirements for them until 2011. Currently, there are twenty-three municipalities which meet these conditions.

837. The capital city, Budapest, has a special two-level local government system: besides housing the capital city government, there are also twenty-three district governments. All of them are municipal governments, and there is no hierarchical relationship between them. Budapest is an extremely big city in Hungary, having with about 1.7 million inhabitants being a population more than eight times greater than the second largest city, Debrecen.

Table 8 The Number and Types of Local Authorities

Types of Municipalities	*Number of Municipalities*	*Proportion of Municipalities*	*Population of Municipalities (%)*
Communes with a population under 500 people	1,064	33.5	2.8
Communes with a population between 500 and 999 people	674	21.2	4.8
Communes with a population between 1,000 and 2,999 people	855	26.9	14.4
Communes with a population of 3,000 people or above	110	3.5	4.2
Total number of communes	2,809	88.4	30.2
Towns with a population under 5,000 people	89	2.8	3.0

Types of Municipalities	*Number of Municipalities*	*Proportion of Municipalities*	*Population of Municipalities (%)*
Towns with a population between 5,000 and 9,999 people	112	3.5	7.8
Towns with a population of 10,000 people or above	121	3.8	22.1
Total number of towns	322	10.1	32.9
Towns with county rank	23	0.7	19.9
Capital city and its districts	24	0.8	17
Total number of municipalities	3,178	100.0	100.0

838. The country has been divided into nineteen counties since 1950 (*see* Figure 4). Counties represent the middle level of public administration (i.e., the level between the central government and the municipalities). The Fundamental Law does not list the counties; the county division, the modification of county borders, and the seats of counties are determined by law.

839. While the county boundaries were not changed in 1990,[322] the range of powers of the counties was reduced so significantly that they are frequently featured as 'levitating counties' seeking a place in the existing local government system.[323] This arose as a result of the 'municipality-centred' local government system.[324] The counties were deprived of most of their functions in 2011, when the central government took over the maintenance of their institutions, together with the accumulated debts of the county governments.

322. In political discussions, many refer to the 'thousand-year-old' counties, because already at the time of the foundation of the historical Hungarian kingdom, the country was divided into counties (*comitatus*). In reality, the basic arrangement of the current administrative division of the counties was established in 1950.
323. Gábor Zongor, *A lebegő megye* (Comitatus Könyv- és Lapkiadó 1994).
324. Ilona Pálné Kovács, *Integráció és dezintegráció a területi közigazgatásban*, in *Egy évtized önkormányzati mérlege és a jövő kilátásai* (Imre Verebélyi ed. 2000) 90.

Figure 4 The Counties of Hungary

§14.03 Electoral Systems of Local Governments

840. All councils are directly elected, but using different voting systems. In the case of municipalities having 10,000 or less inhabitants, there is a 'shortlist' system in which the whole municipality constitutes only one election ward. All candidates are put on the ballot-paper, and the candidates who receive the largest number of votes are elected. The number of candidates to be elected by this method depends on the number of members of the local council. In those municipalities with more than 10,000 citizens (and in the districts of the capital city), a 'mixed' system is used. Around 60% of representatives are elected by a simple plurality (first-past-the-post) system in individual electoral constituencies, and about 40% of the local councillors are elected with a proportional system among candidates on 'compensation lists'[325] comprising party candidates.

841. In Budapest, the capital city, the electoral system of the twenty-three districts where local authorities exist is identical to that of the municipalities, including the election of mayors. As to the election of the chief mayor of Budapest, 5,000 recommendations are required to become a candidate, and the candidate with the

325. The voters do not vote directly on these lists; the candidates will be elected from the compensation lists in proportion of the surplus votes cast for the candidates of the individual electoral constituencies.

most votes in the one-turn election will be the chief mayor. The way in which members of the general assembly of the capital city are elected changed in December 2023, when the pre-2014 pure party-list election system was reinstated. This means that from 2024, the thirty-two seats will be allocated in proportion to the votes cast for the party lists. Those parties can set up lists that have a candidate for mayor in at least three districts of the capital city or have a candidate for chief mayor in Budapest. Only parties that get at least 5% of votes could send representatives to the general assembly.

842. Mayors and local representatives are elected for five years.

843. The turnout rate of local government elections is normally lower than that of parliamentary elections. In 2019, it was 48.58%; in 2014, 44.30%; in 2010, 46.64%; in 2006, 53.12%; and in 2002, 51.11%.[326]

§14.04 THE INTERNAL ORGANIZATION OF LOCAL GOVERNMENTS

844. The Fundamental Law recognizes the right of local authorities to determine their organization and operation. Nevertheless, this power must be exercised within the limits of the law. The Local Government Act of 2011 determines the basic organizational structure of local authorities. The new legislation did not make deep changes in the organizational system of local authorities, so the internal structure of the municipalities and counties looks more or less like that in 1990.

845. According to this Act, the major decision-making and legislative body of local governments is the representative body, the council. The council has the right to manage independently 'local public affairs'. Its decisions in this area may be reviewed only by a court on grounds of legality. The representative body exercises ownership rights over local government property; it manages – within the limits of the law – its own revenues and imposes local taxes. It determines the annual budget of the municipality and may decide whether to take out loans and obtain credit, although such decisions have been controlled by the central government since 2011. The council decides on the organizational structure of the municipality (e.g., whether it maintains a separate mayor's office or not). The body may establish local government institutions and may associate with other local authorities. It may issue local decrees, which cannot be in conflict with higher-ranking legal norms.

846. The size of the representative body depends on the number of local inhabitants: the smallest councils have only three members, while the biggest representative body exists in Debrecen (the second largest city of the country), where the council consists of thirty-four members and the mayor (*see* Table 9).

326. Source: National Election Office, 2011.

Table 9 The Size of Representative Bodies

Population of the Municipalities	*Number of Councillors Elected from Lists*	*Number of Councillors Elected from Individual Electoral District*
Voting for uniform shortlist		
100 or less	2	–
101–1,000	4	–
1,001–5,000	6	–
5,001–10,000	8	–
Mixed voting system		
10,001–25,000	3	8
25,001–50,000	4	10
50,001–75,000	5	12
75,001–100,000	6	14
100,001–	+1 for each 10,000 inhabitants	+1 for each 25,000 inhabitants

847. The Local Government Act prescribes that the representative body must hold sessions as needed, but must do so at least six times a year. As a rule, these sessions are open to the public. Each representative body has to hold a public meeting each year, where they inform the local population directly about the policies of the municipal government.

848. The council may set up committees. Local authorities may freely determine the number and types of their own committees, although the municipalities with more than 2,000 inhabitants are obliged to set up a committee for financial control. The composition of the local government committees reflects the parties' proportional weight on the council. These bodies may have non-elected members too, although elected representatives must be in a majority in the committees. In some cases, the committees may play an important role because – on the basis of delegated power from the council – they may be entitled to take decisions on certain local public matters.

849. The mayor, who is elected directly by local voters, is the chairman of the council. Although the mayor is the figurehead of the local executive, he is not politically accountable to the representative body. The direct legitimacy of the mayor puts him in a very strong position even in those cases where there is a 'cohabitation' between the majority in the council and the mayor, each having different party-affiliations. The only power of the council to remove the mayor from office is via an application to the court. The court may suspend a mayor from office if it finds that the mayor has repeatedly acted illegally or has not complied with his duty to declare his personal financial interests.

850. The mayor represents the municipality and directs – through the chief administrator – the mayor's office. The mayor's office is led by the chief administrator, who is appointed for an indefinite period by the mayor[327] (until 2011, by the council). The chief administrator is the senior civil servant in each municipality and has to meet professional requirements as laid down by law. He is responsible for preparing and executing the decisions of the council and performs state administrative tasks and functions which are conferred on him by law. So far, the chief administrators of local authorities have had a significant role in carrying out the latter tasks, but most of these functions were taken over by the recently established state administrative district units under direct subordination to county government offices.[328] The chief administrator is a legal 'watchdog' of local government because he must warn the council, its committees and the mayor when he finds that their decisions have the potential to violate, or have violated, the law. This task of giving legal advice may sometimes produce a situation of conflict between the chief administrator and the political bodies of the municipality. The chief administrator may find himself in a difficult position since he works under the control and the direction of the mayor and his tenure also depends on him.

851. The mayor's office is the administrative organization of local authorities. The major functions of these offices are the preparation and implementation of the decisions of the representative body and the management of the day-by-day local administration. In addition, they administer several state administrative tasks which have been transferred by the central government to the mayor or the chief administrator. Remarkably, the latter functions will significantly decrease from 2013, when the new district bodies of the central government took over most of them. The size of the mayor's offices varies from three to a few hundred civil servants.

852. The Local Government Act of 1990 encouraged small municipalities (with less than 1,000 inhabitants) to establish or join 'rural district administrative offices' (*körjegyzőség*), which are joint executive bodies of the participating municipalities, leaving the freedom of local authorities to do so or to run a mayor's office of their own. In the early 1990s, roughly half of the municipalities (altogether 1548) established a separate mayor's office, while the other half of local authorities (1526) founded altogether 529 rural district administrative offices.[329] Until the late 2000s, the number of these offices grew to 762, embracing 63.6% of the municipalities of Hungary. Nevertheless, from 2013, the municipalities having less than 2,000 inhabitants have been obliged to establish joint executive bodies. These joint mayor's offices will serve at most seven adjacent municipalities (which belong to the same administrative district), and are financed proportionally by them. In some cases, the

327. In those municipalities which belong to a joint executive body, the chief administrator is appointed by the body of the respective mayors.
328. Similar boards as parts of state administration existed between 1950 and 1983 in Hungary.
329. Ernő Szigeti, *A körjegyzőségi rendszer térszerkezeti jellemzői* (ECOSTAT 2009) 7 (http://www.kozigkut.hu/doc/szigeti_09okt.pdf)

bigger municipalities can be bound to be the seat of the joint executive body, so, to a degree, their organizational freedom is also restricted. In 2023, 554 municipalities had a separate office.

853. Another restriction of the organizational freedom of local authorities comes from the fact that the operation of the mayor's offices is financed directly by the central budget. Thus, the central government may control the staff management (e.g., the number of staff), seeing as local governments are reluctant to provide additional funding for this aim.

854. The internal organization of the county governments is broadly similar to that of the municipalities, with only minor differences. The deliberative body of the counties is called a 'county assembly'. It is presided over by a chairman, who is elected by the members of the assembly. It is a frequently discussed peculiarity of the county assembly membership that the voters of the towns with county rights (which are usually the biggest cities and the traditional seats of the counties) cannot vote for the representatives of the county assemblies, but only for their own municipal council members. But since the counties have lost their primary functions in public service delivery, this issue has become quite irrelevant.

§14.05 Local Government Responsibilities

855. When the Local Government Act of 1990 was under preparation, it was not put in question that the new local authorities would have a general competence at the local level, and only in exceptional cases could a matter of local public affairs be conferred on organ other than the municipal government. In other words, the basic conception of the effective local government law closely reflected the principles of the European Charter of Local Self-Government of 1985, an international treaty under the aegis of the Council of Europe. In the last two decades, the scope of responsibilities of local authorities has slowly but surely increased, frequently generating complaints from municipalities that they are burdened more and more with compulsory tasks but without adequate financial resources. This trend seems now to have broken, seeing as municipalities are losing some basic functions. As of 2020, the management of public schools were taken over by the central government, except the maintenance of the school buildings in municipalities with more than 3,000 inhabitants, and the inpatient and outpatient care, the hospitals and clinics are also gradually being nationalized.[330] By transferring some of the biggest and most costly tasks, as well as state administrative functions from local authorities to central government agencies, the balance of local responsibilities is moving away from local self-government towards a much greater role of the State.

856. Local authorities still perform many tasks which can be mandatory or voluntary. As to the former, only an act of Parliament may confer such responsibility

330. These losses are not counterbalanced by the new functions of the care of homeless people and public safety which were conferred by the new legislation on municipalities.

on local government. When a law transfers a new obligatory task to local authorities, it must also ensure the financial means necessary for its execution. It is a recurrent complaint of local authorities that, in contrast to the principle of adequate finance, the central government has not provided sufficient resources for fulfilling the responsibilities transferred.

857. The Local Government Act of 2011 and other laws regulating specific administrative areas have transferred a number of tasks and functions to municipal governments. While the earlier legislation required all municipalities to provide certain public services for their local population, the new law is based on the principle of differentiated allocation of responsibilities to local authorities, depending on:

- their population;
- their economic capacity; and
- the size of their administrative territory.

858. In other words, the inherent logic of the regulation is that municipalities with different capacities must have different tasks and functions.

859. Typically, the larger municipalities perform many more functions than the smaller ones, like housing management, provision of public transport, waste disposal and local fire protection, which the smaller communes are not bound to provide. Larger municipalities, with a larger number of inhabitants, participate in the management of local energy supplies, run public utilities, and maintain public service institutions providing local services beyond the compulsory range of responsibilities, and so on.

860. In the spirit of an approach that local governments enjoy as much freedom and autonomy as possible, all local authorities, including the smallest ones, have the right to undertake any responsibilities that are mandatory only for the larger municipalities in their own area.

861. The law stipulates that local governments can voluntarily undertake any local public function which is not assigned to the exclusive competence of other administrative bodies. Under these terms, the only limitation on this right is that the undertaking of non-mandatory functions cannot endanger the fulfilment of the tasks that municipalities are under a duty to perform. Typically, larger municipalities are in the position to undertake local functions beyond their mandatory tasks, such as encouraging and supporting the local economy, launching local programmes for the creation of jobs, promoting tourism (e.g., by organizing festivals), or founding and managing institutions for their own sake (e.g., baths).[331]

862. The 'compulsory' character of tasks and functions means that local authorities are responsible for organizing public services. As a general rule, they can freely

331. Some greater cities launched very ambitious projects, like establishing local industrial parks, or founding common corporations with private investors to build motor race tracks or airports.

choose how or in which form they comply with this requirement. Nonetheless, an act of Parliament may prescribe that certain public services can be provided only by public authorities or public corporations. The stronger a municipality is, the better the chance it has to provide local public services through its own institutions. Conversely, smaller communes which do not have the capacity to maintain their own institutions are bound to find alternative ways to provide public services. A number of different options exist for smaller communes to deliver public services.

863. The Local Government Act recognizes the freedom of local authorities to establish associations with each other or join international organizations in order to promote their own interests. One of the basic rights of local authorities is to establish associations with other local governments for the performance of their tasks and functions in a more effective way, or freely to join an existing local government association (*önkormányzati társulás*).

864. The 'frozen structure' of the local government system noted above renders it impossible to integrate the small municipalities into larger ones. In this situation, seeing the extreme differences of the various local authorities in their capacity to deliver services, the central government began to encourage an 'integrated' way of performing tasks and functions. The freedom of municipalities to establish special associations with each other to carry out jointly certain mandatory tasks is one instrument for this purpose. In practice, most local government associations exist for the maintenance of public service institutions, and for the exercise of certain administrative authorities. For a long time, the central government encouraged the foundation of such cooperation with financial incentives, but voluntary associations could not offset the fragmentation of the basic level of local government.

865. After 2004, the central government changed its policy, concentrating on a 'differentiated distribution of tasks and functions'. This formula developed a practice through which responsibilities are conferred on local governments depending on their capacity to deliver them. The main direction of this policy was to establish 'multifunctional small districts' (*többcélú kistérségi társulás*) on the basis of the statistical division of the country. A large number of responsibilities were conferred on these districts, which were thought to be more powerful than individual local authorities. The public services which could be provided in this way were basic-level education, social services, family and child protection, local public transport, housing, water management and sewerage, communal services and energy supply, environmental protection, waste management, culture and leisure, assistance for job-seekers, planning and regional development. Some of these services require public service institutions which can be maintained more efficiently by bigger local authorities, whereas others need inter-municipal cooperation and coordination for which the district can be an effective organizational framework. All of these local services were jointly financed by the member-communities, in proportion to their population. Although these small districts could only be established voluntarily, the central government offered financial support to those municipalities which managed their service delivery in this form. This policy encouraged the joint maintenance of local government institutions, abolishing those primary schools, health, social and other institutions which could be operated in an effective way by a single local government.

866. Another way to ensure the provision of compulsory public services was to outsource them to other service providers, for example, to state corporations, private actors, voluntary organizations or churches. In some economic spheres, state-owned companies have a significant role, in particular in the fields of inter-municipal public transport, public utilities, or postal services. However, the contribution of the private sector to local administration is only sporadic and fluctuating. For instance, in the last few years, a number of local authorities have handed over the management of their hospitals and other health institutions to private investors and companies. This development has led to sharp ideological disputes and fierce political resentment. The issue of whether the involvement of profit-oriented organizations endangers the provision of health services or not was put in national referendum in 2008, which refused the privatization of public hospitals and of other health institutions.

867. It was noted above that in 1990 the political climate was not favourable for the counties, and they were deprived of most of their previous functions. In defining the role of the counties, the basic principle was that they execute those tasks and functions that cannot be mandatorily allocated to municipal governments. As a result, they received a subsidiary role, providing public services which are not delivered by any local authority – if these services have a regional character, covering the large part of the whole territory of the county. In the first part of the 1990s, the larger municipalities had ambitions to undertake or take over the responsibility from the county's management of a number of public services (secondary and vocational schools, hospitals, etc.), which served not only their own population but also the inhabitants of the agglomeration. With the worsening of the economic situation, mainly from the early 2000s, they began to return their management to the county governments.

868. All these policy directions have been changed since 2010 as a result of the overwhelming majority of the conservative right. As was said above, instead of supporting the voluntary associations of local authorities, the most costly tasks and functions are and were taken over by the central government. The state administrative authorities (like licences, sanctions, registrations) were taken back by the State. This wave of centralization is based on a new etatism, relying on concentrating the available resources and more effective (and stronger) central control. The counties, loosening their functions and resources, do not count anymore as auxiliary institutions, taking over institutions from local governments in trouble.

869. No doubt, the serious effects of the world economic and financial crisis beginning in 2008 contributed to these changes. Private sector organizations are much less in the position to take part in the delivery of public services, and the privatization or opting-out of these services is not well supported by the new etatist policy of the government.

§14.06 Central–Local Government Relations

870. The strong central tutelage over local councils before 1990 inclined the legislators of the new political parties in the transition period to weaken central control over the newly created local authorities. The dominant view was that local autonomy postulates the primacy of local government decisions, as long as these decisions are not declared unlawful by a court. As a result, there were no controls to ensure the effectiveness or appropriateness of decisions of the representative bodies. In this spirit, the Local Government Act of 1990 acknowledged only a control of legality carried out by territorial offices of the central government on the decisions of local authorities. These offices were the regional representatives of the central government (they were subordinated to the Ministry responsible for local government). Until 1994, eight regionally organized Commissioners of the Republic had been exercising this control. In that year, those offices were abolished and were replaced by county administrative offices.

871. Despite the fact that the legal control of local authorities had been working well for a long time, during the second coalition of the socialist MSZP and the liberal SZDSZ (2002–2009), the government introduced a bill in 2006 on the restructuring of county administrative offices which proposed their replacement with regional offices. This proposal was a step towards the regionalization of public administration. The leftist coalition also desired the setting up of regional self-government, but, as this proposal was not supported by the opposition parties, it started to regionalize the state administration because this action did not require approval of the opposition. Parliament passed a constitutional amendment which empowered the government to decide freely on the establishment and name of the state administrative organs. To exploit this authorization, the government (disregarding the heavy protest of the opposition parties) pushed through Parliament a legislative bill amending the Local Government Act on regional administrative offices. This legislative measure engendered a fiery dispute because the modification of this Act would have required a qualified majority for any amendment. The law was declared null and void by the Constitutional Court on the basis that an act of Parliament whose adoption and modification needs the support of a two-thirds majority of MPs cannot be amended by a simple majority.[332] Surprisingly, in 2008, the government led by Ferenc Gyurcsány issued a similar regulation in a government decree, instead of restoring the original situation. This regulation was also annulled by the Constitutional Court for the same reason.[333] On that occasion, the Court also set a deadline for the approval of a regulation on the legal control of local

332. Decision 90/2007. (XI. 14.) of the Constitutional Court.
333. Decision 131/2008. (XI. 3.) of the Constitutional Court.

authorities. Because until that time no new regulation had been adopted, between 2009 and 2010 no legal control over the actions of local authorities existed.

872. The new conservative government first restored the former status of the county administrative offices and then transformed them into county government offices in 2010. In doing so, most regional state administration agencies were integrated into these offices, and the government appointed a commissioner for each of them. This entailed that powerful regional sub-centres of central government were set up, and they were placed under strong political control. Furthermore, the Local Government Act of 2011 has provided new (and stronger) supervisory powers for the county government offices over local authorities.

873. Legal control means only an *ex post* examination of the lawfulness of the local decisions without the power to annul or suspend them. All local governments had to send their decrees and individual resolutions to the competent office so that it could control their compliance with the law. If this office found a piece of legislation or a measure to be illegal, it could call upon the respective local authority to end the violation of law, setting also a deadline for it. When the local government did not revise its measure, the county government office had to turn to the courts to obtain an amendment of a resolution, and, in the case of local government decrees, the office could only bring an action before the *Kúria* or the Constitutional Court in order to repeal it.[334] Since 2011, under special circumstances, the head of the county government office may issue a local decree or other measure instead of the local council, and may impose fines on the mayor or the chief administrator if they fail to fulfil their legal obligations.

874. The economic management and the spending powers of local governments are supervised by the State Audit Office. With regard to the great number of local authorities, it is the explicit target of the State Audit Office to implement an overall control of economic management once a year in each municipal government. Although this kind of control extends also to the efficiency of the financial management of local governments, the report of the SAO may only make recommendations, but it is not binding upon the municipalities.

875. Pursuant to the relevant law, the county self-governments and the bigger local authorities are bound to commission an independent auditor to audit their financial management.

§14.07 Local Government Finance

876. The Local Government Act of 2011 determines the main sources of local government revenue. After 1990, the basic aim was to ensure effective powers and

334. The Constitutional Court has jurisdiction only if the local government decree violates the Fundamental Law. In every other case (i.e., when the decree is in conflict with any other higher-ranking legislation) the *Kúria* has the power to review the legality of the local decrees.

useful rights, as well as a large local asset base for local authorities in order to enable them to obtain their own revenue. It was rightly thought that local autonomy must be guaranteed through a corresponding level of economic independence from the central government. Another legal safeguard of local self-government was the requirement of budgetary support (from the central government) for local authorities in proportion to the compulsory tasks and duties that the law confers on them.

877. Local revenue has four basic categories:

(i) own revenues:
  – local taxes;
  – fees and charges for local public services, duties and fines;
  – revenues from business profits;
(ii) central grants:
  – general (block) grants;
  – specific grants;
  – other subsidies and transfers;
(iii) shared taxes;
(iv) loans, credits and bonds.

878. The most important sources of own revenues are local taxes. All municipal governments are entitled to impose them in accordance with the law. County governments do not have this power. The relevant law[335] enumerates the types of local taxes and determines their limits. Local governments are free to choose which taxes they wish to levy and their amount. It can be said that almost all municipalities have revenues from local taxation.

879. Municipalities usually obtain some revenue from the users of public services in the form of fees and charges. In addition, they are entitled to get money from duties, and certain fines imposed by their organs. They also rely on business-like revenue, that is, on profits, dividends, interests, concession fees, rents, and so on, stemming from the business activities undertaken by local governments or income from their own properties and property rights.

880. Local authorities may take out loans, obtain credit and may issue bonds. The new Local Government Act prescribed some debt-ceiling provisions for local authorities in 2011. Thus, local authorities may not plan operational deficits in their annual budget. Besides that, all development loans of local governments have to be approved by the central government. The relevant law[336] prescribes also that the debt burden of municipalities may not exceed half of their local revenues.

335. Act C of 1990.
336. *See* the Act CXCIV of 2011 on the economic stability of Hungary.

Part III: Fundamental Rights

Chapter 1: The Constitutional Bases of Fundamental Rights and Obligations

§1.01 The Constitutional Nature of Fundamental Rights

881. The chapter 'Freedom and responsibility' of the Fundamental Law contains the provisions on the constitutional rights. The title of this chapter suggests that there is a connection between fundamental rights and duties, as if the fulfilment of the citizens' obligations would be a condition for exercising the basic rights. Although this wording reflects a conservative value order, this is nonetheless meaningless from a constitutional point of view, seeing as the constitutional provisions on the various individual rights do not make the exercise of these rights dependent on the fulfilment of the obligations.

882. Article I section (1) declares the respect and defence of the fundamental rights 'as a primary obligation' of the State. According to this article, these rights are not only 'inalienable', but are 'inviolable' too. This is clearly an unprecise formulation, as section (3) of the same article specifies the general conditions of the legitimate basic rights-limitation. In this light, this provision is likely to the commitment of the State to the human rights as 'inalienable' property of every person. In academic literature, some derive from this formulation that the State only 'acknowledges' rather than establishes and bestows the basic rights, but this differentiation does not have significance in codified constitutional law.[337]

883. The next article claims that Hungary recognizes the individual as well as the 'community' rights. This kind of differentiation is based on the premise that as long as individual rights are available to everyone, collective rights can only be exercised by special groups of people (i.e., more than one person together). The Hungarian political establishment has attached great importance to this approach since the regime change because of the large Hungarian minority beyond the state borders.

884. The subjects of constitutional rights are primarily natural persons. Although the Fundamental Law protects foetal life, from the point of view of fundamental

337. Bernadette Somody, Máté Dániel Szabó, Beatrix Vissy and Dalma, Dojcsák, *Alapjogi tanok I* (HVG-ORAC 2018) 17.

rights, the legal capacity of human beings begins with live birth. Self-evidently, first and foremost, human beings have human rights, but at the same time, certain fundamental rights and obligations which do not only apply to people by their nature are also guaranteed for legal persons established by an act of Parliament (Article I section (4)). Notwithstanding this, according to a decision of the Constitutional Court, public authorities do not have basic rights, so they are not entitled to submit constitutional complaints.[338] However, this decision was overruled by an omnibus law adopted in 2019, which allowed public authorities to lodge a constitutional complaint with the Constitutional Court if a final administrative or judicial limits their powers in a way that is contrary to the Constitution.[339]

885. Under certain circumstances, fundamental rights have a horizontal effect, which means that certain legal claims for constitutional rights are generally enforceable between private parties (*Drittwirkung*). In this field, in a landmark case of the Constitutional Court, the Court upheld a judicial decision which declared illegal the entrance policy of a nightclub according to which the women could enter for free, but men had to pay an entrance fee.[340]

§1.02 Constitutional Limitations of Rights

886. According to the dominant view, the Fundamental Law contains certain 'absolute' (i.e., 'non-restrictable') rights. The jurisprudence of the Constitutional Court in the 1990s found the right to human dignity and life such a basic right. The core elements of human dignity, like the prohibition of torture, inhuman or degrading treatment or punishment, servitude and human trafficking, are also untouchable by legal restrictions, as well as the prohibition on human cloning and medical or scientific experiments on human beings without their informed and voluntary consent. The absolute nature of these rights implies primarily that they cannot be suspended even under special legal orders. The most important criminal law guarantees also belong to this group of rights, which means that the presumption of innocence, the right to defence, the principle of *nullum crimen sine lege* (i.e., the prohibition on retroactive punitive legislation) and double jeopardy may not be set aside even during extraordinary situations.

[A] The Necessity/Proportionality Test

887. Apart from the 'absolute' or 'non-restrictable' rights, the Constitution defines the general conditions for limiting fundamental rights. The so-called necessity-proportionality test was developed by the Constitutional Court in the early

338. Decision 3307/2012. (XI. 12.) of the Constitutional Court.
339. Act CXXVII of 2019.
340. Decision 3001/2016. (I. 15.) of the Constitutional Court.

1990s, and this method has been incorporated into the constitutional text. In fact, this method specifies the constitutional standards of the legitimate restrictions of fundamental rights.

888. The first requirement is that every limitation of basic rights must have a legitimate aim. This can be the exercise of another fundamental right or the protection of 'any constitutional value'. While the first case relates to the possible collisions of constitutional rights, the second refers to any interests that can be directly deduced from the Fundamental Law (such as the maintenance of the operability of the State, the environmental protection or the provision of healthy work conditions).

889. The next standard is that the restriction of a basic right must be necessary for the attainment of the legitimate aim. As a matter of fact, the constitutional text contains the strong necessity standard saying that basic rights can be limited only 'to the extent absolutely necessary' for this purpose. This means that always the least restrictive manner must be chosen from several possible limitations. However, it seems only a formal requirement, as the Constitutional Court usually does not make such a strict scrutiny.

890. The third requirement is the proportionality of the restriction. It means that the right-limitation must be proportionate to the desired goal. In other words, the legitimate aim must be valuable enough for justifying the requested restriction of a basic right.

891. The last component of the test claims that the 'essential content' of the particular fundamental right must be respected. This provision is probably a remnant of the former Constitution and the jurisprudence of the Constitutional Court, which declared that the 'essential content' of the basic rights cannot be restricted even by law. Presumably, this approach was taken over from the German constitutional law concerning the core of the fundamental rights which are untouchable for the legislature. However, there is no relevant jurisprudence on the precise meaning of the 'essential content'.

892. Despite the fact that the necessity-proportionality test is the most commonly used technique of the Constitutional Court for reviewing the constitutionality of rights-limitations, the Court has never developed a doctrinally sound methodology for its application. So in practice, the mere reference to the proportionality/disproportionality of the restriction is used as an ultimate argument in constitutional reasoning in Constitutional Court's rulings. Previously, therefore, when the Court was willing to undertake conflicts with the legislative power, in cases of the collision of basic rights, it was often accused of arbitrarily choosing the right which prevails over the other one.

[B] Other Standards

893. Although the Fundamental Law does not provide for other requirements for limiting basic rights, the Constitutional Court over time has developed some other methods for reviewing the constitutionality of legal restrictions of rights. These have the common feature that they are not used in general but applied only when reviewing restrictions on specific rights. However, from a doctrinal point of view, they are just as poorly grounded and elaborated as the necessity/proportionality test; the Court only selectively applies these constructions referring to them without clear evidence or detailed reasoning. Yet it might be useful that the Constitutional Court announces what aspects it considers in principle when examining the constitutionality of a legal restriction of fundamental rights.

894. The so-called public interest test relates to the protection of private property and seeks to determine whether property rights were restricted in the given case in the public interest.

895. The 'rationality test' applies to rights that cannot be classified as fundamental rights. In these cases, it is examined whether the restriction has been made on an objectively reasonable ground.

896. The clear and the present danger test as well as content-neutral constitutional protection are roughly in line with the original American pattern used in some freedom of expression cases.[341]

[C] Formal Requirement for Rights-Limitations

897. The Fundamental Law also imposes a formal requirement on the restrictions of basic rights declaring that such rights may be limited only by act of Parliament which means that these regulations belong to the scope of exclusionary legislative subject matters. Beyond this, certain fundamental rights, namely the freedom of the press, the rights of national minorities, and the right to vote may be regulated only by cardinal acts. In other cases, the laws governing the legal status of institutional guarantees of fundamental rights must be cardinal acts, i.e., laws adopted by a qualified majority. Thus, the detailed regulation of:

- the independent authority supervising the application of the right to the protection of personal data and to access data of public interest;
- the religious communities and the churches;
- the political parties;
- the organ supervising media services, press products and the communications market,

341. Decision 30/1992. (V. 26.) of the Constitutional Court.

are specified by the chapter 'Freedom and responsibility' about which Parliament may only pass a law by a two-thirds majority of the MPs present. However, according to the practice of the Constitutional Court, provisions that are only indirectly and remotely related to a substance of fundamental rights can be regulated in legal norms of lower levels.[342]

898. It is to be noted that in the chapter 'State', the Constitutional Court, the Judiciary and the Prosecution Service, which play an important role in the protection of fundamental rights, are listed as public authorities whose regulation also requires a cardinal act.

899. It is peculiar that certain fundamental rights may be limited only by a cardinal act, but in spite of the appearance, in some cases, the reason for this requirement was not to make the restriction of rights more difficult but conversely to cement the rights-limitations. So, for example, the campaign limitation rule that political advertisements may only be published in media services free of charge must be laid down in a cardinal act.

900. The Constitution also states explicitly that not only natural persons but also other 'subjects of law' (such as organizations) can have rights and obligations, unless they relate by nature only to natural persons.

901. It is important to note that the level of constitutional protection of fundamental rights has been significantly reduced since March 2020 due to the continuing special legal order. In such cases, the Constitution provides the government with exceptional powers to derogate from the provisions of the law by decree, and also relieves the standards for the restriction of rights, as far as the exercise of basic rights and liberties, except the right to human dignity, the prohibition of torture, inhuman or degrading treatment or punishment, servitude and human trafficking, as well as the constitutional guarantees of criminal proceedings, may be suspended, or restricted beyond the extent defined by the necessity-proportionality test. In the five successive states of danger declared so far, the government has often used this power to restrict a whole series of fundamental rights.

§1.03 Constitutional Obligations

902. The Fundamental Law also specifies the essential obligations of natural persons. It is to be noted that some abstract obligations are defined by the first chapter of the Constitution named 'Foundation'. Article C) says, for example, that everyone is obliged to resist against the seizing and exercise power by force 'in a lawful way'. However, this provision is rather a symbolic remnant of an old public law tradition (the so-called resistance clause of the Golden Bull of 1222), without any practical significance. In 2012, a non-governmental organization filed a constitutional

342. Decision 64/1991. (XII. 17.) of the Constitutional Court.

complaint with the Constitutional Court arguing that the Orbán government's measures aimed at the exclusive exercise of power, but the Court rejected the petition on formal grounds.[343]

903. At first sight, Article O) contains a no less general or abstract obligation according to which everyone is responsible for himself or herself and is 'obliged to contribute to the performance of State and community tasks according to his or her abilities and possibilities'. The second part of the sentence formulates the principle of burden sharing between the members of the society providing constitutional ground for the State to impose taxes and other financial obligations. In this field, Article XXX has also a relevance establishing everyone's obligation to contribute to covering common needs according to his or her capabilities and to his or her participation in the economy. This burden may legitimately be relieved for parents, in a way that the costs of raising children may be taken into consideration.

904. Article P) obliges everyone to protect, maintain and preserve natural resources, in particular arable land, forests and the reserves of water, biodiversity, in particular native plant and animal species, and cultural artefacts for future generations.

905. In the chapter 'Freedom and responsibility', the constitutional text specifies some other obligations. Article XII, together with the right of people to choose their work and employment freely, states that everybody is obliged 'to contribute to the enrichment of the community through his or her work, in accordance with his or her abilities and potential'. This clause does not have any real constitutional effect.

906. Article XVI section (3) obligates parents to take care of their minor children, including the provision of their schooling. It is quite a special provision which says that adult children are also obliged to take care of their parents if they are in need. While the former clause on the parents' responsibility is enforced by a number of legal measures, the latter seems to be a dead letter of the Constitution, and no relevant case law (or any application) is known.

907. A specific obligation is formulated in Article XXI section (2) stating that anyone who causes damage to the environment has to restore it or bear the costs of restoration. This provision is completed by a general prohibition to transport pollutant waste into the territory of Hungary for the purpose of disposal.

908. According to the Constitution, the defence obligation lies only with the citizens. Still, its contents are most fully explained in the constitutional text (*see supra* Part II, Chapter 11, §11.04).

909. Below, expounding the constitutional rights, we will follow the traditional classification of basic rights, distinguishing the first-, second- and third-generation

343. Order IV/02532/2012 of the Constitutional Court.

rights, although the structure of the Fundamental Law only by and large corresponds to this conceptualization. Nonetheless, as we will see, some categories of this chapter are not considered constitutional rights anymore, but, like the social rights, are merely state aims imposing the commitments on the State to strive to achieve them, but which do not provide enforceable rights for people. However, since these 'quasi-rights' are not separated from the 'real' ones, they will be discussed here. The construction of this chapter of the Constitution is not based on a coherent approach of fundamental rights, and, owing to the amendments of the recent years, it looks like by now as a patchwork.

Chapter 2: The Right to Life and Human Dignity

910. Although the Constitution does not establish a hierarchy of the fundamental rights, the constitutional jurisprudence, especially the early practice of the Constitutional Court tried to establish a hierarchy between certain rights.

911. In this approach, human dignity is in inseparable unity with the right to life because these rights mutually assume each other, and they express the human quality of every natural person. In addition, the right to human dignity is the source of all other rights. Some scholars claimed that the Court represented a Christian approach of life and dignity.[344] However, the doctrine of the inseparability or unity of these two fundamental rights became doubtful when the constitutional problem of passive euthanasia arose, in which case human dignity was in conflict with the right to life.

912. Since the repeal of all Constitutional Court decisions made before the entry into force of the new Fundamental Law in 2012, there has not been relevant constitutional jurisprudence on the relationship between these two basic rights.

§2.01 The Right to Life

913. As it has been said, the Fundamental Law acknowledges everyone's right to life together with the right to human dignity (Article II). Its content is everyone's right not to be killed. This comprises the constitutional requirement that public institutions and officials exercising public authority cannot deprive anyone of their lives. In the landmark case of this right, the Constitutional Court annulled the death penalty as a punishment with reference to the fact that the capital punishment irrevocably deprives the man of his right to life and human dignity.[345] Although the previous constitutional text prohibited only the 'arbitrary deprivation' of life, the Court found that the death penalty – because it necessarily deprives the man of all his human rights – is conceptually an arbitrary action in all cases. In this way, the decision was an apparent *contra constitutionem* ruling which the Court tried to compensate by arguing that Article 8 section (2) of the 1949/1989 Constitution (saying that the laws may not restrict the basic meaning and contents of fundamental rights) was later incorporated as Article 54, which prohibited only the arbitrary deprivation of life. Since the *lex posterior derogate legi priori* principle is not valid within the Constitution, the Court has never used such argumentation anymore.

914. After the Constitutional Court found the death penalty incompatible with the Constitution, Hungary undertook international legal obligations not to apply capital punishment. Thus, the 13th Protocol of the European Convention on Human Rights was promulgated by Act III of 2004, as well as Article 2 paragraph 1 of the

344. Attila Tóth Gábor, *Az élethez való jog* in Emberi jogok (Gábor Halmai and Attila Tóth Gábor eds., Osiris Kiadó 2003) 310.
345. Decision 23/1990. (X. 31.) of the Constitutional Court.

Charter of Fundamental Rights of the European Union stating that no one can be condemned to death penalty and executed, is also binding on Hungary.

915. Despite the Court having pronounced the right to life as an absolute liberty, it upheld the legislation which in some cases allowed the use of weapons by policemen or soldiers, and also found that legal rules are constitutional that permit killing in self-defence and exigency as an ultimate device. The Constitutional Court also defended legal regulations that required the risk of sacrificing life from the members of armed services.

916. From the right to life comes the State's constitutional obligation to protect human lives. This can be mainly achieved by legal regulation, like prescribing the binding use of safety helmets or belts.

917. The problem of legitimate limitation of the right to life was also raised in the abortion cases. The basic rules of abortion are regulated by Act LXXIX of 1992 on the Protection of Foetal Life. This regulation came to the Constitutional Court twice in the 1990s. In these cases, the Court did not undertake the responsibility of deciding whether or not the foetus is a human being, or, in other words, the human life begins with conception, or from a later date (e.g., from birth). It stated that this decision falls within the competence of Parliament. Nevertheless, the State's obligation to provide legal protection for life extends also to the foetus' life too.[346] The Court identified the collision of the right of the pregnant woman to her physical self-determination and the foetus' right to life. In any case, until the foetus' right to life is not the same as that of the born man, the right to physical integrity of the mother is preferred. This right, however, is not unlimited; as pregnancy advances in time, the right of the foetus to life is becoming more and more prevalent.

918. The Fundamental Law states that the life of the foetus must be protected 'from the moment of conception' without clarifying the starting point of human life. Since this part of sentence is connected to the provision of the right to life of every human being, during and after the constitution-making process, many worried that Article II of the Fundamental Law can be interpreted as meaning that the foetus has all fundamental rights, and this can lead to the abolition of abortion. However, the rules of abortion have remained unchanged since the new Constitution came into force.

919. According to the Abortion Law,[347] pregnancy may only be terminated until the twelfth week of the gestational period in the following cases:

(a) In the event of a 'serious crisis situation of the pregnant woman', under the conditions specified in this legislation. In the sense of this law, the 'serious crisis situation' is the result of physical or psychological distress or social inactivity. The pregnant woman herself has to make statement about the existence of the

346. Decisions 64/1994. (XII. 17.) and 48/1998. (XI. 23.) of the Constitutional Court.
347. Act LXXIX of 1992 on the protection of foetal life.

crisis situation. The family protection service may not overrule this statement, but it must give information to the pregnant woman about the consequences of abortion.
(b) It is justified by a serious risk to the health of the pregnant woman.
(c) If the foetus is likely to suffer serious disabilities or other impairments.
(d) The pregnancy is the consequence of a criminal offence.

920. In certain cases, the pregnancy can be interrupted until the eighteenth week if the pregnant woman has a limited capacity or she missed the twelve-week deadline beyond her own fault, or the abortion can be performed even later, when the probability of genetic damage of the foetus is too high. Eventually, the pregnancy may be interrupted at any time before giving birth if the life of the woman is endangered by health reason, or in the event of an abnormality which is incompatible with the postnatal life of the foetus.

921. Another legal challenge to the right to life was the constitutional controversy about the permissibility of euthanasia. The Act CLIV of 1997 on Health Care introduced passive euthanasia in the Hungarian legal system. According to this law, the refusal of life-support treatment and life-saving intervention is possible only if the patient suffers from a serious and incurable illness which, according to the state of the art of medicine, leads in a short time, even with proper healthcare, to death. In this case, the patient or in case of mental incapacity his or her legal representative may refuse such medical treatments if a three-member medical committee examines the patient and unanimously confirms that the patient's decision was made aware of its consequences. Any adult person, in his/her full legal capacity, for the case of his or her possible mental incapacity, may refuse all life-supporting and life-saving interventions in writing if he or she is suffering from an incurable illness and as a result of this illness, he or she cannot physically provide himself/herself, or the pain cannot be relieved by appropriate treatment. It is to be added that pregnant women cannot refuse the life-supporting and life-saving intervention even if the conditions of passive euthanasia otherwise exist.

922. The Constitutional Court in 2003 refused the petition according to which the Act on Health Care unconstitutionally restricted the patients' right to self-determination by not allowing them to complete their lives by medical assistance (i.e., active euthanasia). The Court maintained its earlier interpretive practice that the rights to life and human dignity are inseparable from each other, and as such, they cannot be restricted. It stated that the decision of the incurable patient that he or she does not want to suffer and therefore refuses the medical treatment needed to maintain his or her life is a part of his/her right to self-determination. However, it applies only to voluntary passive euthanasia. In this case, the State's obligation to protect life is to ensure the integrity of the patient's decision-making process so that the patient cannot be disturbed by illegitimate influences. At the same time, the Constitutional Court took the view that active euthanasia does not belong to the sphere of the right to self-determination of the patient, as it needs the contribution of the doctor who becomes an active participant in the decision-making process. In fact, the Court did not exclude the constitutional permissibility of active euthanasia forever, but only as long as its social conditions are assured.[348]

§2.02 Human Dignity

923. After Article I defining common and general rules on fundamental rights, among the specific rights, the Fundamental Law first declares the right to life and human dignity. This expresses that these rights have a special place and role in the legal system. Notably, the National Avowal also states that 'human existence is based on human dignity'. This postulation is interpreted in constitutional law that human dignity is the basic source of human rights.

924. As it has been said above, from the beginning of its existence, the Constitutional Court evolved the so-called indivisibility doctrine of human dignity, according to which this right cannot be separated from the right to life of human beings and, in their unity, these rights are absolute and cannot be restricted. The Court needed this special doctrine to declare the unconstitutionality of the death penalty claiming that the capital punishment forever and irrevocably deprives the man from his/her life and human dignity.[349] This approach was, however, frequently criticized, arguing that, on the one hand, in some cases these two rights can be in conflict with each other (as in case of euthanasia), and, on the other hand, the right to life was not unlimited in the living law (as the killing can be justified in exigency). The Fundamental Law eliminated this problem defining only the human dignity as inviolable right (Article II).

925. During the 1990s, the right to human dignity had a prominent role in the jurisprudence of the Constitutional Court. The dominant approach of this right was imported from the practice of the German Federal Constitutional Court.[350] According to this interpretive way, the right to human dignity is a 'general personality right', which is the right to unfold human personality.[351] In the understanding of the Constitutional Court, the right to human dignity has a core area which is untouchable to the state intervention, but the Court has never clarified the content of this sphere. It had a greater practical significance that the body considered human dignity as a 'mother right' from which further constitutionally unenumerated rights can be derived. Thus, the Court read out of the human dignity clause of the 1949/1989 Constitution the freedom of marriage, the right to self-determination, the right to bodily integrity, the right to personal name and others.[352] These derived rights were

348. Decision 22/2003. (IV. 28.) of the Constitutional Court.
349. Decision 23/1990. (X. 31.) of the Constitutional Court.
350. Catherine Dupré, *Importing the Law in Post-Communist Transitions: The Hungarian Constitutional Court and the Right to Human Dignity* 65–87 (Hart 2003); Kinga Zakariás, *Az emberi méltósághoz való alapjog. Összehasonlító jogi elemzés a német és a Magyar alkotmánybírósági gyakorlat tükrében* (Pázmány Press, 2019).
351. Decision 8/1990. (IV. 23.) of the Constitutional Court.
352. *See*, in detail, Kinga Zakariás, *Az élethez és az emberi méltósághoz való jog* in Az Alkotmány kommentárja II. kötet (András Jakab (ed.), Századvég Kiadó 2009) 1908–1909.

considered as rights which can be restricted in the usual way. It is to be noted, however, that the Court refused to derive some other rights from human dignity, such as the 'right to intoxication' or the right to particular human reproduction procedures (like artificial insemination or surrogacy). In doctrinal terms, it was unclear how the Constitutional Court derived certain rights, and why rejected others from the dignity clause of the Constitution. By all means, the Court later abandoned this practice, partly because some previously unenumerated rights had been codified by statutory law, partly because the renewed Court conducted a more moderate interpretive practice.

926. In this field, another important finding of the Court was that the right to human dignity is a so-called subsidiary right which can always be invoked to protect individual autonomy if none of the fundamental rights referred to in the Constitution applies to the particular case.[353] In practice, the Court frequently referred to the right to dignity when it did not find any textual basis for justifying its view often attracting the criticism of judicial activism. But just like in case of the interpretation of the right to human dignity as a 'mother right' of all other fundamental liberties, up to now the 'subsidiary right doctrine' has been abandoned and forgotten.

927. Drawing conclusions from the criticisms of the 'indivisibility doctrine' postulating the full unity of the right to life and human dignity, the text of the Fundamental Law specifies only the latter as an absolute right. Today, the prohibition of torture, inhuman or degrading treatment or punishment, as well as servitude and human trafficking are unrestrictable components of the right to human dignity (Article III section (1)). Similarly, the unconditional prohibition of any practice aimed at eugenics, the use of the human body or its parts for financial gain, and human cloning (Article III section (3)) also protects the untouchable sphere of human dignity.

928. The early jurisprudence of the Constitutional Court on human dignity had a significant impact on legislation. For example, the Health Act of 1997 stated that '[t]he dignity of the patient must be respected in health care'. As part of this, it stated that, in exercising his or her right to self-determination, the patient may freely decide whether or not he or she resorts to health services, and if yes, which medical treatment he or she consents or refuses. In every case, in the course of medical attendance, the patient's rights may be restricted only to the extent and in the manner provided by law, for a period justified by his/her state of health.[354]

929. In recent years, the Constitutional Court has only rarely referred to human dignity, which has lost its prominent role in constitutional review. Then, the Court has shown much more deference to legislative intent than earlier. This new practice can be exemplified by a recent decision declaring that the criminalization and imprisonment of homeless people do not conflict with the Fundamental Law of

353. Decision 8/1990. (IV. 23.) of the Constitutional Court.
354. Act CLIV of 1997.

Hungary, as homelessness 'is not part of the right to human dignity'.[355] Nevertheless, in a decision from December 2021, the Constitutional Court put its practice on the right to human dignity on a completely new foundation, by making human dignity a community-based concept, as opposed to the previous individualistic one. Although this decision, at the initiative of the government, was aimed at an abstract interpretation of the EU clause (Article E section (2)) of the Fundamental Law, it explained in detail in its reasoning that human dignity is the source of the right of individuals to self-identity and self-determination, which are realized in the 'traditional social environment' into which the individual is born. The protection of this social environment is a constitutional obligation of the State. And this is violated when 'foreign populations (...) reside permanently and en masse on the territory of Hungary'.[356]

930. In fact, the right to legal capacity can be also deduced from the right to human dignity. According to the Fundamental Law, every human being has legal capacity which means that all men have rights and obligations (Article XV section (1)). Everyone's legal capacity begins from conception and lasts until the moment of his or her death.[357] The legal capacity of foetus is conditional, where the condition is the fact of birth. The right to legal capacity is of an absolute nature too; it may in no way be restricted, so even any demise of this right is null and void.

355. Decision 19/2019. (VI. 18.) of the Constitutional Court.
356. Decision 32/2021. (XII. 20.) of the Constitutional Court.
357. According to civil law, the time of death is indicated by the disappearance of brain functions, which in fact is justified by a medical certificate.

Chapter 3: Equality

§3.01 The Non-discrimination Principle in Hungarian Constitutional Law

931. The Fundamental Law states that everyone is equal before the law (Article XV section (1)). Section (2) specifies the core content of this right, saying that Hungary guarantees fundamental rights to everyone without discrimination and in particular without discrimination on the grounds of race, colour, sex, disability, language, religion, political or other opinion, national or social origin, property, birth or any other status. The enumeration of the personal attributes on which basis the discriminative treatment is especially prohibited is only an exemplary list focusing on the most frequent bases of discriminative treatment. This formulation reflects the approach that the primary content of equality is that everyone is entitled to the same basic rights and to the same extent. This implies also the prohibition of arbitrary discrimination.

932. The constitutional requirements of equality before the law were evolved by the Constitutional Court in the early 1990s. In the first relevant landmark case, the Court found that the prohibition of discrimination does not mean that any differentiation, including those which aim at the greater social equality, is prohibited. The non-discrimination principle signifies that the law must treat everyone equally; that is, the rights and benefits must be allocated in a way that everybody's interests are taken into consideration with the same respect and prudence, in respect to individual circumstances.[358] In this way, the Court extended the effect of the non-discrimination principle to the entire legal system, while the constitutional text referred only to the equality in fundamental rights – after which the body began to use diverse tests for equality cases, depending on whether they affect basic rights or other legal relationships. It is to be noted that this early judgment was probably inspired by the enthusiasm of the system change, as this approach was undoubtedly much wider than the existing constitutional provision of the time when this decision was taken. This broad interpretation lent a wide range of discretionary power to the Court which frequently used it in the course of constitutional review of legal norms. Biological reasons were sufficient to endorse laws, for instance, restricting compulsory military service obligation to men,[359] or providing retirement pension for women earlier than for men.[360]

933. Nevertheless, according to the interpretative practice of the Court, any differentiation is constitutionally prohibited if it is arbitrary, that is, if it is not reasonably justified. From this point of view, the reason for differentiation between the persons who are in a similar legal position (they constitute, in the terminology of

358. Decision 9/1990. (IV. 25.) of the Constitutional Court.
359. Decision 46/1994. (X. 21.) of the Constitutional Court.
360. Decision 32/1997. (V. 16.) of the Constitutional Court.

the Constitutional Court, a 'homogenous group') has always to be examined. Differentiation is only permissible if there is a legitimate and rational reason related to the purpose of the regulation; that is, the use of irrelevant criteria, like protected personal properties, is not allowed.

934. It is worth noting that the constitutional jurisprudence of non-discrimination principle was criticized not only for opening the way to judicial activism but also for implicitly preferring a specific – Dworkinian – reading of equality.[361]

935. Although discrimination based on sex is explicitly prohibited by the Equality Clause, the constitutional text emphasizes that women and men have equal rights. This provision, which appears to be superfluous, obviously intended to offset the traditionally disadvantaged position of women. Similarly, it is also raised separately that the government has to protect families, children, women, the elderly and persons living with disabilities by means of special measures. This provision allows that the State apply positive discrimination in order to improve the situation of socially vulnerable groups and to provide equal opportunities. Besides that, Article XV section (4) contains a general obligation of the State to 'promote the achievement of equality of opportunity and social inclusion' 'by separate measures'. This clause is often considered as one providing 'positive discrimination'. The next section immediately highlights groups in which the application of reverse discrimination appears to be a constitutional command. In another place, the Fundamental Law goes a step further when it states the requirement for stronger protection for women in the course of defining the conditions of entitlement to a state pension (Article XIX section (4)).

936. The principle of equality is also generally recognized and sought by sectoral laws. For example, the Civil Code states 'that spouses are equal in marriage and family matters; their rights and obligations are equal'.[362] The Labour Code refers to the requirement of equal treatment as a basic principle of labour law.[363] The same principle is enshrined in the law on national education.[364] The Act on Health provides that '[a]ll patients have the right (…) to receive health care (…) in accordance with the principle of equal treatment'.[365] Notably, this law prefers the reverse discrimination stating that '[e]qual opportunities must be ensured in the use of health services'.[366] The latter principle is the explicit objective of the Act on the rights and equal opportunities of persons with disabilities.[367]

---

361. Kriszta Kovács, *Equality: The Missing Link*, in *Constitution for a Disunited Nation: On Hungary's 2011 Fundamental Law* 173–174 (Attila Tóth Gábor ed., Central European University Press 2012).
362. Art. 4:3 of Act V of 2013 (Civil Code).
363. Art. 12 of Act I of 2012 (Labour Code).
364. Art. 1 s. (2) of Act CXC of 2011.
365. Art. 7 s. (1) of Act CLIV of 1997.
366. *Ibid.*, Art. 2 s. (2).
367. *See* Arts 1 and 3 of Act XXVI of 1998.

§3.02 Forms of Discrimination

937. However, the Act of equal treatment and the promotion of equal opportunity[368] have the utmost importance for the enforcement of the right to equality. This law declares that all natural persons and organizations under the jurisdiction of Hungary must be treated with equal respect and care taking personal interests into consideration equally. Although the scope of application of the law basically covers the operation of public authorities and public service producers, it applies also to private parties which offer goods and services to the public, as well as it is applicable to labour relations. However, its effect does not extend to family relationships and relationships between relatives, religious activities of churches and memberships of private organizations.

938. The law defines the forms of discrimination. According to these definitions, direct discrimination means the violation of equal treatment of persons in an arbitrary way, which is based on, *inter alia*, gender, race, colour, nationality, political view or sexual orientation. The discrimination is indirect when, even though the persons in the same situation are seemingly treated in the same way, members of certain groups defined on the basis of protected characteristics get to a considerably disadvantaged situation compared to others. Harassment is an intimidating or degrading behaviour that violates human dignity and is associated with a protected characteristic of the person concerned. Segregation is an unlawful separation of a group of people specified by their protected personal characteristics, while the retribution is a threatening or injurious conduct against somebody who has complained against the violation of the equal treatment.

939. Until 2020, any behaviour which infringed the principle of equal treatment may have been brought before the Equal Treatment Authority, an autonomous state administration body which may, within its competence, investigate such complaints and may, if it finds the contested action or conduct discriminatory, prohibit the discriminatory conduct, and impose a fine on the offender. Its decisions were subject to judicial review. In 2020, this body was merged into the Office of the Commissioner for Fundamental Rights, and since then the Commissioner has been carrying out this task.

940. The aforementioned positive discrimination is not considered a breach of equal treatment. It is the case when an action aims at eliminating the inequality of a social group and the preferential treatment is provisional or lasted until a condition is met. In the Hungarian legal system, there are some areas where affirmative actions are used. For instance, the Labour Code provides protection for women for the period of maternity against dismissal, while those who are in disadvantaged situation can receive extra points during the university admission process. Yet, the application of affirmative actions does not have a clear and predictable doctrinal base. The Constitutional Court, for instance, upheld the government decree automatically ensuring extra points in the university admission process to those who

368. Act CXXV of 2003.

were in disadvantaged social situation arguing that this measure had a legitimate aim, and it did not infringe the equal dignity of those people detrimentally affected by this admission system.[369]

§3.03 CONTESTED ISSUES

941. Although non-discrimination is a highly emphasized principle of the Hungarian constitutional law, in particular in recent years, a number of constitutional disputes have arisen regarding the practical application of this precept. One of the most controversial issues has been the constitutional definition of marriage and family. In Hungary, same-sex marriage has never been allowed. The Constitutional Court already in its formative years upheld the traditional concept of marriage, claiming that 'the institution of marriage has traditionally been a life community of men and women in our culture and in our law. This cohabitation typically aims at the birth and raising of children in the family',[370] even if the constitutional text of that time neither the marriage nor the family defined in this way. The Fundamental Law lays down the institution of marriage alike, 'as the union of a man and a woman established by voluntary decision', while 'family ties' are 'based on marriage or the relationship between parents and children' (Article L) section (1)). Whereas the constitutionalization of the classical form of marriage *expressis verbis* excludes same-sex marriage and thus makes a difference on account of sexual orientation, the definition of family allows discrimination on the basis of the private way of life, as the preferred family model is not only constitutionally protected, as opposed to other forms of relationships, but must be expressly favoured by the State. It is to be noted that the definition of family was built into the constitutional text by the Fourth Amendment in 2013 after that the Constitutional Court invalidated a provision of the act on the protection of families,[371] which defined the family as an emotional and economic relationship based on marriage between women and men, on parentage or adoption. Nevertheless, the Court recognized the lawmaker's right to adopt different rules on marriage and other forms of relationship stipulating that the State must also protect those relationships which are 'emotional and economic communities based on mutual care for the same purpose'.[372] Notwithstanding, the Hungarian legal system does not ensure fully equal rights for gay and lesbian couples, as they cannot marry and adopt children. It is to be added that the proposed Ninth Amendment to the Fundamental Law and the connecting legislation would continue the gender-based discrimination recognizing only the sex by birth and establishing constitutional obstacles of adoption of same-sex couples (*see supra* Part I, Chapter 2, §2.02, [C] [4] [i]).

369. Decision 635/B/2007. of the Constitutional Court.
370. Decision 14/1995. (III. 13.) of the Constitutional Court. Notably, the Court in its some other judgments abolished the discrimination based on sexual orientation. *See*, e.g., Decision 37/2002. (IX. 4.) of the Constitutional Court.
371. Act CCXI of 2011.
372. Decision 43/2012. (XII. 20.) of the Constitutional Court.

942. A gender-based discrimination is allowed by the Constitution also in terms of pension entitlements, providing that an act of Parliament 'may lay down the conditions for entitlement to state pension also with regard to the requirement for stronger protection for women' (Article XIX section (4)). On this ground, the act on social security pension system[373] enables women to retire if they worked for at least forty years, even if they have not reached the compulsory retirement age. Since this kind of differentiation, presumably as a preferential treatment, has been sanctioned by the Constitution, the Constitutional Court did not allow a national referendum to abolish this kind of discrimination.[374] There is also a differentiation between men and women in terms of defence obligation, as only adult males are obliged to armed service as a part of defence obligation. However, it is important to note that in practice, the gender gap has not been eliminated in many areas, which are most often characterized by a low proportion of female politicians and the fact that on average, women earn less for the same work than men.

943. In 2021, the so-called Child Protection Act made it possible to register the perpetrators of sexual offences against children in order 'to monitor those in direct contact with children'.[375] The law was heavily criticized for banning the promotion and display of homosexuality and gender reassignment, the portrayal of sexuality 'for its own sake' and 'deviation from the identity of the sex of birth' for those under 18 years, claiming that the law thereby confuses homosexuality with paedophilia.

944. The Fundamental Law authorizes the National Assembly to provide in a cardinal act that only persons with domicile in Hungary may be granted the right or the full right to vote and to be voted for, which breaks through the principle of the equality of citizenship as well as the equal right to vote (Article XXIII section (4)). On this basis, the Hungarian citizens who do not have a residence in the territory of Hungary may vote only for party lists but not for individual candidates. Or, among Hungarian citizens staying abroad on election day, only those who do not reside in Hungary can vote by mail.

945. The different legal status of religious communities also raises the problem of discrimination based on religion because treating these communities differently, the State ultimately considers certain religious communities to be more valuable than others (*see* outlined *infra* in Part III, Chapter 6, §6.02).

373. Act LXXXI of 1997.
374. Decision 28/2015. (IX. 24.) of the Constitutional Court.
375. Act LXXIX of 2021.

Chapter 4: The Right to Personal Liberty

§4.01 Constitutional and Statutory Guarantees of Personal Liberty

946. The first-generation rights include those that protect the freedom of individuals against state interference. The Fundamental Law safeguards that everyone has the right to liberty and security. For this purpose, no one can be deprived of liberty except for reasons specified in an act of Parliament and in accordance with the procedure laid down by law (Article IV sections (1)–(2)). Since the major threat to personal liberty is the State's criminal justice powers, the Constitution contains the most important guarantees of criminal procedure.

947. For criminal proceedings, the right to fair trial provides constitutional frameworks, according to which everyone has the right to have any charge against him or her:

- adjudicated by an independent and impartial court;
- established by an act of Parliament;
- in a fair;
- and public trial;
- within a reasonable time (Article XXVIII section (1)).

948. All these guarantees are specified by law, like the Act on organization and administration of courts,[376] the Act on Prosecution Service,[377] the Penal Code[378] and the Act on Criminal Proceeding.[379]

949. The traditional habeas corpus is included in the constitutional text in a way stating that 'any person suspected of having committed a criminal offence and taken into detention must, as soon as possible, be released or brought before a court'. In this case, the court is obliged to hear the person brought before it and have to make a decision, without delay, with a written statement of reasons to release or to arrest that person (Article IV section (3)).

950. A further constitutional safeguard is included in section (4) of the same article prescribing compensation for those persons whose liberty has been restricted without a well-founded reason or unlawfully.

951. One of the Fundamental Law's most controversial provisions refers to life imprisonment without parole, in a strange way, as a guarantee stating that this punishment may only be imposed for the commission of intentional and violent criminal offences (Article IV section (2)). However, the heavy international and domestic

376. Act CLXI of 2011.
377. Act CLXIII of 2011.
378. Act C of 2012.
379. Act CX of 2017.

criticisms have focused on the fact that the Constitution allows for a real-life imprisonment as a legitimate criminal sanction. The Penal Code clearly states that 'imprisonment lasts for a definite time or for life'.[380] According to the related rules in effect, in the case of life imprisonment, conditional leave may be allowed by a court after twenty-five years, but this possibility may be excluded in the life imprisonment sentence. It should also be noted that in certain cases the judge is obliged to impose life imprisonment on the offender.

952. The presumption of innocence is also safeguarded, declaring that no one can be considered guilty until his or her criminal liability has been established by the final and binding decision of a court (Article XXVIII section (2)).

953. Article XXVIII section (3) formulates the right to defence at all stages of criminal proceedings. This right is supported by the provision which protects the defence counsels exempting them from liability for their opinion expressed while providing legal defence.

954. The Constitution includes the principle of *nullum crimen sine lege*, specifying that no one can be held guilty or be punished on the basis of a retroactive legislation. It means that nobody has criminal liability for an act which, at the time when it was committed, was not qualified as a criminal offence. It is considered that this wording includes the *nulla poena sine lege* (no punishment without a law) as well as *nulla poena sine crimine* (no punishment without a crime). Nevertheless, the Fundamental Law allows some exceptions to these principles. First, the prohibition of retroactive criminal legislation does not prejudice the prosecution and conviction of any person for any act which, at the time when it was committed, was a criminal offence according to the generally recognized rules of international law. Furthermore, Article U) makes other exceptions in case of crimes committed under the communist dictatorship if they were not persecuted for political reasons (*see also supra* Part I, Chapter 2, §2.02, [B] [3]).

955. Article XXVIII section (6) is the double jeopardy clause of the Constitution. As specified by this provision, no one can be prosecuted or convicted for a criminal offence for which he or she has already been finally acquitted or convicted in Hungary or, within the scope specified in an international treaty and a legal act of the European Union, in another State. This prohibition does not relate to extraordinary legal remedies.

956. The right to appeal also belongs to the constitutional construction of fairness of legal procedures. This entails everyone's right to seek legal remedy against any judicial decision which violates his or her rights or legitimate interests.

957. It should also be pointed out that a number of guarantees of criminal proceedings are established and detailed in statutory law, like the right to use of mother tongue during the procedure, the obligation of public authorities, including courts,

380. Art. 34 of the Penal Code.

to give reasons for their decisions, the principle of equality of arms, or the right to access to the relevant documents of the case.

958. It is noteworthy that some other guarantees of the right to fair trial apply also to other legal procedures (like administrative or disciplinary proceedings).

§4.02 The Freedom of Residence and Movement

959. The other crucial province of the right to personal liberty is the freedom of residence and movement. Everyone who has a valid legal entitlement to reside in Hungary has the right to freely move in the whole territory of the country. Self-evidently, the private properties and public institutions having restricted areas are limitations on this right.

960. In this respect, however, there are certain differences between the rights of Hungarian citizens and foreigners, inasmuch as the citizens of Hungary may not be expelled from the territory of the country and may return from abroad at any time. At the same time, foreigners who reside in the territory of Hungary are also protected as far as they may only be expelled under a lawful decision. Moreover, collective expulsion is constitutionally prohibited, which means that an expulsion order may be issued only as a result of an individual procedure governed by law (Article XIV section (2)).

§4.03 Legitimate Limitations on the Right to Personal Liberty

961. Personal liberty can be restricted for several different reasons. The most usual restriction is the imprisonment imposed by a final judicial decision. As it has been said above, the Fundamental Law, under special circumstances, applies life imprisonment without parole. Hence, the constitutionality of this form of penalty may not be questioned, even if it means the complete denial of the right to liberty, not just the restriction of it.

962. Imprisonment can only be carried out within the frameworks of law, as a penalty imposed for a crime, on the basis of a final judicial decision made in a lawful procedure.

963. In addition, there are other coercive measures taken in a criminal proceeding, involving provisional deprivation of personal liberty. Such kind of coercive measures affecting personal liberty are detention, injunction to stay away, criminal supervision, arrest, pre-emptive enforced treatment and home detention.

964. The Act on Criminal Proceedings determines the conditions and duration of these measures. While detention may be ordered by courts, the Prosecution Service and the investigating authority, and may last up to seventy-two hours, arrest needs judicial decision, and its maximum duration can be four years.

965. Besides these, there are some sorts of police actions like catching, arrest under warrant or public safety custody. Some coercive measures restricting liberty are also applied in cases of misdemeanours (administrative offences), like short-term confinement or administrative detention. The legal conditions of the application of these measures are laid down in the Act on misdemeanours.[381]

966. Personal liberty may be restricted for public health reasons too. This may occur in case of the compulsory treatment of psychiatric patients, or in the event of an epidemic risk (quarantine, lockdown, social distancing). These compulsory actions are regulated by the Act on public health.[382]

967. The right to movement as a derived right from personal liberty has a specific limitation which was interpolated into the constitutional text by the Seventh Amendment to the Fundamental Law. The new provision, in line with the anti-migrant campaign of the government majority, prohibits the settlement of foreign population in Hungary. A foreign national, except if he or she has a legal entitlement to free movement and residence, may only live in the territory of Hungary under an application individually examined by the Hungarian authorities (Article XIV section (1)).

968. Finally, it should be noted that Hungary has on several occasions been condemned by the Court of Justice of the European Union for the conditions of imprisonment of convicted persons. This is mainly due to the overcrowding of prisons. On the other hand, over the last few years, there have been regular criticisms of the detention of asylum seekers and of the circumstances of their detention.

381. Act II of 2012.
382. Act CLIV of 1997.

Chapter 5: Privacy Rights

§5.01 Right to Private and Family Life, Home and Good Reputation

969. Privacy rights explicitly emerge in the text of the Fundamental Law. Article VI says that everyone has the right to have his or her private and family life, home, communications and good reputation respected. Another provision of the same article, which has recently been included in the text, appears to attribute a privileged role to the protection of privacy, which means that at least in some cases, it trumps over other basic rights. According to this rule, the exercise of the right to freedom of expression and assembly cannot impair the private and family life and home of others. Section (2) of this article draws the conclusion stating that the State provides legal protection for the tranquillity of homes. Besides these, the Constitution includes explicitly only the protection of personal data in the scope of privacy rights.

970. Originally, the Constitutional Court deduced the right to inviolability of a private home from the principle of human dignity, as one of its specified forms. This right protects every user's private home who has a legal title to a specific home.[383] The right to private home is protected by the civil, criminal and administrative law guarantees. In contrast, it may be restricted in cases determined by law, for example, in the course of a criminal proceeding or as a measure of police authority, as well as for health reasons, such as house-search, for secret information gathering or in case of emergency calls.

971. The right to good reputation may also be derived from the right to human dignity. In private law, it belongs to the personality rights which may be infringed upon by false allegation or rumour which offends a natural person or an organization. The persons whose right has been violated may be entitled to rectification and compensation for personal injury. This right is also under criminal law protection, as libel and defamation are crimes.

972. The law banning the showing of homosexual content to people under 18 was a serious intrusion on the right to privacy,[384] accompanied by an intense anti-LGBTQ campaign in the pro-government press.

§5.02 Personal Data Protection

973. Article VI section (3) of the Fundamental Law states that everyone has the right to the protection of his or her personal data. The Constitutional Court already in its formative years elaborated a rich case law in relation to personal data protection. The landmark decision was made as early as in 1991, when the Court declared the uniform system and general use of personal identity number unconstitutional.

383. Decision 1115/B/1995. of the Constitutional Court.
384. *See supra* n. 382.

The body formulated in this judgment the so-called right to informational self-determination, an unwritten constitutional principle which is a special form of the right to self-determination, an integral part of the right to human dignity.[385]

974. The later legislation codified the jurisprudence of the Court in this field, including the pertinent cardinal act, which regulates this right together with the freedom of information.[386] Although this law does not define the concept of 'right to informational self-determination', it is a generic term of the rights of personal data protection. Its core content is that everyone possesses his or her personal data, which can be handled by public authorities only if the person concerned has consented to the processing it, or is required by law to serve a purpose in the public interest. Besides informational self-determination, the other basic principle of personal data processing is that such kind of data may be collected, stored or used only for specific purpose set by law, to the extent and for the time necessary to achieve that purpose.

975. In this scope, the concept of personal data embraces all information and data relating to a person, from which he or she can be identified, as well as the conclusions that can be drawn from these data. Among these, the so-called specific data are under enhanced legal protection, like racial origin, nationality, religious faith or other conviction, criminal record, sexual orientation, state of health, political opinion and party affiliation, membership of an interest organization. As a major rule, state authorities may not register and process such data, unless authorized to do so by law. However, even in the cases of the specific data, the data processing of public authorities is not unlawful, if the person concerned has consented to it, it aims at pursuing public interest, and it is anonymous.[387]

976. Pursuant to the right to the protection of personal data, the concerned person may request information on what kind of personal data are kept by public authorities on him or her. He or she may request rectification of incorrect data, and in the case of unauthorized data processing, he or she may request the erasure of the unlawfully stored data. There are narrowly tailored exceptions to these rights; for example, it is not required to give information about the personal data kept as a result of secret surveillance, or there is a lower-level protection of personal data of prisoners.

977. Legal claims relating to personal data enjoy special judicial protection; in case of infringements of the right to personal data, the courts of appeal have a jurisdiction which acts in expeditious proceeding. A further peculiarity of such procedures is that the burden of proof is on the data controller. In the event of a breach of the right to the protection of personal data, the individuals concerned may be entitled to get financial compensation, while the abuse of personal data is a criminal offence sanctioned by the Criminal Code.

385. Decision 15/1991. (IV. 13.) of the Constitutional Court.
386. Act CXII of 2011.
387. Decision 74/1992. (XII. 28.) of the Constitutional Court.

978. In some areas where the exercise of certain professions inevitably requires the processing of sensitive personal data, such data are subject to special legal protection, such as medical secrets, lawyers' professional secrecy, bank secrets, and journalists' sources.

§5.03 Right to Self-Defence

979. The Fundamental Law has constitutionalized the right to self-defence. In Article V, it declares that everyone has the right to repel any unlawful attack against his or her person and property, or one that poses a direct threat to them, as provided for by an act of Parliament. This provision was controversial in the years following the new Constitution's entry into force, fearing that it would open the way to disproportionate action against any attack, but in essence, judicial practice has not changed compared to the past.

Chapter 6: Freedom of Religion

§6.01 The Scope and Limitation of the Freedom of Religion

980. The freedom of religion is guaranteed by the Fundamental Law which prescribes also that the detailed rules relating to religious communities and established churches must be laid down in a cardinal act[388] (Article VII section (5)). The oddity of this regulation is that it requires a law adopted by a qualified majority only for the regulation of the legal status of the churches, while the scope and limitation of religious freedom may be determined by ordinary law.

981. The Constitution defines freedom of religion as everyone's right to freedom of thought, conscience and religion. This right includes the freedom:

– to choose or change one's religion or other belief;
– to manifest or abstain from manifesting it;
– to practise or teach religion or other belief through religious acts, rites or otherwise;
– either individually or jointly with others;
– either in public or in private life (Article VII section (1)).

982. The Act on churches compliments this definition that freedom of conscience and religion is a fundamental right of everyone that may not be linked to the requirement of any legal form. The law also states that no one can gain any advantage or suffer a disadvantage on account of the exercise of religious freedom. Then, the parents (and the legal guardians) have the right to decide and take care of their child's moral or religious education.

983. The legal guarantees of this right are also specified by the law. Thus, freedom of religion has to be safeguarded also for the people in education, health, social, family, child care and youth protection institutions as well as for those in prison both individually and together with others. Besides that, no specific data on the religious belief can be collected by a public authority which means that the personal data relating one's faith or conviction are under special legal protection. As a reaction to the State Church Office that exercised strong political control over churches in the decades of the party-State before the system change, the law prescribes that the State may not operate or establish a body for the management and supervision of religious communities.

984. As to the limits of the freedom of religion, the law contains only a general clause, providing that the religious community may only engage in religious activities that are not contrary to the Fundamental Law, do not violate the law, and do not violate the rights and freedoms of other communities. Nevertheless, the legislative

388. Act CCVI of 2011.

empowerment granted by the Constitution for the legislature without any stipulation has opened the way for Parliament to impose strict restrictions on the freedom of religion.

985. In reality, this was achieved through the regulation of religious communities. Certainly, the right of individuals to practise their religion with others in a community is an inherent part of religious freedom. This is recognized also by the Fundamental Law, declaring that those people who share the same faith may, for the practice of their religion, establish religious communities operating in the organizational form specified in a cardinal act.

§6.02 The Legal Status of Religious Communities

[A] The Types of Churches

986. The legal regulation of religious communities is based on several different principles. First, as it has been said, the religious communities can freely be established, and the practice of religion in a community is also guaranteed. Second, the series of new legislation on churches has abandoned the basic principle of the equality of religious communities (and churches) represented by the church legislation after the system change. The Fundamental Law of 2011 openly makes a distinction between the different religious communities. In principle, this differentiation is justified by the fact that the acquisition of different church statuses depends on the fulfilment of the objective criteria laid down by law. But these conditions distinguish between the various religious communities on the base that how long they have operated, and how much their social support is. Then, the new Constitution has preserved the principle of separation of State and church, though in a modified form. As the Fundamental Law formulates, the State and religious communities 'operate separately', and, consequently, religious communities are autonomous organizations. Nonetheless, the Constitution explicitly permits the cooperation between the State and religious communities 'to achieve community goals'. According to the constitutional text, the religious communities should request such a cooperation on which the National Assembly decides. Interestingly, while the first sentence of Article VII section (4) refers to 'religious communities' as potential counterparts of the State in such a cooperation, the same provision reserves this opportunity only for the established churches. In the frameworks of such a privileged relationship, the State may provide specific rights and advantages to established churches 'with regard to their participation in the fulfilment of tasks that serve to achieve community goals'.

987. The law on churches defines religious communities as communities of natural persons, irrespective of their organizational form, which have been established for the practice of religion and primarily engage in religious activities. Moreover, they are autonomous, self-governing organizations composed of natural persons sharing the same beliefs. As a result of the political zeal for eliminating the so-called business churches (organizations that use church form only as a disguise), the law provides that the political, psychic or parapsychic, medicinal, economic or entrepreneurial, educational, health, charitable, child, youth or family protection, environmental and nature conservation, and cultural activities in themselves are not recognized as religious activities.

988. The law defines also the religious activity in a way that the religious communities carry out activities related to a worldview that targets supernatural, systemic beliefs, doctrines that relate to the entirety of reality, and encompasses the whole human personality with specific behavioural requirements.

989. Then, the Act specifies the religious communities as legal entities. It is worth noting that freedom of religion covers the right to form and run religious communities in an informal way, that is without legal personality, but these communities are not entitled to the benefits provided for the formalized churches.[389]

990. The religious communities having legal entity are the religious associations (*vallási egyesület*), listed churches (*nyilvántartásba vett egyház*), registered churches (*bejegyzett egyház*), and established churches (*bevett egyház*).

991. Among them, the religious association is the loosest organizational form. As a matter of fact, it is a special kind of civil associations as far as its aim is to practise religious activity. The State can enter into an agreement with a religious association for a limited period of time (up to five years, but the contract is renewable) to perform certain public activities or to support religious activities.

992. The religious association is entitled to a portion of the personal income tax paid and determined by individuals under a separate law. This is a particularly precious privilege, as all personal income taxpayers may offer 1% of their income tax to a church or a non-governmental organization, and significant revenue may be obtained from this source.

993. The next church ranks depend on the supporters of the respective churches, measured by the number of those taxpayers who offered certain amount from their personal income tax on the average of the previous years. Thus, those religious communities are entitled to be the so-called listed churches which have earned at least 1,000 private individuals' tax donations on the average of the previous three years, and have been operating at least five years as a religious association, or have at least 100 years of independent international operation in an organized form. The religious associations may also request registration as a 'listed church' if they have at least 1,000 registered members of residence in Hungary, have been a religious association for at least five years, and declare that, for the purpose of its religious activities or its public service activities, they do not use support from public finances, the European Union or international sources. The listed churches are also entitled to

389. Renáta Uitz, *Freedom of Religion and Churches: Archeology in a Constitution-Making Assembly*, in Constitution for a Disunited Nation: On Hungary's 2011 Fundamental Law 226 (Attila Tóth Gábor ed., Central European University Press 2012).

gather tax donations from personal income tax, and they may make a contract with the State for a maximum period of ten years.

994. The registered churches are those religious communities which have gained at least 4,000 taxpayer's donations on the average of the previous five years, and have been existing at least twenty years as a religious association, or have at least 100 years of independent international operation in an organized form. The listed churches may request this rank if they comply with the stricter conditions, such as they have at least 10,000 registered members with a residence in Hungary or have been operating as a religious association for at least twenty years. The registered churches may become a party to an agreement with the State for up to fifteen years, which can also be extended, and they are entitled to get tax donations too.

995. The highest church rank is the established church of which twenty-seven are existing in Hungary. The State may enter into a comprehensive agreement with registered churches on cooperation for community purposes. A registered church becomes established one by such an agreement which must be promulgated by law. These churches have special privileges. They are entitled to get tax donations from the individuals' personal income tax, and its supplement from the state budget, if its amount is less than the revenue of the previous year. Then, the established churches receive tax reliefs and state subsidies.

[B] State–Church Relationship

996. As a consequence of the principle of separation of State and church, the State cannot interfere in the life of religious communities; internal decisions made in the scope of the church autonomy cannot be overridden or changed by the State, and state bodies have no power to adjudicate disputes raising within religious communities. At the same time, the institutional separation means not only the protection of the internal autonomy of the churches against state intervention but also that the decisions of the religious communities cannot be enforced by using public authority. Then, churches may not exercise public power, although the debate arises from time to time that the State should recognize the Church's wedding, but it still has not yet happened.

997. As it has been said, the Fundamental Law allows the cooperation between the State and the churches to pursue public good. In this context, the State may contract with the religious communities with legal personality for different purposes, mainly for the preservation of historical and cultural values, education, health, charity, social, family, child and youth protection, cultural or sports activities. It has also been described that the State may enter into an agreement with the various churches under different conditions depending on their legal status. In addition to this, determining the conditions of the agreement, the State may legitimately take into account the historical and social role of the respective religious communities, their social acceptance, embeddedness, organization, and experience gained through their traditional public activities.

998. The first general agreement (Concordat) was concluded by an international treaty between Hungary and the Holy See in 1997; then the State concluded a bilateral agreement with several churches, primarily with the so-called historical churches. The term 'historical churches' is largely an informal naming of the four traditional Hungarian churches, the Catholic Church, Reformed Church, the Evangelical Lutheran Church and the Federation of Hungarian Jewish Communities. However, already in the 1990s, efforts were made to bring the historical churches into a privileged position, and the Constitutional Court did not object to this favouritism.[390] For example, it has not proved unconstitutional that only these churches could provide religious services in the army.[391]

999. All churches with legal personality are entitled to state subsidies, not only for public services they provide (which may be transferred from the State) but also for the support of their religious activities. It is a constitutional requirement that if churches perform a public task (e.g., maintain a school or a health institution), the budget support provided to them must not be lower than that of public bodies carrying out a similar task.

1000. In practice, since 2010, the government has strongly supported the greater social engagement of churches, even at the expense of state institutions. For example, between 2001 and 2016, the proportion of the church-maintained secondary education institutions increased from 8.2 to 22.8%, and the growth largely took place from 2010 to 2015.[392] Whereas in the 1990s, the Constitutional Court stated it as a constitutional requirement that '[w]here the state transfers the state school building into church property, for those who do not wish to attend a church school, the state has to provide them for a public school in a way that does not impose a disproportionate burden on them'.[393] Compared to this, in 2015, in almost 5% of the municipalities, only non-state schools operated.[394]

1001. The requirement of the neutrality of the State is not explicitly mentioned in the constitutional text, as it was not specified in the previous Constitution either. Nevertheless, this was postulated by the Constitutional Court as a constitutional principle in 1993.[395] However, this principle has been much less effective since 2010 than before. The Fundamental Law has subject to fierce criticism for its references to Christianity which is allegedly incompatible with the principle of neutrality of State.[396] The Fundamental Law begins with the motto that 'God bless Hungarians', and the National Avowal explicitly refers to the role of Christianity 'in preserving nationhood'. The Seventh Amendment of the Constitution declares the

390. Decision 8/1993. (II. 27.) of the Constitutional Court.
391. Decision 970/B/1994. of the Constitutional Court.
392. Tamás Hajdu, Zoltán Hermann, Dániel Horn and Júlia Varga, *A közoktatás indikátorrendszere 2017* (MTA 2018) 136.
393. Decision 4/1993. (II. 12.) of the Constitutional Court.
394. Hajdu et al., *supra* n. 399, 104.
395. Decision 4/1993. (II. 12.) of the Constitutional Court.
396. Uitz, *supra* n. 396, 202, 234.

religious commitment of the State more openly than ever before, obliging all state organs to protect the 'Christian culture of Hungary' (Article R) section (4)).

1002. Beyond these general postulations, the State may support religious activities from budget sources and cover the costs of religious education in public schools (students must choose between divinity and general ethics).

1003. Churches also enjoy privileges that other types of private law associations are not entitled to. For example, they have the right to set up and operate educational, health and social institutions, in which case they are entitled to the same amount of budget support as state or local government institutions engaged in similar activities. Their economic activities are subject to beneficial rules. Churches can collect donations and receive budget and European Union subsidies. Their religious income and its use may not be controlled by any public body, even if it comes from a budget source or income tax offers (as they are entitled to receive 1% of personal income tax offerings from taxpayers). In the case of churches, the sale of religious publications and items and the provision of church services are not considered economic-entrepreneurial activities. They have the right to establish private law companies and non-governmental organizations.

1004. As far as the operation of religious communities is concerned, a religious community with legal personality is registered by the Court of Appeal of the Capital City, provided that the applicant is engaged primarily in religious activities, has a religion and a liturgy, and does not pose a national security risk. The only exception is the established church because such a legal status can be endorsed only by Parliament in law. Religious communities operate on the basis of their own internal rules, beliefs, and liturgy. Their institutions, denominations and symbols receive increased legal protection.

§6.03 Constitutional Practice

1005. It is not surprising at all that after forty years of communist dictatorship, it was particularly important to ensure religious freedom. The Act LXXIII of 1993 on freedom of conscience and religion, and the churches introduced a state-of-the-art regulation that guaranteed the separation of State and churches, and the free exercise of religion, on which a rich constitutional jurisprudence was built. For example, the Constitutional Court declared the neutrality of the State in religious and worldview issues as a basic constitutional principle, even though it was not explicitly included in the constitutional text.[397] The Court stated in another decision that Christian holidays and Sunday rest days were constitutional because their religious character had faded and, in line with traditions, they had become social conventions.[398] Then, even if not in the text of the Constitution, the differentiation between the various religious communities emerged in Hungarian constitutional law

397. Decision 4/1993. (II. 12.) of the Constitutional Court.
398. Decision 10/1993. (II. 27.) of the Constitutional Court.

when a government decree authorized four specified denominations (Roman Catholic, Calvinist, Lutheran and Jewish churches) to establish and operate army chaplaincies. The Constitutional Court upheld this legislation arguing that the social status and acceptance, as well as the role of churches in Hungarian history, can legitimately be taken into account when the State shapes its relationships with the churches.[399]

1006. Religious freedom and the regulation of the legal status of churches have been at the centre of intense political and public debates since 2010. In 2011, a new legislation deprived more than 300 former churches of their church status, and imposed new requirements for their recognition as churches. This legal re-registration was conditional on prior approval by the legislature by a two-thirds majority vote, although an exception was granted to 'historic churches' and some other religious associations, altogether fourteen former churches which did not have to apply for recognition (shortly afterwards, Parliament restored the church status to a further eighteen former churches). It should also be noted that the new law did not provide any legal remedy for those religious associations whose applications were rejected by Parliament without any reasoning being offered. The Venice Commission held that the new regulation limited the freedom of religion,[400] and the Hungarian Constitutional Court invalidated certain provisions of the Church Law in February 2013.[401] However, only two weeks later, the Fourth Amendment to the Fundamental Law incorporated the same rules into the text of the Constitution, so all the basic elements of the highly controversial regulation remained in effect. The European Court of Human Rights also stated that the relevant legislation does not treat the various religious communities as equals, and some measures, like Parliament's decision on the recognition of churches or the absence of any right to appeal against the legislature's decision, violate the corresponding provisions of the ECHR.[402]

1007. Although the relevant rules have changed in the meantime, and the religious associations, listed churches and registered churches are registered by a court, the highest church rank is donated by Parliament, i.e., a political body which may provide this status by law on the basis of a general agreement between the government and the concerned registered church. Eventually, in this way, the government has a definitive influence over which religious community can achieve this privileged status.

399. Decision 970/B/1994. of the Constitutional Court.

400. Venice Commission, Opinion on Act CCVI of 2011 on the right to freedom of conscience and religion and the legal status of churches, denominations and religious communities of Hungary, CDL-AD(2012)004-e, Opinion 664/2012.

401. Decision 6/2013. (III. 1.) of the Constitutional Court.

402. ECHR Case of *Magyar Keresztény Mennonita Egyház and Others v. Hungary*, Application Nos 70945/11, 23611/12, 26998/12, 41150/12, 41155/12, 41463/12, 41553/12, 54977/12 and 56581/12 (2014).

Chapter 7: The Right to Assembly

§7.01 THE LEGAL SOURCES, THE CONCEPT AND THE SCOPE OF THE RIGHT TO ASSEMBLY

1008. The Fundamental Law guarantees the right to assembly in Article VIII together with the right to association. According to the Constitution, everyone has the right to 'peaceful assembly'. The detailed rules are laid down in Act LV of 2018 which replaced the earlier Act III of 1989 which was one of the very few laws that had been enacted during the system change. Secondary legislation regulating freedom of assembly also exists, including the Decree of the Minister of Interior on the duties of the police related to assuring the order of assemblies.

1009. The Act on the right to assembly defines the content of this basic right circumscribing its scope as well. According to this law, everyone has the right to organize and participate oneself or together with others in marches and demonstrations without approval or, in cases set by law, prior notice. As it has been said, this right covers only the peaceful assemblies which means that participants may not be armed with weapons or objects capable of causing bodily harm. The Act covers mainly meetings held in public areas, stating that in case of assemblies held in non-public ground, only the approval of the owner and user of the property is needed. It acknowledges also the right to participate in so-called spontaneous assembly, that is such occasional public meetings which occur spontaneously (i.e., without prior organization) as a result of an event. Self-evidently, such assemblies do not need any prior notification.

1010. In legal sense, assemblies are public gatherings of two or more people with the aim of expressing views on public matters. A gathering is 'public' if anyone can freely join it. Although the right to assembly is a constitutionalized human right, and it extends to both the organization of demonstrations and the participation in public gatherings, its scope is restricted by the Act cited above, inasmuch as only the Hungarian citizens or foreigners having a residence permit are entitled to organize an assembly.

1011. The freedom of assembly embraces all lawful acts of freedom of expression, including to make speeches, display signs, distribute flyers, shouting political slogans, and singing songs.

§7.02 THE LIMITS OF THE FREEDOM OF ASSEMBLY

1012. If somebody wants to organize an assembly on public ground, he or she must notify the event to the competent police department not earlier than three months, but not later than forty-eight hours prior to the date of the meeting. The notification must contain the name(s) and address(es) of the organizer(s), or if the assembly is announced by an organization, the same data of its authorized representative. In addition, the police authority must be informed about the location of the demonstration and its route, the start and end time, the purpose of the assembly and the expected number of participants.

1013. The right to assembly has for a long time dubiously limited in Hungarian law. The legal terminology seems to insist persistently that public meetings must be only notified, rather than approved by public authorities. However, under certain circumstances, the competent police authority may prohibit the demonstration within forty-eight hours of receipt of the notification. This is the case when it is reasonably presumed, on the basis of the information available after the consultation, that the demonstration would directly, unnecessarily and disproportionately affect public security or public order. The police may also ban the assembly if it would presumably cause unnecessary and disproportionate harm to the rights and freedoms of others. All these reasons are specified by the law. Thus, public security is endangered in particular, if the holding of the public gathering involves a criminal offence or it instigates to commit crimes. Public order may also be jeopardized if the public meeting may disturb the functioning of the courts or disturb the traffic. While these restrictions have for the entire time included by law, the Act on the right to assembly expanded the limitations in 2018 for the sake of privacy. According to this law, other people's rights and freedoms may be hurt in particular, if the street demonstration – due to the duration or the technical means employed – violates their private and family life, home, human dignity, or if it offends the dignity of the Hungarian nation, and other national, ethnic or religious communities. It is to be noted that these are only exemplary enumerations heightening the most typical abuses of the right to assembly. The participants of the demonstrations cannot hide their faces and cannot possess a weapon.

1014. The police authority may also prohibit the holding of an assembly if it would be held in a historic memorial site or on a day of commemorating the victims of inhuman crimes committed under the rule of a national socialist or communist dictatorship. Even the 'direct risk' that the inhuman crimes committed by the national socialist or communist dictatorship can be denied at the assembly gives the opportunity for the police to ban the announced public gathering.

1015. Although the decision of the police authority is not subject to administrative appeal, the organizers may contest it in court within three days. The court may change or invalidate the decision of the police authority also within three days of receipt of the request.

1016. If the assembly has been noticed by police, the organizers have a particular responsibility for the lawfulness of the demonstration. On the one hand, they must ensure the peaceful organization of the meeting and, on the other hand, they are jointly liable, together with the persons causing damage, for the harm caused to the injured third party by the participants. If the organizers fail to fulfil their obligations, the police authority may impose administrative fine on them.

1017. When the assembly is held, it may be dissolved by the organizer(s) if the behaviour of the participants endangers the legality of the demonstration. In particular, this is the case if the assembly loses its peaceful nature, or the rights or freedoms of others are violated, and 'the order may not be restored otherwise'. The police authority may dissolve the assembly, if it has not been approved beforehand (excluding the 'spontaneous' gatherings), the assembly has been prohibited, the organizers fail to fulfil their obligation to do so in the cases specified above, or the demonstration is held at a different location, route, or time than that was specified in the licensing decision.

1018. The exercise of the right to assembly is also protected by criminal law. On the one hand, the Criminal Code punishes those who obstruct others to exercise their right of assembly by force or threat, or those who prevent or seriously disturb the holding of a demonstration. On the other hand, the participants of the public gatherings may also be punished if they contravene the instructions of the organizers, or hurt the organizers while they perform their duties.

§7.03 Constitutional Practice

1019. The doctrinal bases of the right to assembly were elaborated by the Constitutional Court from the early 1990s. The Court tried to incorporate the freedom of assembly into the framework of its general approach of fundamental rights. In doing so, it argued that this right, is one of the so-called communication rights, and as such, it is in association with freedom of expression. The constitutional significance of communication rights is that they provide freedom for the self-realization of human beings.[403] The demonstrations facilitate the collective expression of opinions in public affairs. The freedom of assembly is not only an individual right, but it also imposes an obligation on the State to ensure its free exercise.[404]

1020. Otherwise, the Act on the right to assembly of 1989[405] with its liberal regulation provided a proper framework for a long time for the organization of demonstrations. Nevertheless, from the 1990s, the demonstrations of the neo-Nazi association 'Blood and Honour' addressed challenges to the legal groundwork of the right to assembly. These demonstrations often led to public outrage, which led sometimes the police to ban them on trumped-up bases. The violent police actions during the street riots in 2006 evoked an even more political and social outcry.

1021. After that the European Court of Human Rights declared in 2007 that the lack of prior notification itself does not necessarily make a demonstration illegal,[406] the Constitutional Court stated that the right of assembly also extends to gatherings

403. Decision 30/1992. (V. 26.) of the Constitutional Court.
404. Decision 55/2001. (XI. 29.) of the Constitutional Court.
405. Act III of 1989.
406. Case of *Bukta and Others v. Hungary*, Application No. 25691/04 (2007).

without prior organization, if, due to the event giving rise to the demonstration, cannot be announced three days beforehand. The obligation of prior announcement should not apply to flash mobs or spontaneous gatherings either, as they have not organizers.[407]

1022. As it has been said above, the 1989 law on the right to assembly was replaced by a new legislation in 2018.[408] Although the practice has shown some legal gaps of the old law, strange antecedents led to the adoption of the new statute. In December 2014, the police banned a demonstration planned to hold in front of the house of the Prime Minister Viktor Orbán. Because the police authority justified the refusal on grounds other than those set out in the law, the organizers challenged the prohibitory resolution, but the courts upheld the police decision. Against the final judicial judgment, a constitutional complaint was submitted to the Constitutional Court, but the Court surprisingly held that the police prohibited lawfully the demonstration, even if it used a new, non-codified reason to do so. At the same time, the Court instructed Parliament to harmonize legal rules on the protection of privacy and the freedom of assembly.[409] It was even more surprising that the Court, in another ruling, adopted on the same day, annulled a judicial decision which had confirmed a prohibitory resolution of the police authority, arguing that a demonstration may not be forbidden on the basis of hypothetical grounds (assuming that the planned gathering would be dangerous and would violate others' rights).[410]

407. Decision 75/2008. (V. 29.) of the Constitutional Court.
408. Act LV of 2018.
409. Decision 13/2016. (VII. 18.) of the Constitutional Court.
410. Decision 14/2016. (VII. 18.) of the Constitutional Court.

Chapter 8: The Right to Association

§8.01 The Legal Sources, the Concept and the Scope of the Right to Association

1023. Under the constitutional recognition by the Fundamental Law, the detailed rules pertaining to the right to association are laid down in the Act CLXXV of 2011 on the Right to Association, the Legal Status of Organisations of Public Utility and the Operation and Support of the NGOs. This law does not cover all non-governmental organizations, as separate cardinal acts regulate the operation and financial management of political parties,[411] the legal status of the churches[412] and the business organizations (companies),[413] while special acts make the legal regulation complete, like the Labour Code defining the rights of trade unions,[414] the Civil Code determining the conditions of the foundation of various types of civil organizations,[415] the Act on transparency of organizations supported from abroad,[416] or the law on the court registration of non-governmental organizations and related procedural rules.[417]

1024. The right to association is guaranteed by the Fundamental Law stating that everyone has the right to establish and join organizations. This right also includes that political parties, trade unions and other interest representation organizations 'may be formed and may operate freely' (Article VIII, sections (2)–(3) and (5)). Non-governmental organizations may be established for any lawful objectives, even though organizations with a particular purpose can have a special status, as political parties and trade unions. In the wording of the act cited above, 'by virtue of the right of association, an organization may be founded for the purpose of carrying out any activity which is in conformity with the Fundamental Law and which is not prohibited by law'.[418]

1025. Not only natural persons have the right to association, but legal persons and other organizations without legal personality have also this right, except that only natural persons may be members of a political party and a trade union.

1026. The Act on the right to association defines the limits of the right to association. Thus, the exercise of this right may not aim at the violent seizure and exercise of power, or its exclusive possession, it may not realize or call for a criminal offence, and may not breach others' rights. No armed organization may be established on the basis of the right to association. This right may not be exercised for the primary purpose of economic-entrepreneurial activities. A special restriction is

411. Act XXXIII of 1989.
412. Act CCVI of 2011.
413. Act V of 2013.
414. Act I of 2012.
415. Act V of 2013.
416. Act LXXVI of 2017.
417. Act CLXXXI of 2011.
418. Art. 3 s. (4) of the Act CLXXV of 2011.

imposed on the right to association of the members of the Hungarian Armed Forces, the police, the National Security Services, the judges and the prosecutors inasmuch as they may not be members of political parties.

§8.02 Types of Organizations Formed on the Basis of the Right to Association

1027. On the basis of the right to association, several different organizations may be formed. In legal terminology, the 'civil organization' is an umbrella term embracing all NGOs founded on the basis of the right to association. One of the major types of civil organizations is the association which can be formed voluntarily by at least ten founding members who must adopt the statute of the association and to elect its managing and representative body. An association may come into existence by judicial registration. Any other community of natural persons whose operation is not regular or which have no registered membership or organization is not considered to be an association.

1028. Natural persons may set up also a civil society organization for achieving their common goals of non-economic interest and to coordinate their activities for community purposes. In spite of the association, the civil society organization is not a legal person.

1029. The third major form of civil organizations is the foundation whose legal status is regulated by the Civil Code. The foundation is a legal entity created by the founder for the permanent realization of the specific goals defined in the founding charter.

1030. Other organizational forms founded on the basis of the right to association are the political parties and the trade unions regulated by specific laws.

1031. A civil organization can be qualified as a public benefit organization (PBO) if it is registered in Hungary and has sufficient resources to meet the common needs of society, and whose appropriate social support can be demonstrated. The services of the PBOs must be available not only to their own members, employees or volunteers of the organization, but also to others. The PBOs may be entitled to tax and duty exemption or relief.

§8.03 Working Rules of Civil Organizations

1032. In theory, the NGOs have a wide range of structural and operational autonomy; nevertheless, the law determines the members' rights and requires a democratic minimum for their internal organization when it prescribes that the most fundamental decisions (like the adoption of the founding charter, merger with another organization or the abolishment of the NGO) have to be made by the highest body of the respective civil organization, which must be the assembly of all members or an elected body.

1033. The Prosecution Service exercises legal supervision over the NGOs, and may turn to court for dismissal of a civil organization if it operates against its own statute, it commits a crime or calls for a criminal offence, and its operation violates others' rights and freedoms. In addition, the court may state the termination of an NGO if it has not been working for at least one year or the number of its members drops below ten people.

1034. Civil organizations manage their assets independently and they may have own financial resources, but they cannot be funded primarily for the purpose of carrying out economic and business activities. NGOs may legitimately receive budgetary subsidy from the State through a specialized budget fund, the National Cooperation Fund under the limitation that political parties and trade unions cannot get finance from this source.

§8.04 Recent Constitutional Development

1035. The Act on the right to association adopted in 1989 during the regime change provided a liberal regulation and an appropriate framework for guiding and administering the enthusiasm of founding civil organizations. Some of the constitutional issues raised in the first decade after the transition to democracy, still reflected the specific problems of the transition period to democracy. For example, due to the negative experiences of the party-State, or more precisely, the direct control of armed organizations by the Communist Party, the ban on party membership of soldiers and policemen was considered so important that this limitation was enshrined in the Constitution in 1989. When in 1994 the Police Independent Trade Union filed a constitutional complaint arguing that the constitutional ban infringed constitutional rights of career members of the police, the Constitutional Court refused the complaint holding that it had no competence to annul a provision of the Constitution itself.[419] In another decision, the Court held that the compulsory registration of associations is not unconstitutional, as it is a necessary precondition of the legal personality of these organizations.[420]

1036. In 1996, the Constitutional Court declared that it is a constitutional duty of the State to provide the conditions necessary for the proper physical and mental development of children, which provides a constitutional basis for limiting the right of association of children by the legislature or the judiciary. With this ruling, the

419. The European Court of Human Rights recognized in this case that the historic past and the special situation of a given state are legitimate conditions to be taken into consideration determining the limitation of a civil right. *See* ECHR Case of *Rekvényi v. Hungary*, Application No. 25390/94 (1999).

420. Decision 1487/D/1995. of the Constitutional Court.

Court upheld the ban on children being allowed to join a homosexual association.[421] Another decision said that the legal ban on the establishment of criminal organization is constitutional.[422]

1037. It is a matter of course that the civil organizations must also comply with the legal rules. In addition, operation of the NGOs may be restricted if their activities are not in accordance with their statutes. In 2007, the Court of Appeal of Budapest dissolved a neo-Nazi movement (Movement of Hungarian Guard, *Magyar Gárda Mozgalom*), because their events (mainly marches in small settlements where Roma people were in majority in the population) had directly and effectively challenged public order and public peace by expressing racial and discriminative views, and had gone far beyond the limits of free expression.

1038. After 2010 the right of association was restricted in several respects. In 2014, the government launched a political smear campaign and took administrative measures against some NGOs sponsored by international funds, the EEA Grants and Norway Grants. The government accused the aid mechanism of indirectly supporting one of the opposition parties and asked the donor countries to let the Hungarian government to decide on the distribution of all funds. The conflict lasted for years, and several criminal and administrative investigations were launched against the NGOs that received aid. After the Hungarian authorities found no crime or irregularity, the case ended at the end of 2015, when the Hungarian government promised that it would not harass NGOs supported from these funds in the future. However, since this conflict, the government has pursued political attacks and campaigns, in particular against those civil organizations which deal with human rights and/or provide legal aids for refugees and other vulnerable groups, and a legislative package restricting their activities have been adopted. The package, which was inspired by the heavy anti-migrant and Eurosceptic campaign of the government, consisted of three laws, named 'Stop Soros' referring to the government's accusations that the NGOs support immigration and are financed by George Soros, an American billionaire of Hungarian origin. One of them was adopted by Parliament in 2017,[423] which required all associations and foundations that receive funding from foreign sources (individuals, foundations, governments or agencies) above a certain amount in a tax year to notify the court in order to be registered as an 'organization supported from abroad'. Beyond this stigmatization, some other administrative measures were prescribed for the affected NGOs, like their obligation to publish the fact that they are financed from abroad on their own, as well as on a governmental homepage. The sport clubs and religious communities are exempt from the effect of this law.[424]

1039. In 2018, another legislation introduced the so-called special immigration tax which must be paid by NGOs helping or supporting immigration. The tax rate

421. Decision 21/1996. (V. 17.) of the Constitutional Court.
422. Decision 58/1997. (XI. 5.) of the Constitutional Court.
423. Act LXXVI of 2017.
424. The Act was found by the Court of Justice of the European Union in 2020 to be in breach of EU law because it had 'introduced discriminatory, unjustified and unnecessary restrictions on foreign donations to civil society organizations'. *Commission v. Hungary*, C-78/18, 18 June 2020.

was 25% of all financial support they receive. In the scope of this law, 'activities helping immigration' covered all programmes, actions and activities that directly or indirectly lead to immigration, including media campaigns or education.[425] Finally, the Penal Code was amended in 2018, introducing a new type of crime called 'facilitation and support of illegal immigration'.

1040. Although all pieces of the legislative package triggered heavy international criticism, only the criminalization of the assistance of migrants by the Penal Code has been brought to the Constitutional Court, which upheld the contested provision stipulating that it is a constitutional requirement that the effect of the law should not extend to unselfish behaviours to assist vulnerable and poor people which behaviours are unrelated to the purpose of the law.[426] Nevertheless, the European Court of Justice decided in 2021 that Hungary breached EU law by criminalizing the activity of helping people who were not eligible for international protection under national law, to initiate asylum procedures.[427] As a result, Parliament repealed the law stigmatizing the NGOs concerned.[428]

425. Act XLI of 2018.
426. Decision 3/2019. (III. 7.) of the Constitutional Court.
427. *Commission v. Hungary*, Case C-821/19, 16 Nov. 2021.
428. Act XLIX of 2021.

Chapter 9: Freedom of Expression

§9.01 The Content of Freedom of Expression

1041. According to Article IX section (1), everyone has the right to freedom of express. This right embraces not only the freedom of speech, but it includes also the freedom of the press, provided that a distinction can be made between these terms at all.[429] Freedom of expression, in principle, protects all kinds of opinions, irrespective of the form in which they are expressed. Some special fields of the right are enumerated by the Constitution separately, such as the freedom of scientific research and artistic creation (Article X section (1)).

1042. The Constitution acknowledges the State's obligation to provide institutional protection for this right when it says that Hungary recognizes and protects the freedom and diversity of the press and ensures 'the conditions for free dissemination of information necessary for the formation of democratic public opinion' (Article IX section (2)).

1043. The Fundamental Law provides that the detailed rules relating to the freedom of the press and the organ supervising media services, media products and the communications market must be laid down in a cardinal act.

1044. In this field, the law on freedom of the press and fundamental rules of media content (so-called media constitution)[430] and the law on media services and mass communication (so-called media law)[431] have the greatest importance. While the former law contains the primary scope[432] and general limitations[433] of the freedom of the press and regulates, among others, the rights of the audience (as consumers of media services) like the press rectification rights, and the obligations of the media service producers, the latter comprises the rules of the market authority and competition supervision of the media market.

1045. It can be clearly seen that the contemporary constitutional concept of freedom of expression goes far beyond the traditional content of this right, that is the prohibition of state interference in the freedom of speech and freedom of the press

429. These terms are often used as synonyms in Hungarian constitutional terminology. *See*, e.g., András Koltay, *A véleménynyilvánítás szabadsága, a sajtószabadság és a közérdekű adatok nyilvánossága*, in *Az Alkotmány kommentárja II. kötet* (András Jakab ed., Századvég Kiad 2009) 2223; Gábor Halmai, *A véleményszabadság határai* (Alantisz 1994); András Sajó, *A szólásszabadság kézikönyve* (KJK_Kerszöv 2005).
430. Act CIV of 2010.
431. Act CLXXXV of 2010.
432. Providing that the freedom of the press extends to the independence of the press from the State and any organization and interest group.
433. Declaring that the freedom of the press may not realize a crime or a call for committing a crime, must not violate public morality, or impinge on the privacy of others.

(prohibition of censorship), and it embraces also the State's institutional duty to protect actively this right and provide framework for the free information flow, primarily by maintaining public service media and protecting the rights of certain vulnerable groups.

1046. As an institutional guarantee of these State's obligations, the media law has established the National Media and Infocommunications Authority, an autonomous regulatory body which is responsible for regulating and supervising this sector of the market. Within the framework of this authority, the so-called Media Council whose primary task is to ensure the functioning of democratic publicity in the media and the legal operation of media service providers in order to maintain a pluralistic media market. It is also the Council's responsibility to keep track of the media market processes and, if necessary, to prevent market concentration that violates the law. In addition, the Council investigates the complaints about media content, including objections to the impartiality of public media. The chairman and the four members of the Media Council are elected by the National Assembly with a two-thirds majority of the MPs for nine years.

§9.02 The Limits of Freedom of Expression

1047. While the Constitution only briefly refers to the content and the protected area of the freedom of expression, it contains some restrictive provisions. Thus, it says that '[i]n the interest of the appropriate provision of information as necessary during the electoral campaign period for the formation of democratic public opinion, political advertisements may only be published in media services free of charge, under conditions guaranteeing equal opportunities, laid down in a cardinal act' (Article IX section (3)).

1048. Beyond that, the Constitution comprises also content-based limitations stating that '[t]he right to freedom of expression may not be exercised with the aims of violating the human dignity of others' and 'the dignity of the Hungarian nation or of any national, ethnic, racial or religious community'. These provisions were interpolated in the text by the Fourth Amendment to the Fundamental Law in 2013 with the justification that human dignity may restrict the freedom of expression, and the objective was to lay the constitutional foundations for the possibility of penalizing certain forms of hateful expressions if the dignity of communities is violated.[434] In accordance with this constitutional provision, human dignity is protected against hate speech also by a whole system of legal tools. The Penal Code provides that anyone who incites violence or hatred against (a) the Hungarian nation, (b) a member of a national, ethnic, racial, religious group or a member thereof, or (c) certain groups of the population or their members, in particular with regard to disability, gender identity and sexual orientation, is punishable by a term of imprisonment

434. Fruzsina Gárdos-Orosz, *The Regulation of Offensive Speech in the New Hungarian Civil Code*, 3(1) ELTE L.J. (2015) 111–112.

of up to three years.[435] In addition, according to the Civil Code, any member of a community so violated may go to court within thirty days to defend their personality rights,[436] and may file a complaint with the Equal Treatment Authority under the Act on equal treatment for the prohibition of the infringement.[437]

1049. National symbols are also under enhanced legal protection. The Penal Code punishes those who use offensive or derogatory expressions on the national emblems, or abuse otherwise the anthem, flag, coat of arms or the Holy Crown.[438] The curiosity of this provision is that it includes the Holy Crown among the protected items, although it is not a national symbol under the Fundamental Law. The Constitutional Court, abandoning its previous interpretive practice which emphasized the content-neutral protection of freedom of speech, upheld this restriction, arguing that the national symbols representing the unity of the country embody substantial constitutional values that are out of the protected area of freedom of expression.[439]

1050. The prohibition of the public use of authoritarian symbols is also an existing restriction on freedom of expression. The distribution, public use or display of swastika, SS badge, arrow cross, hammer and sickle and five-pointed red star are qualified criminal offences by the Penal Code.[440] This content-based limitation was also upheld by the Constitutional Court, referring to the special historical circumstances of the country.[441]

1051. Freedom of expression does not extend to defamation and libel, either, which are prohibited by the Penal Code, and are protected also by civil courts. Scaremongering, threat with public danger and some other crimes are also content-based limitations sanctioned by the Penal Code. The qualified data (professional and state secrets) are also protected by law, so these are legitimate limitations of freedom of speech and freedom of the press.

§9.03 Constitutional Practice

1052. After forty years of a socialist party-State, freedom of expression had a specific significance in the new constitutional arrangement. The revised Constitution guaranteed the freedom of expression, and the Constitutional Court enthusiastically began to elaborate the doctrinal bases of this fundamental right. The Court developed an interpretative practice in the early 1990s, according to which this right was a part of an even more general 'mother law' under the name of 'basic communication rights' which was thought to include freedom of the press, freedom of

435. Art. 332 of the Penal Code (Act C of 2012).
436. *See* details in Gárdos-Orosz, *supra* n. 441.
437. Act CXXV of 2003.
438. Art. 334 of the Penal Code.
439. Decision 13/2000. (V. 12.) of the Constitutional Court.
440. Art. 335 of the Penal Code.
441. Decision 14/2000. (V. 12.) of the Constitutional Court.

expression, the right to be informed, freedom of conscience and religion, freedom of assembly, freedom of artistic and scientific creation, as well as other rights ensuring the social communication. Then, the Constitutional Court allotted specific importance and constitutional rank to the freedom of expression, emphasizing that this 'right has actually to allow precedence to only a few [other] rights'.[442] In fact, the body set a sort of ranking among constitutional rights, in which freedom of expression was placed just after the right to human life and dignity. This interpretative practice was likely one of the typical examples of judicial activism since the constitutional text did not know the concept of 'communication rights' and did not rank among the fundamental rights. The landmark decision of the Constitutional Court on the freedom of expression was made in 1992, when the Court stated that this right protected all kinds of views and opinions, regardless of their 'value and truth', which was justified by the constitutional principle of the State's ideological neutrality: '[i]n this process, there is a place for every opinion, be good and harmful, both pleasant and offensive'.[443] This liberal approach of the freedom of expression was probably due to the democratic enthusiasm at the outset of the system change, but in fact, it was not entirely true at the time of its formulation, as the freedom of expression was limited in many ways on the basis of the content of the speech (e.g., in the case of libel and defamation, or breaching state secrets). Later on, both the relevant legislation and constitutional jurisprudence have gradually moved away from this broad interpretation. The prohibition of wearing totalitarian symbols, the protection of national symbols, the prohibition of public denial of the crimes of the national socialist and communist systems, and the protection of the dignity of the Hungarian nation, and the national, ethnic, racial or religious communities not only have restricted the freedom of speech based on its content but also have applied criminal law sanctions to certain kinds of speeches. The constitutionality of these content-based limitations has been accepted by the subsequent practice of the Constitutional Court, rendering the thesis of the content-neutral protection of opinions illusory.

1053. The limits of the freedom of expression have been defined and redrawn in a number of constitutional disputes. The tightening of constitutional practice can be observed with regard to hate speech cases. The landmark decision of the Constitutional Court in 1992 meant the adoption of the American clear and present danger test, stating that the pure danger of disturbing public peace was not a sufficient reason to criminalize hate speech. According to this approach, incitement to violence and hatred was a legitimate limit on freedom of speech only if it could lead to violence.

1054. Another landmark judgment of the Constitutional Court declared unconstitutional the rule that imposed stricter penalties for defamation and libel of a public authority or an official person than a citizen.[444] In effect, by way of this decision, the Court has incorporated the jurisprudence of the European Court of Human

442. Decision 30/1992. (V. 26.) of the Constitutional Court.
443. Decision 30/1992. (V. 26.) of the Constitutional Court.
444. Decision 36/1994. (VI. 24.) of the Constitutional Court.

Rights, which provides broader protection for the political speeches in public discourse. In addition, the so-called New York Times rule, imported from the American law, has also been introduced in the Hungarian constitutional law, when the Court ruled that even defamatory statements against politicians can only be punished if the offender knew that he or she alleged false things. According to the Court, a distinction must be made between the opinions and the facts, but at the same time, it has been argued that even false statements are inevitable attendants of public debates.

1055. In 2001, the Constitutional Court repealed legislation providing the right to respond to press releases because it considered it to be a disproportionate restriction on freedom of expression while not considering the institution itself to be unconstitutional.[445] The Court extended the constitutional protection to parliamentary speeches too.[446]

1056. Since 2010, the Constitutional Court has reaffirmed the broad interpretation of freedom of expression with regard to public disputes and criticism of public figures.[447] There has been lengthy litigation about whether the face of police officers performing their duties can be published in the press, as in these cases, they usually did not consent to the recording and publishing of their faces, and the protection of the image is a matter of personality rights under the Civil Code. The conflict was caused by the fact that the Constitutional Court defined the concept of public participation more broadly[448] than the *Kúria*.[449] In any case, the issue is still unresolved.

1057. However, in recent years, the Constitutional Court has not addressed the major problem of the Hungarian situation of the freedom of the press, namely the requirements of impartiality of public service media and its balanced news service. In fact, the public broadcasters, including public televisions and radios, as well as the official news agency, are tools of political campaigns of the government and the government parties, which are seriously biased and do not meet the requirements of balanced information service.[450] The media authority, which is responsible for supervising public media, has not objected to this practice since Parliament elected all the members of the board from among the candidates of the government parties for nine years in 2010, even though the previous constitutional case law stressed the public function of the press to provide comprehensive, balanced and realistic information on public affairs. As a counterweight to power, the press should control the exercise of public power and play a role as a public watchdog.[451]

---

445. Decision 57/2001. (XII. 5.) of the Constitutional Court.
446. Decision 34/2004. (IX. 28.) of the Constitutional Court.
447. Decision 7/2014. (III. 7.) and Decision 13/2014. (IV. 18.) of the Constitutional Court.
448. Decision 28/2014. (IX. 29.) of the Constitutional Court.
449. Uniformity Resolution 1/2012. BKMPJE, and its replacement in Uniformity Resolution 1/2015. BKMPJE.
450. *See*, e.g., *Report: Hungary dismantles media freedom and pluralism*, International Press Institute (2019), https://ipi.media/report-hungary-dismantles-media-freedom-and-pluralism/.
451. Decision 165/2011. (XII. 20.) of the Constitutional Court.

1058. It is worth noting as well that after 2010, the Hungarian press market was radically transformed. It is often believed that freedom of the press has been restricted by market tools rather than legal instruments. The main trend has been the acquisition of a significant part of the media market by businessmen who are allegedly closely associated with government parties. In 2016, the largest opposition newspaper, *Népszabadság* was closed by the new owner without legal successor. In 2018, many businessmen offered free of charge more than 400 press products to the newly created Central European Press and Media Foundation, classified by the government as 'strategically important' organization exempting it from the investigation of the Hungarian Competition Authority. The new media holding, which has a large share in the media market, has enabled a unified and centralized control of pro-government press products. In 2020, the independence of the largest online newspaper, the government-critical *Index* was abolished. Although *Index* was a market-leading online outlet, its owners wanted to change its operating model referring to market interests and then dismiss the editor-in-chief. Subsequently, in protest, the entire editorial staff resigned collectively. They were replaced by journalists less critical of the government.[452]

1059. It is a further constitutional problem that while the State plays a decisive role in the advertising market, public money ads are distributed not on an objective but on a political basis, thus keeping alive some pro-government press products that would otherwise be unsustainable. Concerning political campaigns, the constitutional debates of recent years have revolved around issues such as campaign restrictions, the lack of equal opportunities and the relationship between the political campaigns of the government and the government parties. While the Fundamental Law has limited the publication of political advertisements in commercial media during campaign periods,[453] the constitutional requirement of equal opportunity has become an empty slogan in the past years. For example, neither the media authority nor the courts have complained that the government conducted campaigns with unlimited use of public resources outside the legally specified campaign period (which may begin fifty days before the day of the respective election or referendum), as they have considered the publicly financed propaganda as 'information campaigns'. This issue became especially controversial after 2015 when government campaigns started to attack the European Union's migration policy. In addition, while the law on referendums[454] stipulates that electoral procedures must be applied to referendum procedures, the judicial practice makes a distinction between the two procedures requiring the safeguard of equal opportunity only for electoral process. In this way, the *Kúria* has not required the government to be neutral during the national referendums and thus opened the way for the use of public resources to

452. In a similar scenario, the then market-leading portal called *Origo* became a pro-government internet newspaper through an acquisition in 2014.
453. Art. IX s. (3).
454. Act CCXXXVIII of 2013.

support the government's position.[455] This was especially worrying because the government-sponsored campaigns were largely identifiable with the political advertisements of the government parties.

1060. In 2021, Parliament passed a salad law amending several previous laws to ban the publication of pornography and any other content that depicts sexuality for its own sake, promotes or displays gender non-conformity, gender reassignment or homosexuality for children under 18.[456] As a result of the law, sex education in primary and secondary schools has been abolished, and many bookshops only sell fiction depicting homosexual relations in a separate place and format (e.g., wrapped).

455. Decision Kvk.III.37.901/2016/2. of the *Kúria*.
456. Act LXXIX of 2021.

Chapter 10: Cultural Rights

1061. According to the Fundamental Law, Hungary ensures cultural rights, including:

(a) the freedom of scientific research; and
(b) the artistic creation;
(c) of learning (or right to education); and
(d) teaching.

§10.01 Freedom of Scientific Research

1062. Article X of the Constitution recognizes academic freedom (freedom of scientific research) and freedom of artistic creation. The State must be neutral in scientific questions. It is clearly expressed by section (2) of the same Article declaring that the 'State shall have no right to decide on questions of scientific truth; only scientists shall have the right to evaluate scientific research'. One important institutional guarantee for academic freedom is formulated in Article X section (3) in a way that higher education institutions are 'autonomous in terms of the content and the methods of research and teaching'. The only limitation imposed on this autonomy is that the organization of universities is regulated by an act of Parliament, and the government may, within the limits of that law, lay down the rules governing the management of public institutes of higher education and supervise their management.

1063. The Constitutional Court has in several decisions elaborated in detail the constitutional content of the freedom of scientific research, teaching and learning and the requirements of their regulation. According to these rulings, these are not only fundamental constitutional values but also 'subjective rights'. 'In a more general sense, academic freedom is a part of freedom of expression'.[457] In addition, the Constitutional Court has consistently held that 'the freedom of teaching and learning is a guarantee of the freedom of scientific (…) life from external interventions, [which] is realized by the way of the assessment of scientific (…) questions (…) by the scientists or their bodies'.[458]

1064. Article X section (3) expresses also that Hungary protects the scientific and artistic freedom of the Hungarian Academy of Sciences and the Hungarian Academy of Arts. In theory, the former is another institutional guarantee of academic freedom. The Hungarian Academy of Science was founded by the Act XI of 1827 for the establishment of a scientific society and the attendance of the domestic language, after that the great landowner count István Széchenyi offered the one-year income of his estate for this purpose. Today, the Academy is a public body

457. Decision 34/1994. (VI. 24.) of the Constitutional Court.
458. Decision 41/2005. (X. 27.) of the Constitutional Court.

which performs public tasks related to the maintenance, support and representation of science. It is financed by the state budget and regulated by the Act XL of 1994.

1065. The early practice of the Constitutional Court traced back academic freedom to the freedom of expression (as a 'mother right').[459] The neutrality principle does not exclude the State from setting preferences through institutions and finance.

§10.02 Freedom of Artistic Creation

1066. Freedom of artistic creation includes the creation of artworks with the free choice of subject, material and genre, that is, all forms of artistic self-expression, the exhibition and dissemination of artworks.[460] The State must refrain from judging the value of the artworks, and 'must make possible and ensure the diversity of the works of art, and may not make any art genre or artistical exclusive'.[461] However, preliminary artistic review of artworks displayed in public spaces is allowed.

1067. The State also guarantees the freedom of scientific research and freedom of artistic self-expression through the regulation of authors' copyrights.

§10.03 Freedom of Learning and Teaching

1068. In terms of the constitutional text, freedom of learning means that every Hungarian citizen has the right to education. This formulation clarifies that it is a citizen's right. In fact, not all citizens are entitled to all benefits of this right, as the university student status may be subject to conditions set by law.

1069. The Constitution recognizes the freedom of learning 'for the acquisition of the highest possible level of knowledge' (Article X section (1)). In the next section, it prescribes that the State must ensure this right by public education, which constitutes a complex institutional system. First, the right to education is provided through:

(a) free and compulsory primary education;
(b) free and generally accessible secondary education; and
(c) higher education accessible to everyone according to his or her abilities; and, finally
(d) financial support as provided for those receiving education, within the limits of the law.

1070. In an early ruling, the Constitutional Court declared that parents have the right to decide whether their children attend church or public school. However, it is

459. Decision 30/1992. (V. 26.) of the Constitutional Court.
460. Decision 24/1996. (VI. 25.) of the Constitutional Court.
461. Decision 18/2014. (V. 30.) of the Constitutional Court.

also a constitutional requirement that the State must ensure primary education in public schools everywhere.[462] Another decision stated that access to higher education for persons who have been banned from public affairs or have a criminal record may be restricted but not excluded.[463]

1071. The State is obliged to establish and manage the institutional system of public education.[464] However, church and private schools can participate in primary and secondary education on the basis of an agreement with the State. Free education in primary and secondary schools basically means that there is no tuition fee in these schools. It is to be noted that there is compulsory education up to 16 years age so it is not only a right, but an obligation to attend school. Equal treatment of every pupil is a fundamental requirement in public schools.

1072. As to the universities, such institutions can be founded by churches, business organizations and foundations.[465] State grants are provided for the catholic universities on the basis of the Concordat between Hungary and the Vatican, but the Hungarian government concluded similar agreements with some other historical churches. Universities established in a foreign country may also operate; today, there are more than twenty foreign-funded higher education institutions. Certainly, there are some legal requirements for establishing and maintaining universities. Thus, they have to offer accredited doctoral programmes in at least two fields of study. At least half of their teaching and research staff must have a doctoral degree. All universities must have at least three faculties. Hungary introduced the Bologna system gradually from 2005, so the typical education programme consists of a bachelor and master training. However, there are some exceptions to the Bologna system in the field of medical, legal, architectural and agricultural studies, where the undivided 5–6-year education programmes have remained untouched.

1073. The Fundamental Law authorizes Parliament to adopt a legislation that financial support of higher education studies is subject to participation for a definite period in employment and/or to exercising for a definite period of entrepreneurial activities, regulated by Hungarian law.

1074. Freedom of teaching does not establish enforceable right to everyone to teach in schools, as the appointment may be dependent on professional qualifications and appointments; basically, this right protects, within the limits of law, the freedom of teachers to decide what and how they teach within the limits of the law.

---

462. Decision 4/1993. (II. 12.) of the Constitutional Court.
463. Decisions 35/1995. (VI. 2.) and 12/1996. (III. 22.) of the Constitutional Court.
464. Act CXC of 2011.
465. Act CCIV of 2011.

§10.04 Recent Constitutional Development

1075. Among cultural rights, academic freedom has been mostly exposed to challenges since 2010. In higher education, a new management system was introduced in 2014 in which the university leadership has been doubled or separated into two parts along functional aspects at institutional level: since that time, the university chancellor has been responsible for the economic, financial, controlling, accounting, labour, legal, administrative, Information Technology activities of the higher education institutions and the financial management of the respective universities. Since the chancellors are appointed by the Prime Minister, and are subordinate to a Minister, they are the extended arms of the central government. Another organizational innovation was to establish so-called consistoriums: these are consistorial bodies consisting of five members of which three are delegated by the line minister, and the rector and chancellor of the institution are also members. These bodies set long-term strategic goals for the institution, and decide on medium-term institutional development plans and the annual budget programme. All these changes have strengthened the central control of universities raising the problem of spillover effect on professional issues. It revealed itself when in 2018 the government abolished the gender studies at the state-owned universities for ideological reasons.

1076. In 2017, a new legislation for the operation of the foreign-funded universities set impractical and unprecedented conditions for the respective universities, which have made the establishment and operation of foreign-funded universities dependent on an intergovernmental agreement between the governments of the source country and Hungary. The new regulation allows the operation of the foreign-funded universities only if they have a campus in their source country, unless this country is within the European Economic Area. This legislation has been enacted admittedly in order to expel the Central European University (CEU), an American-Hungarian higher education institution which has been working for twenty years in Hungary. The university is sponsored by George Soros, outcried a public enemy by the public and pro-government media. Although the CEU complied with all legal conditions, the government refused to sign a treaty with the State of New York (the host State of the CEU), and the university was forced to move its American courses to Vienna in 2019. In 2020, the European Court of Justice ruled that Hungary, by adopting and applying a law restricting the operation of foreign universities, has failed to fulfil its obligations under the EU law.[466] Although the so-called lex-CEU was brought to the Constitutional Court for a constitutional review still in 2017, the Court did not made any decision, but it declared it a moot case after that Parliament amended the contested law in line with the ECJ ruling,[467] and terminated the proceeding in 2021. However, despite the legal obstacles being removed, the Central European University, which in the meantime moved to Vienna, has not returned to Hungary.

466. *Commission v. Hungary,* Case C-66/18, 6 Oct. 2020.
467. Act LIV of 2021.

1077. From 2019, the Government has transformed several public universities into quasi-private entities, placing them under the management of non-profit foundations. Since then, most public universities have been transferred to so-called public interest foundations. These transformations have been heavily criticized because while the central government has lost control over the universities that were transferred, leading politicians of the government parties and people loyal to them were appointed to the boards of trustees of the new foundations.[468] In addition, the transformation of the University of Theater and Film Arts in August 2020 provoked a great protest since all management competences were transferred from the university leadership to a board of trustees appointed by the Government. The restructuring was accompanied by months of protests, and most teachers of the university resigned, establishing an alternative institution, whose degrees are recognized by several foreign universities. However, the outsourcing of state universities to public interest foundations continued: by the end of 2022, twenty-one former state-run high education institutions had been transferred to such foundations, and only five remained under state control. In December 2022, the European Commission suspended Erasmus+ and Horizon funds for Hungarian universities under the management of public interest foundations because this would pose a 'serious risk' to the EU budget due to the rule of law concerns, in particular corruption risks.

1078. Academic freedom was frequently invoked also against the government's plan to take over the whole network of research institutes of the Hungarian Academy of Sciences (HAS). HAS is a public body functioning as a self-regulatory legal entity which carries out a duty by practising, supporting, overseeing and representing science. Until 2019, it consisted of academicians, that is, members of the Academy elected by domestic members, and a network of research institutes covering all spheres of science. In this year, by a legislative package, all research institutes were transformed into a newly created public body of which members are elected by the Prime Minister. In this way, the central government has acquired a decisive influence over the whole spectrum of scientific research. The new legislation required the HAS to give the property of research institute (the greatest part of its own assets) to the use of the newly established public body free of charge. This issue has been also submitted to the Constitutional Court for the alleged violation of academic freedom and the right to property.

1079. In this context, it should be mentioned that in recent years the government has begun to establish a kind of parallel system of scientific institutions. In doing so, the government funded, among others, the Institute for Hungarian Studies (researching 'Hungarianness'), the Institute for the History of Regime Change, the Research Institute for National Strategy (for reuniting the nation divided by state borders), and the Veritas Institute (for historical studies), and the Ferenc Mádl Institute (for comparative law studies).

1080. In general, the cultural policy of the State and the system of cultural subsidies have been constantly centralized in recent years. Today, all cultural fields

468. Acts VIII and IX of 2021.

(including performing arts, public collections, memory politics, visual arts) are overseen by government-run 'cultural strategy institutions', which are also responsible for distributing budget support to the relevant cultural spheres. Governmental control is exercised by the National Cultural Council.[469]

469. *See* Act CXXIV of 2019.

Chapter 11: Economic Rights

§11.01 Freedom of Enterprise

1081. Among economic rights, the freedom of enterprise is of paramount importance, at least in the sense that it is not only an individual right but also a fundamental principle of economic life. As it has already been said, Article M) section (1) of the Fundamental Law declares that 'Hungary's economy is based on value of (…) freedom of enterprise'. Having regard to the fact that the National Avowal of the Constitution replaced the reference to the social market economy in the former constitutional text, this statement presumably plays the same role, that is, to declare the principle of market economy otherwise. As a matter of fact, this foundation of the country's economic life is corroborated by the freedom of enterprise as an individual right.

1082. In its early practice, the Constitutional Court regarded this right as an aspect of the right to free choice of occupation and work,[470] although it was explicitly included already in the previous Constitution, where this right was linked to the basic principle of freedom of competition.[471] In theory, the core function of this right is to enable people to establish and proceed freely with economic activity, but the Constitutional Court has ever been cautious to recognize it, stressing that 'no one has the right to exercise a particular profession in the form of an undertaking', but the right to free enterprise means only that the State should not prevent the citizens from becoming entrepreneurs.[472] This enigmatic argumentation justified the judgment of the Court which upheld a local government decree that limited the number of taxi cars in the capital city of Budapest.

1083. Despite the uncertainties in the protected areas of this right, it is certain that the exclusive economic activities of the State restrict the freedom of enterprise. In this field, the State has a wide-ranging discretionary power to define economic areas where only the State can carry out economic activities or which are subject to strict state supervision. In this respect, there is only a formal requirement limiting the freedom of action of the State, namely that these economic areas or activities must be specified by cardinal acts. In fact, the government since 2010 has interpreted the scope of exclusive state economic activities in a very broad way, cutting out more and more economic activities from the domain of free market economy. In many cases, it does not mean that only a state organization or a state-owned company can carry out certain activities; since 2010, the government has pursued a so-called orthodox economic policy, as part of which it is admittedly striving to change the economic elite in several economic sectors and branches, and to gain majority Hungarian ownership. The first can be exemplified by establishing state monopoly on the gambling industry, then giving gambling concessions for a few private enterprise, or the reallocation of state land tenures and tobacco retail

470. Decision 54/1993. (X. 13.) of the Constitutional Court.
471. *See* Art. 9 s. (2) of the Constitution of 1949/1989.
472. Decision 21/1994. (IV. 16.) of the Constitutional Court.

licences. There are a number of legal and non-legal tools for creating majority ownership for Hungarian investors and entrepreneurs. For example, the government may declare an economic project 'investment of national importance' by government decree in order to simplify or hasten the necessary administrative procedures and to make easier to obtain administrative licences.[473] This legal instrument together with the granting of state subsidies to certain business organizations or investments, as well as the extensive practice of 'managed public procurements', have already rendered the early jurisprudence of the Constitutional Court illusory, according to which it is unconstitutional if the State, by means of public authority, creates a more advantageous position for itself (or for others) over other actors of economic life.[474]

1084. The constitutional jurisprudence also knows the freedom of contract, even though this is not explicitly recognized by the Fundamental Law. The substance of this right is that in the scope of private legal relationships, the parties are free to conclude contracts and, within the limits of law, freely determine its content. Just because this right does not have a constitutional rank, the level of state intervention is much higher, and the freedom of contract can be restricted more than constitutional rights. However, even in this constitutional context, the possibility of state intervention has significantly expanded in recent years. It can be demonstrated by the Constitutional Court's decisions in foreign currency loan-related cases. The antecedent of these cases was that, as a result of the financial crisis beginning in 2008, the debt burden of loans previously denominated in foreign currencies increased significantly due to the depreciation of the *forint*, placing thousands of debtors in a difficult situation. In order to ease their situation, Parliament has retroactively amended such loan agreements by law. In its Decision 34/2014 (XI. 14.), the Constitutional Court examined the constitutionality of the legislative act regulating the nullity of exchange rate margins in foreign currency loan contracts and the presumed unfairness of provisions enabling banks to unilateral amendment interests, fees and costs in foreign currency consumer loan contracts.[475] Although the Court acknowledged that the act did have a restrictive effect on the fundamental rights in question such as on the freedom to contract, the right to property, the right to fair trial and, furthermore, the act might raise concerns with regard to its *ex tunc*, retroactive effect, which is against the rule of law, the act is not unconstitutional as the legislative solution was proportionate with the aim to protect the citizens in desperate financial situations. Giving priority to substantive justice before procedural justice is a new phenomenon in the Hungarian constitutional jurisprudence. The Court emphasized in this case the responsibility of the State to provide help for people in desperate situations, and do justice for them, overruling former principles developed by the Constitutional Court related to the constitutional relevance of procedural fairness, legal stability, predictability and the ban on retroactive legislation.

473. *See* Act LIII of 2006.
474. *See* Decisions 50/1991. (XI. 19.) and 59/1992. (XI. 6.) of the Constitutional Court.
475. Act XXXVIII of 2014.

§11.02 PROPERTY RIGHTS

1085. The right to property and inheritance is also under constitutional protection (Article XIII section (1)). While the Constitution does not specify the protected area of this right, the Constitutional Court built up a sophisticated jurisprudence on property rights in the 1990s. However, in contrast with some other constitutional rights, the interpretative practice of the Court has substantially changed in recent years.

1086. It is worth noting that the constitutional definition of the right to property is not the same as its civil law definition. The Constitutional Court elaborated a specific rights-based justification for it, instead of the traditional approach which considered the right to property as a set of disposition rights, like use, exploitation or rental. In the view of the Court, the right to property is an important component of the human personality providing the material basis for individual autonomy. As such, it enjoys the same rights protection than other constitutional rights.[476] In addition, the Court expanded this level of protection from its classical domains (like moveable and immovable property) to rights representing assets, like pension savings or bank accounts.[477] Beyond this, property rights cover ownership rights of companies, while only the insurance-based social entitlements. Nevertheless, the constitutional protection applies only to existing statutory entitlements and it does not provide an unconditional right to acquire any property.

1087. The Fundamental Law contains a special restriction of the right to property, stating that property entails 'social responsibility'. Although the precise content of this provision is unclear, it is to be noted that this right does not protect the personal assets as a whole; it means that constitutional protection cannot be invoked against public payment obligations (like paying taxes).

1088. Nevertheless, the Constitutional Court traditionally applies public interest test to constitutional controversies related to property rights, which is a milder analysis compared to the necessity/proportionality test, examining whether restrictions imposed on the right to property is really based on public interest. This examination has a crucial role in adjudging the constitutionality of expropriation, the conditions of which are determined by the constitutional text, presumably because it results in complete deprivation of property rights. According to these requirements, property 'may only be expropriated exceptionally, in the public interest and in those cases and ways provided for by an Act, subject to full, unconditional and immediate compensation'. These guarantees protect primarily the private property; however, it is disputed whether it can be invoked in defence of other forms of property. The 1990s were accompanied by controversies over the constitutionality of restrictions on local government property, and in 2019, an amendment to the Higher

476. Decision 64/1993. (XII. 22.) of the Constitutional Court.
477. Decisions 17/1992. (III. 30.), 64/1993. (VI. 3.), 867/B/1997., 1138/B/1995., 51/2001. (IX. 15.), 109/2008. (IX. 26.) of the Constitutional Court.

Education Act obligating the Hungarian Academy of Sciences to transfer the greatest part of its assets free of charge to the use of a newly established state organization.

1089. Noteworthy, the traditional constitutional view that emphasized the equality of property forms can no longer be maintained; the state and local government properties, which are classified by the Fundamental Law as 'national assets', are subject to much stricter restrictions than property of individuals or private organizations. Within this category, certain movable and immovable properties (like the Holy Crown and the coronation jewels, the building of Parliament, minerals, rivers and lakes, national parks, etc.) belong to the exclusive state properties.

1090. It can also be noted that the authorization of the people by Article V of the Fundamental Law to repel any unlawful attack and threat covers also the defence of property.

1091. Since the political turn of 2010, the level of protection of property rights has significantly decreased compared to the previous years. This was partly due to the fact that in 2011, the Constitutional Court was deprived of the power of constitutional review of public finance laws (*see* outlined *supra* in Part II, Chapter 6, §6.03, [B]). The decreasing protection of property rights opened the way for the so-called unorthodox economic policy of the government, including the distraction of the assets of private pension funds (which had been working from 1998). These funds had about three million members, and collected almost three trillion HUF (about 10% of the Hungarian GDP). In the autumn of 2010, Parliament adopted a law to divert the private pension contributions to the state budget temporarily for the next fourteen months.[478] Besides that, the law contained a set of provisions to force the people to leave the private pension funds, transferring their savings to the state budget by returning to the state pension scheme, prescribing that people who opt to stay in the private funds will lose their future pension claim from the State, even though their employer is bound to pay social security contributions for them also in the future. In fact, it was a nationalization of the assets of the private pension funds confiscating of their members' savings, but the legal way for constitutional review has disappeared in the meantime.

1092. In another decision, the Constitutional Court upheld the extremely controversial law[479] which had completely restructured the tobacco retail trade market, withdrawing the state concessions from the earlier tobacconists, and redistributing the government approvals through a highly debated application system. The Court argued that the earlier licences had not established a vested right for the tobacco sellers to continue their activity without any limitation. Furthermore, it spectacularly turned away from its earlier practice when declared that the tobacco seller's licence does not fall within the scope of the property rights. Notably, in contrast with this decision, the European Court of Human Rights held that the withdrawal of

478. Act CLIV of 2010.

479. Decision 3194/2014. (VII. 14.) of the Constitutional Court.

the prior licences by law without compensation was such a breach of property rights which was a violation of Article 1 of the Protocol No. 1 of the European Convention of Human Rights.[480]

1093. It is to be noted that in certain economic spheres and activities (tenancy of state-owned lands, gambling, etc.), a quite similar development has taken place, when public concessions were withdrawn from the former beneficiaries and redistributed them to new ones by law.

§11.03 The Right to Free Choice of Work and Occupation

1094. Whereas in the past, the Constitutional Court needed significant creativity to render meaningless the previous constitutional provision on the right to work, which had been rooted in the original text of the Constitution of 1949, the Fundamental Law corrected this mistake, and, according to the former Constitutional Court practice, it provides that everyone has 'the right to choose his or her work, and employment freely and to engage in entrepreneurial activities' (Article XII section (1)). But the change is not just about replacing the right to work with the right to freely choose a job. On the one hand, a general obligation is attached to this right stating that everyone is 'obliged to contribute to the enrichment of the community through his or her work, in accordance with his or her abilities and potential'. Furthermore, the right entrenched in this article is not a real one; as it turns out in section (2), this is not a constitutional right, but only a state objective because Hungary 'strives' 'to create the conditions that ensure that everyone who is able and willing to work has the opportunity to do so'.

1095. Even in this weakened form, one could think that this right has a preeminent role as the Fundamental Law handles the work as a basic constitutional value. As Article M) section (1) enunciates, '[t]he economy of Hungary shall be based on work which creates value'. Nevertheless, in reality, this constitutional declaration was inspired by the objective of a 'working society' as embedded in the political ideology of government parties and has no practical significance.

1096. As a matter of fact, the only constitutional meaning of the right to free choice of work and occupation is the ban of forced labour.

1097. The concerning jurisprudence of the Constitutional Court was based primarily on the earlier constitutional text and was largely linked to the social aspects of this right, such as the decision that the right to free choice of work and occupation does not guarantee a social benefit for unemployed persons, but it is a possible element of the social welfare system.[481]

---

480. ECHR Case of *Vékony v. Hungary*, Application No. 65681/13. (2015).
481. Decision 45/B/1997. of the Constitutional Court.

§11.04 Employee's Rights

1098. From a theoretical point of view, the employee's rights are at the crossroads of social and economic rights. Yet, they are discussed here because the relevant rights as they are laid down in Article XVIII of the Fundamental Law are real constitutional rights, whereas social rights at the constitutional level appear only as state objectives.

1099. The Constitution provides the possibility of concluding collective agreements between the employees and employers and the right 'to take collective action to defend their interests, including the right of workers to discontinue work'. The detailed rules of the right to strike are determined by law.[482] It is a right protected by the Constitution: while no one may be obliged to cease to work (i.e., the participation is voluntary in such an action), it is illegal to compel anyone to abstain from taking part in a lawful strike.

1100. The right to strike has a number of limitations. In exercising this right, the employees and employers must cooperate with each other. Before the strike begins, the parties must go through a negotiation procedure, and only if it does not lead to a compromise within seven days, is allowed to stop working.

1101. Strike may be organized only for protecting economic and social interests, so it is not allowed for political goals. Similarly, no strike can be held against individual employer actions or omissions which are subject to judicial review. It is prohibited to go on strike in the courts, the Hungarian Defence Forces, the law enforcement agencies and the national security services, while special rules apply to the administrative bodies. No strike may be initiated or held if it would directly and severely endanger life, health or the environment.

1102. Further restrictions are put on certain public service producers, particularly in the areas of public transport and telecommunications, as well as in the supply of electricity, water, gas and other energy. In these cases, any strike may be held only after an agreement about the minimal level of service delivery. The extent and conditions of sufficient service may be determined by law. In the absence of legal regulation, the scope and terms of sufficient service need to be agreed during pre-strike consultation; in this case, the strike may be sustained if the parties have entered into the agreement or, in the event of failure thereof, at the request of either of the parties, the court decides on the extent and conditions of the service delivery.

1103. It is to be noted here that the Fundamental Law explicitly recognizes that trade unions and other interest representation organizations may be formed and may operate freely on the basis of the right of association (Article VIII section (5)). The rights of trade unions are specified by the Labour Code. Thus, for example, trade unions have the right to represent their members vis-à-vis the employer, initiate and

482. Act VII of 1989.

organize strikes (including solidarity strike). Among these rights, the prohibition of discrimination based on the trade union membership can be highlighted which is guaranteed by judicial protection.

1104. Every employee has also the right to working conditions which ensure respect for his or her health, safety and dignity, as well as to daily and weekly rest periods and to a period of annual paid leave.

1105. In 2022, after the teachers' trade unions organized a countrywide strike in March 2022 to demand a pay-rise for teachers and the reform of public education, the government, using the exceptional power conferred on it in an emergency, has set the level of so-called sufficient services almost the same as in the normal case. For example, this regulation prescribed that primary schools must provide the same supervision as usual, and 100% of lessons of compulsory subjects must be held for students preparing for matriculation. In this way, the emergency legislation has completely removed the teachers' right to strike. This legislation was confirmed by Parliament in May 2022 with a 'salad law' amending more than forty laws. The law was challenged by opposition MPs before the Constitutional Court. The ruling in this case gave the Court another opportunity to prove its loyalty to the government. In its decision, the Constitutional Court rejected the petition but did not feel the need to give detailed reasons for its ruling. By stating that, according to the Constitution, '[e]very child shall have the right to the protection and care necessary for his or her proper physical, mental and moral development', it simply declared that the right of teachers to strike was restricted for legitimate purposes, in a necessary and proportionate manner.[483]

1106. The Twelfth Amendment to the Fundamental Law significantly restricted the labour rights of soldiers when it stipulated that 'no trade union may be formed and operate in connection with the status of a professional member of the Hungarian Defence Forces'.[484]

483. Decision II/1665/2022. of the Constitutional Court.
484. *See supra* Part I, Chapter 2, §2.02 [C] [4] [l].

Chapter 12: Social Rights

§12.01 The Constitutional Nature of Social Rights under the Fundamental Law

1107. The constitutional status of social rights has substantially changed with the entry into force of the Fundamental Law. While they were considered constitutional rights in the previous Constitution, the Fundamental Law specifies them only as state aims.[485] It should be noted, however, that the status of social rights as real fundamental rights was not clear before under the 1949/1989 Constitution either. For example, the Constitutional Court did not consider it unconstitutional that the State did not guarantee the right to housing.[486] In fact, the constitutional jurisprudence recognized only the minimum subsistence level as a constitutional requirement.[487] The Court derived this right from the right to human dignity. But even in this case, the precise level of minimum subsistence level could not be defined by judicial tools, so the State had a wide margin of appreciation to determine the forms and extent of social services. Then, social rights have always been linked to the citizenship.

1108. As Article XIX section (1) formulates it, Hungary 'strives' 'to provide social security to all of its citizens'. Still, it provides also that every Hungarian citizen, within the limits of the law, is entitled to assistance in the event of maternity, illness, invalidity, disability, widowhood, orphanage and unemployment for reasons outside of his or her control. It means that those citizens who are not able to take care of themselves without their own fault must receive certain social benefits from the State.

1109. According to section (2), the State fulfils this obligation primarily through the system of social security embracing social institutions and measures. However, the forms and extent of social care depend on the economic performance of the State.

§12.02 The Subjects and Content of Social Rights

1110. The Constitution specifies certain groups of people which are deemed to be particularly in need, and, therefore, are the main target groups of social benefits. These are the elderly people who can be helped and supported by a general state pension system based on social solidarity and by allowing for the operation of voluntarily established social institutions. In addition, women may get 'stronger protection' in regard to the conditions for entitlement to state pension (Article XXI section (4)). Finally, here it can be referred to Article XV section (5) declaring that

485. Zsolt Balogh, Fruzsina Gárdos-Orosz, *Gazdasági, szociális és kulturális jogok* in Alkotmányjog (Iván Halász, Dialóg Campus 2018) 262.
486. Decision 42/2000. (XI. 8.) of the Constitutional Court.
487. Decision 32/1998. (VI. 25.) of the Constitutional Court.

by means of separate measures, the Hungarian State protects 'families, children, women, the elderly and those living with disabilities'.

1111. The past constitutional debates could inspire the constitution-makers to specify the objective to provide legal protection for homes. For this purpose, the State strives 'to ensure decent housing conditions and access to public services for everyone' (Article XXII section (1)). The Constitution counts on local authorities in these efforts, not only in contributing to creating decent housing conditions but also in 'protecting the use of public space for public purposes by striving to ensure accommodation for all persons without a dwelling'. Probably, this provision was devoted to counterbalance the frequently contested next paragraph according to which the use of public space as a habitual dwelling is prohibited. The criminalization of homelessness, especially among the constitutional provisions on social rights, is a surprising idea (*see supra,* Part I, Chapter 2, §2.02, [C] [4] [g]).

1112. Another troubling limitation is formulated in section (3) stipulating that the 'nature and extent of social measures may be determined in an Act in accordance with the usefulness to the community of the beneficiary's activity'. Indeed, this rule may have been born in the spirit of linking the rights and duties, even if only in case of social rights rather than classical liberties.

1113. As it has been mentioned, the State provides social care through the system of social security operating social institutions, social benefits (payments) and services in kind (like home nursing). In Hungary, a mixed system of social security works consisting of solidarity-based and insurance-based components. Most social services are provided *ex gratia* which depend on the economic performance (and political will) of the State, while its freedom of discretion is much narrower in case of 'purchased' services. It has already been explained how the protection of property rights has weakened since 2010, which has also led to a weakening of social rights. As a very recent development, for example, an act of Parliament restricted access to healthcare stating that if a person who is obliged to pay healthcare contribution fails to do so, and the resulting arrears exceed three times the monthly amount of his or her contribution, lose the right to free healthcare which means that his/her insured relationship ceases until the debt is settled.[488]

1114. The legal frameworks of social services are laid down primarily in the Act on the protection of families[489] and the Act on social administration and services.[490]

488. Art. 46 s. (2) of Act CXXII of 2019.
489. Act CCXI of 2011.
490. Act III of 1993.

Chapter 13: Third-Generation Rights

1115. The third-generation rights are not separate from other basic rights in the constitutional text, either. Still, those rights can be classified into this category which have been invented in the past decades, and protect certain vulnerable groups, or have been brought about by scientific and technical progress.

§13.01 The Rights of Children and the Protection of Families

1116. The Fundamental Law declares the right of every child 'to the protection and care necessary for his or her proper physical, mental and moral development' (Article XVI section (1)). The institution of marriage also enjoys constitutional protection (Article L) section (1)). The children's right 'to receive the protection and care of their family, and of the State and society' as well as the protection of family and marriage was recognized already by the former Constitution.[491]

1117. However, as far as the protection of the institutions of family and marriage, the new Constitution has brought about several innovations. On the one hand, it tries to give a kind of ideological fundament for the marriage defined 'as the union of a man and a woman established by voluntary decision', while the family is acknowledged 'as the basis of the survival of the nation'. Beyond that, family ties are 'based on marriage or the relationship between parents and children' (Article L section (1)). Surprisingly, this solemn assertion has not been placed in the Preamble of the Fundamental Law, but it is entrenched in the norm text of the Constitution. True, the National Avowal (the Preamble) also contains a reference to the family in an even solemn form expressing that '[w]e hold that the family and the nation constitute the principal framework of our coexistence'.

1118. The constitutional definition of the family and marriage triggered heated debates. In particular, it was criticized for its strong ideological content, and because, by reinforcing the traditional family and marriage model, the Fundamental Law narrowed the legal concept of these social institutions, thereby differentiating between citizens on the grounds of the type of cohabitation they chose in their private lives. In fact, by defining marriage according to its traditional model the Fundamental Law imposes a constitutional ban on the legal recognition of same-sex marriage for the future and, furthermore, it prefers the conventional family model against over other forms, such as cohabitation, single form of life or childless marriage.

1119. As a matter of fact, the discrimination based on sexual orientation is not a new phenomenon in Hungarian constitutional law. Although the Court declared in

491. Art. 67 s. (1) and Art. 15 of the Constitution of 1949/1989.

the early 1990s that human dignity enshrines the right of individuals to self-determination which includes the right to freedom of marriage,[492] it did not extend this right to same-sex couples, although the concept of family was not defined in the former Constitution and by the family law in that time. In fact, the Constitutional Court stated that 'the institution of marriage in our culture and in our law is a symbiosis of a man and a woman', and the Constitution provides protection only for this kind of marriage.[493] The Constitutional Court has always insisted on this interpretation of marriage,[494] although the previous constitutional text, as I have already pointed out, did not define its concept.

1120. The Parliament adopted a law in 2007 for the legalization of the relationship of same-sex partners.[495] Although this was a great progress towards the equal rights of gay and lesbian people, the law did not eliminate all discrimination, as it did not recognize the same-sex marriage, and did not allow the adoption of a child for same-sex couples.[496]

1121. Both the legal literature and the constitutional practice seem to agree on the fact that the constitutional protection covers only the cohabitation of two persons by marriage.[497] The Constitutional Court pointed out in a case that no national referendum may be held on the introduction of polygamy.[498]

1122. The Fundamental Law prescribed that the protection of families must be regulated by a cardinal act. On this basis, the National Assembly passed the relevant law in 2011 (Family Law).[499] According to this law, the State protects the institutions of family and marriage as self-values, and encourages the families as the primary frameworks of having children. On this ground, the law created the opportunity to give special support to the traditional family model in budgetary, social and tax policy.

1123. The content of the children's right to protection and care aims at ensuring their 'proper physical, mental and moral development'. This is not only the responsibility of the parents, who are obliged to take care of their minor children, including the provision of their schooling, but also of the State, which is bound to operate child protection institutions.

---

492. Decision 22/1992. (IV. 10.) of the Constitutional Court.
493. Decision 14/1995. (III. 13.) of the Constitutional Court.
494. Decision 65/2007. (X. 18.) and 75/2007. (X. 19.) of the Constitutional Court.
495. Act CLXXXIV of 2007.
496. For this, *see* Orsolya Szeibert-Erdős, *Same-Sex Partners in Hungary: Cohabitation and Registered Partnership* 4(2) Utrecht L. Rev. 212–221 (2008); and András Jakab, *Az Alkotmánybíróság első határozata a bejegyzett élettársi kapcsolatról* 1 Jogesetek Magyarázata (2010) 9–16.
497. Balázs Schanda, *A házasság intézményének védelme a magyar alkotmányjogban* 4 Iustum Aequum Salutare (2008) 68.
498. Decision 75/2007. (X. 19.) of the Constitutional Court.
499. Act CCXI of 2011.

1124. As a part of child protection, the Fundamental Law prohibits the employment of children, except in those cases specified by law, where there is no risk to their physical, mental or moral development. The Constitution declares also that Hungary ensures the protection of 'young people and parents at work' 'by means of separate measures' (Article XVIII sections (1)–(2)).

1125. The children's rights are listed in a special law,[500] and in the Family Law. Thus, all children have the right to be cared and to grow up in a family. Those children, who are in a disadvantaged situation, have the right to special assistance in increasing the chances of their development. They have to be protected against any physical, sexual or psychological violence. Unless otherwise provided by law, the children have the right to know their family of origin.

1126. The Fundamental Law provides for parents the right to choose the way of upbringing to be given to their children. Besides that, the Family Law enumerates a number of other parents' rights relating to their children.

1127. It is a very special constitutional provision that adult children are also obliged to take care of their parents if they are in need (Article XVI section (4)), but this constitutional command is a dead letter in practice.

§13.02 Rights of Persons with Disabilities

1128. Several provisions of the Fundamental Law relate to the rights of persons with disabilities. Article XIX section (1) enumerates also disability as an entitlement to social benefits set by law. Article XV section (2) specifies it among the protected characteristics as regards the prohibition of discrimination. Article H) states that Hungary protects the Hungarian Sign Language 'as a part of the Hungarian culture'.

1129. The specific rights of disabled persons are entrenched in an act of Parliament.[501] The most important of these are the right to equal treatment, that is the right to non-discrimination based on disability, the right to a barrier-free, perceptible and safe built environment, and the right to equal opportunities providing independent way of life, active participation in social life, and equal access to public services for disabled persons. Since a number of fundamental rights may be limited on the basis of mental incapacity, like the right to self-determination, privacy, property, the right to choose freely vocation and work, or the right to vote, the rules of guardianship of mentally disabled persons must be adopted by law.

---

500. Act XXXI of 1997.
501. Act XXVI of 1998.

§13.03 THE RIGHT TO PHYSICAL AND MENTAL HEALTH

1130. Article XX of the Fundamental Law has a very special content, forasmuch as the two sections of the article, in a sense, seem to be contradictory. Whereas section (1) states that everyone has the right to physical and mental health, the next paragraph shows that this is merely a state objective. Section (2) describes the way in which the State has to promote the realization of this right. Accordingly, this aim is pursued by the State:

- through agriculture free of genetically modified organisms (which means a constitutional ban on GMO agricultural production);
- by ensuring access to healthy food and drinking water;
- by organizing safety at work;
- by healthcare provision;
- by supporting sports and regular physical exercise; and
- through environmental protection.

1131. The standards of these state activities are entrenched in sectoral laws, like the Act on CLIV of 1997 on healthcare, which specifies the patients' rights. Some of these rights (like the right to informant consent to medical treatments) can be deduced from the right to self-determination, an integral component of human dignity, while others impose obligations on the State to provide proper health services. Then, whereas everyone has the right to life-saving medical care in case of urgent need, other care for preventing severe or permanent health damage, and pain relief, most forms of healthcare are based on an insurance or contractual relationship.

1132. According to the constant practice of the Constitutional Court, there are no constitutional standards for the level of physical and mental health; it depends on the capacity of the State.[502]

§13.04 THE RIGHT TO HEALTHY ENVIRONMENT

1133. The healthy environment is definitely one of the conditions for the physical and mental health of people. Although Article XXI of the Constitution postulates it as a fundamental right, in constitutional jurisprudence, it is considered as a state objective. In any case, it is hardly possible to derive or enforce specific, individual and enforceable rights from this abstract right. The constitutional text does not specify the protected area of this right, but sections (2) and (3) of this article only impose general obligations that can contribute to maintaining a healthy environment. Thus, section (2) states the well-known principle of environmental protection, namely that anyone who causes damage to the environment is obliged to restore it or to bear the costs of restoration as provided for by an act of Parliament. The next paragraph prohibits the transport of pollutant waste into the territory of

502. *See*, e.g., Decision 1316/B/1995. of the Constitutional Court.

Hungary for the purpose of waste disposal. The Fundamental Law contains an obligation in this respect elsewhere, in the chapter 'Foundation', where it states that it is the obligation of the State and everyone to protect and maintain natural resources, in particular, arable land, forests and the reserves of water; biodiversity, in particular, native plant and animal species and to preserve them for future generations (Article P) section (1)).

1134. It can be considered a constant approach of this constitutional right that it is closely related to the right to life and the right to physical health. In addition, this right implies obligations on the State rather than particular enforceable rights. Even though the Constitutional Court ruled in an early decision that it is not possible to retreat from the level of protection once achieved, unless it is necessary for another fundamental right, but even in this case, not disproportionately,[503] this requirement is mostly meaningless, because it apparently does not mean the invariability of environmental standards.

§13.05 The Right to Biological Self-Determination

1135. Although the constitutional text does not know the right to 'biological self-determination', it comprises some provisions which can be clearly derived from the right to human dignity, and within it, from the right to self-determination. Apart from the content of these rights, it is indicated by their placement in the Fundamental Law.

1136. Article III of the Fundamental Law specifies some prohibitions which are unconditional requirements of the right to human dignity. Among these rights, the Constitution prohibits the performance of medical and scientific experiments on human beings without their informed and voluntary consent, as well as the practices aimed at eugenics and the use of the human body or its parts for financial gain, as well as human cloning (Article III sections (2)–(3)). The prohibition of eugenics, human organ trafficking and human cloning are innovations which were not included in the previous Constitution. Beyond the relevant legal rules, so far, no specific constitutional jurisprudence has evolved in respect of these rights.

503. Decision 28/1994. (V. 20.) of the Constitutional Court.

Chapter 14: The Right to Vote

§14.01 THE CONTENT OF THE RIGHT TO VOTE

1137. Article XXIII of the Fundamental Law guarantees the right to vote for every adult Hungarian citizen. This right comprehends both the active (to cast a vote in elections) and passive (the right to be elected in elections) right to vote. The only exception to this rule is that those who have been sentenced to imprisonment without being disqualified from public affairs as an additional penalty, or to compulsory medical treatment by a final judicial decision in a criminal proceeding, are entitled only to cast a vote in the elections, but are not eligible.

1138. As it can be seen, this is basically citizens' right, but in the case of the elections of local government representatives and mayors and of members of the European Parliament, the right to vote is extended also to every adult citizen of another Member State of the European Union with domicile in Hungary. In addition, those foreigners who have a refugee, immigrant or resident status in Hungary are entitled to participate in local elections as voters (i.e., they have active right to vote).

1139. As far as Hungarian citizens are concerned, their right to vote extends to the parliamentary elections, the elections of the members of European Parliament and local elections. Evidently, the right to vote in local elections is restricted to those citizens who have a domicile in the settlement or county where local election is held or have a registered place of residence there.

1140. The constitutional regulation of right to vote is based on five fundamental principles: the right to vote is general, equal and free which is exercised in direct and secret voting.

§14.02 CONSTITUTIONAL PRINCIPLES OF RIGHT TO VOTE

[A] Universal Right to Vote

1141. The basic principles of right to vote in their entirety are set out in respect of the general elections, saying that members of the National Assembly are elected 'by universal and equal suffrage in a direct and secret ballot, in elections which guarantee the free expression of the will of the voters, in the manner laid down in a cardinal act' (Article 2 section (1)).

1142. The universal suffrage is guaranteed for every election by Article XXIII section (1), but section (6) of this article comprises also its limits. Besides the Hungarian citizenship, the other requirement of general right to vote is the majority (full age) which means reaching the age of 18. In addition, according to the Civil Code, a minor is considered of full age if he or she – with the permission of the guardianship authority, after reaching the age of 16 – has married.

1143. One who is banned from public affairs, or does not have mental capacity necessary to exercise the right to vote, may be excluded by a final judicial decision from the right to cast a vote or eligibility in elections. As a matter of fact, it has a constitutional safeguard that any Hungarian citizen may be disenfranchised only by court for a criminal offence or limited mental capacity. Before 2010, mentally disabled citizens were excluded from the right to vote by law. However, the European Court of Human Rights ruled in a Hungarian-related case that the practice which does not provide for individual proceeding in such cases is contrary to the European Convention on Human Rights.[504]

1144. The central registry of voters is kept by the National Election Office. The legal rules of managing the registry are laid down in Act XXXVI of 2013 on the electoral procedure.

[B] Equal Right to Vote

1145. The equality of the right to vote means, on the one hand, that everyone has the same number of votes in the election, and, on the other hand, everyone's vote has to be taken into account in the same way (every vote is equivalent).[505]

1146. However, the Fundamental Law itself makes an exception to the first criterion when it allows Parliament to provide in a cardinal act that only persons with domicile in Hungary may be granted the right or the full right to vote and to be voted for, and may specify further requirements for the eligibility to be voted for. Indeed, this stipulation which puts a limitation on the equality of the right to vote, has opened the way to grant suffrage for the Hungarian citizens who live abroad who may vote only on party lists, but, in the absence of Hungarian residence, they may not vote for individual candidates. In the lack of this provision, this kind of differentiation would be unconstitutional, as it was concluded by the Constitutional Court when similar one had been made between voters who had had residence in Hungary.[506]

1147. The second criterion sets the requirement for the electoral system that individual constituencies must be designed so that each of them has approximately the same number of voters. N.B., some differences are permissible if they have constitutional reasons (such as consideration of administrative boundaries or nationality ratios), but the greater the difference in the number of voters in the various constituencies, the stronger the justification required.[507] It is also a constitutional requirement that the boundaries of constituencies be prescribed by law.[508] When the

504. ECHR Case of *Alajos Kiss v. Hungary*, Application No. 38832/06 (2010).
505. Decision 809/B/1998. of the Constitutional Court.
506. Decision 6/1991. (II. 28.) of the Constitutional Court.
507. Decision 22/2005. (VI. 17.) of the Constitutional Court.
508. Decision 193/2010. (XII. 8.) of the Constitutional Court.

electoral districts were redrawn in 2013, the recommendation of the Venice Commission was mostly followed according to which the average difference between the size of individual constituencies should not be more than 10%, but should not exceed 15%.[509] However, the Court's practice has been less strict in recent years in this area. In a decision, the Court stated that the principle of equal right to vote is 'not a fundamental right, but a constitutional principle, a guarantee governed by the Fundamental Law, and cannot therefore be judged according to the necessity/proportionality test which is applied to fundamental rights'.[510] According to the current legal rules, the number of voters entitled to vote in single-member constituencies may not differ by more than 20% from the national arithmetical average of voters.

1148. Another concern about the equal right to vote was a differentiation made by the electoral procedural rules between the Hungarian citizens on the basis that they had a residency in Hungary or not. While the Hungarians living beyond the borders were allowed to vote by postal voting, it was not permitted for those who resided in Hungary but were abroad on election day. However, the Constitutional Court did not object this differentiation holding that this difference did violate neither the right to free elections nor the right to non-discrimination. The Court argued that the residence requirement expresses a more intensive connection to the political community so it can be expected that those voters will be at home on election day or go to an embassy or a consulate to cast a vote. Then, the undoubted advantage of the possibility of postal voting for non-resident voters was a form of compensation for them for disadvantage of having only one vote in the parliamentary elections.[511]

[C] Direct and Secret Voting

1149. Direct voting means that voters cast their vote directly to the candidates, rather than an elector or an electoral body. This principle prevails in all kinds of elections. The only exception is the election of the Assembly of the Capital City, where the mayors of the capital districts are ex officio members of the representative body, but the Constitutional Court found constitutional this election method.[512]

1150. Sometimes this principle is interpreted as a requirement that voters may cast their vote only in person, not by proxy. Although this is indeed the case, conceptually, direct right to vote refers to the direct relationship between voters and candidates.

509. Act XXXVI of 2013.
510. Decision 3141/2014. (V. 9.) of the Constitutional Court.
511. Decision 3086/2016. (IV. 26.) of the Constitutional Court.
512. Decision 26/2014. (VII. 23.) of the Constitutional Court.

1151. Secret voting is guaranteed by the electoral procedural rules, where the voters anonymously cast their votes in a closed booth in polling stations. The vote counting committees may record only the appearance of the voters and the fact of voting.

[D] Free Right to Vote

1152. This principle was introduced *expressis verbis* into the Hungarian constitutional law by the Fundamental Law. Although there is no well-elaborated jurisprudence about this requirement, its evident content is that all voters may freely decide whether or not they take part in the elections and whom they vote for.

Chapter 15: Other Political Rights

1153. The Fundamental Law recognizes some other rights which enable citizens to participate in the decision-making processes of public affairs.

§15.01 THE RIGHT TO VOTE IN REFERENDUMS

1154. In addition to the right to vote in the elections, the participation in local and national referendum is also a form of direct exercise of public power deriving from the principle of popular sovereignty. Accordingly, the Fundamental Law, in parallel with the right to vote in general and local elections, provides everyone's right to participate in national and local referendums (Article XXIII section (7)). This means that this right can be exercised by the same persons who have the right to vote, and the procedural rules to be applied are the same, as they are laid down in the Act on Electoral Procedure.[513]

§15.02 THE RIGHT TO HOLD A PUBLIC OFFICE

1155. Although the right to hold a public office is an important, constitutionally recognized form of citizens' participation, it can be classified neither as a fundamental human right, nor as an enforceable entitlement of the citizens to hold an office. In fact, this right offers a possibility for the citizens to participate in the indirect exercise of public power, not as a principal, but as an agent in the system of power-sharing.

1156. The subjects of this right are Hungarian citizens; the laws governing legal status of the categories of public service (government officials, judges, prosecutors, etc.) stipulate Hungarian citizenship among the general conditions of employment.

1157. From a legal point of view, this right provides an equal opportunity for everybody to be elected or appointed to a public office. In the wording of the Fundamental Law, every Hungarian citizen 'has the right to hold public office according to his or her aptitude, qualifications and professional competence'. On the basis of this right, in theory, everyone may apply for any public office, including the elected representatives of the National Assembly or local governments, and all positions of public service. 'A public office is to be understood as any activity which presupposes direct participation or contribution to the exercise of public power (in particular, acting on behalf of the State), whether or not it is an "occupation" in constitutional term.'[514]

1158. Since nobody has a personal privilege to hold a specific public office, it is not a limitation on this right if the occupation of public offices is subject to election

513. Act XXXVI of 2013.
514. Decision 52/2009. (IV. 30.) of the Constitutional Court.

or certain qualifications. Even a legitimate election or appointment does not constitute an unconditional right to hold a certain position, as the term of office may be terminated for statutory reasons and in specific legal procedures (e.g., in case of disgrace or as a result of disciplinary action or if the conditions for election or appointment are no longer met).

1159. Nonetheless, the Fundamental Law empowers Parliament to determine in cardinal act public offices that may not be held by members or officials of political parties. The legal limitation of the term of office or the exclusion of the possibility of re-election for specific representative functions is considered also rational and justified restrictions on the right to hold public office.

1160. According to a decision of the Constitutional Court, the legislative permission for administrative agencies to dismiss government officials without justification violates the right to hold public office.[515] However, this judgment did not provide any legal protection for government officials fired after the change of government in 2010, as the legislator enacted the 'loss of confidence' as a legitimate reason for dismissal which does not request further justification.

§15.03 Freedom of Information

1161. The Fundamental Law declares the freedom of information together with the right to protection of personal data. This connection (which already existed in the previous Constitution) was probably motivated by the view that these rights often emerge as a barrier to one another. The content of freedom of information appears in the constitutional text as everyone's right to access and disseminate data of public interest. The Fundamental Law also set up a joint body to ensure the application of the right to the protection of personal data and to access data of public interest in the form of an independent authority which must be established by a cardinal act. This is the National Authority for Data Protection and Freedom of Information regulated by an act adopted in 2011 on informational self-determination and freedom of information.[516]

1162. This law defines the data of public interest as information or knowledge, in any way or by any means, arising out of or in connection with the activities of state administration agencies, local governments or other public authorities, which do not fall within the scope of personal data. It is a legal obligation of the public authorities to publish these data in their scope of responsibility. Beyond this, there is another category of data which do not belong to the scope of data of public interest, but the law orders their disclosure in the public interest.

1163. According to the law, all public authorities must allow anyone to have access to the public interest data in their possession. Anyone may request it orally,

515. Decision 8/2011. (II. 18.) of the Constitutional Court.
516. Act CXII of 2011.

in writing or electronically, and the request must be discharged within fifteen days, or denied within eight days with written justification. The refusal of the request may be challenged before the court. It is a special guarantee that the burden of proof is on the public authority in these cases.

1164. Freedom of information has a number of legitimate limitations. First and foremost, the protection of personal data restricts the access to data of public interest. In addition, the so-called qualified data (i.e., state or professional secrets) are protected against publicity according to the level of secrecy and the duration (which may last up to thirty years) of this qualification, set by law.[517] In short, those data are to be 'qualified' the publicity of which would be detrimental to the public interest (including interests of sovereignty, foreign affairs, constitutional order, defence, national security, criminal, public finance, national economy). It is important, however, that only an act of Parliament may restrict the publicity of data which would be otherwise data of public interest.

1165. In recent years, the legal tools of the freedom of information have significantly weakened. In 2011, the aforementioned law on this right abolished the institution of the Parliamentary Commissioner for Data Protection, that is, the ombudsman who was independent of the Executive. The newly established National Authority for Data Protection and Freedom of Information is an autonomous administrative agency, integrated into the executive power, whose chairman is not elected by Parliament but appointed by the Head of State. This institutional change was consolidated by the Fundamental Law. As a result of the amendment of this law in 2015, the access to data of public interest became more difficult than beforehand. Since then, public authorities may charge a fee to cover the costs of the supplying the requested data. In certain cases this can be a very large amount, which may deter both citizens and NGOs from requesting data.

1166. Moreover, in recent years, there have been several debates about the public interest nature of certain data and whether they can be disclosed. The most well-known case of these was when the Hungarian National Bank established several foundations and companies from its business profits, and refused all data requests arguing that the funds of these organizations 'have lost their public money nature'. However, the Constitutional Court declared that these are public funds, so information regarding their expenditure is to be qualified as data of public interest. According to the Court, companies owned by the National Bank are indirectly owned by the State, while the foundations are financed from public funds and they perform public tasks, that is why there was no legitimate aim to limit the freedom of information in this respect.[518] Public authorities frequently query the public nature of certain payments and state aids, like the subsidies paid by private and public companies for sport or cultural activities, albeit these can be deduced from their corporation tax.

517. Act CLV of 2009.
518. Decision 8/2016. (IV. 6.) of the Constitutional Court.

§15.04 THE RIGHT TO PETITION

1167. This right implies everyone's entitlement to submit, either individually or jointly with others, written applications, complaints or proposals to any organ exercising public power. It is an inherent content of the right that nobody can be disadvantaged for having filed a petition with a public body. In a proper sense, this is an auxiliary tool besides the right to appeal and, at the same time, it might be an effective way of inclusion of citizens in decision-making processes of public bodies.

1168. This right, by its very nature, can be exercised not only by individuals but also by organizations and communities. Since the contacted public authorities apparently are not bound by the petitions, there are only a few relevant procedural rules. However, it makes sense that the requested bodies have to reply to the petitions within thirty days.

Selected Bibliography

Bakó Beáta, *Challenges to EU Values in Hungary – How the European Union Misunderstood the Government of Viktor Orbán* (Routledge, 2023).

Balogh Zsolt, Gárdos-Orosz Fruzsina. *Gazdasági, szociális és kulturális jogok* in Alkotmányjog (Iván Halász, Dialóg Campus 2018).

Bánkuti Miklós, Halmai Gábor and Scheppele, Kim Lane. 'From Separation of Powers to a Government without Checks: Hungary's Old and New Constitutions'. In *Constitution for a Disunited Nation: On Hungary's 2011 Fundamental Law*, edited by Gábor Attila Tóth. Central European University Press 2012.

Chronowski Nóra and Varju Márton. 'Constitutional Backsliding in Hungary'. *Tijdschrift voor Constitutioneel Recht* 6 no. 3 (2015).

Chronowski Nóra. *The Post-2010 'Democratic Rule of Law' Practice of the Hungarian Constitutional Court under a Rule by Law Governance,* 61(2) Acta Juridica Hun. J. Leg. Stud. (2020).

Chronowski Nóra, Ágnes Kovács, Zsolt Körtvélyesi and Gábor Mészáros, *The Hungarian Constitutional Court and the Abusive Constitutionalism,* 7 MTA Law Working Papers (2022).

Csink Lóránt, Schanda Balázs and Varga Zs. András (eds). *The Basic Law of Hungary: A First Commentary.* Clarus Press–National Institute of Public Administration 2012.

Detre László, Jakab András and Lukácsi Tamás, *Comparing Three Financial Conditionality Regimes and their Application to Hungary: The Conditionality Regulation, the Recovery and Resilience Facility Regulation, and the Common Provisions Regulation,* Max Planck Institute for Comparative Public Law & International Law (MPIL) Research Paper No. 2023/23.

Dezső Márta et al. *Hungary.* Wolters Kluwer 2010.

Dupré Catherine. *Importing the Law in Post-Communist Transitions: The Hungarian Constitutional Court and the Right to Human Dignity.* Hart 2003.

Fazekas Mihály and Tóth István János. 'From Corruption to State Capture: A New Analytical Framework with Empirical Applications from Hungary'. *Political Research Quarterly* 69 no. 2 (2016).

Gárdos-Orosz Fruzsina. 'The Hungarian Constitutional Court in Transition – From Actio Popularis to Constitutional Complaint'. *Acta Juridica Hungarica, Hungarian Journal of Legal Studies* 53 no. 4 (2012).

Gárdos-Orosz Fruzsina and Szente Zoltán (eds). *Alkotmányozás és alkotmányjogi változások Európában és Magyarországon* (NKE Közigazgatás-tudományi Kar 2014).

Selected Bibliography

Gárdos-Orosz Fruzsina. 'The Regulation of Offensive Speech in the New Hungarian Civil Code'. *ELTE Law Journal* 3 no. 1 (2015).

Gárdos-Orosz Fruzsina, *The reference to constitutional traditions in populist constitutionalism – The case of Hungary,* Hungarian Journal of Legal Studies 61(1) (2020).

Gárdos-Orosz Fruzsina. Constitutional Interpretation under the New Fundamental Law of Hungary, in *Populist Challenges to Constitutional Interpretation in Europe and Beyond* (Fruzsina Gárdos-Orosz and Zoltán Szente eds, Routledge, 2021).

Gárdos-Orosz Fruzsina and Kinga Zakariás. Organisational, Functional and Procedural Changes of the Hungarian Constitutional Court 1990–2020, in *The Main Lines of the Jurisprudence of the Hungarian Constitutional Court. 30 Case Studies from the 30 Years of the Constitutional Court (1990 to 2020)* (Fruzsina Gárdos-Orosz and Kinga Zakariás eds, Nomos 2022).

Győry Csaba & Nyasha Weinberg, *Emergency powers in a hybrid regime: the case of Hungary,* The Theory and Practice of Legislation, 8(3) (2020).

Hajdu Tamás, Hermann Zoltán, Horn Dániel and Varga Júlia. *A közoktatás indikátorrendszere 2017* (MTA 2018).

Halász Iván and Schweitzer Gábor. *Szimbolika és közjog: Az állami és nemzeti jelképek helye a magyar alkotmányos rendszerben* (Kalligram 2010).

Halmai Gábor. *A véleményszabadság határai* (Alantisz 1994).

Halmai Gábor. 'The Hungarian Approach to Constitutional Review: The End of Activism? The First Decade of the Hungarian Constitutional Court'. In *Constitutional Justice, East and West. Democratic Legitimacy and Constitutional Courts in Post-Communist Europe in a Comparative Perspective*, edited by Wojciech Sadurski. Kluwer Law International 2002.

Halmai Gábor. *Ungarn* in Handbuch Ius Publicum Europaeum. Band I. Grundlagen und Grundzüge staatlichen Verfassungsrechts (Armin von Bogdandy, Pedro C. Villalón and Peter M. Huber (eds) C. F. Müller Verlag 2007).

Halmai Gábor. *The Invalid Anti-Migrant Referendum in Hungary.* Verfassungsblog 2016 https://verfassungsblog.de/hungarys-anti-european-immigration-laws/.

Halmai Gábor. 'Illiberal Constitutionalism? The Hungarian Constitution in a European Perspective'. In *Verfassungskrisen in der Europäischen Union*, edited by Stefan Kadelbach. Nomos 2018.

Illés Gábor, Körösényi András and Metz Rudolf. 'Broadening the Limits of Reconstructive Leadership: Constructivist Elements of Viktor Orbán's Regime-Building Politics'. *The British Journal of Politics & International Relations* 20 no. 4 (2018).

Jakab András and Cserne Péter. *A kétharmados törvények helye a magyar jogforrási hierarchiában* 5 no. 2 Fundamentum (2001).

Jakab András. 'The Republic of Hungary: Commentary'. In *Constitutions of the Countries of the World*, edited by Rüdiger Wolfrum and Rainer Grote. Oceana 2008.

Jakab András and Szente Zoltán. *Az Országgyűlés hatáskörei, 19.§* in Az Alkotmány kommentárja I. kötet (Jakab András (ed.) Századvég 2009).

Jakab András. Az Alkotmánybíróság első határozata a bejegyzett élettársi kapcsolatról, 1 no. 2 Jogesetek Magyarázata (2010).

Jakab András and Szilágyi Emese. *Sarkalatos törvények a magyar jogrendben* in A magyar jogrendszer állapota (András Jakab and György Gajduschek (eds) MTA TK JTI 2016).

Jakab András and Gajduschek György. 'The Rule of Law, Legal Consciousness and Compliance'. In *Social Report [of Hungary]*, edited by István György Tóth. TÁRKI Social Research Institute 2019.

Kelemen Katalin, *The New Hungarian Constitution: Legal Critiques from Europe,* 42 Review of Central and East European Law (2017).

Kilényi Géza. *Az alkotmányozás és a 'kétharmados' törvények* Jogtudományi Közlöny 49 no. 5 (1994).

Koltay András. *A véleménynyilvánítás szabadsága, a sajtószabadság és a közérdekű adatok nyilvánossága*, in Az Alkotmány kommentárja II. kötet (András Jakab (ed.) Századvég Kiad 2009).

Kovács Kriszta and Tóth Gábor Attila. 'Hungary's Constitutional Transformation'. *European Constitutional Law Review* 7 no. 2 (2011).

Kovács Kriszta. 'Equality: The Missing Link'. In *Constitution for a Disunited Nation: On Hungary's 2011 Fundamental Law*, edited by Attila Tóth Gábor. Central European University Press 2012.

Körösényi András, Parlamentáris, vagy 'elnöki' kormányzás? Az Orbán-kormány összehasonlító perspektívából Századvég 6 no. 20 (2001).

Kukorelli István (ed.). *Alkotmánytan* (Osiris, 5th ed. 1998).

Küpper, Herbert. *A kétharmados/sarkalatos törvények jelensége a magyar jogrendszerben* MTA Law Working Papers (2014).

Majtényi László and Zsugyó Virág (eds). *Harcz az Alkotmányért* (Kalligram 2019).

Mezey Barna and Szente Zoltán. *Európai alkotmány- és parlamentarizmustörténet* (Osiris Kiadó 2003).

Molnár Csaba and László Róbert. *Hány szavazó kell az Összefogásnak a parlamenti többséghez?* http://www.valasztasirendszer.hu/?p=1942632&_ga=2.225841500.751485544.1561494981-851406330.1561494981.

Molnár Kálmán. *Magyar közjog* (Danubia 3d ed. 1929).

Nagy Ernő. *Magyar közjog* (3d ed. 1890).

Paczolay Péter. 'The New Hungarian Constitutional State: Challenges and Perspectives'. In *Constitution Making in Eastern Europe*, edited by Dick Howard. The Woodrow Wilson Center Press 1993.

Pálné Kovács Ilona. *Integráció és dezintegráció a területi közigazgatásban* in Egy évtized önkormányzati mérlege és a jövő kilátásai (Imre Verebélyi (ed.) 2000).

Pálné Kovács Ilona. *Helyi kormányzás Magyarországon* (Dialóg-Campus Kiadó 2008).

Petrétei József. Magyarország alkotmányjoga I: Alapvetés, alkotmányos intézmények (Kodifikátor Alapítvány 2013).

Pogány István. 'Constitutional Reform in Central and Eastern Europe: Hungary's Transition to Democracy'. *International and Comparative Law Quarterly* 42 no. 2 (1993).

Rady Martyn (ed.). *Customary Law in Hungary: Courts, Texts, and the Tripartitum.* Oxford University Press 2015.

Sajó András. *A szólásszabadság kézikönyve* (KJK_Kerszöv 2005).

Schanda Balázs. *A házasság intézményének védelme a magyar alkotmányjogban*, Iustum Aequum Salutare 4 no. 3 (2008).

Schiemann John W. *The Politics of Pact-Making. Hungary's Negotiated Transition to Democracy in Comparative Perspective.* Palgrave Macmillan 2005.

Schwartz Herman. *The Struggle for Constitutional Justice in Post-Communist Europe.* The University of Chicago Press 2000.

Schweitzer Gábor. A magar királyi köztársaságtól a Magyar Köztársaságig: Közjog- és tudománytörténeti tanulmányok (Publikon Kiadó, 2017).

Sólyom László. Az alkotmánybíráskodás kezdetei Magyarországon (Osiris Kiadó 2001).

Somody Bernadette, Szabó Máté Dániel, Vissy Beatrix and Dojcsák Dalma. *Alapjogi tanok I* (HVG-ORAC 2018).

Sulyok Gábor. 'Incorporation of International Law into Domestic Law under the Fundamental Law of Hungary'. In *The Transformation of the Hungarian Legal System 2010–2013*, edited by Péter Smuk. Complex 2013.

Szabó Miklós. *A jogforrás* in Bevezetés a jog- és államtudományokba (Miklós Szabó (ed.) Bíbor Kiadó 1997).

Szájer József. Szabad Magyarország, szabad Európa: Újabb tizenöt év. Beszédek, írások, dokumentumok 1998–2013 (2014).

Szeibert-Erdős Orsolya. 'Same-Sex Partners in Hungary: Cohabitation and Registered Partnership'. *Utrecht Law Review* 4 no. 2 (2008).

Szente Zoltán. 'Functions of the National Assembly Within the Constitutional Tradition of Hungary'. *Historia Constitucional* 8 (1997).

Szente Zoltán. *A törvénykezdeményezési jog* in Az Alkotmány kommentárja: I. kötet (András Jakab (ed.) Századvég Kiadó 2009).

Szente Zoltán. *Az Országgyűlés tagjainak jogállása* in Az Alkotmány kommentárja: I. kötet (András Jakab (ed.) Századvég 2009).

Szente Zoltán. *Verfassung und Verfassungsmäßigkeit im ungarischen Parlamentsrecht*, Jahrbuch für Ostrecht 50 no. 1 (2009).

Szente Zoltán. *Kormányzás a dualizmus korában* (Atlantisz 2011).

Szente Zoltán. *A historizáló alkotmányozás problémái: A történeti alkotmány és a Szent Korona az új Alaptörvényben*, Közjogi Szemle 4 no. 1 (2011).

Szente Zoltán. 'The Doctrine of the Holy Crown in the Hungarian Historical Constitution'. *Journal on European History of Law* 4 no. 1 (2013).

Szente Zoltán. 'Breaking and Making Constitutional Rules: The Constitutional Effects of Financial Crisis in Hungary'. In *Constitution in the Global Financial Crisis: A Comparative Analysis*, edited by Xenophon Contiades. Ashgate 2013.

Szente Zoltán. 'The Interpretive Practice of the Hungarian Constitutional Court: A Critical View'. *German Law Journal* 14 no. 8 (2013).

Szente Zoltán. 'The Political Orientation of the Members of the Hungarian Constitutional Court between 2010 and 2014'. *Constitutional Studies* 1 no. 1 (2016).

Szente Zoltán. *The Controversial Anti-Migrant Referendum in Hungary Is Invalid.* https://constitutional-change.com/the-controversial-anti-migrant-referendum-in-hungary-is-invalid/

Szente Zoltán. 'Challenging the Basic Values? Problems in the Rule of Law in Hungary and the Failure of the EU to Tackle Them'. In *The Enforcement of EU Law and Values: Ensuring Member States' Compliance*, edited by András Jakab and Dimitry Kochenov. Oxford University Press 2017.

Szente Zoltán and Gárdos-Orosz Fruzsina. 'Judicial Deference or Political Loyalty? The Hungarian Constitutional Court's Role in Tackling Crisis Situations'. In *New Challenges to Constitutional Adjudication in Europe: A Comparative Perspective*, edited by Zoltán Szente and Fruzsina Gárdos-Orosz. Routledge 2018.

Szente Zoltán. *A parlamentek története: A korai rendi gyűlések kialakulásától a modern népképviseleti törvényhozásokig* (Országház Könyvkiadó 2018).

Szente Zoltán. *The Twilight of Parliament – Parliamentary Law and Practice in Hungary in Populist Times*, 1 International Journal of Parliamentary Studies (2021).

Szente Zoltán, From guarding the constitution to serving politics – the decline of the Hungarian Constitutional Court, in *Constitutionality of Law without a Constitutional Court A View from Europe* (Miroslaw Granat ed, Routledge, 2023).

Szente Zoltán, *Constitutional identity as a normative constitutional concept,* Hungarian Journal of Legal Studies 63(1) (2022).

Szigeti Ernő. *A körjegyzőségi rendszer térszerkezeti jellemzői* (ECOSTAT 2009) http://www.kozigkut.hu/doc/szigeti_09okt.pdf.

Szikinger István. 'Hungary's Pliable Constitution'. In *Democratic Consolidation in Eastern Europe*, Volume I. Institutional Engineering, edited by Jan Zielonka. Oxford University Press 2001.

Takács Albert and Kmetty Ildikó. *Az eutanáziához való jog: Indítvány az Alkotmánybírósághoz,* Fundamentum 7 no. 1 (2003).

Tomcsányi Móric. *Magyarország közjoga* (Királyi Magyar Egyetemi Nyomda, 5th ed. 1943).

Tóth Gábor Attila. *Az emberi méltósághoz való jog és az élethez való jog* in Emberi jogok (Gábor Halmai and Attila Tóth Gábor (eds) Osiris Kiadó 2003).

Tóth Gábor Attila. *Az élethez való jog* in Emberi jogok (Gábor Halmai and Attila Tóth Gábor (eds) Osiris Kiadó 2003).

Tóth Gábor Attila (ed.). *Constitution for a Disunited Nation: On Hungary's 2011 Fundamental Law.* Central European University Press 2012.

Tóth Gábor Attila. *A jogok törvénye: Értekezések az alkotmányos szabadságról* (Gondolat 2014).

Trócsányi László. *The Dilemmas of Drafting the Hungarian Fundamental Law: Constitutional Identity and European Integration.* Schenk 2016.

Uitz Renáta. 'Freedom of Religion and Churches: Archeology in a Constitution-making Assembly'. In *Constitution for a Disunited Nation: On Hungary's 2011 Fundamental Law*, edited by Attila Tóth Gábor. Central European University Press 2012.

Varju Márton, Chronowski Nóra, Sulyok Gábor and Bárd Petra. 'Hungary: Constitutional (R)evolution or Regression?'. In *The Role of National Constitutions in European and Global Governance. National Reports*, edited by Anneli Albi and Samo Bardutzky. T.M.C. Asser Press 2019.

Vörös Imre. 'The Constitutional Landscape after the Fourth and Fifth Amendments of Hungarian Fundamental Law'. *Acta Juridica Hungarica* 55 no. 1 (2014).

Vörös Imre. *A történeti alkotmány az Alkotmánybíróság gyakorlatában,* Közjogi Szemle 7 no. 4 (2016).

Selected Bibliography

Zakariás Kinga. *Az élethez és az emberi méltósághoz való jog* in Az Alkotmány kommentárja II. kötet (András Jakab (ed.), Századvég Kiadó 2009).

Zakariás Kinga. *Az emberi méltósághoz való alapjog. Összehasonlító jogi elemzés a német és a Magyar alkotmánybírósági gyakorlat tükrében* (Pázmány Press, 2019)

Zongor Gábor. *A lebegő megye* (Comitatus Könyv- és Lapkiadó 1994).

Documents

Bertelsmann Stiftung Transformation Index BTI, https://www.bti-project.org/en/reports/country-reports/detail/itc/HUN/.

European Parliament, P8_TA-PROV(2018)0340, The Situation in Hungary. European Parliament resolution of 12 September 2018 on a proposal calling on the Council to determine, pursuant to Article 7(1) of the Treaty on European Union, the existence of a clear risk of a serious breach by Hungary of the values on which the Union is founded (2017/2131(INL)).

Freedom House, Democracy in Retreat. Freedom in the World 2019, https://freedomhouse.org/report/freedom-world/freedom-world-2019/democracy-in-retreat; World Justice Project Rule of Law Index 2019, https://worldjusticeproject.org/sites/default/files/documents/WJP-ROLI-2019-Single%20Page%20View-Reduced_0.pdf.

Hungarian Helsinki Committee, Blurring the Boundaries. New Laws on Administrative Courts Undermine Judicial Independence (Hungarian Helsinki Committee 2018).

National Statistical Office, http://www.ksh.hu/docs/hun/xstadat/xstadat_eves/i_wnt001c.html.

National Statistical Office, http://www.ksh.hu/docs/hun/xstadat/xstadat_eves/i_wdsd008.html.

Organization for Security and Co-operation in Europe, Hungary parliamentary elections 6 April 2014 OSCE/ODIHR Limited Election Observation Mission Final Report, OSCE Office for Democratic Institutions and Human Rights, Warszaw, 11 July 2014.

Organization for Security and Co-operation in Europe, Hungary parliamentary elections 8 April 2018 OSCE/ODIHR Limited Election Observation Mission Final Report, OSCE Office for Democratic Institutions and Human Rights, Warszaw, 27 June 2018.

Venice Commission, Opinion on Act CCVI of 2011 on the right to freedom of conscience and religion and the legal status of churches, denominations and religious communities of Hungary, CDL-AD(2012)004-e, Opinion 664/2012.

Venice Commission, Opinion on the Cardinal Acts on the Judiciary that were amended following the adoption of Opinion CDL-AD(2012)001 on Hungary, CDL-AD(2012)020-e, Opinion 683/2012.

Venice Commission, Opinion on the Fourth Amendment to the Fundamental Law of Hungary, CDL-AD(2013)012, Opinion 720/2013.

Table of Cases

Constitutional Court

Kúria (Supreme Court)

European Court of Human Rights

Table of Legislation

These are the list of important acts of Parliament in effect on 31 December 2023.

Table of Legislation

Index

The numbers here refer to paragraph numbers.

Index

Index

Index

Index

www.ingramcontent.com/pod-product-compliance
Lightning Source LLC
Chambersburg PA
CBHW071421230926
51846CB00001B/102
9789403511283